Technology for Early Childhood Education and Socialization:
Developmental Applications and Methodologies

Sally Blake
University of Memphis, USA

Satomi Izumi-Taylor
University of Memphis, USA

Information Science REFERENCE

INFORMATION SCIENCE REFERENCE

Hershey · New York

KH

Director of Editorial Content:	Kristin Klinger
Senior Managing Editor:	Jamie Snavely
Assistant Managing Editor:	Michael Brehm
Publishing Assistant:	Sean Woznicki
Typesetter:	Sean Woznicki
Cover Design:	Lisa Tosheff
Printed at:	Yurchak Printing Inc.

Published in the United States of America by
Information Science Reference (an imprint of IGI Global)
701 E. Chocolate Avenue
Hershey PA 17033
Tel: 717-533-8845
Fax: 717-533-8661
E-mail: cust@igi-global.com
Web site: http://www.igi-global.com/reference

Library of Congress Cataloging-in-Publication Data

Technology for early childhood education and socialization : developmental applications and methodologies / Sally Blake and Satomi Izumi-Taylor, editors.
     p. cm.
  Includes bibliographical references and index.
  Summary: "This book provides readers with valuable and authentic research on how technology relates to early childhood growth"--Provided by publisher.
   ISBN 978-1-60566-784-3 (hardcover) -- ISBN 978-1-60566-785-0 (ebook) 1. Early childhood education--Computer-assisted instruction. 2.
Education--Effect of technological innovations on. 3. Children--Effect of technological innovations on. 4. Child development.
5. Social learning.
 I. Blake, Sally, 1949- II. Izumi-Taylor, Satomi, 1948-
  LB1139.35.C64T39 2010
  372.133'4--dc22
                            2009007013

British Cataloguing in Publication Data
A Cataloguing in Publication record for this book is available from the British Library.

6/07/11

Table of Contents

Detailed Table of Contents

Chapter 1
Reflections Concerning Technology: A Case for the Philosophy of Technology in Early
Childhood Teacher Education and Professional Development Programs 1
 Andew Neil Gibbons, New Zealand Tertiary College, New Zealand

The philosophy of technology underlies how people view and use technology. The historic relationship of
humans to technology is important to explore when developing a context for current technology applications. Within such a context, this chapter outlines the core components, philosophy and debate contributing
to sessions run with early childhood education student teachers and early childhood educators.

Chapter 2
Computer Technology in Taiwan Kindergartens 20
 Yu-Yuan Lee, University of Memphis, USA & Nan Kai University of Technology, Taiwan

Taiwan has become a global high-tech center. The success of becoming the leading country of high-tech
and information technology is accredited to the efforts of the government and of all citizens. In addition,
Chinese highly value in academic success, and this has contributed to the success of Taiwan. Parents
believe the success of life is rooted in a good education, especially in the early years. This chapter
presents an overview of early childhood education in Taiwan and explores how Chinese culture had
influenced the value of parents' expectation in education, as well as how children learn through the use
of technology. The last part of the chapter discusses the discrepancy between current early childhood
education situations and teachers' professional development.

Chapter 3
Tech-Knowledge in Japanese Early Childhood Education 49
 Tetsuya Ogawa, Kawasaki Futaba Kindergarten, Japan
 Satomi Izumi-Taylor, University of Memphis, USA

This chapter describes how Japanese early childhood education promotes children's socialization through the use of technology and play in group-oriented environments. The chapter also presents the traditional Japanese view of the child and of early childhood education, Japanese strategies in developing children's socialization skills, changes in the use of technology in the field of early childhood education, and recommendations for educators.

Chapter 4

The last nine years have seen major change in the Mexican Educational System as sweeping reforms across all levels have been implemented. In particular the early years of education have become the focus of legislation to increase quality, open access, and improve curriculum. How technology shaped these sweeping reform efforts will change the future of Mexico in a global community. Early childhood education must support the use of technology if the population is to move into a techno-society.

This chapter discusses technology and its role in teacher education. In order for technology to reach the early childhood classroom, it must first reach the classroom of the teacher education programs. The effect of self-efficacy on preschool teachers use and understanding of technology may influence their instructional applications. Early childhood faculty come from the same career pool as early childhood teachers and may share the same beliefs that practitioners have concerning technology. Teacher education programs have a responsibility to produce professionals who are literate in technology tools and applications.

Chapter 6

This chapter explores how technology is used with young children with special needs in the United States. It also discusses the legal issues and mandates and the reality of how teachers and schools are dealing with children with special needs in early childhood settings. Information resources and how assistive technology fits into developmentally appropriate practice is included in this discussion.

Chapter 7

This chapter discusses the roles of technology in instruction and assessment of young children. The influx of technology in schools and homes has been rapid and wide spread. Most children today have seen or used a computer or other technological tool before they enter school. As the student-to-computer ratio has improved from 60-to-1 in 1983 (OTA, 1988) to an average 4-to-1 nationwide in 2007 (Nagel, 2007) the question is no longer whether computers can assist in early childhood learning in general, but rather how computers can and should be used and to what end (Johnson, 1998; Cuban, 2001).

In this chapter the authors have provided an overview of some of the ideas about families and technology use in early childhood programs. The four authors are university faculty and provide their thinking and some experiences with family involvement and teacher training. The chapter is framed with the idea that families are the first teachers of children and play a major role in learning. There is a special introductory section written by Denise Winsor, who piloted the Family Builders and Family Preservation grants in the 1980's. Winsor provides insight into the role of family in early childhood education. The next section explores technology that is used to facilitate family involvement and building family involvement through technology. The authors briefly discuss some of the issues, problems and solutions to technology within family relationships and the role you might play as a professional. They try to address the advantages and disadvantages of family/school communication approaches to developing technology relationships with caregivers. They have included some real world examples from practitioners and how they help our students conceptualize technology use with families. The last section includes helpful advice for families concerning appropriate use of technology with their child. The authors hope this chapter helps you think about the role of families in your classroom and how technology can work for the development of stronger relationships as well as academic support.

Chapter 9

Calls for increased use of technology in early childhood and primary classrooms have not gone unanswered. However, recent research findings report little technology integration with computers continuing to be unavailable. This descriptive study looked to explore to what extent and in what ways technology is integrated into early childhood and primary classrooms. Findings corroborate previous dated research that trivial technology is being used. Technology use, computer access and styles of pedagogy remain critical in the debate to whether teachers will integrate computers for teaching and learning.

It is evident from the information in the previous chapters in this book that there is much to be learned about how technology fits into the world of early childhood education (ECE). This chapter discusses some exciting new thinking about epistemology and how children and teachers learn and how this could relate to technology and all learning with young children and their teachers. The new understanding of preschool education potential demands new approaches to these vital years of schooling if we are to prepare our children to succeed in the increasingly demanding academic environments.

Technology is being designed for children of all ages, even as young as nine months (Morrison, 2007). The software market is growing rapidly for children from infant to preschool age, with programs for children under five representing the fastest-growing educational softwarea area (Morrison 2007). The Internet provides access to a great collection of resources available for young children and teachers. The following pages may be of interest to educators of young children. There are web sites included for software and articles of interest related to issues concerning technology and young children selected by all authors of our book.

Foreword

Is there a link between technology and good teaching to young children? Will it help their development? One can find out by reading this book, *Technology for Early Childhood Education and Socialization: Developmental Applications and Methodologies*. The book has left me with an indelible impression confirming the notion that there is a strong linkage between technology and early childhood education. The readers will obtain valuable information that deals with this issue. The recommendations regarding computer technology to help children learn are worth considering, because technology opens up many doors to the future.

It is undeniable that technology is here to stay as a tool of instruction and discovery for years to come. As we are advancing technologically, regressing to the old ways of doing things is not an option any more. The emergence of computers and its impact in our daily lives is unquestionable.

As I often speak to my science methods students that, at one time, pencil, a chalk, and even slide-rules were the mainstay of our education. In fact, many scientists and engineers who put the man on the moon learned their science subjects in high school and in college using a slide-rule. Today, a calculator is more powerful in its computing abilities than a computer that was built in the 1950's and 1960's. Without being able to predict its rapid growth, the overall technology advanced quickly throughout the 60's, 70's, 80's, and 90's. Consequently, one example of technological advancement is the computer that is prevalent and dominant -- impacting education as well as daily transactions throughout today's society.

In this first decade of the 21st century, we are finding out that children at pre-K, kindergarten, and lower elementary levels are already computer savvy. Many learn to play games on the computer at home, at school, or at a day-care. Many also learn their subject matter using educational software. Now, the question is: Are our children keeping up with the use of computers and the rapidly growing technology? We must explore this question in depth. Generally, young children encounter and engage in the use of technology in all forms such as electronic games, watching an adult using the U-Scan at a grocery store, listening to their teacher's power point presentation, and so on. As teachers, we should facilitate the use of technology as a tool of meaningful teaching and learning. Therefore, the onus is on the teachers to be creative, innovative, and user-friendly as they incorporate technology with other methods of instruction.

The multiple chapters in this book are a product of many hours of diligent research and relevant writing. These chapters can promote critical discourse and analytical dialogue on the issue of constructive approach to technology use in early childhood years. The authors' tireless efforts signify the notion that technology is here to stay. Although controversial, we must find diverse approaches to its use in the classroom, especially among young children. These chapters will provide food for thought among many early childhood educators and teachers. As you read each chapter, your background will be enhanced and enriched, however, I encourage you to pause for reflection.

By reading this book, you will ascertain that technology has widely spread throughout the educational system of many countries. In particular, the Japanese educational system encourages the use of technology to promote learning and development among children at home and at school. Use of technology in the classroom is imperative anymore, however, it requires unflinching teacher supervision. Many teachers have a penchant for self-improvement. Use of computers in their daily teaching is one avenue to achieve this objective.

Finally, writing a book is not a frivolous pursuit. It requires tremendous amount of hard work reading, writing, and synthesizing related information to strengthen and anchor one's own research. I believe a good book in teacher education should be useful as well as user friendly and devoid of platitudes. I think the editors and the many authors of this book have made an exceptional contribution in this arena: application of technology with young children.

In summary, in today's highly technological society, it is imperative that teachers integrate computers in their instruction on a daily basis effectively and efficiently. We must help children to become competitive, as they will enter the global economy as adults. Therefore, young children must become acquainted with the use of computers from a very young age, especially during the early childhood years. This book provides valuable insights, current trends, necessary tools, and a theoretical framework to accomplish this goal. Students of early childhood education will find it useful.

S. Wali Abdi
Professor of Science Education
The University of Memphis
September 2008

S. Wali Abdi *is a Professor Science Education at the University of Memphis. He has been a science teacher, researcher, consultant, speaker & author. He has taught Science & Mathematics to elementary/middle school students. Since joining The University of Memphis (1993), Dr. Abdi has received numerous awards, notably, The University of Memphis Alumni Distinguished Teaching Award. He has presented at summer institutes and national/state conferences on science education & multicultural education. Dr. Abdi is teaching and training preservice/in-service teachers. His areas of interest are: assessment of prior knowledge, tackling children's misconceptions in science, & active science teaching and learning. Having degrees in Biology & Science Education (Virginia Tech), he has worked on teacher training grants funded by The NSF, The Assisi Foundation, The U.S. Department of Education, & The Tennessee Department of Education. Dr. Abdi has presented at NSTA, NAEYC, SCST, & AETS conferences. He edits the Book Reviews Section of the journal, School Science & Mathematics. Dr. Abdi passed away soon after he wrote our introduction.*

Preface

"Any sufficiently developed technology is virtually indistinguishable from magic." This famous quote by Arthur Clarke brilliantly describes how technology has advanced in our current global society. Technology has progressed to such an extent that it affects people of all ages, and the field of early childhood education also has been greatly influenced by its progress. However, there has been much controversy about the use of technology and the overall effects on children's development. While almost every early childhood program has a computer, the controversies continue as to how best use technology when working with young children. Not every use of technology is appropriate or beneficial and research is limited. Before implementing any technology in the classrooms of young children, the design of the curriculum, social setting, teacher technology competence, and program requirements must be examined. Teachers must also consider how to meet the needs of young children from diverse populations. Although many teachers use technology and have such tools available, little is known about how to train teachers or how technology fits into early childhood classrooms.

Since technology is constantly changing, the goals of education have changed, and in turn, technology has changed the notion of what it means to be educated (Morrison, 2007).

Even very young children are exposed to technology in their homes. Therefore, early childhood teachers need to be aware of the influence of technology on children, and they also need to develop their skills in using technology to benefit children (NAEYC, 1996). The influence of technology on early childhood education is reflected in research indicating that developmentally appropriate educational computer programs promote young children's social, emotional, and cognitive development (Blagojevic, 2003; Clements & Sarama, 2003; Fisher & Gillespie, 2003; NAEYC, 1996, Wortham, 2006). However, historically, the use of technology in the early childhood classroom has been debated (Wartella & Nancy, 2000). Some educators note that children can make powerful discoveries through technology, while others report that technology takes children away from traditional concrete activities. In the midst of such arguments, this book can contribute to how early childhood educators as well as early childhood teacher educators can implement and assess developmentally appropriate technology and play for all children.

Computers are increasingly present in early childhood education settings. Toward the end of the 1980s, only one-fourth of licensed preschools had computers. Today almost every preschool has a computer, with the ratio of computers to students changing from 1:125 in 1984 to 1:22 in 1990 to 1:10 in 1997. Not every use of technology, however, is appropriate or beneficial. The design of the curriculum and social setting are critical (Clements, 2006). Teachers of young children are the technology gatekeepers in childcare programs. They are vital to the appropriate use of technology yet little is documented concerning training and understanding of teachers' use in classrooms. Teachers need to understand how to develop learning, what types of learning should be facilitated, and how to serve the needs of diverse populations using technology. Computers are more than tools for bringing efficiency to traditional approaches; they can open new and unforeseen avenues for learning.

Most educators of young children advocate for a constructivist approach to teaching. This approach supports Developmentally Appropriate Practice for pedagogy applications. During the last 13 years, perspectives on the principle of developmental appropriateness have become more sophisticated The National Association for the Education of Young Children (NAEYC) is considered the professional society for educators of young children. NAEYC adopted a position statement concerning the appropriate use of technology with children ages 3-8 in 1996. This document primarily addressed the use of computer technology and other technology integrated with computer technology in early childhood settings. NAEYC believes that in any given situation, a professional judgment by the teacher is required to determine if a specific use of technology is age appropriate, individually appropriate and culturally appropriate (NAEYC, 1996). This indicates that the teachers need training and experience in technology applications and analysis.

In writing this book, Technology for early childhood education and socialization: Developmental applications and methodologies, our intention is to provide a guide for all educators who are involved in the lives of young children and are considering how to implement technology in their classrooms. We hope this work helps practitioners examine their beliefs about technology and think about issues that seem relevant across cultures. This book is for educators across the continuum including teacher trainers, university faculty, and classroom practitioners. Some strategies and suggestions described may be well accepted in classrooms already and others provide new insights and ideas for classrooms. Like children, educators have developmental levels of technology understanding and we have tried to address all levels of thinking and skills. We hope to inspire the exploration of different technology applications for teaching young children. Our goal is to address the major issues surrounding technology from an international perspective in order to provide a holistic portrait of technology and early childhood education.

This book offers a critical discussion of how early childhood educators use technology in different cultural settings and how college and university faculty members focus on the appropriate use of technology to provide meaningful and productive learning for children and their teachers as well. The eighth chapter is an overview of what is happening in real schools after our children leave their early childhood programs in the United States. Early childhood teachers' perceptions and understanding of technology greatly influence the kinds of experiences for and outcomes of young children in the classroom; thus, all educators need to be informed about this topic. To fill this need, we present this book that focuses on international perspectives concerning practical applications of, controversies surrounding and of technologies in order to promote young children's learning and development. Chapter authors are international and were enthusiastic to share their observations and experiences to make a positive impact on the lives of children and of educators at all levels. Each author's diverse experiences, pedagogical views, educational practices, and discoveries can support all educators in implementing the innovative use of technology in early childhood education classrooms.

This book, consisting of nine chapters, presents four international perspectives from Japan, New Zealand, Taiwan, and the United States; the relationships between teacher education and technology; special early childhood education and technology; the roles of technology in instruction and assessment of young children; and family involvement and technology. We also describe some helpful links to Online Resources on Technology as a Learning Tool (NAEYC and Authors) in Chapter IX.

ORGANIZATION OF THE BOOK

Chapter 1 offers a case for the philosophy of technology in early childhood teacher education and professional development programs in New Zealand. It is represented in the following six themes: 1) the importance of critical reflection in teaching practice; 2) the philosophy of technology; 3) the weaving of technology in Aotearoa/New Zealand; 4) the professional development session, A brief history of ICT advocacy in ECE; 5) the teacher education sessions, critical understandings of technology in the curriculum, and 6) the concluding statements, visions, and questions concerning technology. This chapter outlines the core components and philosophy of sessions run with early childhood education student teachers and early childhood educators to encourage critical reflection of the role of new technologies in early learning environments. The student teachers were participating in a field-based diploma of teaching program while the educators were participating in a professional development network. The teachers were introduced to key assumptions about technology in early childhood education and the impact of these assumptions on teacher self-perceptions and on their development of strategies to ensure careful introduction of new technologies into the learning environment

Chapter 2 explores how Japanese early childhood educators implement technology to promote children's socialization skills. Japanese early childhood educators integrate play and technology in order to support young children's development and learning in group-oriented environments. The main focus of Japanese early childhood education is to guide children to develop basic human attributes rather than to teach them academics, and teachers provide children with age-appropriate technology in order to enhance play rather than to focus on their academic skills. Through children's requests, teachers support their play by providing opportunities to engage in technology-related activities. Examining the ways Japanese teachers use such activities can provide some insight as to how to implement play and technology for young children. The use of play as a pedagogical approach is maintained in all Japanese early education programs. The teachers of Japan are highly skilled and provide experiences and environments that teach through play. This approach does not include direct teaching which is common in many programs in the United States. Children develop higher order thinking skills needed for science and technology development which is evident and well documented through international tests results of older children who have come through the Japanese educational system. The role of early childhood in this academic success may be one of the influencing variables.

Chapter 3 focuses on technology and early childhood education in Taiwan and describes how young children use technology in the classroom. This chapter presents an overview of early childhood education in Taiwan and how Chinese culture has influenced the value of parents' expectation in education, as well as how children learn through the use of technology. Children in Taiwan enjoy different kinds of interactive video games and develop a love of learning. This chapter explains how early childhood teachers provide developmentally appropriate video games for young children in classrooms. One interesting aspect of the Taiwan educational system is the high level of government support for technology. Technology education has become a competitive aspect of preschool enrollment and many parents are placing their children in private schools that use and teach technology rather than public preschools. Some teachers in these programs have technology degrees. How the early childhood programs combine development and technology to support the government technology requirements is an interesting story. The role of parents and their expectations of children to succeed is another factor of interest in Taiwan. Along with technology instruction the parents of most young children want their children to learn English in these educational programs. Taiwan is another country that consistently scores high on international tests that measure mathematics and science inquiry thinking. The impact of early childhood programs is unknown concerning how these countries continue to succeed in the global economy. It is well documented that both Taiwan and Japan consistently outscore students from the United States on international comparisons.

Chapter 4 takes an in-depth look at the sweeping reform in preschool education in Mexico. The complexities of the Mexican educational system are explained in this chapter. Mexican preschool education started with two distinct programs. One to serve social needs and one to serve educational academic development. New reform requires all preschools provide academic focus through appropriate developmental approaches. However, the teacher now must be the deciding influence on how a program works to accomplish this blend of social reform and academic success. There is an overview of technology in Mexico, a comprehensive explanation of new reform efforts, and a description of how technology is used in some of the preschool programs. Mexico is of particular interest because up until 10 years ago it was considered a "developing country" but the Mexican economy has expanded to become the ninth largest in the world. Technology has played a major role in this change. Schools struggle to keep up with the needs of the economy which demands more and more sophisticated technology education. Mexico is a country of contrasts. There are 62 indigenous towns in Mexico, where one of the 80 languages and their variants is spoken. This extensive diversity influences education and how technology is used. While the United States and Mexico are considered different countries they share a common 2,000-mile-long border area where the socio-economic dynamics of two interacting cultures have a strong influence on the educational resources for young children. This area is almost a country within a country. This chapter includes some of the issues concerning the border areas.

Chapter 5 presents ways teacher education institutions use technology to educate and train pre-service teachers of young children. This chapter describes how teacher educators can prepare their in-service teachers to develop technology literacy since all young children need an opportunity to experience and to explore technology at early ages in order to prepare for life in a modern society and to deepen their creative problem-solving and thinking skills. Because technology plays a great role in young children's learning and development, early childhood educators need to know how to implement technology in their programs and to develop technological literacy for their charges as well as for themselves. The resistance to technology is evident in teacher education programs as well as in the classroom. A teacher education program is only as good as it's faculty. If the United States wants to produce techo-literate children they have to make sure that their teachers accept and use technology. This chapter includes a brief discussion of the role self-efficacy plays in teacher's belief systems and gives information about teachers of young children in the United States. Chapter 10 shares new research into what influences teacher's instructional choices.

Chapter 6 examines how technology is used with young children with special needs. It also includes the legal issues and mandates and the reality of how teachers and schools are dealing with children with special needs in early childhood settings. Information resources and how assistive technology fits into developmentally appropriate practice is described. This chapter explains how early childhood educators can endorse global education which is inclusive through the use of technology. Such education should support children and families with special needs, improve social and political conditions, and move towards a more equity educational process. The role of technology in the assurance of equal access is major. New technologies allow children previously left in resource rooms or grouped in special schools with limited curriculum opportunities to participate in a fuller range of educational opportunities. Technology development continues to insure the global opportunity for all children in early childhood programs to have an equal opportunity for educational and social success. The schools of today must address these issues and provide children the "best possible" learning environment. Technology has been the key influence on this progress in schools.

Chapter 7 describes the roles of technology in instruction and assessment of young children. The chapter also explores current use of different forms of technology in early childhood classrooms and discusses some of the problems that have been encountered in technology use with a focus on computers, including three main issues associated with instruction and assessment with young children: developmentally appropriate use of computers, instructional use of computers and equity issues. There is an overview of technology used for assessment of early childhood programs and some discussion of appropriate use in instruction. There is advice on how to develop an approach to technology assessment in the classroom and the teacher's role. A chart that identifies the levels of technology use recommended for children is in this chapter and the different instruction modes recommended for technology instruction is included. An in-depth discussion of the debate about how technology influences development is included in this chapter. Readers will take a close look at how the general population develops tech-fear from undocumented reports and reflect on the difference in opinion and research supported ideas about technology.

Chapter 8 illustrates how early childhood educators can promote family involvement through the use of technology. Parent/family involvement is a key to children's success in their school lives. This chapter explains the complexities of the relationship between parents or caregivers and children and how these interactions influence learning. Research on literacy acquisition and development is used as an example of how first environments build learning and it is hypothesized that this would apply to technology learning. This chapter looks at three main issues that influence family and children's technology relationships. These include the Digital Generation Gap which threatens the traditional respect system in families; Equity Issues which are evident between socioeconomic classes and give suggestions for how teachers and schools can help bring equal technology opportunity; and Open Access which is becoming a growing problem as the internet continues to grow and more websites not appropriate for young children are available.

When primary caregivers know how to be involved in their children's everyday activities in schools, parent and family members are more likely to support their children's performance. Through the use of technology, parents and family members can be valued sources of children's successful school lives. For these reasons, this chapter includes ways for early childhood educators to get parents and family members to be involved in their children's school lives.

Chapter 9 shares the results of a research study concerning use of technology in American schools. The purpose of this study was to examine the current state of technology integration and describe access, instructional activities and use in early childhood and primary classrooms in the United States. The primary research question was: To what degree and in what ways have teachers integrated technology with instruction in early childhood and primary grades? This snapshot shows the actual environment our American children move into after they leave early childhood programs. It gives a clear overview of the realities teachers and children encounter in American schools and summarizes technology use, access, and pedagogy. The compelling evidence from this study that technology use in schools is trivial and that teachers are not using available technology is a grave concern if we are to prepare our children for the Digital Society in which they are not a part. Another concern that is evident from this study is the use of technology for lower level thinking activities that require skill practice and repetitious assignments in the United States. Unlike countries like Japan which integrate technology into play the trend in the United States is to use computers like glorified worksheets. This lower level approach to active cognitive engagement could have a major impact on future academic success for children. One reason we have included this study is to allow readers to see the difference in a research study about technology and a personal opinion piece. Most early childhood practitioners and programs identify research as any article published in an early childhood journal. This, again influences how teachers learn and use technology in their classrooms.

Chapter 10 is Building Epistemic Awareness in the Early Childhood Classroom: Theory, Methodology, and Technology looks at the epistemological influences on technology use of early childhood professionals, children and how conceptual change occurs. Teacher belief's about learning are a major influence on their instructional behaviors. This chapter helps teachers explore their belief systems about learning and how to approach conceptual change in themselves and young children. This should help teachers face their "technology demons" as they move into a new era of digital change in early childhood classrooms. The reflective approach to epistemology is important if we are to prepare our children for the challenges they face in the global environment. This chapter connects the ideas from the other chapters and helps teachers understand some of the reasons they made instructional decisions in regards to technology.

Chapter 11 is a resource chapter for early childhood professionals. It was compiled by all contributing authors and contains sources of information the readers might find helpful. It includes website, articles, and books that provide additional information about the topics from our book. This chapter includes developmentally appropriate websites, software, and programs for children and teachers. It also provides comments from children and teachers who have experience with programs and websites. We hope the readers find this useful.

The appendices in this book include reflective checklist, a personal epistemology survey, a graphic organizer to analyze different web sites, and a planning guide for technology use.

Audience: The proposed audience for this book would include university faculty for use in an Early Childhood Technology course, Head Start and Child Care Center teachers and professional development personnel, and public school teachers and administrators working with young children. We propose an international market also for similar childhood programs.

College students and college educators will be our target audience. For example, this book will be part of our early childhood education courses, including ECED 8107/7107 Constructivism in early childhood education, ECED5440/4540 TEP (Teacher Education Program) admission courses and other courses. Also, this book will be highly suitable as a personal reference for early childhood practitioners, for administrators, and for parents of young children. Early childhood educational organizations such as Head Start programs and the National Association for the Education of Young Children, childcare centers, preschools, kindergartens, and primary schools (1st through 3rd grades) would purchase this book for their library use. As a secondary market, both public and university libraries, book stores, book clubs as well as educators, school personnel, educators, and university libraries in Japan, New Zealand, and Taiwan will purchase this book.

It is acknowledged that technology plays a significant role in all aspects of modern society. However, there has been much controversy about the use of technology and the overall effect on student achievement. School districts spend millions of dollars on new technology that they believe will improve student achievement. Many studies indicate that using technology in the classroom does not have a significant impact on student performance (Clark, 1983, 1994; Ravitz et al., 2002). Others indicate technology is valuable in classrooms. In Preparing Teachers for a Changing World, Darling Hammond and others (2005) acknowledge the importance of technology for today's students and tomorrow's citizens. While most classrooms have technology tools available and many teachers are using them, teachers need to incorporate the opportunities of the emerging technological infrastructure into their overall curricular thinking (Darling Hammond et. al, 2005). For teacher preparation institutions to ensure that teachers know how to use the technologies that are part of professional communities of practice, these need to be infused into the content pedagogy courses that teachers complete.

While we prepare teachers to work in the fast paced world of technology we hope our book helps them gain a better understanding of how important the role of cyber learning is becoming to all children. Most children come to our classrooms aware of technology and comfortable with it. It is up to us as professionals to help them build on their knowledge and prepare them for the communication systems of the future. In order to do this we must overcome any anxiety we have about technology. It is essential that teachers become better prepared to apply and integrate new technology in the service of helping children learn and develop socially, emotionally, and intellectually. We thank you for this opportunity.

REFERENCES

Beisser, S.R., & Gillespie, C.W. (2003). Kindergarteners can do it so can you: A case study of a construc-tionist technology-rich first year seminar for undergraduate college students. *Information Technology in Childhood Education Annual* (pp. 243-260).

Blagojevic, B. (2003). Funding technology: Does it make cents? *Young Children, 56*(3), 28-33.

Clements, D. H. (2002). Computers in early childhood mathematics. *Contemporary Issues in Early Childhood, 3*(2), 160-181.

Clements, D. H. (1999). Young children and technology. In G. D. Nelson (Ed.), *Dialogue on early childhood science, mathematics, and technology education* (pp. 92-105). Washington, DC: American Association for the Advancement of Science.

Clements, D. H. (1991). Current technology and the early childhood curriculum. In B. Spodek & O. N. Saracho (Eds.), *Yearbook in early childhood education, Volume 2: Issues in early childhood curriculum* (pp. 106-131). New York: Teachers College Press.

Clements, D. H. (1993). Computer technology and early childhood education. In J. L. Roopnarine & J. E. Johnson (Eds.), *Approaches to early childhood education* (2nd ed.) (pp. 295-316). New York: Merrill.

Clements, D. H. (1993). Early education principles and computer practices. In C. G. Hass & F. W. Parkay (Eds.), *Curriculum planning: A new approach* (6th ed.). Boston: Allyn and Bacon.

Clements, D. H., & Nastasi, B. K. (1992). Computers and early childhood education. In M. Gettinger, S. N. Elliott, & T. R. Kratochwill (Eds.), *Advances in school psychology: Preschool and early childhood treatment directions* (pp. 187-246). Hillsdale, NJ: Lawrence Erlbaum Associates.

Clements, D. H., & Nastasi, B. K. (1993). Electronic media and early childhood education. In B. Spodek (Ed.), *Handbook of research on the education of young children* (pp. 251-275). New York: Macmillan.

Clements, D. H., Nastasi, B. K., & Swaminathan, S. (1993). Young children and computers: Crossroads and directions from research. *Young Children, 48*(2), 56-64.

Clements, D., & Sarama, J. (2003). Young children and technology. *Young Children, 58*(6), 34-40.

Clements, D. H., & Swaminathan, S. (1995). Technology and school change: New lamps for old? *Childhood Education, 71*, 275-281.

National Academy of Education (2005). L. Darling-Hammond, J. Bransford,

M.A. Fischer, & C.W. Gillespie (Eds.), *Development and computers: One Head Start classroom's experience. Young Children, 58*(4), 85-91.

Gillespie, C.W. (2004). Seymour Papert's vision for early childhood education? A descriptive study of preschoolers and kindergarteners in discovery-based, Logo-rich classrooms. *Early Childhood Research and Practice, 6*(1). Available online at http://ecrp.uiuc.edu/.

Gillespie, C.W., & Beisser, S.R. (2001). Developmentally appropriate LOGO computer programming with young children. *Information Technology in Childhood Education* (pp. 232-247).

Morrison, G. (2007). *Early childhood education today* (10th Ed.). Upper Saddle River, NJ: Merrill Prentice Hall.

NAEYC position statement: Technology and young children-ages three through eight. (1996). *Young Children, 51*(6), 11-16.

Wartella, E. A., & Nancy, J. (2000). Children and computers: New technology-old concern. *Children and Computer Technology, 10*(2), 31-43. Available at www.futureofchildren.org.

Wortham, S. (2006). Early childhood curriculum (4th ed.). Upper Saddle River, NJ: Pearson Merrill Prentice Hall.

Acknowledgment

We would like to express our gratitude to our Advisory and Review Board and all of our authors for their time and input. As we were finishing the work one of our contributing authors died. We would like to dedicate this book to his memory.

This book is dedicated to the loving memory of our esteemed colleague, friend, and mentor at the University of Memphis: S. Wali Abdi. He has had a profound influence in everything we do. The world was a more joyful and meaningful place because of his sense of humor, positive disposition, boundless kindness, wisdom, playfulness, and zest for life. We miss him more than words can express. Wali lost his battle with cancer soon after he completed the introduction to this book. He was a brave and courageous colleague who never gave up hope.

He was a science teacher, researcher, consultant, speaker and author. Dr. Abdi was a Professor of Science Education in the College of Education. Since joining The University of Memphis in 1993, Dr. Abdi received numerous awards: The University of Memphis Alumni Distinguished Teaching Award; Science Educator of the Year Award for Higher Education presented by Tennessee Science Teachers Association; and The Outstanding Teacher of the Year Award presented by Memphis Organization of Science Teachers. Dr. Abdi also received The Outstanding Award of the Year for Teaching and for Service in the College of Education.

"To provide effective science instruction, a teacher should first and foremost make learning meaningful and useful. Inquiry-based instruction is a relevant and an essential component of effective teaching. Furthermore, students should be given multiple and continual opportunities to manipulate objects in order to construct meaning from what they learn and experience" (Abdi, 2005, p.18).

Wali, you gave us meaning and we shall always remember and respect you.

Chapter 1

Reflections Concerning Technology
A Case for the Philosophy of Technology in Early Childhood Teacher Education and Professional Development Programs

Andrew Neil Gibbons
New Zealand Tertiary College, New Zealand

An important feature of a learning machine is that its teacher will often be very largely ignorant of quite what is going on inside, although he may still be able to some extent to predict his pupil's behavior. (Turing, 1992, p. 158)

ABSTRACT

The philosophy of technology underlies how people view and use technology. The historic relationship of humans to technology is important to explore when developing a context for current technology applications. Within such a context, this chapter outlines the core components, philosophy and debate contributing to sessions run with early childhood education student teachers and early childhood educators.

INTRODUCTION

Humans have a complex relationship to technology. Watching children playing with technologies, old and new, in early childhood centers, teachers amaze in the child's abilities and passions. And they often reflect that they do not really know what is going on inside those seemingly well-connected learning machines: the child and the technology. Alan Turing, widely regarded as one of the central figures in the development of intelligent machines, established a strong connection between the child and the machine. When constructing machines that might display human attributes in a condition requiring some form of intelligent response he looked to the behaviors of young children as they learn. If he could replicate the child's behaviors in a machine he might take great leaps towards constructing an artificial

DOI: 10.4018/978-1-60566-784-3.ch001

intelligence. However, as Arthur C. Clarke warned us in 2001, such a prize comes with associated costs (see Kubrick, 1968), and Clarke's message remains relevant some forty years on. From the ape's use of a bone as a weapon (the dawn of technology?), to the intelligent computer HAL 9000's unswerving dedication to a predetermined task despite the cost to human life (the dusk?), we are confronted with metaphors of the impact of technology on our lives.

What then are the benefits and costs associated with technology in the early childhood curriculum? This is a question that has attracted an immense amount of popular and scholarly opinion and research, particularly with regards to technologies such as personal computers, educational software, the Internet, digital cameras and more. This book provides an important contribution to such opinion and research. However it is a question that is not the focus of this chapter. Given that there is already much said about both the pitfall and possibilities of technology, of interest here is 'how do teachers make sense of it all?'

Within such a context, this chapter outlines the core components, philosophy and debate contributing to sessions run with early childhood education student teachers and early childhood educators. The sessions encouraged critical reflection of the role of new technologies, particularly Information and Communication Technologies (ICT), in early learning environments. They reflected a commitment to weaving the philosophy of technology into teacher education and professional development. In particular attention is drawn to the ways in which the early childhood educator is constructed in ICT literature. These constructions may have varying affects on the role of the teacher, the experiences of children, and the 'progress' of communities and societies. Philosophy can contribute to understanding constructions of the teacher and their effects.

Understanding and engaging with philosophy should not be considered a luxury or superfluous in early childhood education if we are to remain committed to the idea of the teacher as a reflective and critical pedagogue. Within this context that chapter first establishes the importance of critical reflection in early childhood education. The second section gives a brief overview of three key philosophies of technology and additionally relates key philosophical themes to popular fiction to evidence how a wide range of resources can be employed to encourage teachers and student teachers to reflect critically on technologies in their educational environments.

The chapter builds around the author's reflections on his development and delivery of the sessions and not on the reception and evaluation by the participants. Such contributions would be valuable components of further research, as noted in the concluding section of this chapter. The student teachers were participating in a field-based diploma of teaching program whilst the educators were participating in a professional development network. Research from the past three decades is drawn into the discussion to emphasize key themes, and their relative stability over time. Much of the literature refers to the use of computers in early childhood education and primary education. In general the terms technologies or new technologies are applied here acknowledging that understanding technology in a wider and more philosophical sense provides the scope and aim of this chapter. Finally, the problem of constructing the teacher as technologically weak is explored, with attention to more positive constructions that draw upon the philosophy of technology.

BACKGROUND: ISSUES, CONTROVERSIES AND PROBLEMS

The Importance of Critical Reflection in Teaching Practice

Rachel Bolstad's (2004) Government-funded research The Role and Potential for ICT in Early Childhood Education: A review of New Zealand

and international literature argues for a culture of critique when considering the role of ICT in early childhood education. In Aotearoa/New Zealand, like elsewhere, early childhood discourse highlights the importance of the reflective educator. A meaningful and positive education for young children requires, it is generally accepted, a teacher who can critically reflect on their practice (Vossler, Waitere-Ang, & Adams, 2005). Emphasis of the importance of critical reflection frequents various and dissonant discourses regarding the aims and outcomes of early childhood education. For instance, both advocates for developmentally appropriate practice, and the many critics of developmentally appropriate practice establish critical reflection as a key characteristic of an educator.

While the NAEYC's 1996 statement on developmentally appropriate practice does mention the importance of reflective practice in teachers, it does acknowledge the importance of supporting a child's reflective practice. In addition it is recognized that knowledge is socially constructed – a key component of a contemporary understanding of reflective practice – and that early childhood programs must be sensitive to local and cultural contexts – again a key component of reflective practice. Hao (2000) suggests that a key component of a quality early childhood curriculum is reflective practice. Quality is here understood in terms of developmentally appropriate practice. For the teacher, Hao follows, reflective practice is essential in order to make sense of and apply their teacher 'training' where their training involves developing familiarity with research and theory of appropriate practices.

Developmentally appropriate practice required [sic] teachers to engage in practices which better reflect what is known about how children develop and practices that are more sensitive to individual a [sic] cultural diversity. To reach such a goal, teachers must make constant efforts to

make sense of what is happening to children and frequently consider underlying assumptions and implications when analyzing classroom practices (Hao, 2000, p. 8).

Moss (2006) presents contending models of the early childhood worker, very much based around the teacher's reflective practice. His contribution to the philosophy of early childhood education is significant in that he views the teacher as a constructed subject. In other words, through our values and beliefs, and the language that we use, we fashion our knowledge of what a teacher should be like, and this knowledge then contributes to how a society views and defines a teacher, and importantly how teachers view and define themselves. This is not an unusual or troubling situation, it is that which makes it possible to have teachers, and to be teachers – however it is important to understand this possibility in order to examine different constructions of the teacher and how these constructions impact upon society.

Two constructions relevant to this chapter are that of 'worker as technician' and 'worker as researcher'. The technician is the dominant model, according to Moss, linked to expectations that quality early childhood education is measurable, and that wider social, economic and political gains can be realized through effective management of a quality environment. Here there is a strong link to the notion of education as a production line – hence the teacher articulated as technician. Evidence of the technical nature of the teacher is observed in the increasing classification, observation and regulation of teachers and teaching practice, a form of quality assurance again linked with the production line.

Technicians may have varying levels of skill and qualification. But their role is to apply a defined set of technologies through regulated processes to produce pre-specified and measurable outcomes. In the field of early years, the technologies and processes include working with detailed and prescriptive curricula (or similar practice guidelines), programmes and similar procedures to regulate methods of working, and using observation and other methods to assess performance against developmental norms and other standardised outcome criteria (Moss, 2006, p. 36).

The teacher as technician is also assumed to be somewhat neutral. They apply the curriculum without interfering in its purpose. Underpinning such expectations are egalitarian as well as economic goals: all children will receive a fair and transparent education where teachers are able to systematically apply the curriculum. The worker as researcher, in contrast, is believed to engage in her work at a deeper, more critical, and more meaningful level than the technician:

The worker as researcher is constantly seeking deeper understanding and new knowledge, in particular of the child and the child's learning processes. Research is part of everyday practice and can be conducted by everyone – not only the researching teacher, but the researching child and the researching parent (Moss, 2006, p. 37).

The worker as researcher weaves together constructivist notions of learning and post structural theories of knowledge. A critically reflective teacher cannot be determined by a list of measurable and universal characteristics. Engaging in critical reflection then requires an understanding of oneself as a particular kind of contextualised learner. In other words, it is not easy to say exactly what one must be in order to be critically reflective. There is an expectation that a teacher engage in dialogue and negotiation in order to be critically reflective; however there will be many different manifestations of negotiation and dialogue given the many contexts in which one is an educator.

The most significant difference between the two models Moss provides is the view of the teacher as either impartial and objective, or im-

plicated and subjective. These characteristics are essential to the practices of reflection – how one understands and observes the learning and teaching environment, and how one positions oneself as a teacher within it. However there is less dissonance between the models of Hao and Moss. While they would almost undoubtedly conflict over the issue of developmentally appropriate practice, the value of contextualized and critical reflection seems somewhat consistent. The purpose here is not to provide a lasting definition of critical reflection; it is to show that critical reflection is widely understood as being a key component of teaching (Vossler et al., 2005). As such, it has then to be considered in relation to the use of technology in early childhood education.

The remaining sections of this chapter consider the relationship between critical reflection and technology in early childhood education. Being a critical professional may indeed be enhanced by technology. For instance, debates around key educational questions, and practices, may be wider and more inclusive thanks to online forums (Buckleitner, 1999). However in the field of early childhood education there is a tendency, and perhaps not exclusively associated with the early childhood sector, to perceive educators as 'low-tech' and/or resistant to new technologies (see for instance Bolstad, 2004). Dating back to the sixties, teachers were expected to be resistant to new technologies through a conservative desire to protect the traditions they were comfortable with (see for instance Skinner, 1965; Papert, 1993). The argument that follows is that such characteristics do not blend well with expectations of critical reflection. I suggest it might not be a bad thing to hold on to some outdated values, principles and practices at worst, and at best to critically question the ways in which teachers are characterized as low-tech or unskilled. Philosophy contributes to both possibilities.

THE PHILOSOPHY OF TECHNOLOGY

As noted above the importance of an educator's practices of critical reflection is widely, perhaps even universally, accepted. One might reasonably expect then that an educator's critical reflection be informed by relevant discourse. For instance reflecting upon technology in the early childhood curriculum will require some familiarity with knowledge and debate relevant to technology, and this might include:

- Research related to the use of technology in early childhood settings, including the home, and in other education settings such as primary schools;
- Popular opinion regarding technology, both general and specific to early childhood education, published in the news media, through advocacy groups and the corporate sector;
- Academic discourse relevant to technology, including analysis of government policies, and philosophical works exploring deeper questions and implications associated with using a wide range of technologies in early childhood education; and
- Literary accounts of the relationships between human and machine.

It is these last two points that provide the scope of this section, given a perception that the first two are more widely disseminated and that student teachers and teachers are more familiar with arguments for and against technology in the curriculum that are based upon either popular opinion or empirical research of the use of technology in early childhood settings.

Humans have an essential relationship to technology; hence there is a very strong body of work that considers policy and philosophy related to technology. While very little is known or 'taught' about this work in teacher education

and professional development, it provides the most substantial tools with which to engage critically in reflection upon the technologies in our centers: how we use them, why we use them, and what happens when we use them. For all the value of the philosophy of technology in enriching our thinking, arguments are often complexly structured and articulated, engendering limitations to their accessibility. However in fiction, whether literary classics or contemporary pulp fiction and cinema, many key questions associated with technology are both explicitly and subtly introduced to a wider range of audiences, encouraging a deeper understanding of the human-technology bond.

With regard to academic discourse, the respective works of Martin Heidegger, Chet Bowers, and Andrew Feenberg provide many critical positions to consider carefully when thinking about technology in early childhood education. Their work offers different ways of thinking about technology, and is generally focused upon considering the ways in which we perceive and value human (and other) life, and how one, put simply, is human. In theoretical terms, each provides what is known as a substantive (as opposed to instrumental) approach to questioning technology:

Instrumental theories offer the most widely accepted explanations of technology based on the view that technologies are tools for human purposes, neutral in value, universally applicable, and with the only problem being the use to which they are put. This theory is also referred to as the anthropological explanation ... The substantive theories of technology hold that a technology is anything but neutral; rather it has a substantive value bias and through this bias transforms what it is to be human ... modern technology subjugates humanity to its own essence (Fitzsimons, 2002, p. 173).

In an instrumental view, air conditioners are simple machines that will be turned on and off by a human who is hence responsible for the effect the air conditioner has on the immediate and wider environment. In the substantive view, the air conditioner is a machine designed and used with culturally specific expectations regarding control of the environment; and it is a machine that fundamentally transforms human behavior. The philosophers below do not, generally, propose that the air conditioner be unplugged, rather that its affect on human being be more critically appreciated.

Heidegger is arguably one of the most significant, controversial, and confusing philosophers who questioned technology. His most relevant work was named, conveniently, 'The Question Concerning Technology' and was, and is, a rather amazing and unsettling exploration for the essence of technology. Now I noted earlier that humans have an essential relationship to technology. Heidegger took this assumption very seriously. So much so that he explained the essence of technology as being that which gives humans a sense of who they are. For instance, the ancient Greeks had the characteristics of ancient Greeks because of the ways in which they perceived, made, and used technologies. And 'modern man' is in some way defined by his and her relationship to technology (in fact 'his' and 'her' are in some way constructed around relationships to technology – think of those technologies that contribute to a wide range of gender stereotypes). Heidegger was very interested, and concerned, by the differences between the ancients and the moderns. He argued that the former generally understood technology as creative and nurturing, while the latter saw, and see, technology as exploitative – technology enables humans to take advantage of the world. Modern technology, Heidegger (1977, p. 14) argued, "puts to nature the unreasonable demand that it supply energy that can be extracted and stored as such." The purpose is to continue to consume nature – the 'standing reserve'.

Through modern technology everything becomes 'standing reserve', meaning that 'natural' resources such as water, or 'human' resources such as the child are categorized and measured for their value, and that this value can be stored and used at a later date. For example, water is stored in lakes to generate electricity, whilst children are educated in order to extract value at a later date, when they contribute to the economy. These might not seem like behaviors that warrant criticism of modern societies; many benefits are extracted for positive outcomes through the generation of electricity and the education of the child.

Heidegger is critical of such storing and exploiting; however, these applications of technology are of less concern than the tendency to forget that there are other relationships to technology that do not require maximization of potential and exploitation. He is concerned by a will to progress that obscures the possibilities of what he considers to be a more creative and poetic existence. For example, Heidegger peers through a philosophic microscope at the bridge and the jug, to give evidence of how essential, how complex, and how poetic, the relationship between human and technology might be. He explores how these two 'things' give presence to a myriad of experiences, assumptions, values, relationships and more.

Each culture has its own understanding of technology yet such differences are often seen as problems to be solved by 'educating' those who, when judged by certain assumptions about technological advancement, appear ignorant or less developed. Think for instance of the impact of modern technology on nomadic cultures. Once regions were cyclically returned to at appropriate seasons – no such cycles are possible as a result of the advance of modern 'developed' societies. For instance, the notions of ownership of land and resources, and compulsory schooling (all essential notions to a technological society) have contributed to the demise of nomadic cultures.

Heidegger (1977) offers a view of technology that is positive, but that it is hard to see the positive values of technology in the contemporary will to progress. Bowers (1988, 2000) has a similar focus on the exploitative purposes of technology, however where Heidegger's focus is on the philosophy of being human, Bowers is more concerned with the social, political and economic relationships that produce, are produced by, and are hidden by technology. The prevalence of computer technologies in education contributes strongly to his critique of technology, as are a concern for the environment and a concern for the protection of community relations. Bowers has particular relevance to philosophy in that he explains the relationship between knowledge, values, and technology. At the nexus of these is the belief that technology is neutral, that it has no 'culturalness'.

Bowers (1988, 2000) refutes claims that technology is neutral because residual knowledge is transmitted by technology. More than this, it is important to consider the transmission of values and beliefs embedded in technology discourses. Such discourses in constituting the scope and purpose of ICT, impact upon the adult's understanding of, structuring, planning for and reflecting upon the young child's play with technology. In other words, how one defines technology in general, or specific classifications of technology such as ICT, reflects certain decisions made, and these decisions will vary between and within communities and cultures. It is generally accepted that the global village made possible by new technologies is not an homogenous village. Bringing people closer together is not about making everyone the same, so it is consistent to expect that however connected we might feel because of mobile phones and the Internet, such connections will vary in quality. However the new technologies, and our understanding of their importance, are not global, they are specific to certain cultures. Hence where the importance of computer technologies and the Internet are articulated in international educational discourse and policy, a question of power arises. To return to nomadic cultures, the 'civilization' of such cultures relies on assumptions of 'we know best'. That which tells us we know best is often our technology.

Where groups or communities are measured by so-called developed nations and communities as being under developed, normally based upon access to technology, these groups are often then targeted as needing more advantage. Such campaigns as 'one laptop for every child' (go to http://laptopfoundation.org/en/index.shtml) are examples of the tendency of the west to perceive, and then seek to address,' technological deficit syndromes'. For Bowers such strategies are very problematic. For instance, questions raised would be: which laptop companies stand to benefit; how are cultural knowledges and culturally specific practices affected when 'foreign' technologies are introduced; what is the environmental impact of such strategies, and, why does any child need a laptop?

If the answer to the last question is for educational and economic advantage then the argument turns back to the Heideggerian concern that human being is becoming quite limited in its purpose. Perhaps given a democratic bent we would wish all children to have laptops to simply enhance their knowledge and wonderment. Bowers (2000) would suggest that this is not the real purpose of such strategies. Additionally, the likely outcomes are of concern for him. Technologies such as laptops, and information networks such as the Internet and educational software, are culturally specific and endanger the points of difference that engender communities as communities. Bowers also challenges that the very purpose of education emerges as technologically oriented, or technocentric. Education is in this sense itself a technology designed to enhance a technological society. Educational questions (questions essential to critically reflective practice) become narrowly defined in technical and economic terms, and not "concerned with how technology as an area of study can be situated into a wider cultural, social, ethnic, intellectual and political milieu" (Marshall, 1999, p. 168). Patrick Fitzsimons (2002, p. 184) argues:

When we take education primarily as a technology for national economic development, that 'technology' is focused on some predetermined goal, itself already evaluated as of value. Education so configured does not suggest or ask about education's purpose. The process to the ends is purely to produce the predetermined ends, and the human is part of that structure.

One could be forgiven for assuming that the philosophy of technology leads to a rather grim view of the world in which every act is about exploitation and every one of us is simply a cog in the big machine of a technological society, somewhat like The Matrix. However this is not the case. Feenberg's (1999) critique of technology suggests that there is much evidence to refute any suggestion of human slavery. He argues that our real lives are full of difference and that these differences engender positive and unique relationships to technology.

Feenberg (1999) challenges the philosophy of technology to ensure that key questions about technology move from the broad and essentialising to the specific and pragmatic. Like Bowers and Heidegger he is concerned with how one lives a good life given one's technological environment. In particular he is concerned with how we might "intervene in the design process in the defence of the conditions of a meaningful life and a livable environment" (Feenberg, 1999, p. xiv). Here, assumptions that a teacher is trained in a predetermined role are challenged. Feenberg requires that we ask how teachers contribute to the design of technologies that are used in their classrooms; and in this context remembering that there is no universal classroom. So how do teachers around the world negotiate with the technologies they use? Feenberg accepts that this will happen as each teacher will interpret and apply their resources differently. However in a paradigm of professionalism teachers are confronted with incessant expectations to display certain standards, skills and qualities. Teachers need some encouragement to

resist such pressures if they are to engage in the essential considerations that enhance reflection upon the use of technology include:

* What counts as technology?
* Is technology neutral?
* How does technology impact on our lives?

As argued above, these questions are prevalent in the world of fiction. The philosophy of technology does not reside solely in the complex worlds of scholars and hence there are many strategies that can be employed to encourage teachers, and children, to engage with critical questions associated with technology. In science fiction educators and children are presented with accessible and important 'questions concerning technology'. Some examples …

The storylines in both Digimon (2000) and Transformers (2007) orient around relations between humans and technology. In Digimon the human characters develop symbiotic relationships with digital world characters, and work together to save the digital world, and then the 'real world' from oppressive and dictatorial regimes. Meanwhile in Transformers Autobots and humans work together to preserve the planet's limited energy resources. Both narratives draw out important questions around the impact of technology on our lives, the ways in which different people use technology, and the emotional links between humans and technology (links that shape who we are, and how we perceive ourselves).

In AI (2001), an adaptation of Brian Aldiss' short story Supertoys Last all Summer Long, the viewer engages with parents who replace their son with an artificial boy whilst the son's illness is untreatable. With the return of the son the AI boy is confronted with questions of his own existence, and the story of Pinocchio is revisited. We are asked to consider what counts as a real boy (Ghiraldelli, 2002), and we are again confronted with emotional connections with a machine. Such issues are extremely important for teachers to engage with in classrooms. A critical component of reflection is the ability to ask ourselves, what is real, and has become central to the emergence of philosophy for children (see Haynes, 2002).

In the Star Wars (2005) series adults and children are confronted with more important questions regarding the nature of real and artificial, human and machine. For instance C3P0, the famous translator droid, regularly engages with questions of his own limitations as merely a machine, and grapples with the problems of having a personality. The limitations of machines are also raised. As cloning technologies develop, galactic alliances turn to clone armies as more efficient and effective weapons than droid armies. Countless reproductions of one man can be made, and while each is valued for his ability to act independently, is his death of any great concern? And what does genetic science suggest about the constructed nature of the human machine?

In the world of literature Samuel Butler's Erewhon (1970) devotes a chapter to the question of whether machines are alive, in the context of a society that has refused the advances of technology. Martian Time Slip (1964), by Philip K Dick introduces the limitations of advanced teaching machines that have limited options to choose from in their responses to children. Yet the human characters reveal themselves to be limited in their options too – Dick reveals a tendency to view our own failings in the actions of others, and to make assumptions that lack reflexivity.

All these sources of questioning relationships to technology provide rich terrain in which to develop early childhood teaching practices that are both informed and sensitive. The development of these qualities underpins the purpose of the two sessions outlined and discussed in the remains of the chapter.

THE PROFESSIONAL DEVELOPMENT SESSION

The purpose of the professional development session was to emphasise and discuss the importance of critical reflection upon ICT discourse, particularly in terms of how such discourse might construct the early childhood educator as a technologically deficient subject. I introduced, through reference to policy and research, assumptions of the ICT competencies of educators, arguing that such assumptions undermine the ways in which educators might actively engage in critique.

The session began with images of a well known idiom: don't throw the baby out with the bath water. I have been cautioned of this danger, most likely because of my tendency to question practices. I take the advice quite seriously, it is important to consider what progress has given us, and not to dismiss it. And being resistant to change brings with it the possibility that change will be affected more carefully and meaningfully. Colin Gibbs (personal communication, March 11, 2008) perhaps best sums this perspective up: if there is too much resistance to a new idea, it is probably not the right time to introduce it.

During the session I ask participants to engage with suggestions that preschoolers will need to 'graduate' in computer literacy in the future if they wish to enter school (see Hughes, 1998). Technological literacy is widely regarded as essential for a successful life. One might argue that this has always been the case. Whilst technologies change, the importance of familiarity and capacity to utilise technology remains a consistent value for, and outcome of, education. Yet the suggestion that children might need to graduate from preschool as computer literate is a conflation of science fiction and curriculum advocacy that raises interesting tensions around what might be considered essential about a child's learning before school. Such debates need not be restricted to the latest software or hardware. Thinking about such claims, or prophesies, provides valuable space from which to interrogate wider assumptions about school readiness and early childhood competence. During the presentation these claims are situated in a historical context, referring to provocative quotes from the 60s – a period of intensive invasion of new technologies into homes and institutions (see Bagrit, 1965). The teachers are asked to define in their own terms the meaning of 'technological change' and consider why some might see change as invasion, and others as salvation that social institution such as education might seek immunisation from it?

The presentation then introduces definitions of technology in order to pull apart what does and does not counts as technology by definition, and how these definitions impact upon education. Participants are asked to consider why it might be valuable to be critically reflective in relation to definitions and assumptions, before being introduced to the following quote, in order to emphasise my concerns regarding the ability of teachers to implement technologies in their center. *"Without good guidance, examples, and support for their own professional learning, early childhood educators will make their own decisions about the nature and extent of ICT use in children's learning"* (Bolstad, 2004, p. ix).

I ask the educators: "why might a teacher's 'own decisions' be a problem for researchers and policy makers?" My concern here was a perception that teachers (many of whom had been working in the sector for many years) identified themselves as lacking proficiency (at best) or techno-illiterate (at worst). Now, whether this was in any way an accurate self assessment, the impact of such an assessment has serious implications for the meaningful and reflective incorporation of any technologies, let alone new technologies into early childhood educational settings. From where do such negative perceptions of self come? And what is their impact on the educator's qualities as a critically reflective practitioner?

The idea that teachers might be in technological debit is often alluded to in the calls to 'educate' teachers of the importance of their role, and of the need to adopt certain values, beliefs, and practices. Teachers are presented with the argument that their attitude and ability will negatively impact on the child's learning. New technologies such as computers are expected to facilitate new forms of learning for children (Papert 1993, Yelland, 2002), and the teacher must be primed in order to facilitate these outcomes (Yelland, 2002). Yet their existing beliefs are regarded as a central obstacle to effective integration of new technologies. More than simply learn the facts about computers, for instance, and how to use them most effectively in the classroom, teachers need to relate better to computers (Clements, 1999). Otherwise their professional development may engender more resistance. Hence professional development may best be oriented towards encouraging a positive attitude towards technology (Bolstad, 2004). A positive attitude requires a positive sense of self, a sense that is arguably unlikely to develop out of a sense of inadequacy and/or weakness.

While almost a decade has passed since Clements made the above recommendations, they are very relevant for their focus and contribution, and in a fast paced world of technological transformation, they also enable us to reflect upon how beliefs regarding the role of teachers have developed. Bolstad's research suggests that there is a growing distancing of literature from stigmatization to a more strengths-oriented construction of the teacher. The competing constructions contributed to my development of sessions that encouraged educators and student teachers to think about how they felt about these issues. In so doing I was hoping to not only raise awareness of the importance of thinking critically about technology, but also the importance of thinking about how one is, as an educator, discursively constructed. What this means is that through discourse the educator comes to know herself as having particular characteristics and qualities. This is not to suggest that she is imprisoned in these characteristics, but it is to say that she is strongly influenced by them. And in the instance of technoliteracy (Lankshear, Snyder, & Green, 2000), this influence generates concerning tensions between the notion of the skilled and critical and empowering educator, and the technicist teacher trained to do a specific task.

In terms of technical application, the 90s saw many guidelines generated, featuring considerable sensitivity to the existing assumptions of a quality and appropriate natural learning environment. For instance Bredekamp and Rosengrant (1994, p. 54) argue that computers should not "replace highly valued early childhood activities and materials" and are not inherently an educative necessity. Teachers must ensure that the computer is integrated into the classroom in such a way as to encourage social activity, child-direction, and exploration and problem solving (Davidson & Wright, 1994). The early years curriculum is generally understood in a holistic sense. As such the complex role for the teacher is to ensure that any new technology is introduced "without jettisoning sound values and education ideals" (Cook & Finlayson, 1999, p. 5) – or, don't throw the baby out with the bath water. Technology in the curriculum should not be narrowly understood as a means of preparing children for the needs of the nation as a competitive economy in a global information age and hence not be sensitive to the wider principles of early childhood education.

Bredekamp and Rosengrant (1994) suggest that where computers do not augment an integrative curriculum, it is likely because teachers are not integrating them properly. To integrate the computer properly, they continue, teachers must critically engage with research on, for instance, quality software and then introduce the children through a process of "awareness, exploration, inquiry and utilization" (ibid. p 55). Ainsa, Murphy, Thouvenelle and Wright (1994) additionally argue that it is the role of the professional to filter appropriate software for parents. Teachers should be responsible for advising parents of good practice when it comes to using the computer. The importance of reaching out to the home reflects a wider expectation that the early childhood teacher ameliorate social and economic disadvantage. Teachers can, in other words, help to address issues of disadvantage in access to technology. Hence it is not just teachers who are constructed as needy. ICT discourse constructs and colonises whole communities and cultures as in need of ICT solutions. The concern here is not that such groups are not needy, or that they should not be identified as needy, rather that emphasis on amelioration of need through access to technology can obscure the factors that contribute to need, and does very little to address the power and knowledge relationships that lead to need. In other words, some children are targeted as in need of a head start with computers, but the reasons that some children might be 'needy' are forgotten in the will to give them access to computers through their early childhood education. With or without computers, the more substantial factors that contribute to disadvantage for certain groups will continue to disadvantage those groups. In sum, teachers are responsible for ensuring children and parents and communities have positive attitudes to and experiences with new technologies. Yelland (2002) emphasises that such positivity leads to enhanced relationships to education as a whole. Such emphasis is quite particular to technology in the curriculum. If teachers do not like to sing or lack ability in art, it is unlikely you will be accused of affecting the child's attitude to the curriculum, and to learning in general.

The session then outlines the claims of critics of new technologies in early childhood education. Following Bowers, it is suggested that ICT advocacy in education has the vested interests of private corporations who are developing 'brand loyalty' at earlier and earlier ages. For instance children playing with cell phones in centres, whether the phone works or not, are developing desired behaviours and preferences. Critics also suggest that while economic vested interests are flourishing, the vested interests of teachers, communities, parents, and children regarding technology are subordinate to expert opinion and research. Teachers' own opinions about using computers in preschool environments are marginalised given that their knowledge and attitudes are constantly questioned.

These criticisms are far outweighed by the literature promoting the benefits of and best practices with new technologies. Understanding of such criticism is nevertheless critical to the constitution of the early childhood teacher as a reflective practitioner who is able to effectively integrate new technologies in a range of early childhood settings.

Critical engagement, however, has a tendency to be marginalised as moral panic ... Where analysis of the nature and purpose of new technology on existing and future practices and philosophies in education is stigmatised as negative, traditionalist, Luddite and/or moral panic, meaningful critique if limited (Gibbons, 2006, p. 12).

The story of the Luddites is very relevant. Being a Luddite tends to mean being either afraid or ignorant in relation to new technologies. While the story of the Luddites has far more depth to it, the effectiveness of the will to progress has limited interpretation of their machine breaking and rioting – the diversity of human experiences and actions are in this way undermined and obscured. Professional development for teachers provides time and space to collaborate with colleagues in making sense of technology. Teachers are encouraged to value their own perspectives, experiences and aspirations in relation to technology. They are in addition discouraged from beginning their development with the attitude that they are in need of learning how to implement technology in their centres. They would not be encouraged, in Aotearoa/New Zealand, to devalue a child's contribution in such ways. Much of their teacher education is focused on providing a learning environment that is sensitive to the needs of each child, valuing each child's contributions, and protect-

ing the child from standardised expectations of developmental measurement. In what ways then should teacher education introduce technology to student teachers?

TEACHER EDUCATION

The contending discourses that contribute to the politics and philosophy of early childhood education generally find their strongest manifestations in early childhood teacher education. Whether discussions of the importance of a theory of learning, or of the importance of an area of the curriculum, it is often through the context of teacher education that such discussions are given voice. For discussions on technology then, it follows that the student teacher be introduced to arguments for and against the importance and contribution of technology.

Teacher education is generally regarded as the period of time in which a student teacher develops favourable perceptions of, and skills with, implementing new technologies in the early childhood environment. Teacher education in this sense can ameliorate the low-tech deficit, engendering a techno-credit. In the late 80s and early 90s teacher education (more generally) was very much focused on training the teacher to use specific technologies (Dunn & Morgan, 1987). This concerned some advocates who argued that student teachers need to be able adaptable in a constantly transforming technological environment, and require an understanding of the wider social contexts in which technologies are developed and applied (Gwynn, 1986). Hence students should not develop specific skills in, for instance, certain software, rather they should learn about how to learn about technology once out in the field – they should, in other words, perceive themselves as in a constant state of 'becoming' (Vossler, et al., 2005).

This importance of critical reflection guided my development of lectures for student teachers studying both three year diplomas and degrees in early childhood education. The purpose of classroom lectures I delivered to early childhood student teachers was to introduce the students to technology in the curriculum. Teacher education often focuses on strategies of how to use new technologies to benefit the development of their children, and how to ensure children develop with socially-desirable behaviours in regards to the use of technology (Ainsa et al., 1994), such as not using cell phones at inappropriate times. For early childhood student teachers the key word is 'integration'. New technologies are not expected to cause too much disruption to the environment. Integrating new technologies then requires careful and reflective practice.

The class engages with the sort of questioning believed necessary to make sense of the literature in each student's past, current, and future contexts. This was achieved through practical activities and through connection of the Aoteaora/New Zealand national curriculum for early childhood Te Whāriki (Ministry of Education, 1996) with each student's views on technology. The practical exercise of note was an informal piece of empirical research during the session. I asked the students to raise their hands if they had a cell phone. I then asked them if their cell phone was on, and quickly followed this with the request that all cell phones be activated. This generally meets with some humorous responses not the least because it is normally quite a surprising command given the traditional context of a tertiary lecture. As the lecture proceeds the students are asked to identify when they have been sent a text message (otherwise known as an SMS) or have been called. What I do not do is tell students what to do when their phones receive the message or call.

As we proceed through the session the core principles and strands of the curriculum are discussed in relation to technology. For instance, in what ways can teachers integrate computers and the Internet into the centre in order to support children's connections with their family and community, or their relationships with each other? In addition as texts and calls are received (and they invariably are received), the student teachers must make some critical decisions: what should I do if the phone rings or if someone texts; and how will this impact on the class and the lecturer? Such questions contribute to a critical literacy, in that student teachers are being encouraged to think carefully about the implications of using technology in their personal and professional lives. Importantly, they are not being told what to do.

Critical reflection contributes to the student teacher's wider understanding of the world. Through exploring relationships to technology student teachers are confronted with many social, cultural, political and economic questions. Student teachers must also consider the relationships between learning, education and technology. These deeper questions orient around the purpose of education. Critical reflection draws, as noted above, from issues around technology in the early childhood setting, to an expansive and productive practice of reflecting upon one's teaching practice. In this sense, there is immense value to new technologies for they encourage rather than discourage critical reflection. Student teachers are confronted with the assumptions that they make regarding technology. Common sense becomes open to questioning, and questioning is a not simply an important quality of a teacher, it is, according to Heidegger,(1977) an important quality of being human.

It is important to think about the values and beliefs that are transmitted through technology. For instance, how does a cell phone impact on a child's perception of their society, their environment, their relationships, and their own identities? How do we view people because of their access to certain technologies? And more than how we think about the world, how do technologies actually change the ways in which we think? New technologies can significantly alter both the child and adult's educational experiences, and their experiences of being a child or adult. Hence technology provides an important scope for introducing student teachers to the deep questions about society and self. The difference between teacher training and teacher education becomes an important focus for the development of a teacher's ability to critically reflect upon technology and self. Where training might be seen as providing computers to student teachers to help train them in the necessary skills, teacher education requires more engagement with the notion of being in a constant state of becoming (Vossler et al., 2005), an engagement that gives presence to a more poetic understanding of one's self (or perhaps selves) as teacher. The crux of the issue is then the tension between the need for supporting student teachers to think carefully and critically about technology, and the impact of labeling the same students as traditionally technologically poor. Somewhat ironically, there is a sense that an early childhood educator's stereotypical strengths, their passion for connecting with and nurturing children, is fundamentally associated with their stereotypical weakness – their lack of knowledge and passion regarding new technologies. Yet if teachers engage with the meanings of technology in a wider sense then they may have quite different conceptions of what it means to be a technophobe or a technophile. Focusing on their technological strengths might then be an important and reflective introduction to technology in the curriculum (see for instance Buckingham, 2007).

Now, the idea that advocates for technology wish teachers to be 'mindless consumers' (O'Neill & Jolley, 2004) seems fairly farfetched. It is unreasonable to claim that any literature that seeks to enhance a teacher's knowledge of technology wishes to generate an army of mindless teaching machines. If this is not the intention, then let us discontinue with the negative characterizations of early childhood teachers.

The impact of such labeling is concerning, as already noted above, in the context of the reflective practitioner. The challenge is to refrain from simply expecting to construct a more able student through enhancing their technological skills. Student teachers do not need to become more able than children at understanding and applying all the fancy gadgetry, software, and online environment. They do need to be aware of how their understanding of technology and of themselves is in some way a product of the discourses that have influenced and shaped them, that confront them through their teacher education, and that define their day to day experiences. Such awareness can be explored through a turn to philosophy, and particularly in this context the philosophy of technology, but in a wider sense to the philosophy of education.

For student teachers, an introduction, at the very least, to the philosophy of technology can have a significant impact on their development as a critical and reflective practitioner. Following Heidegger, the many diverse contexts of early childhood teachers give presence to who they are, to the time and place in which they themselves were children, and had different relationships with technology. Following Bowers, their cultural knowledge needs to be protected, and their awareness of the cultural nature of technology needs to be developed. Following Feenberg, their understanding and use of technology should not result in their perception of themselves as inadequate. Student teachers do not then need to develop in themselves, or in the child, a sense of expertise (Bers, New & Boudreau, 2004) when such expertise devalues their own contributions and/or knowledge (Castellani & Tsantis, 2002). In this way they might contribute to educational debates, keeping educational questions open (Gibbons, 2006). If teachers are not contributing to such discussions then where resides the critical pedagogue?

CONCLUDING STATEMENTS, VISIONS AND QUESTIONS CONCERNING TECHNOLOGY

By degrees, the universal right to be educated has mutated into a universal obligation to be assessed, and it is easy to forget that these are, in fact, quite distinct objectives (Brown, 2002, p. 165).

Brown's critique of education reminds us that technology is not simply changing the role of the teacher. Technology is questioning the presence of the teacher and school. Some research and commentary suggests that new technologies will not just change the role of teacher; it will negate the role of the teacher as we know it. While the locus of such views tends to come from critiques of education and not advocacy for technology – the technology is regarded generally as a tool to enable a vision of learning and education free from forms of schooling that emerged during the industrial revolution – these are 'real' concerns. In a 'technological age' education is understood as a technology. The teacher too becomes a tool to affect certain outcomes. Critics such as Ivan Illich (1976) might have argued, in the 70s, that the human teacher had already been replaced by a human teaching machine in the evolution of state schooling. The 'deschooling' movement perceived new technologies as means to affect preservation of the identities and independencies of communities and cultures. However, more recently Bowers has challenged this assumption, arguing that computer technologies are equally as homogenizing as school systems. I would not hope to convince a teacher of the merits of either argument. Rather this chapter stresses the importance of student teachers and teachers having space to make their own decisions. The wider issue is that of the status of teaching and teachers – two common positions are to suggest that increased status will be achieved through instigating more surveillance and regulation of teachers, or alter-

natively more status will be achieved through paring back the level of governance of teachers. This chapter has supported the latter, through appealing to the literature on reflective practice in early childhood education. I suggest it might not be a bad thing then to hold on to some outdated values, principles and practices at worst, and at best to critically question the ways in which teachers are constructed as both strong and weak players in hi-tech and low-tech worlds. Philosophy contributes to both possibilities.

If early childhood education is not to be understood as technocentrically configured into the wider 'diploma mills' of the 21st century (Peters, 1998), teacher educators and professional development facilitators might think carefully about how and why they are introducing new technologies into the worlds of teachers. Their own critical reflection might encourage a sense of caution and informed critique when considering the purpose and role of technology in the centre's life. ICT is very exciting for many who consider the benefits for education, and this is as it should be. I do not wish to stifle the passion for technology, I wish such passions to be enlarged and enlivened through drawing in more voices. Sadly, the voices that are missing in this chapter of those of the student teachers and teachers themselves. It is time then to provide more space for their stories about technology.

Some philosophical questions for reflective practitioners:

1. How does technology affect how I think about myself as a teacher, and about the child as a learner?
2. How do new technologies affect my values and beliefs regarding early childhood education?
3. How do the technologies I implement in my teaching practice reflect the cultures represented in my community?
4. Who should I involve in introducing and evaluating technology in the early childhood

curriculum?

5. What literature and cinema impacts upon how I think about technology?
6. What is my philosophy of technology in early childhood education settings?

Brown's critique of education reminds us that technology is not simply changing the role of the teacher. Technology is questioning the presence of the teacher and school. Some research and commentary suggests that new technologies will not just change the role of teacher; it will negate the role of the teacher as we know it. While the locus of such views tends to come from critiques of education and not advocacy for technology – the technology is regarded generally as a tool to enable a vision of learning and education free from forms of schooling that emerged during the industrial revolution – these are 'real' concerns. In a 'technological age' education is understood as a technology. The teacher too becomes a tool to affect certain outcomes. Critics such as Ivan Illich (1976) might have argued, in the 70s, that the human teacher had already been replaced by a human teaching machine in the evolution of state schooling. The 'deschooling' movement perceived new technologies as means to affect preservation of the identities and independencies of communities and cultures. However more recently Bowers has challenged this assumption, arguing that computer technologies are equally as homogenizing as school systems. I would not hope to convince a teacher of the merits of either argument. Rather this chapter stresses the importance of student teachers and teachers having space to make their own decisions. The wider issue is that of the status of teaching and teachers – two common positions are to suggest that increased status will be achieved through instigating more surveillance and regulation of teachers, or alternatively more status will be achieved through paring back the level of governance of teachers. This chapter has supported the latter, through appealing to the literature on reflective practice in

early childhood education. I suggest it might not be a bad thing then to hold on to some outdated values, principles and practices at worst, and at best to critically question the ways in which teachers are constructed as both strong and weak players in hi-tech and low-tech worlds. Philosophy contributes to both possibilities.

If early childhood education is not to be understood as technocentrically configured into the wider 'diploma mills' of the 21st century (Peters, 1998), teacher educators and professional development facilitators might think carefully about how and why they are introducing new technologies into the worlds of teachers. Their own critical might encourage a sense of caution and informed critique when considering the purpose and role of technology in the centre's life. ICT is very exciting for many who consider the benefits for education, and this is as it should be. I do not wish to stifle the passion for technology, I wish such passions to be enlarged and enlivened through drawing in more voices. Sadly, the voices that are missing in this chapter of those of the student teachers and teachers themselves. It is time then to provide more space for their stories about technology.

REFERENCES

Ainsa, P. A., Murphy, D., Thouvenelle, S., & Wright, J. L. (1994). Listen to the Children: Observing Young Children's Discoveries with the Microcomputer. In J. L. Wright, & D. D. Shade (Eds.), Young Children: Active Learners in a Technological Age (pp. 3-17). Washington D.C.: National Association for the Education of Young Children.

Bagrit, L. (1965). The age of automation. *The Reith Lectures, 1964.* Harmondsworth: Penguin Books.

Bers, M. U., New, R. S., & Boudreau, L. (2004). Teaching and learning when no one is expert: Children and parents explore technology. *Early Childhood Research and Practice, 6*(2). Retrieved 22 January, 2005, http://ecrp.uiuc.edu/v6n2/bers.html

Bolstad, R. (2004). *The role and potential for ICT in early childhood education: A review of New Zealand and international literature.* Wellington: New Zealand Council for Educational Research.

Bowers, C. (1988). *The cultural dimensions of educational computing: Understanding the non-neutrality of technology.* New York: Teachers College Press.

Bowers, C. (2000). *Let them eat data: How computers affect education, cultural diversity and the prospects of ecological sustainability.* Athens, GA: The University of Georgia Press.

Bredekamp, S., & Rosengrant, T. (1994). Learning and teaching with technology. In J. L. Wright, & D. D. Shade (Eds.), *Young children: Active learners in a technological age* (pp. 53-61). Washington D.C.: National Association for the Education of Young Children.

Brown, K. (2002). *The right to learn: Alternatives for a learning society.* London: Routledge Falmer. Buckingham, M. (2007). *Go put your strengths to work: 6 powerful steps to achieve outstanding performance.* New York, NY: Free Press.

Buckleitner, W. (1999). The state of children's software evaluation: Yesterday, today, and in the 21st Century. *Information Technology in Childhood Education Annual.* Retrieved March 21, 2002, from http://web2.infotrac.galegroup.com

Butler, S. (1970). *Erewhon.* Harmondsworth: Penguin Books.

Castellani, J., & Tsantis, L. (2002). Cross-cultural reactions to using computers in the early childhood classroom. *Contemporary Issues in Early Childhood, 3*(2). Retrieved October 14, 2003, from http://www.triangle.co.uk/ciec/

Clements, D. H. (1999). *The future of educational computing research: The case of computer programming.* The Association for the Advancement of Computing in Education. Retrieved October 20, 2001, from http://web7.infotrac.galegroup.com

Cook, D., & Finlayson, H. (1999). *Interactive children, communicative teaching: ICT and classroom teaching.* Buckingham, UK: Open University Press. Limits of Software. Reading, MA: Addison-Wesley.

Davidson, J. I., & Wright, J. L. (1994). The potential of the microcomputer in the early childhood classroom. In J. L. Wright & D. D. Shade (Eds.), *Young children: Active learners in a technological age* (pp. 77-91). Washington D.C.: National Association for the Education of Young Children.

Dick, P. K. (1964). *Martian Time Slip.* London, UK: Millenium.

Dunn, S., & Morgan, V. (1987). *The impact of the computer on education: A course for teachers.* Hemel Hempstead: Prentice Hall.

Feenberg, A. (1999). *Questioning technology.* London: Routledge.

Fitzsimons, P. (2002). Enframing education. In M. A. Peters (Ed.), *Heidegger, education, and modernity* (pp. 171-190). Lanham, MD: Rowman & Littlefield Publishers.

Ghiraldelli, P. Jr. (2000). The fundamentals of Gepeto's philosophy of education: Neopragmatism and infancy in the postmodern world. *Educational Philosophy and Theory, 32*(2), 201–207. doi:10.1111/j.1469-5812.2000.tb00444.x

Gibbons, A. N. (2006). The politics of technology in early childhood in Aotearoa/New Zealand: Fitting early childhood educators in the ICT grid. *Australian Journal of Early Childhood, 31*(4), 7–14.

Gwynn, R. (1986). Towards a pedagogy of information. In R. Ennals., R. Gwyn, & L. Zdravchev (Eds.), *Information technology and education: The changing school* (pp. 29-44). Chichester: Ellis Horwood Ltd.

Hao, Y. (2000). *Relationship between teachers' use of reflection and other selected variable and preschool teachers' engagement in developmentally appropriate practice.* Retrieved 25 February, 2008, from http://www.eric.ed.gov/ERICDocs/data/ericdocs2sql/content_storage_01/0000019b/80/16/e2/3b.pdf

Haynes, J. (2002). *Children as philosophers: Learning through enquiry and dialogue in the primary classroom.* London: RoutledgeFalmer.

Heidegger, M. (1977). The question concerning technology. (W. Lovitt, Trans.). In M. Heidegger (Ed.), *The question concerning technology and other essays* (pp. 1-49). New York: Harper & Row.

Hughes, D. R. (1998). *Kids online: Protecting your children in cyberspace.* Minnesota: Fleming H. Revell.

Illich, I. (1976). *Deschooling Society.* Harmondsworth: Penguin Books.

Kennedy, K. (Producer). (2001). *AI.* US: Warner Brothers.

Kubrick, S. (Writer/Director). (1968). *2001: A space odyssey.* US: MGM.

Lankshear, C., Snyder, I., & Green, B. (2000). *Teachers and technoliteracy:- Managing literacy, technology and learning in schools.* St Leonards, NSW: Allen & Unwin.

Lucas, G. (Executive Producer and Director). (2005). *Star wars episode III: Revenge of the Sith.* US: Twentieth Century Fox.

Marshall, J. D. (1999). Technology in the New Zealand curriculum. *New Zealand Journal of Educational Studies, 34*(1), 165–175.

Ministry of Education. Te Tahuhu o te Matauranga (1996). *Te whāriki: He whāriki matauranga mō ngā mokopuna o Aotearoa, early childhood curriculum.* Wellington: Learning Media.

Moss, P. (2006). Structures, understandings and discourses: Possibilities for re-visioning the early childhood worker. *Contemporary Issues in Early Childhood, 7*(1), 30–41. doi:10.2304/ciec.2006.7.1.30

Murphy, D. (Producer). (2007). *Transformers.* US: Paramount.

National Association for the Education of Young Children. (1997). Developmentally appropriate practice in early childhood programs serving children from birth through age 8. Washington, DC, USA: National Association for the Education of Young Children. Retrieved March 18, 2008, from http://www.naeyc.org/about/positions/pdf/PSDAP98.PDF

Papert, S. (1993). *The children's machine: Rethinking school in the age of the computer.* New York: BasicBooks.

Peters, M. A. (1998). Education and the shift from knowledge to information: Virtual classrooms or automated diploma mills? *Access, 17*(1), 65–78.

Seki, H. (Producer). (2000). *Digimon: The movie.* US: Twentieth Century Fox.

Skinner, B. F. (1965). Reflections on a decade of teaching machines. In R. Glaser (Ed.), *Teaching machines and programmed learning: Data and directions* (pp. 5-20). Washington: Association for Educational Communications and Technology.

Turing, A. (1992). *Mechanical Intelligence: Collected Works of A M Turing*. Amsterdam: North Holland.

Vossler, K., Waitere-Ang, H., & Adams, P. (2005). Becoming an educator. In P. Adams, K. Vossler, & C. Scrivens (Eds.), *Teachers work in Aotearoa New Zealand* (pp. 17-27). Victoria, Australia: Thomson/Dunmore Press.

Yelland, N. (2002). Playing with ideas and games in early mathematics. *Contemporary Issues in Early Childhood, 3*(2). Retrieved October 23, 2002, from http://www.triangle.co.uk/ciec/

Chapter 2
Computer Technology in Taiwan Kindergartens

Yu-Yuan Lee
University of Memphis, USA & Nan Kai University of Technology, Taiwan

ABSTRACT

Taiwan has become a global high-tech center. The success of becoming the leading country of high-tech and information technology is accredited to the efforts of the government and of all citizens. In addition, Chinese highly value in academic success, and this has contributed to the success of Taiwan. Parents believe the success of life is rooted in a good education, especially in the early years. This chapter presents an overview of early childhood education in Taiwan and explores how Chinese culture had influenced the value of parents' expectation in education, as well as how children learn through the use of technology. The last part of the chapter discusses the discrepancy between current early childhood education situations and teachers' professional development.

INTRODUCTION

Determining the best methods for adapting school curriculum to address the continuous changes in society has always been one goal that schoolteachers and administrators endeavor to achieve. This task has become even more difficult than before because today's students, growing up in an environment of rich digital media and advanced technologies, have available more sophisticated ways of learning. Prensky (2001a) has highlighted the discrepancy of

learning methods between today's generations and their previous generations, which is called "digital immigrants." Today's generations are digital media literate. Their experiences of communicating, processing information, and socialization through digital technology will be brought into the schools, impact traditional instructions and teachers' roles in the classroom as well (Foreman, 2003; Prensky, 2001b; Tapscott, 1998).

Knowing how to read and write is not enough to survive in a rapid changing society. The traditional meaning of literacy includes the ability to read and write. However, as technology advances, we are

DOI: 10.4018/978-1-60566-784-3.ch002

moving towards an age that strongly demands technological literacy beyond the traditional meaning of basic reading and writing skills (Kajder, 2004). Knowing how to get information from the vast data base on the Internet is imperative; and this competence should be enhanced in schools. Papert (1998) asserts that technology should not only be used to empower the quality and content of learning; but also, and most importantly, it should be used as an integral tool to cultivate innovative knowledge, which is considered a necessity for functioning in a modern society (Shaffer & Gee, 2005). Thus, to better prepare students with skills to adapt to the changing world, schools are encouraged to integrate technology into the teaching and a learning process in an early stage.

Taiwan has been a leader in the production of electronic semiconductors since 1999, and has become a global high-tech center today (Babb, 1999; Taiwan Review, 2004). Its output of electronic/computer products, such as personal computers, monitors, and scanners, has given it prominence in the world community (Babb, 1999). According to Dahl and Lopez-Claros (2005), Taiwan was ranked as the world's fifth most competitive economic country and has become a leader of the widespread use of information and communications technologies. Under the impacts of economic globalization; the government, parents, and educators in Taiwan strive to maintain the competitiveness of its citizens. They are strong proponents and advocates and catalysts in providing education for computer literacy and the knowledge of information technology. Indeed, technological education has been flourishing in Taiwan. For instance, new curricula and objectives of curricula emphasizing technological literacy and foreign language proficiency have been implemented since 2000. Computer literacy has become an important core curriculum in all levels (Ministry of Education (MOE, 2003; 2005a). The government has even promoted media as a second curriculum (MOE, 2006) to reinforce students' education in information and internet technology.

In addition to government's reforms and policies, Chinese cultural values and parents' expectations have also contributed to the flourish of technology education. Having long been influenced by Confucianism, which honors scholars and literati in the Chinese society, most parents highly value children's academic achievement and take this goal as their responsibilities (Zhang & Carrasquillo, 1995; Lin & Tsai, 1996). In this sense, parents are desperate to educate their children at early ages. They expect them to succeed academically and become well-rounded persons in the future. Children in their early ages are taught to read, write, and to do simple arithmetic skills before they begin school (Schneider & Lee, 1990; Zhang & Carrasquillo, 1995). It is common that kindergarteners are taught to read and write and some are assigned written homework (Lin & Tsai, 1996). In addition, children are sent to attend all kinds of skill classes after schools to meet their parents' expectations. These lessons include dancing, drawing, mental arithmetic, piano, English, or even computer skills and such lessons can easily be found in kindergarten curricula in Taiwan. To meet parents' needs, not only has English been requested as a common course in kindergarten, but computer classes have also been included to recruit new students in many private kindergartens. In fact, as Fang (2003) argues, with the prevalence of computers, many young children have ample opportunities to access computers at home. Young children already have possessed various background knowledge related to multi-media and computer technologies before they attend preschools or kindergartens.

Accessing internet or playing with computer software/video games is a very popular leisure activity for children and young adolescents in Taiwan (Tseng & Liang, 2002). Besides its entertaining function, computers have been considered as multifunctional learning tools and toys to help children's cognitive development in many studies. Yang (1998) accredits its family educative function of computer software. He believes computers are versatile tools that can assist children's growth at home. Likewise, Fang (2004) concludes that children demonstrate their love and active participations in learning through the implementing information technology in kindergarten. Children also learn how to negotiate and take turns through computer use. Lü, Zhang, Lin, and Xu (2007) promote children's literacy abilities through the use of international pen pal e-mail and blogs.

This chapter illustrates how computer technologies have been used to promote children's learning by tapping into three aspects related to current technology education in Taiwan. The first section highlights the importance of computer literacy and the new use of technology for learning for the new generations; the second part delineates current early childhood education in Taiwan, and how technology is viewed as the first concern to connect to global success from the viewpoints of culture, economics and government policies in Taiwan. The last part presents how computer technologies have promoted children's cognitive development in Taiwan, as well as how such technologies caused some early childhood educators to be concerned about its use in the classroom. Implications for future efforts will also be discussed.

The Importance of Technology Literacy for Today's Generations

The evolution of computer technology has had profound impacts on our daily lives. The most obvious impacts are the ways people process information, think, learn, and even socialize, especially when we view how players interact with each other in the gameplay world (Prensky, 2001; Shaffer, Squire, Halverson, & Gee, 2005). To illustrate, people use instant messaging, blogs, online phoning, or videoconferencing to overcome the constraints of time and space. People may even practice engage in tasks and portray identities, which cannot be assessed in reality, in the virtual community of massive multiplayer online video game worlds (Shaffer et al, 2005).

Computer literacy is essential for our new generations. Indeed, our new generations, which are entitled "Net Generation" (Tapscott, 1998), "digital native", or "Game-Generation" (Prensky, 2001a) will be the dominating population in our future job market; and their experiences in communicating, doing things or even learning with advanced computer technologies will reshape our future society (Tapscott, 1998). In his book *Growing up Digital: the Rise of the Net Generation,* Tapscott (1998) states that digital technology is a natural part of life for today's generations. He predicts the new generation will reshape a future society because of their experience of immersion in digital technology. He argues that the technological dependence of the new generations and the multimedia environment afforded by their high-tech resources will eventually be brought into classrooms and help transform educational methods. In fact, these shifts in the learning environment have already begun to occur. Technology-based curricula are popular and even video games are integrated into classrooms (see Squire, 2004; Van Eck, 2006) to meet how the new generations learn.

Learning environments and classroom instruction is enriched with the advances in computer technologies and networking. So-called "blogs", personal websites in which students can amass data, share their opinions and discuss their viewpoints, have become common place. Nowadays, students can "blog" their thoughts on-line, and interact with classmates and even people from different countries. As an added benefit, while students are engaging in these interactive activities, they can also learn other languages and cultures (Purushotma, 2005). Immersing in such activities, students actively learn rather than passively receive knowledge and information (Tapscott, 1998). On the other hand, technology-based learning also allows students to access real-time data, which are often more in-depth, accurate, and more visually stimulating than traditional classroom lectures. In fact, there are some educators who argue that traditional education methods which emphasize lecturing and professor-centered classroom methods cannot engage and motivate students to learn. They suggest the use of digital game-based learning environment to customize the classroom to each student's need (e.g. Foreman, 2003; Prensky, 2001).

Knowing how today's "digital native" generations learn can add its importance to adopt technology-based learning in school curricula. Prensky (2001a) claims that today's teachers are confronted with motivating today's students to learn because the traditional instructions cannot meet the way they learn and assess information. He urges today's teachers to adopt "digital native" methodology, to "learning new ways to do old stuff." (p.5). In other words, digital technologies are encouraged in school curricula. Shaffer and Gee (2005) argue that schools should provide students with more opportunities to cultivate innovative knowledge. Only with innovative knowledge can students become creative thinkers and have the competitive edge and competency needed in the 21st century. The innovative knowledge needs to be trained from the kindergarten level (Shaffer & Gee, 2005). Innovative knowledge can be transmitted through the application of computer technology, such as epistemic games (Shaffer & Gee, 2005). Epistemic games are games that can help students "learn to work and, thus, to think as innovative professionals" (Shaffer & Gee, 2005, p. 15). Many computer games, such as simulation games, provide good opportunities for the development of innovative knowledge. When students are immersing in such games, they are encultured into that community and learn to innovate (Shaffer & Gee, 2005). These issues illustrate how the advancement of technologies has influenced schools and teachers concerning education. There is a need to integrate computer technology into school curricula.

Computer Software as a Powerful Tool for Learning

Video games, besides their entertainment value, have raised much attention in education and research because of their embedded advantages for learning. Although many educators and parents are skeptical about video games, studies are now reveling that some entertaining games can help students' development of cognitive skills, such as critical thinking, reasoning, and problem-solving skills (Gee, 2003; Shaffer & Gee, 2005). Researchers and educators praise the education power and, therefore, advocate the application of digital game-based learning in school settings (Prensky, 2001; Foreman, 2003; Gee, 2003; Shaffer & Gee, 2005; Shaffer, Squire, Halverson, & Gee; 2005; Van Eck, 2006).

Game-like learning activities are effective in motivating children to access learning tasks and in retaining their attention (Rosas et al., 2003), not only because of the sensory-rich learning characters, but also the embedded educational power that promotes learning (Foreman, 2004; Prensky, 2002; Shaffer et al, 2005; Van Eck, 2006). Shaffer, Squire, Halverson, and Gee (2005) claim that video games provide situated learning environments, in which knowledge is initiated and transformed in "learning by doing environments" (p.108), rather than by rote learning. In the game world, knowledge is constructed and acquired through responding to the world that players are interactive with and situated in (Shaffer et al., 2005; Van Eck, 2006).

Playing video games/online games is a very common activity among teens in Taiwan. There are almost 60 million online video game players in Taiwan, and 43 percent of the players are under the age of 19 (Tseng & Liang, 2002). Playing video games has become one of their daily activities, and much game software has been found to be helpful to students in developing math and science concepts, as well as problem-solving and languages skills (Rosas et al, 2003; Dylak &

Kaczmarska, 2001). Students in Taiwan are motivated to learn while playing video games in their leisure time. In a study conducted by Lee, Cheon, and Key (2008), it was found that students have played video games since they are in elementary schools. These students perceive video games to be helpful for learning a second/foreign language (Lee et al., 2008). Students in Taiwan use different language learning strategies to solve language barriers while playing video games (Lee & Key, 2008). This implies that video games can be used for learning outside classrooms. Despite the fact that video games still have negative influences on players, such as aggression and addiction, (Ballard & West, 1996; Hauge & Gentile, 2003), playing such games has become a common activity among teens. Instead of worrying about how videogames can deteriorate children's minds, educators need to put more effort into evaluating appropriate games for classrooms and teaching them how to select good games for effective learning.

CURRENT PRESCHOOL EDUCATION IN TAIWAN

Early Childhood Education in Taiwan

Children at age six are required to attend schools since the inauguration of the nine-year compulsory education in 1968 by the Ministry of Education (MOE, 2005). Although preschool education has not been included as mandatory in Taiwan; previously, the awareness of the importance of preschool education has become the main focus of education innovation in the past decades. The policy of ten-year mandatory compulsory education, which includes one year of preschool education, has become the focus of the government education reforms (Fang, 2004).

The curriculum standards issued in 1987 for preschool education include six core areas: health education, play, music, work, language arts, and general knowledge. Thematic teaching or unit teaching is adopted by most preschools to integrate the six core areas (Zheng, 2004). Preschool education in Taiwan mainly falls into two categories: kindergartens and childcare centers. Childcare centers are social welfare organizations and are supervised by the social departments, while kindergartens are educational organizations and are supervised by the Ministry of Education (MOE, 2005b). Kindergartens are managed privately or publicly. Teachers who work for kindergartens are known as *kindergarten teachers*, while teachers in childcare centers are called *caregivers* (Hsieh, 2004). Private owned kindergartens dominate the majority of preschool education organizations, and childcare centers are all run by private organizations. On the other hand, public kindergartens are either affiliated with elementary schools or run by the local government. Preschoolers (age three to six) are expected to attend at least one year of kindergarten or preschool before they attend elementary schools. However, many young children attend preschools at the age of three. Some preschools mix children of different ages; others have three level classes for different ages of children. Children are grouped into different classes. Each class has a name, such as Sunflower Class, Kangaroo Class, Elephant Class, etc. Most children eat lunch and take naps at schools.

Because there are no standard textbooks for preschool education, schools have their own choice of contents and instructions. This makes early childhood curricula rich and more flexible. Most preschool curricula are designed to meet the needs of parents and the society (Fang, 2004; Hsieh, 2004). In order to distinguish their programs and to recruit more students, many private-run kindergartens adapt preschool education programs from other countries. These programs include *Montessori, Waldorf, the Reggio Emilia approach, and High-Scope* (Hsieh, 2004; Zheng, 2004). In terms of curriculum design, although the MOE has issued the preschool education standards, many kindergartens develop their programs heavily based on the needs of parents (Hsieh, 2004).

Table 1. Weekly timetable

Day/Time	Monday	Tuesday	Wednesday	Thursday	Friday
8:00 ∫ 9:00	Learning Corner	Learning Corner	Learning Corner	Learning Corner	Learning Corner
9:00 ∫ 11:30	Songs & Chants Math Reading	Reading Phonics Storytelling	Reading Phonics Science	Math Phonics Songs & Chants	Reading Math Social Studies
11:30 ∫ 14:20	Lunch and Nap				
14:20 ∫ 16:20	Thematic Teaching Snack Time Art	Science Snack Time Music	Computer Snack Time Art	Chinese Phonics Snack Time Music	Handwriting Snack Time Art
16: 30 ∫ 18:00	Go Home				

In this sense, activities, such as handwriting, English, art, mental arithmetic, and mathematics are introduced into kindergartens (Hsieh, 2004; Lin & Tsai, 1996). Computer activities are also introduced to children and used as a recruiting incentive to lure more students to programs (Lai & Chiu, 2006). Bilingual kindergartens or even only English speaking kindergartens are very prevalent and popular in Taiwan (Zheng, 2004).

A Day in a Private Preschool in Taiwan

To provide a picture of preschool education in Taiwan, the following section will describe a day in a private preschool. Children go to preschool for five days a week and stay until 4:30 PM. The curricula in preschools are very compact and exciting (see Table 1). Table 1 is an example of a weekly schedule in a bilingual kindergarten in central Taiwan. In general, preschools have their own school buses to serve their students. Schools normally open at 7:30 which allows parents to send their children to schools before they go to work.

When children arrive, they choose their own activities, such as playing with blocks, toys, or reading, or choosing different learning centers. During this period, teachers interact with children individually. Formal classes from 9:00 to 11:30 are designed for the development of children's English/Language Arts skills in reading, speaking, listening, and writing. Children listen to story, sing songs and chants, and read books together. Math, science, social studies, and language art are integrated into thematic teaching. Each period is about 30-35 minutes.

During lunch time, teachers and children eat together. Children learn social behavior at the table; they also learn the responsibilities of helping by cleaning up the tables when they finish lunch. After lunch, teachers and children take naps together. Classes designed in the afternoon are to develop children's competence in reading, speaking, handwriting, and math and science concepts in Chinese. In addition, music, art, and computer classes are offered. In the thematic teaching period, different media including projectors, PowerPoint, and the internet, are used to present the teaching materials. In computer classes, children learn how to operate basic computer devices and to play with software. Normally, children are paired by two in the computer class, take turns operating the computer, and share their experiences together. Classes end around 4:20 in the afternoon. After that, children either attend other skill-related classes (English, music, art, dance, and mental arithmetic) or play in the playground while waiting for their parents to pick them up. Many preschools offer these afternoon classes.

CULTURAL VALUE OF EDUCATION

Parents' beliefs and values of education influence the ways they raise their children. Education in Taiwan is strongly influenced by the traditional Chinese culture, in which the values of education and family function are emphasized. Confucianism values education. Being a well-educated person has the most prestigious social status in Chinese culture. Therefore, educating children to be well-rounded persons is always the primary concern for parents in Taiwan. Education is seen as a path to success and a brighter life. The majority of parents believe that to have a brighter and a successful future is to achieve success in academic performance. Chinese people value academic achievement, and under the influence of traditional cultural values, parents take the education of their children seriously and expect them to achieve academic success (Lin & Tsai, 1996). As described in an ancient classical book called *San Tz Jing* from the *Sung* dynasty, to teach and educate one's young child is a parental responsibility. Parents believe that earlier learning is related to a brighter life. Thus, to achieve academic success, most parents start to plan children's education at a very young age. There is a strong belief prevalent in Taiwanese society: "Do not let your child lose at the starting point" (Lin & Tsai, 1996, p.162). Helping children to excel in academic performance is the predominant expectation for most parents.

The prevalence of cram schools (or so-called Buxiban) for all kinds of after school learning activities is the mirror of most parents' expectations. Furthermore, due to the influence of the global village and globalization of the economy, computer technology literacy and English competence have been perceived the essential skills to connect to the international community. These two subjects are the most requested by parents in the cram schools. Hung's (2004) study gives a vivid picture of how learning English has become a national movement:

As e-generation comes. ...With the rapid advance of technology, the development of international economy and business, ...Not only has English been taught for the fifth grade of elementary schools, but also students and adults hurry to a short-term language institutes to learn English after school or work (p.1).

Although learning about computer skills has not provoked as much debate as the appropriateness of learning English in kindergartens, providing both English and computer programs has become a selling point to recruit children for most preschools and kindergartens in Taiwan. Moreover, because of the declining rate in birth in Taiwan, parents tend to have one or two children, and parents are desperate to educate their children to become the outstanding students. Allowing young children to have access to computer technology has become a prevalent trend among Taiwanese families (Yang, 1998). In Lai and Chiu's (2006) study, more than 60 percent of parents agree to have computer programs in kindergarten. To meet their needs, most kindergartens offer such programs (Lai & Chiu, 2006). In Fang's (2004) study, most teachers and administrators agree about the need of integration of information technology into early childhood curriculum. They believe that integrating information technology into curriculum is far more important than discussing the appropriateness of introducing computer programs into schools since young children already have access to computers outside school settings (Fang, 2004).

Government's Support of Technology Literacy

There are two key points that the Taiwanese government has made that defines their focus on technology. These include the many educational reforms and policies such as standards and the government's support of the establishment of *high tech parks,* such as *Hsinchu Science-based Industrial Park,* to attract talented electronic engineers to work in Taiwan (Babb, 1999).

Increasing the economic and educational competitiveness of e-generations is one of the leading goals among the Taiwanese government's policies. For instance, the new curriculum standards of *Grade 1-9 Curriculum* highlights the importance of technology education in the following seven major learning areas, which are: Language Arts, Health and Physical Education, Social Studies, Arts and Humanities, Mathematics, Science and Technology, and Integrative Activities (MOE, 2003). To cultivate students with a capacity for lifelong learning, one of the goals of the *Grades 1-9 Curriculum* is to cultivate students to "… Acquire the ability to utilize technology and information," in which students are capable of using technology to access, analyze, and evaluate information for lifelong learning (MOE, 2003). To meet this goal, science and technology is identified as a major learning area in the *Grades 1-9 Curriculum* for Elementary and Junior High School Education. Elementary students need to meet technology standards by the third grade.

Additionally, to meet the needs of a rapidly changing society and the advance of technology, the government even promotes media as a second curriculum (MOE, 2006). The administrative plan: *Policy White Paper on Media Literacy Education* outlines the role of media education:

The majority of educators. … As the hours children and youth are exposed to the media (including the Internet and computer games) already exceeds that the time they spend in the classrooms of elementary and high schools, it could be claimed that the media is the first education curriculum rather than the second. (MOE, 2006, Part 1, para. 1)

To increase students' competitiveness, educational authorities should "pay special attention to - education through the media", and are encouraged to create a digital learning environment (MOE, 2006).

Engineering or computer technology-related disciplines have become the top choices for students' majors in universities in Taiwan (Babb, 1999). The establishment of the *Hsinchu Science-based Industrial Park* and the success of the industries in the park also make technology or computer-related disciplines the most selected programs in most universities. Students are eager to get into computer technology-related or information technology-related departments because they would have a better chance to work at the *Science-based Industrial Park* and make good money.

COMPUTER TECHNOLOGY AS A TOOL FOR CHILDREN'S COGNITIVE DEVELOPMENT

As the increase of household penetration of computers in Taiwan, computers play an important role in family activities. Playing computer/video games is very popular among teens and children (Tseng & Liang, 2002). The computer is an important tool for children's cognitive development and the development of family literacy (Nelson, Duvergé, Gary, & Price, 2003; Young, 1998). Yang (1998) supports the educative value of computer in family activities. He asserts that computers are helpful for children's cognitive development, and they can promote children development at home because computers can be used as story books (digital books), tape recorders, TVs, or even toys (video games) (Nelson et al, 2003; Young, 1998). Computers can be used as multifunctional learning toys/tools, which can engage children in learning through visual (pictures and animations) and auditory (sound and music) interactions. They can provide different stimuli to children of different ages at different times to promote cognitive development (Yang, 1998).

In addition to the educational value of computer technology in the family, many studies have demonstrated how kindergarten teachers apply computer technologies to help children's cognitive development (Fang, 2004; Liang, Wang, & Cui, 2005; Lü et al, 2007). Computers have been introduced into kindergartens in two ways: learned as a skill in a computer classroom, and integrated into teaching (Lai & Chiu, 2006). According to Chiu's (2003) study, 70% of kindergartens in central Taiwan teach children computer skills in computer classrooms. Children learn basic computer skills using computer software, and most instructors are computer teachers rather than kindergarten teachers (as cited in Chiu & Chuang, 2004).

In Fang's (2004) study, it was found that computers are integrated into thematic teaching by the kindergarten teachers. Students not only learn the basics of computer hardware but also learn how to use computer to draw pictures, to print their works, and to watch movies. Through the implementation of information and computer technology, children develop their abilities to negotiate with others. They also learn to be patient with each other while waiting for their turns to play with the computers. Further, computers also help them to develop the concept of shapes, symbols, and the sequence of numbers. Computers are used as toys to motivate them to learn, and at the same time children's social and cognitive skills can be developed through the use of computers (Fang, 2004).

Similarly, a study conducted by Lü and others (2007) also found that computers promote children's cognitive development and social skills. In this study, they implemented the "International Netpal Project" into their thematic teaching. Chil-

dren in Southern Taiwan have been netpals with a kindergarten class at a Montessori school in the United States and with a picture book writer in Japan through e-mail. The e-mail contexts include pure texts, pictures, and pictures with texts. The results indicated that children understand that computers can be used to find information through the internet, to write (type), to draw pictures, to see pictures on other's websites, and to send e-mails. They also learned that computers can be used for video conferencing. From the authors' observations of children's conversations in a computer center, they have found that children love using computers and have rich peer interactions. Children helped each other in solving problems while using computers and shared their own experiences. In terms of the development of literacy skills, Lu and others (2007) conclude that children have increased their interests in print words and improved the comprehension skills in reading. They also have better concepts of writing styles and sometimes create symbols of their own to express their ideas in writing (Lü et al, 2007).

Kindergarten teachers in Taiwan have tried to introduce computer and information technology to their classrooms. The results have revealed a positive improvement in children's cognitive and social development. These studies imply that computer and information technology should be implemented in kindergarten curricula. To achieve higher success of such implementation, kindergarten teachers' competence in integrating such technology also needs to improve (Fang, 2004; Lai & Chiu, 2006).

TEACHERS' CONCERNS REGARDING THE USE OF COMPUTER TECHNOLOGY

Although the government's policies value the role of media education, the focuses are only on elementary and middle school curricula. Media and technology integration curricula in kindergarten levels are always neglected (Chiu, 2004), and there is no standard for technology curricula in kindergartens and preschools in Taiwan. Debates surrounding issues of the introduction of computer technologies in early childhood education school curricula have never ceased. Some early childhood administrators, teachers, and caregivers worry that the exposure of computer technology in the early years may impede the development of young children. They dispute that introducing computers to young children may result in poor eyesight for young children and negatively impact social interactions. Moreover, computer software is not age appropriate for children's development (Chiu, 2002; Fang, 2004). Certainly these concerns would be diminished if the technology opponents had a better understanding of the benefits of technologies in education.

Though media and information technology have not been included in preschool curricula and government regulated that public kindergartens are not allowed to teach English and computer skills, private preschools do have the freedom to include computer technology programs in their curricula. Nearly 70% of private kindergartens have implemented computer curricula, according to Chiu's (2003) study (as cited in Chiu & Chuang, 2004). All children still have the opportunities to access computer technologies outside the school settings.

The absence of English and computer skill classes in public kindergartens makes it difficult for public kindergartens to compete with the private ones. Private kindergarten enrollments have exerted a certain amount of competitive pressure on public kindergartens. Yang (2005), a teacher in a public kindergarten, indicates that public kindergartens are confronted with the serious problems of recruiting enough students because of the influence of a declining birthrate in recent years and of the disadvantages of their curricula. She encourages the application of multimedia and websites in public kindergarten curricula (Yang, 2005).

Despite the flourishing of computer skills-related programs in private preschools, some early childhood experts and teachers still have a negative view of the integration of technology into the curricula. The discrepancy between school curricula and parents' expectations forces teachers to rethink their approach to technology. There are two main issues concerning this gap in expectations. First, the problem of qualified early childhood teachers for teaching computer skills-related activities needs to be solved. Chiu (2006) concludes that integration of computer technology in the kindergarten still has its difficulties. For instance, in her (2006) study, computer classes are taught either by computer technicians/ teachers or early childhood teachers in private preschools. She concludes that most early childhood teachers lacked confidence in their abilities to integrate technology into classrooms. However, computer technicians/teachers do not have sufficient knowledge about early childhood education (Chiu, 2006). This dilemma leads to the second critical issue.

Second, the standards for evaluating and selecting appropriate technology-related activities and software needs to be established. According to Chiu and Chuang's (2004) study, computer technicians/teachers and the administrators of the kindergarten, rather than teachers, dominate the choice of appropriate computer software for computer integration curricula. This will lead to the discrepancy between the effective application of technology and children's development in all areas. Although computer technicians/teachers are experienced in all kinds of software, selecting age-appropriate and developmentally appropriate software for young children are more important. As suggested by Chiu and Chuang's (2004) teachers need to fully participate in the choice of teaching materials (Chiu & Chuang, 2004).

In addition to teachers' practices, when examining and reviewing early childhood educational software, Chiu (2006) finds that the majority of educational software is not appropriate for children in terms of age appropriateness, cognitive development, and educational goals. Most commercial software is for practice-and-drill purposes; they rarely provide an open-ended thinking feature. She claims that inappropriate software will not only affect children's eyesight, it also limits the development of children's creativity. For these reasons, she emphasizes the importance for selecting appropriate software as a learning development tool (Chiu, 2006). This reflects that there is a need to establish technology-related standards for early childhood education. By doing this, the software designers or companies can have the guidelines to make their software effective for children's cognitive and social development.

An opposing view from an early childhood expert, Ms. Chia-Hui Lin expresses concerns about technology in early childhood education. Ms. Lin is an instructor at the department of Early Childhood Education in National Tai-Chuang University in Taiwan. According to her experiences in pre-service and in-service teacher education, there are several major concerns that cause her to hesitate to implement technology in early childhood classrooms. First, according to her, a computer impedes children's cognitive development. She argues that computer software lacks concrete operational experiences which limit children's cognitive development to preprogrammed responses. Knowledge is better built in a constructivist learning environment where children can interact with and respond to their environment. Therefore, concrete experiences are more helpful in promoting children's cognitive development.

Second, from a physical development perspective, computer interactions provide limited opportunity for whole body development. According to Lin, a computer helps only in the development of certain motor skills such as hand and eye coordination, and sitting in front of computer a long period of time will cause harm to children's eyesight. Third, a computer class has limited opportunities for social interactions. Ms. Lin explains computer

technology is not necessary for academic development; children still can develop all kinds of skills for future learning without technology. Before age eight, there is no need to integrate computer technology into early childhood classrooms because there are other activities that can be used to support children's learning.

Ms. Lin's explanations illustrate two main problems in early childhood approaches to technology acceptance. One, early childhood educators are still under the influences of the myths and misconceptions about the use of computer technology. For instance, according to the news report from CBBC (2004) and Fang's (2003) study, poor eyesight in children is not directly caused by the use of computers. Bad reading habits, watching too much TV or genetic problems can be the main factors contributing to worsening children's eyesight (Fang, 2003; Lai & Chiu, 2006; CBBC, 2004). Computers did not impede children's social interaction development and the opportunities of sharing life experiences. Most children are found to increase their interaction with peers and adults (teachers) and learn how to negotiate with peers to take turns when they play with computers (Fang, 2004; Lü et al, 2007).

Two, not only are kindergarten teachers lacking in competency to introduce technology to children, but university programs for early childhood teachers do not prepare their students for the new digital age (Fang, 2004). Fang indicates that pre-service and in-service teacher's training in the integration of technology is the key role to the success of computer and information education in early childhood curricula. When competent teachers understand technology and how it can best be used to enhance learning, they can strategically implement technology to help students learn. The first step to prepare teachers to integrate technology in classrooms is to increase teachers' competence in using technology. Liang and Tsai (2008) have found that pre-service teachers with higher internet-self efficacy demonstrate a higher level of preferences toward an internet learning environment and conduct open-ended inquiries. This implies that if teachers have competence in using technology, they will have more confidence implementing it in their instructions.

However, having sufficient technology skills does not insure successful integration of technology in teaching. Most teachers in kindergartens do not have the competency to integrate computers into their teaching. Likewise, Chiu and Chuang (2004) indicate that many teachers in kindergartens are very capable of using computers and digital cameras; however, this does not mean that they are competent in integrating these technologies into their instruction. Early childhood educators need to be prepared to integrate computer technologies into sound learning theories. Although educational researchers and practitioners credit the potential of technology for learning, technology itself can not facilitate learning. It is the way in which these technologies are properly used as tools for students (Kajder, 2004). To accomplish this goal, more effective training sessions or education courses are needed.

IMPLICATIONS FOR INSTRUCTION AND CONCLUSION

The importance of technology literacy is accepted for our new generations. The demand of integrating technology into teaching will increase its importance in school curricula. Kajder (2004) claims that teachers need not to be "tech savvy," but knowing the "right tool, right task, and right student" is very important (p.7). To use technology effectively, educators need to know how learning theories can be enhanced through technology use.

More in-service teacher training sessions on how to implement technology are imperative. As argued in Chiu's (2006) study, the majority of educational software is not appropriate for children not only because of age inappropriateness, but because of the lack of the standards. To

help teachers seek the appropriate software to foster children's cognitive and social development, teachers need to be prepared with learning theories related to the adaptation of technology. In this way, early childhood educators will know when and how they can best implement the effective use of technology and avoid or modify the dysfunctional use of the software.

Innovative approaches to technology need to be introduced to students at an early age before they are out-paced by constantly changing technology (Shaffer & Gee, 2005). By adopting a technology-based curriculum, teachers become strong proponents and advocates, indeed, catalysts for educational innovation. As shown in early childhood classrooms in Taiwan, young children learn to use technology at early ages. Parents, educators, and other involved in children's education are committed to their education through the use of technology-related activities. The more they understand the appropriate use of such activities, the more they can assist their children's cognitive and social development. In Taiwan, it is time to offer children age-appropriate technology and to train teachers to be effective in the classrooms. When competent teachers understand technology and how it can best be used to enhance learning, they can strategically implement technology to help students achieve academic goals. In doing so, students also become technologically competent which will likely make them more competitive in future job markets.

SOME QUESTIONS FOR REFLECTIVE PRACTITIONERS:

1. What kinds of game type technology might be motivational to your children?
2. The Taiwan teenagers use videogames to improve their second language learning during leisure time. How might this be utilized as an informal education tool for second language learners?

3. How could video games influence motivation in your classroom?
4. The early childhood classes in Taiwan use projectors, PowerPoint, and the internet as instructional tools. How do you use these technology forms in your classroom?
5. Taiwan programs include computer instruction as a part of their curriculum. What types of computer instruction could you include in your program?
6. The role of education as high status in Taiwan may influence the use of technology. Is education considered a status level in your culture? How does your culture influence what is taught in early childhood programs?
7. The Taiwanese government has supported the use of technology through implementation of standards in school curriculum and incentives for economic development. How does your government influence the use of technology in your country?
8. The use of media as a curriculum, not just a delivery system, is evident in the Taiwan approach to technology education. Should technology be included as part of you curriculum or be used as an instructional tool? Why or why not?
9. The Taiwanese culture considers computer technology as an important tool for cognitive development in children. Yet some early childhood experts oppose this idea because they consider computer interaction as not being concrete activities. How do you think technology would influence cognitive development? Are computer interactions concrete experiences for the new generation of children? Why or why not?
10. The private early child hood programs in Taiwan use technology as a means to attract students. This could create a digital learning gap between the groups of students. What should be done to insure all children are prepared to meet the high government and family expectations in Taiwan?
11. As an early childhood professional how can you insure your personal bias is not influencing your approach to technology?
12. How does your curriculum compare to the Taiwan curriculum?

REFERENCES

Babb, J. (1999). Chips with everything. *Taiwan Review*. Retrieved January 20, 2008, from http://taiwanreview.nat.gov.tw/site/Tr/ct.asp?xItem=1440&ctNode=119

Ballard, M. E., & West, J. R. (1996). The effects of violent videogames play on male' hostility and cardiovascular responding. *Journal of Applied Social Psychology, 26*, 717–730. doi:10.1111/j.1559-1816.1996.tb02740.x

CBBC NEWSROUND. (2004, July 30). *Poor Eyesight Links to Genetics*. Retrieved May 28, 2008, form http://news.bbc.co.uk/cbbcnews/hi/sci_tech/newsid_3938000/3938193.stm

Chiu, S. (2005, Feburary). Wan chu zhi hui- ru he shen xuan you zhi de you jiao ruan ti [Playing Games for IQ development - how to select a good education software for young children]. *You jiao jian xun, 28*, 9-13.

Chiu, S. (2006). Zhe pian ruan ti shi wo yao de ma? Cong xiao fei zhe de guan dian kan you jiao ruan ti shi chang [Is this software the one I wanted? Examining the education software market from consumers' perspectives]. *Jiao xiao ke ji yu mei ti, 76*, 4-19.

Chiu, S., & Chuang, M. (2004). Computer integration in kindergarten teaching: Teachers' practices and beliefs. *Journal of Taiwan Normal University: Mathematics &Science Education, 49*(2), 35–60.

Dahl, A., & Lopez-Claros, A. (2005). The impact of information and communication technologies on the economic competitiveness and social development of Taiwan. *Global Technology Information Report 2005-2006*. Retrieved May 23, 2008, from http://www.weforum.org/en/initiatives/gcp/Global%20Information%20Technology%20Report/index.htm

Dylak, S., & Kaczmarska, D. (2001). Foreign language, technology, and science. *TechTrends, 45*(6), 35–39. doi:10.1007/BF02772020

Fang, H. (2003, September). You er xiao dian nao hao bu hao [Using computer: Is it good or bad for young children]? *You jiao zi xun, 154*, 2-10.

Fang, H. (2004). A case study on implementation of computer and information education for public kindergarten. *Journal of National Taipei Teachers College, 17*(1), 51–78.

Foreman, J. (2003). Next-generation educational technology versus the lecture. *EDUCAUSE Review, 38*(4), 12-22. Retrieved June 10, 2006, from http://www.educause.edu/LibraryDetailPage/666?ID=ERM0340

Gee, J. P. (2003). *What video games have to teach us about learning and literacy*. New York: Palgrave Macmillan.

Hauge, M. R., & Gentile, D. A. (2003, April). *Video game addiction among adolescents: Associations with academic performance and aggression*. Paper presented at Society for Research in Child Development Conference, Tampa, FL. Retrieved May 07, 2007 from http://www.psychology.iastate.edu/FACULTY/dgentile/SRCD%20Video%20Game%20Addiction.pdf

Hsieh, C. (2004, January). You zhi yuan ke cheng zhi fan si yu zhan wang [*The introspection and envision of preschool education curriculum*]. *You jiao jian xun, 15*. Retrieved May 13, 2008, from http://www.ece.moe.edu.tw/preschool.html

Hsieh, M. F. (2004). Teaching practices in Taiwan's education for young children: complexity and ambiguity of developmentally appropriate practices and/or developmentally inappropriate practices. *Contemporary Issues in Early Childhood, 5*(3), 309–329. doi:10.2304/ciec.2004.5.3.5

Hung, A. M. (2004). *A study of the effects of phonics instruction on English word pronunciation & memorization of vocational senior high school students in Taiwan*. Unpublished master's thesis. National Taiwan Normal University, Taipei: Taiwan.

Kajder, S. (2004). Plugging in: What technology brings to the English/language arts classroom. *Voices from the Middle, 11*(3), 6–9.

Lai, Y., & Chiu, S. (2006). Examining factors related to Taichung kindergarten mangers' decision-making on selecting computer application approaches. *Proceedings of The Second Conference on Computer and Network Technology in Education (CNTE 2006)*, May 23-24, 2006, Chung Hua University, Hsinchu, Taiwan.

Lee, Y., Cheon, J., & Key, S. (2008). Learners' perceptions of video games for second/foreign language learning. In C. Crawford et al. (Eds.), *Proceedings of Society for Information Technology and Teacher Education International Conference 2008* (pp. 1733-1738). Chesapeake, VA: AACE.

Lee, Y., & Key, S. (2008). Playing videogames: Do students choose specific foreign language learning strategies in playing these games? *TNTESOL Journal*, 30-37.

Liang, J., & Tsai, C. (2008). Internet self-efficacy and preference toward constructivist internet-based learning environments: A study of pre-school teachers in Taiwan. *Educational Technology & Society, 11*(1), 226–237.

Liang, P. H., Wang, J. Y., & Tsuei, E. M. (2005). *Young children and technology: a study of integrating information technology into thematic teaching in kindergarten.* Paper presented at the Academic Conference in Department of Early Childhood and Education, Chaoyang University of Technology, Taichung, Taiwan. Retrieved May 10 2008, from http://atecce.org/d/d1-3.htm

Lin, Y. W., & Tsai, M. L. (1996). Culture and the kindergarten curriculum in Taiwan. *Early Child Development and Care, 123,* 157–165. doi:10.1080/0300443961230111

Lü, S., Zhang, L., Lin, S., & Xu, F. (2007). You zhi yuan da ban jin hang guo ji wang lu jiao bi you huo dong zhi ge an yan jiu [A case study on the implementation of the *"International Netpal Project"* in kindergarten]. *Proceedings of Taiwan Academic Network Conferenc 2007.* Retrieved May 23, 2008, from http://itech.ntcu.edu.tw/Tanet%202007/indexI.html

Ministry of Education. Republic of China. (2005a, January 23). *Information and Internet education.* Retrieved May 23, 2008, from http://english.moe.gov.tw/ct.asp?xItem=7190&ctNode=514&mp=1

Ministry of Education. Republic of China. (2005b, January 23). *Education for preschool children.* Retrieved May 23, 2008, from http://english.moe.gov.tw/ct.asp?xItem=7089&ctNode=502

Ministry of Education. Republic of China. (2005, January 23). *Education for Primary and Junior High School Students.* Retrieved April 02, 2008, from http://english.moe.gov.tw/ct.asp?xItem=245&ctNode=502&mp=1

Ministry of Education. Republic of China. (2006, July 4). *Policy White Paper on Media Literacy Education.* Retrieved February 01, 2008, from http://english.moe.gov.tw/ct.asp?xItem=1282&ctNode=784&mp=3

Ministry of Education, Department of Elementary Education. (2003). *General Guidelines of Grades 1-9 Curriculum for Elementary and Junior high school Education.* Retrieved May 01, 2008, from http://www.edu.tw/eje/content.aspx?site_content_sn=4420

Nelson, C., Duvergé, H. A., Gary, B. M., & Price, G. J. (2003). *Using computers in family literacy programs.* Louisville, KY: National Center for Family Literacy.

Papert, S. (1998). Technology in schools: To support the system or render it obsolete? *The Milken Family Foundation.* Retrieved March 01, 2008, from http://www.mff.org/edtech/article.taf?_function=detail&Content_uid1=106

Prensky, M. (2001). *Digital game-based learning.* New York: McGraw-Hill.

Prensky, M. (2001a). Digital natives, digital immigrants part I. *Horizon, 9*(5), 1–6. doi:10.1108/10748120110424816

Prensky, M. (2001b). Digital natives, digital immigrants part 2: Do they really think differently? *Horizon, 9*(6), 1–6. doi:10.1108/10748120110424843

Purushotma, R. (2005, January). Commentary: you're not studying, you're just... [Electronic version]. *Language Learning & Technology, 9*(1), 80–96.

Rosas, R., Nussbaum, M., Cumsille, P., Marianov, V., Correa, M., & Flores, P. (2003). Beyond Nintendo: Design and assessment of educational video games for first and second grade students. *Computers & Education, 40*(1), 71–94. doi:10.1016/S0360-1315(02)00099-4

Schneider, B., & Lee, Y. (1990). A model for academic success: The school and home environment of East Asian students. *Anthropology & Education Quarterly, 21*(4), 358–377. doi:10.1525/aeq.1990.21.4.04x0596x

Shaffer, D. W., & Gee, J. P. (2005, September). *Before every child is left behind: How epistemic games can solve the coming crisis in education* (WCER Working Paper): University of Wisconsin-Madison, Wisconsin Center for Education Research Retrieved March 10, 2006, from http://www.wcer.wisc.edu/publications/workingPapers/Working_Paper_No_2005_7.hp

Shaffer, D. W., Squire, K. R., Halverson, R. H., & Gee, J. P. (2005). Video games and the future of learning . *Phi Delta Kappan, 87*(2), 104–111.

Squire, K. D. (2004). *Replaying history: Learning world history through playing Civilization III.* Unpublished doctoral dissertation, Indian University.

Taiwan Review. (2004, March, 01). Changing role, a high-tech adventure. [Electronic version] *Taiwan Review, 54*(3). Retrieved May 20, 2008 from http://taiwanreview.nat.gov.tw/site/Tr/ct.asp?xItem=939&CtNode=128

Tapscott, D. (1998). *Growing up digital: The rise of the Net generation.* New York: McGraw-Hill.

Tseng, Y., & Liang, C. (2002). The impact of online game and internet café on the school policy. *Audio-Visual Education Bimonthly, 44*(2), 2–12.

Van Eck, R. (2006). Digital game-based learning: It's not just the digital natives who are restless. *EDUCAUSE Review, 41*(2), 16-30. Retrieved June 8, 2006, from http://www.educause.edu/apps/er/erm06/erm0620.asp

Yang, X. (1998, December). Man tan dian nao zai you er jia ting jiao yu de gong neng [The educational role of home computers in young children's family Education]. *You Jiao Zi Xun, 97,* 50–53.

Yang, X. H. (2005, March). Gong li you zh yuan mian lin de jing zheng ya li [Competitive pressure on public kindergartens]. *Early Childhood Education, 277,* 18–19.

Zhang, S. Y., & Carrasquillo, A. (1995). Chinese parents' influence on academic performance . *New York State Association for Bilingual Education Journal, 10,* 46–53.

Zheng, M. (2004, January). Yin ying jiao gai tan you jiao ke cheng zhi fa zhan cu shi [In responding to education reform: the curriculum development trend in early childhood education]. *You Jiao Jian Xun, 15,* 6–7.

APPENDIX

The author wishes to note that because currently the early childhood educational guidelines set forth by the government are being revised by educators, parents, administrators, and other professionals who are involved in young children's lives, she includes the following general guidelines of grades 1-9 curriculum for elementary and junior high school education in Taiwan for those who might be interested in reviewing them: The source is from The Department of Elementary Education, Ministry of Education (http://www.edu.tw/eje/content.aspx?site_content_sn=4420)

General Guidelines of Grades 1-9 Curriculum for Elementary and Junior High School Education

Ministry of Education

Grade 1-9 Curriculum Guidelines

I. Preface

In keeping with the 21st century and the global trends of educational reform, the government must engage in educational reform in order to foster national competitiveness and the overall quality of our citizens lives.

The Ministry of Education (hereafter referred to as the MOE), therefore, initiated curricular and instructional reforms in elementary and junior high school education. These reforms have been based on the *Action Plan for Educational Reform* (「教育改革行動方案」) approved by the Executive Yuan. As the curriculum is not only the core of schooling but also the foundation on which teachers plan learning activities, the MOE places top priority on the development and implementation of the Grade 1-9 Curriculum. The curriculum reforms are necessary and timely based on the following reasons:

(a) Meeting national development needs: The world is now an international community in which all countries are closely connected and intensively competing with each other. We must, therefore, actively conduct educational reforms to enable individuals to maximize their potential, promote social progress, and enhance national competitiveness. The curriculum, as the major component of schooling, must be reviewed and revised continuously in order to render quality school culture and educational results, thus promoting our national development.

(b) Meeting public expectations: In recent years, public expectations for school reforms have been growing stronger. In response to public opinion, the Commission on Educational Reform (教育改革審議委員會) set up by the Executive Yuan published *The Consultants' Concluding Report on Education Reform* (教育改革總諮議報告書) which included several recommendations on school education such as the de-regulation of elementary and junior high schools, curriculum reform, improving teacher instruction, introducing English to primary students, assisting students to develop the basic academic capacities, etc. In response to social expectations, we need to conduct curricular reform with an innovative perspective so as to improve elementary and junior high schools.

The current *Curriculum Frameworks for Elementary Schools and Junior High Schools* were revised and promulgated in 1993 and 1994 respectively. Although the current *Curriculum Frameworks* have been gradually and properly implemented, the MOE believes that innovative thinking and practice in education are the prerequisites for success in the new century. Therefore, the MOE launched plans for another curricular reform in order to build up consensus and integrate the efforts of education reform, in order to create a new and better environment for school education. The development of a new curriculum was divided into three stages. The duration and major tasks of each stage are detailed as follows:

(a) Stage One (from April 1997 to September 1998): Establishing the *Special Panel on the Development of Elementary and Junior High Schools' Curriculum.* (國民中小學課程發展專案小組) The major tasks of this panel were to:
   1. Research and formulate the guiding principles for developing and revising the curriculum of elementary and junior high schools;
   2. Survey the shared components of the curriculum structure of elementary and junior high schools;
   3. Research and formulate the curriculum structure of elementary and junior high schools, such as requisite learning areas and the proportion of each area for the total learning periods; and
   4. Formulate the *General Guidelines of Grade 1-9 Curriculum of Elementary and Junior High School Education.* (「國民教育九年一貫課程總綱」)

(b) Stage Two (from October 1998 to November 1999): Establishing the *Panel on* Researching and Formulating the Guidelines of Each Learning Area in Grade 1-9 *Curriculum* (which covers the levels of elementary school and junior high school levels of education.) (「國民中小學各學習領域綱要研修小組」). As soon as the *General Guidelines of Grade 1-9 Curriculum* was promulgated in September, 1998, the MOE began Stage Two and established *the Panel on* Researching and Formulating the Guidelines of Each Learning Area in Grade 1-9 *Curriculum* in October, 1998. The major tasks of this panel were to:
   1. Research and formulate the *Guidelines of Each Learning Area in Grade 1-9 Curriculum* (「國民教育各學習領域課程綱要」);
   2. Set up the instructional goals and competence indicators for each learning area; and
   3. Research and formulate the principles for implementing the curriculum of each learning area.

(c) Stage Three (from December 1999 to August 2002): Establishing the *Review Committee on Revision and Formulation of Elementary and Junior High School Curriculum.* (「國民中小學課程修訂審議委員會」) After completing the drafts for the curriculum guidelines for each learning area, the MOE immediately established the *Review Committee on Revision and Formulation of Elementary and Junior High School Curriculum.* The major tasks of this committee were to:
   1. Review and confirm the adequacy of the Curriculum Guidelines for each learning area;
   2. Review and confirm the announcement format and the points of implementation for the guidelines of elementary and junior high school curriculum; and
   3. Plan and confirm the coordinating projects concerning the implementation of the new curriculum.

II. Core Rationale

The aim of education is to foster students' sound mind and character. Students should be taught democratic values, the Rule of Law, and humanitarian ideals; they should develop strong and healthy physiques, learn how to think for themselves and be creative. Every government hopes that the school system will produce outstanding citizens with a sense of patriotism and the ability to adopt a global perspective. In essence, education is a learning process to help students explore their potential as well as develop their capacity of adapting and making necessary efforts to improve their living environment. Given that, the following five basic aspects are emphasized and included in Grade 1-9 Curriculum designed for the new century: developing humanitarian attitudes, enhancing integration ability, cultivating democratic literacy, fostering both indigenous awareness and a global perspective, and building up the capacity for lifelong learning. The core components of each aspect are as follows:

A. "Humanitarian attitudes" include self-understanding and respect for others and different cultures, etc.
B. "Integration ability" includes harmonizing sense with sensibility, a balance between theory and practice, and integrating human sciences with technology.
C. "Democratic literacy" includes self-expression, independent thinking, social communication, tolerance for different opinions, team work, social service, and a respect for the law.
D. "Native awareness and a global perspective" includes a love for one's homeland, patriotism, a global perspective (both culturally and ecologically).
E. "Capacity for lifelong learning" includes active exploration, problem solving, and the utilization of information and languages.

III. Curriculum Goals

The curriculum of elementary and junior high schools will adopt the following principles: (1) to involve all aspects of daily life that correspond to the students' mental and physical development; (2) to encourage the development of individuality and the exploration of one's potentials; (3) to foster democratic literacy and respect for different cultures; (4) to develop scientific understanding and competences, in order to meet the demands of modern life.

The aim of national education is to teach students to obtain basic knowledge and to develop the capacity for lifelong learning, in order to cultivate able citizens who are mentally and physically healthy, vigorous and optimistic, gregarious and helpful to the community, intellectually curious and reflective, tolerant and with vision creative and have a positive attitude, and a global perspective. Schools will achieve such ideals through the promotion of educational learning activities which emphasize humanity, practicality, individuality, comprehensiveness, and modernity. Such activities include interactions between oneself and others, individuals and the community, as well as humans and nature. Regarding this aspect of national education, we must guide our students to achieve the following curriculum goals:

1. To enhance self-understanding and explore individual potential;
2. To develop creativity and the ability to appreciate beauty and present one's own talents;
3. To promote abilities related to career planning and lifelong learning;
4. To cultivate knowledge and skills related to expression, communication, and sharing.

5. To learn to respect others, care for the community, and facilitate team work;
6. To further cultural learning and international understanding;
7. To strengthen knowledge and skills related to planning, organizing, and their implementation;
8. To acquire the ability to utilize technology and information;
9. To encourage the attitude of active learning and studying; and
10. To develop abilities related to independent thinking and problem solving.

IV. Core Competence

In order to achieve the aforementioned goals, the curriculum design of elementary and junior high school education shall focus on the needs and experiences of students and aim at developing core competences which a modern citizen should possess. Such core competences may be categorized as follows:

A. Self-understanding and exploration of potentials, which involves thorough understanding of one's physical conditions, capabilities, emotions, needs, and personalities, loving and caring for oneself, self-reflection on a regular basis, self-discipline, an optimistic attitude, and morality, showing one's individuality, exploring one's potentials, and establishing suitable values.
B. Appreciation, representation, and creativity, which involves the capability of perceiving and appreciating the beauty of things as well as exerting imagination and creativity, developing an active and innovative attitude, and expressing oneself in order to promote the quality of living.
C. Career planning and lifelong learning, which involves the utilization of social resources and individual abilities in order to bring one's talents into full play, plot one's course for the future, and develop the ability of lifelong learning in accordance with the transition of the social environment.
D. Expression, communication, and sharing, which involves making effective use of all kinds of symbols (such as languages in both spoken and written forms, sounds, motions, pictures, and arts,) and tools (such as media and technology) in order to make clear one's thinking, concepts, and emotions as well as listening attentively to and communicating effectively with others, and sharing various perspectives and information with others.
E. Respect, care and team work, which involves being democratically literate, tolerant of different opinions, and equitable to individuals and groups of different identities, having respect for life and caring for the community, the environment, and nature, obeying the rules of the law and the norms of the community, and holding an attitude which is beneficial to team work and cooperation.
F. Cultural learning and international understanding, which involves appreciating and respecting different groups and cultures, understanding the history and culture of one's own country as well as others', recognizing the trend of the globalization in which countries all over the world are integrated into a global village, and developing a global perspective with mutual interdependence, trust and cooperation.
G. Planning, organizing and putting plans into practice, which involves being able to make plans and put ideas into practice in daily life, adopting approaches by which thoughts and practice are incorporated and by which each member can contribute to the community as well as serve the public and one's country with enthusiasm.
H. Utilization of technology and information, which involves the utilization of technology in a correct, safe and effective way so as to collect data, make judgments after thorough analyses of the

data, integrate and sort out useful information, and make use of such information for the purpose of enhancing learning efficiency and living quality.

I.   Active exploration and study, which involves encouraging curiosity and observation, actively exploring and discovering questions, and applying one's learned knowledge and skills in daily life.

J.   Independent thinking and problem solving, which involves cultivating the ability and habit of thinking independently and reflectively, making thoughtful analyses and judgments about questions, and effectively solving problems and resolving conflicts.

V. Learning Areas

For the purpose of fostering core competences in citizens, the curriculum of elementary and junior high school education shall emphasize on three dimensions, including individual development, community and culture, and natural environment. Thus, Grade 1-9 Curriculum encompasses seven major learning areas, which are: Language Arts, Health and Physical Education, Social Studies, Arts and Humanities, Mathematics, Science and Technology, and Integrative Activities.

A.   "Learning Area" refers to the content of learning, not the titles of subjects. Except for the required courses, optional courses relevant to specific learning areas may also be made available in consideration of students' references, needs of the communities, and the features of school development.

B.   Implementation of Learning Areas will follow the principle of integration and adopt Team teaching approaches if necessary. The structure of Learning Areas in Grade 1-9 Curriculum is listed as follows in Table 2.

Table 2.

Grade / Learning Area	One	Two	Three	Four	Five	Six	Seven	Eight	Nine
Language Arts	Mandarin	Mandarin	Mandarin	Mandarin	Mandarin	Mandarin	Mandarin	Mandarin	Mandarin
			English	English	English	English	English	English	English
Health and Physical Education	Health and Physical Education	Health and Physical Education	Health and Physical Education	Health and Physical Education	Health and Physical Education	Health and Physical Education	Health and Physical Education	Health and Physical Education	Health and Physical Education
Social Studies	Life Curriculum		Social Studies	Social Studies	Social Studies	Social Studies	Social Studies	Social Studies	Social Studies
Arts and Humanities			Arts and Humanities	Arts and Humanities	Arts and Humanities	Arts and Humanities	Arts and Humanities	Arts and Humanities	Arts and Humanities
Science and Technology			Science and Technology	Science and Technology	Science and Technology	Science and Technology	Science and Technology	Science and Technology	Science and Technology
Mathematics	Mathematics	Mathematics	Mathematics	Mathematics	Mathematics	Mathematics	Mathematics	Mathematics	Mathematics
Integrative Activities	Integrative Activities	Integrative Activities	Integrative Activities	Integrative Activities	Integrative Activities	Integrative Activities	Integrative Activities	Integrative Activities	Integrative Activities

C.   Major Contents of Each Learning Area
1.   Language Arts includes Mandarin, English, and focuses on listening, speaking, reading and writing of languages, developing basic communicating competences, understanding of culture and social customs.
2.   Health and Physical Education focuses on the learning of mental and physical development and health management, sports and motor skills, healthful environments, fitness and lifestyle choices.
3.   Social studies includes the learning of history and culture, geographical environment, social institutions, morals and norms, politics, economy, interpersonal interactions, civic responsibilities, indigenous education, environmental conservation, and the incorporation of the aforementioned learning into one's daily life.
4.   Arts and Humanities includes music instruction, instruction in the visual and performing arts, in hopes to help students to cultivate an interest for arts and encourage them to enthusiastically participate in related activities, thus promoting abilities such as imagination, creativity, appreciation for the arts, and other abilities.
5.   Science and Technology includes the learning of substances and energy, nature, the environment, ecological conservation, information technology. In addition, it will focus on knowledge and skills of science, research and developing such attitudes as respect for all forms of life, a love of the environment, and the ability to utilize information, as well as applying such knowledge and skills to their daily life.
6.   Mathematics includes acquiring the basic concepts of figures, shapes, and quantity, the ability to calculate and organize, and the ability to apply such knowledge and skills in their daily life. It also includes comprehending of the principles of reasoning and problem solving, the ability to elaborate clearly on math-related concepts, and making the appropriate connections among materials and contents between this and other Learning Areas.
7.   Integrative Activities refers to activities which may guide learners to practice, experience, and reflect upon the learning process as well as to testify and apply what has been learned to real situations. This Learning Area includes courses such as Scout Activities, Counseling Activities, Home Economics, and Group Activities, which have already been implemented in existing school systems as well as other separately-arranged learning activities, which resort to link outside educational resources to the school classroom.
D.   Each Learning Area is divided into several learning stages according to the structure of knowledge concerned as well as the continuity principles of the psychological development of learning. Competence Indicators are set for each learning stage. The stages of each Learning Area are detailed as follows in Table 3.
(a)   Language Arts
1.   Mandarin is divided into three stages: Stage One begins at Grade 1 and ends at Grade 3; Stage Two begins at Grade 4 and ends at Grade 6; Stage 3 begins at Grade 7 and ends at Grade 9.
2.   English is divided into two stages: Stage One begins at Grade 3 and ends at Grade 6; Stage Two begins at Grade 7 and ends at Grade 9.
(b)   **Health and Physical Education** is divided into three stages: Stage One begins at Grade 1 and ends at Grade 3; Stage Two begins at Grade 4 and ends at Grade 6; Stage Three begins at Grade 7 and ends at Grade 9.

(c) **Mathematics** is divided into four stages: Stage One begins at Grade 1 and ends at Grade 3; Stage Two begins at Grade 4 and ends at Grade 6; Stage Three begins at Grade 7 and ends at Grade 9.

(d) **Social Studies** is divided into four stages: Stage One begins at Grade 1 and ends at Grade 2; Stage Two begins at Grade 3 and ends at Grade 4; Stage Three begins at Grade 5 and ends at Grade 6; Stage Four begins at Grade 7 and ends at Grade 9.

(e) **Arts and Humanities** is divided into four stages: Stage One begins at Grade 1 and ends at Grade 2; Stage Two begins at Grade 3 and ends at Grade 4; Stage Three begins at Grade 5 and ends at Grade 6; Stage Four begins at Grade 7 and ends at Grade 9.

(f) **Science and Technology** is divided into four stages: Stage One begins at Grade 1 and ends at Grade 2; Stage Two begins at Grade 3 and ends at Grade 4; Stage Three begins at Grade 5 and ends at Grade 6; Stage Four begins at Grade 7 and ends at Grade 9.

(g) **Integrative Activities** are divided into four stages: Stage One begins at Grade 1 and ends at Grade 2; Stage Two begins at Grade 3 and ends at Grade 4; Stage Three begins at Grade 5 and ends at Grade 6; Stage Four begins at Grade 7 and ends at Grade 9.

(h) **Life Curriculum**: Social Studies, Arts and Humanities, and Science and Technology are integrated as Life Curriculum at Grade 1 and Grade 2.

Table 3.

Grade/ Learning Areas	One	Two	Three	Four	Five	Six	Seven	Eight	Nine
Language Arts	Mandarin	Mandarin	Mandarin	Mandarin	Mandarin	Mandarin	Mandarin	Mandarin	Mandarin
			English	English	English	English	English	English	English
Health and Physical Education	Health and Physical Education	Health and Physical Education	Health and Physical Education	Health and Physical Education	Health and Physical Education	Health and Physical Education	Health and Physical Education	Health and Physical Education	Health and Physical Education
Social Studies	Life Curriculum		Social Studies	Social Studies	Social Studies	Social Studies	Social Studies	Social Studies	Social Studies
Arts and Humanities			Arts and Humanities	Arts and Humanities	Arts and Humanities	Arts and Humanities	Arts and Humanities	Arts and Humanities	Arts and Humanities
Science and Technology			Science and Technology	Science and Technology	Science and Technology	Science and Technology	Science and Technology	Science and Technology	Science and Technology
Mathematics	Mathematics	Mathematics	Mathematics	Mathematics	Mathematics	Mathematics	Mathematics	Mathematics	Mathematics
Integrative Activities	Integrative Activities	Integrative Activities	Integrative Activities	Integrative Activities	Integrative Activities	Integrative Activities	Integrative Activities	Integrative Activities	Integrative Activities

VI. Implementation Guidelines

A. Implementation Schedule

Grades 1-9 Curriculum for Elementary and Junior High Schools was implemented at Grade 1 in the school year 2001. English instruction for Grade 5 and Grade 6 was officially implemented in the school year 2001, with further lowering to Grade 3 and Grade 4 in the school year 2005.

B. Learning Periods

(a)   There will be 200 school days in one school year that Students are expected to attend school five days a week, twenty weeks per semester. This number does not include national holidays and weekends. However, in reality, school days may vary in conformity with relevant regulations concerning the office days of government administrative offices and units, issued by the Central Personnel Administration of the Executive Yuan.

(b)   Total Learning Periods consist of Area Learning periods and Alternative Learning Periods. The number of these three Periods are listed as follows in Table 4.

Table 4. (節數 -- Length of learning periods; 年級 – Grade)

	Total Learning Periods	Area Learning periods	Alternative Learning Periods
One	22-24	20	2-4
Two	22-24	20	2-4
Three	28-31	25	3-6
Four	28-31	25	3-6
Five	30-33	27	3-6
Six	30-33	27	3-6
Seven	32-34	28	4-6
Eight	32-34	28	4-6
Nine	33-35	30	3-5

(c)   By the beginning of each school year, the Committee of School Curriculum Development for each school, will determine the learning periods to be assigned for each learning area based on the following rules:

1.   Learning periods of Language Arts will account for 20%-30% of the Area Learning Periods. However, in Grades 1 and 2, such periods may be counted together with the learning periods of Life Curriculum for the implementation of inter-disciplinary learning activities, if necessary.

2.   Learning Periods of the following six Learning Areas will account for 10%-15% of the Area Learning Periods respectively: Health and Physical Education, Social Studies, Arts and Humanities, Mathematics, Integrative Activities.

3.   Schools will calculate the total number of learning periods for each learning area for the whole school year or semester respectively and according to the aforementioned proportions. They will arrange weekly learning periods according to the real situations and needs of instruction.

4.   Schools will arrange practical training periods for information technology and home economics in accordance with the curriculum guidelines of each Learning Area.

(d)   The time for each period should be approximately 40 minutes for elementary schools and 45 minutes for junior high schools. However, schools may adjust the time for each period, the weeks of each semester, and the arrangements of grades and classes according to the specific circumstances regarding curriculum implementation and the needs of students.

(e) Schools are empowered to organize and conduct activities for Alternative Learning Periods (including activities for the entire school or all the Grades), carry out curriculum or activities designed to correspond to goals and objectives of the school, provide optional courses for learning areas, implement remedial teaching programs, and to conduct group counseling or self-learning activities.

(f) Given that some learning activities may be related to two or more learning areas, learning periods for such activities may be separately and proportionately counted as part of the leaning periods for related learning areas.

(g) Under the condition that all the requirements for area learning periods are met, the Committee of School Curriculum Development for each school may determine and organize its learning periods for each learning area.

(h) Total Learning Periods do not include the tutoring sessions of homeroom teachers, lunch/nap time, and cleaning time. Each school may organize a daily schedule for students, as well as activities, which do not fall under the category of learning periods, in conformity with the relevant regulations regarding school hours and activities (「國民中小學學生在校時間」) enforced by the local government.

C. Implementation

(a) Organization
1. Each school will establish a Committee of School Curriculum Development, which consists of curriculum panels for each Learning Area. The functions of this committee is to complete the school curriculum plan for the coming semester, by the beginning of this semester, determine the learning periods for each earning Area for each grade, review textbooks compiled by the school staff, develop topics and activities for teaching, and be responsible for the curriculum and instruction evaluation. The organization of the Committee of School Curriculum Development shall be resolved during Staff Faculty Meetings.
2. Members of the Committee of School Curriculum Development will include the representatives of school administrators, teachers for each grade and each Learning Area, parents, and the community. Scholars and professionals may also be invited to join the committee for counseling, when necessary.
3. Schools may jointly establish an inter-school Committee of School Curriculum Development in consideration with the features of the community, the sizes of the schools, and continuity between elementary and junior high school education. Schools on a smaller scale may merge several curriculum panels in different Learning Areas and form one curriculum panel, which can covers two or more learning areas.

(b) Curriculum Plan
1. The Committee of School Curriculum Development for each school will consolidate the efforts of all school staff as well as resources provided by the community, to develop a school-based curriculum, and formulate a comprehensive School Curriculum Plan based on thorough consideration of relevant factors, such as school conditions, features of the community, parental expectations, students' needs.
2. The School Curriculum Plan will include curriculum plans of each Learning Area and alternative learning periods, in which relevant items such as "Educational Goals of the School

Year/Semester," "Competence Indicators," "Units Corresponding to Competence Indicators," "Amounts of Learning Periods," "Modes of Assessments" will be specified.

3. The School Curriculum Plan will also contain specified descriptions on how to infuse the six major issues (including Gender Education, Environmental Education, Information Technology Education, Human Rights Education, Home Economics Education, Career Development Education) into the teaching of each Learning Area.

4. The School Curriculum Plan shall be submitted to the proper education administrative authority to be documented before the beginning of the School Year. The Curriculum Plan can be modified in accordance with the specific needs of each school on condition that the modified Curriculum Plan be submitted for approval before the beginning of the second semester. Parents will be notified of the teaching plans for their children's classes within two weeks after the new semester begins.

(c) Optional Courses

1. Elementary and junior high schools shall design and provide optional courses according to the different needs of students.

2. Students will take personal factors into account while taking courses, such as personal academic attainment, and the balance between different learning areas.

3. One of Taiwan's local dialects, i.e. Southern Fujianese, Hakka, or an aboriginal dialect, is required from Grade 1 through Grade 6, whereas in junior high school, such courses become optional. The local government, however, has the option of providing instruction of a selected dialect, other than the aforementioned, based on its special needs/features as well as teaching resources, on condition that its Curriculum Plan has been approved by the by the central government.

4. Schools may provide second foreign language courses in addition to English with consideration to the availability of teaching resources in and outside the school, as well as being able to determine the content and teaching materials of such courses.

(d) Schools are allowed to adjust the subject areas and teaching periods in accordance with the needs and available teaching resources, as long as the total teaching hours of each Learning Area remain unchanged and the general principles of comprehensive and integrative teaching are strictly followed.

D. Compiling, Review, and Use of Teaching Materials

(a) Textbooks for elementary and junior high school education will be compiled in accordance with the curriculum guidelines, and submitted to the authority/agency in charge for review and approval. Schools may select their own textbooks from all of the approved versions.

(b) In consideration of regional features, as well as the characteristics and needs of students, schools may compile alternative textbooks and teaching materials or select teaching materials, other than the approved textbooks, if necessary. However, such teaching materials that are adopted for the whole grade or school for one whole semester or more will be presented to the school's Committee of School Curriculum Development for further review.

E. Curriculum Evaluation

(a) Items of evaluation include teaching materials, instructional plans, achievements of implementation.

(b) Curriculum evaluations will be conducted in a balanced and cooperative way, by which the central and local governments are responsible for specific duties and will provide support for each other, if necessary.

    1. The central government is responsible for

        (1) Establishing and carrying out the mechanism for curriculum evaluations in order to evaluate the effects of curriculum reform and the implementation of other measures, and to apply the evaluation results as reference for further reforms; and

        (2) Setting up the Academic Attainment Indicators of each Learning Area and evaluating the implementation of curriculum of local governments and individual schools.

    2. The local government is responsible for

        (1) Visiting schools on a regular basis in order to understand the implementation of curriculum and providing remedies and solutions to predicaments which occur in the implementation process;

        (2) Arranging and conducting instruction evaluations to assure the effects and quality of teaching; and

        (3) Providing assistance and guidance for school to conduct students' academic achievement assessments for each Learning Area.

    3. Schools are responsible for the curriculum and instruction evaluations as well as students' academic achievement assessments.

(c) Evaluations will be conducted through diversified methods, emphasizing both formative and summative evaluations.

(d) Schools will make the most of the evaluation results, and use them as the basis for reforming the curriculum, forming instruction plans, improving learning effects and conducting follow-up reflections and examinations.

F. Instruction Assessments

(a) Assessment of students' academic performance will comply with relevant regulations promulgated by the Ministry of Education concerning the evaluation and grading of students' performance.

(b) In response to the implementation of *Multi-route Promotion Program for Entering* Senior High Schools and Vocational High Schools (高中職多元入學制度) and for the purpose of examining student's academic performances, the MOE will hold the *Basic* Achievement Test for Junior High Students(「國民中學基本學力測驗)in conformity with Grade 1-9 Curriculum Guidelines. Students' scores on such tests may be used as a reference for admission.

(c) In terms of the Basic Achievement Test for Junior High Students, relevant affairs such as the establishment of a database for examination questions, the standardization and implementation of the test will be subject to the Competence Indicators specified in the Curriculum Guidelines and other relevant rules and regulations.

G. Training of Teachers

(a) The Institutes responsible for teachers' education will provide programs for the purpose of training eligible teachers for the Grade 1-9 Curriculum according to the Teacher Education Act.

(b) Local governments and schools will offer preferential employment opportunities to teachers who have passed the Examination for Certificate of Elementary School's *English Teachers* (「國小英語教學師資檢核」) and possess the certificate for Elementary School Teachers who are, to be responsible for English courses in Grade 5 and Grade 6.

(c) Accreditation of a Teacher's specialty for Learning Areas in Grade 1-9 Curriculum will also be subject to the Regulations on Certification and Educational Practice of Teachers of High Schools, Elementary Schools, and Kindergartens.(「高級中等以下學校及 幼稚園教師資格檢定及教育實習辦法」)

H. Authorities and Responsibilities

(a) The Local Government
　　1. Local governments will draw up budgets for the following:
　　　　(1) Seminars for Grade 1-9 Curriculum for educational administrators, school principals, administrative staff, and teachers.
　　　　(2) Production and allotment of needed teaching aids and media, as well as the purchase of teaching equipment and reference books.
　　　　(3) Granting school subsidies needed for action research on curriculum and pedagogy.
　　　　(4) Establishing instructional consulting teams for each Learning Area and visiting schools regularly in order to provide support for teachers.
　　2. In terms of Indigenous education, local governments may develop teaching materials or authorize schools to compile teaching materials with regard to regional features and relevant resources.
　　3. In addition to requesting schools to submit curriculum plans for record, local governments will supervise schools to assure that such plans are adequately implemented.
　　4. Local governments will enforce regulations concerning school hours and activities (「國民中小學學生在校時間」相關規定) with consideration to regional features and the daily schedules of parents.

(b) The Central Government
　　The MOE will:
　　1. Draw up and actively carry out supporting measures for Grade 1-9 Curriculum in order to facilitate the implementation of the Grade 1-9 Curriculum;
　　2. Make the Curriculum Guidelines of each Learning Area available on the Internet for public reference;
　　3. Coordinate affairs concerning the training of teachers with relevant institutes, and be responsible for the training of seeded teachers for the new curriculum; and
　　4. Review and revise existing laws and regulations, as well as drawing up new and relevant ones, in accordance with the implementation of the new curriculum.

I. Additional Provisions

(a) The implementation of curriculum for special education classes will be subject to the Act of Special Education and relevant regulations.

(b) For detailed instructions concerning each learning area, please consult the implementation points specified in the guidelines of each Learning Area in the Grade 1-9 Curriculum.

(c) When implementing Art/Skill-based Education at Grade 9, schools are allowed the flexibility of adjusting Total Learning Periods in order to offer students hands-on skill-oriented courses.

The source is from: The Department of Elementary Education, Ministry of Education: http://www.edu.tw/eje/content.aspx?site_content_sn=4420

Chapter 3
Tech-Knowledge in Japanese Early Childhood Education

Tetsuya Ogawa
Kawasaki Futaba Kindergarten, Japan

Satomi Izumi-Taylor
University of Memphis, USA

ABSTRACT

This chapter describes how Japanese early childhood education promotes children's socialization through the use of technology and play in group-oriented environments. The chapter also presents the traditional Japanese view of the child and of early childhood education, Japanese strategies in developing children's socialization skills, changes in the use of technology in the field of early childhood education, and recommendations for educators.

INTRODUCTION

The technological revolution has been rapid and fluid in society. While business use was evident, educational applications are just now being explored. Educators are often resistive to computer use in classrooms for different reasons. To understand teachers' perceptions about technology in early childhood education is important because such perceptions directly influence children's technology-related experiences in classrooms. On the other hand, their attitudes and viewpoints toward technology affect their teaching styles and efforts (Levin & Wadmany, 2008; Prairie, 2005). Theories

and research on technology and play are multifaceted and individual teachers' perceptions of what constitutes developmentally appropriate technology and play in early childhood settings vary widely. One source of understanding teachers' perceptions of the appropriate implementation of technology and play is Japanese early childhood education. In these settings technology is implemented to support children's play and is based on the Japanese cultural belief that play is valued for itself rather than how it is related to education. In this sense, teachers consider children to be creators of play activities as well as controllers of such activities. The role of the teacher is to support and to facilitate children's learning and development through the use of play and technology. For these reasons, examining how

DOI: 10.4018/978-1-60566-784-3.ch003

Japanese early childhood education programs and educators implement technology and play in the classroom can contribute to the field of early childhood education.

It is well accepted that the Japanese are fascinated with technology (Better than People, 2005; Hey, Big-Spender, 2005), and that "Japan is considered to be one of the leading countries in terms of persevering in the development of technology" (Izumi-Taylor, 2008a). Some people who have visited Japan comment that "Japan has two faces; one is facing the future, and the other is looking into the past" (Izumi-Taylor, 2008, p. 9). Technology permeates the Japanese culture to such a degree that today some Japanese people utilize robots to care for the sick and elderly as well as to do housework. However, at the same time, Japanese people are rigid about keeping their culture and traditions intact (Iikura, 2007) and value transmission of cultural wisdom and knowledge in a group-oriented environment to generations that follow. Such cultural transmission can be seen in the educational approaches used by Japanese with young children.

Japanese preschools are called kindergartens and are attended by children from three to five years of age (Taylor, 2004). The first two years of Japanese kindergartens are the equivalent of preschools in the United States, and the third year is comparable to that of the American kindergarten. Traditional Japanese preschools strive to offer children relaxed, play-oriented, and child-centered programs in group-oriented environments in order to promote their social skills (Izumi-Taylor, 2006). This educational environment is based on play activities that unify and integrate all elements of children's development and learning. This approach is supported by the National Curriculum Standards for Kindergartens (The Ministry of Education, Culture, Sports, Science, and Technology, 2000), which states that children learn best through play and that play is their everyday activity.

Japanese early childhood educators integrate play and technology in order to support children's development and learning in group-oriented environments. While the main focus of Japanese early childhood education is to guide children in developing basic human attributes (such as social skills, empathy, cooperation skills, etc.) rather than teaching them academics, teachers do use age-appropriate technology in order to enhance cooperative play. This approach is different from traditional skill reinforcement technology as seen in many programs in the United States. The children in Japanese programs guide the selection and use of technology through their interest and play rather than the teacher's interest. The teachers support the children's play by offering ample opportunities to engage in technology-related activities. Examining the ways Japanese teachers use such activities can provide some insight to other early childhood educators as to how to implement play and technology for young children. Studying and researching various cultures' ways of offering education to children suggest a way for teachers to reflect on their own teaching (Taylor et al., 2004). This chapter describes how Japanese educators support children's socialization skills through the use of technology and play.

The organizing perspectives of this chapter will focus on two professionals' perceptions and experiences with Japanese early childhood education: the first author writes from the experiences of a Japanese early childhood educator for over 25 years and the second author from the experiences of a Japanese native who has been enculturated in the United States educational system for over 36 years but works in both systems. The first author provides the practitioner's knowledge from the developing use of technology in Japanese kindergartens across twenty-five years of teaching. The second author, with seventeen years of experience observing and researching early childhood education in Japan, working in the United States provides insights into experiences between both countries. The first author has an insider's knowledge of such an environment, whereas the second author has both an insider's and outsider's knowledge of this environment. Together the authors provide an overall picture of the development of the role of technology in Japanese education. When educators with such varying perspectives offer their views of one phenomenon, people's understanding is richer and authentic. We believe that reality is constructed by the perceptions of viewers and that it is created by their perceptions (Lichtman, 2006; Lichtman & Taylor, 1993).

The organizational structure of this chapter describes a typical day at one kindergarten, the traditional Japanese view of the child and of early childhood education, a current understanding of Japanese early childhood education, the evolution of technology use, and the possible future use of technology, and the recommendations for educators. Each issue will be discussed accordingly.

ONE DAY AT A KINDERGARTEN IN KAWASAKI CITY

To promote readers' understanding of a typical group-oriented kindergarten classroom, we will describe how children and teachers spend a typical day at a kindergarten located in the busy, heavily industrialized city of Kawasaki near Tokyo. It has one classroom for three year olds, three classrooms for four year olds, and three classrooms for five year olds. The enrollment fluctuates at around 200, and the staff consists of eight full-time teachers, the director, the assistant director, the helper to the assistant director, and the school van driver. Additionally, on a part-time basis, the school employs an art teacher, a gymnastics teacher, an accountant, an extended care teacher, a technology teacher, and a special education teacher. The kindergarten is privately owned and is run by the first author, by his mother who is assistant director, as well as by other members of his family.

The teachers at this kindergarten are all females in their early twenties, and the children come to this school five days a week. On Mondays, Tuesdays, Thursdays, and Fridays, the children stay from 8:30 a.m. until 2:00 p.m., and on Wednesdays, from 8:30 a.m. until 11:00 a.m. Since teachers spend every Wednesday afternoon in their in-service training sessions, children remain at the kindergarten in only the morning hours. For those children who need to stay till 5:30 p.m. because of their parents' work schedules, the kindergarten offers extended care. The activities are uniform for each classroom of the same age group, thus, a description of one classroom is a general description of all the classrooms for that age group. Classes are identified in colorful and unique ways: one class is named the pineapple class, another is known as the strawberry class, while others are named after green apples, peaches, etc.

A typical day at this kindergarten begins with the cheerful greetings of the children and their teachers. Like lines of dominoes falling forward to capture the heart, tiny children in their uniforms bow and greet each other and their teachers with a noisy, "Ohaiyo gozaimasu!" (Good morning). It has been noted, however, that the decibel level of children in the typical Japanese classroom is comparable to a 747 during liftoff. One possible reason for the Japanese children's boisterous noise level is that Japanese adults value children's vigor, and considerable classroom noise does not reflect negatively on the teacher (Lewis, 1986). In those rare instances when we are actually able to hear over the noise of children, we are impressed with how the teachers greet everyone. Their "Good mornings" and "Hellos" are spoken in cheerful tones.

Some children arrive by walking, and others come by school van. The school van travels four different routes to pick up the children, and when children arrive, they gather in one classroom to engage in free play such as singing songs and playing games with the teachers. At 9:00 a.m. those children who are already in class go outside to play. By 9:50 a.m., all the children have arrived.

Upon arrival, the children remove their shoes and change into different shoes specifically for inside wear and then go to their own classrooms where they put on their smocks. None of the children we observe, including 3 year olds, have a problem changing their clothes. Each child has a shelf with his or her name on it with a box containing crayons and a pair of scissors, another box containing clay and a plastic board upon which to model the clay, a large drawing book, and a workbook. Next to each child's shelf is another shelf used to store hats. Two different hats are provided for each child, one for coming to school and for going home, and the other for going outside for physical exercise or play. Each child shares with another child a small open cubby in which to hang his or her belongings.

After changing clothes and donning colored caps that denote different classes and make it easy to distinguish where the children belong, they go to either a specified classroom or outside to play. At 9:50 a.m. children change back into their shoes to go outside, and when the music begins, all the children gather in the playground for morning exercise according to their own classroom designations. The morning exercise includes following musical directions while engaging in activities of clapping, stretching, turning, and jumping in place. By 10:00 a.m. exercise is finished, and the children are instructed to go to their own classrooms as a teacher announces their classroom names. Before they enter their classrooms, the children wash their hands and gargle (a common practice in Japan that is reinforced in kindergarten). Children gargle especially after meals or after returning from outside (Shinji, 1996). Also at this time, those children who need to go to the bathroom are allowed to do so.

The classroom of five year olds begins with the teacher playing the piano and the children singing the morning song followed by the school theme song. The lyrics of the morning song are:

It is morning, and the sun is rising.

Sparrows at the window are calling you.

Good morning, chun, chun, chun (sound of birds chirping).

And their school song's lyrics are:

Morning has come, and we are happy.

At Kindergarten friends with smiles gather around.

Good morning to you, teachers, we are happy at Kindergarten.

When singing these songs, the children are unbearably loud as if they are engaged in a contest to see who can shout and scream the loudest. However, the teacher never tells them to stop shouting or to stop being so loud, but instead, she whispers, "I wonder who can sing as softly as a little canary." A hush falls over the classroom as the children strain to hear what the teacher is saying, and then the children begin whispering their songs. In all the schools we have visited, none of the teachers have ever told children to tone it down, even though many of them deliberately sang at maximum volume. Instead, they simply asked the children to see how softly they could sing. Tobin, Wu, and Davidson (1989) referred to this type of noisy classroom as having developmentally appropriate chaos. Here again, we find another example of teachers' appreciation of children being children.

After the songs, everyone greets each other with bows and hearty greetings of "Good morning." Rather than having children's desks in a line, the desks in this classroom of five year olds are arranged in clusters forming individual groups called "han." A han usually includes both boys and girls sitting in adjoining seats so they are able to work as a group by just turning in their seats, and each table is generally made of five or six desks placed together. As for the teacher, she has no desk but uses shelves instead. To begin the class, the teacher does the roll call and asks the children, "Who are the toban today?" The toban are those children who are chosen daily on a rotating basis to help in the classrooms with such responsibilities as giving their classmates vitamin pills and stickers to put on their date books to indicate their attendance. The toban usually consists of one boy and one girl, and everyone has a chance to take a turn at being a toban for the day (Taylor, 2004).

In response to the teacher's question as to who are the toban for the day, two children raise their hands, rush to the front of the class, place necklaces adorned with bears' faces around their necks that indicate that their positions as toban. As they proudly stand beside the teacher and face the class, the teacher announces their names and says to the two children, "You are the toban today, yoroshiku onegaishimasu (I am counting on your help)." The teacher then bows to the toban, and the toban bow to the teacher. Then, the teacher says to the class, "These are your toban, yoroshiku onegaishimasu" (Please cooperate with them; I am counting on you). At this point, the toban bow to the class, and in turn, the class members bow to the toban and say, "Yoroshiku onegaishimasu" (Please take care of us, we are counting on you for proper guidance). One can observe in the aforementioned situations that the phrase, "yoroshiku onegaishimasu" is based upon interdependent relationships and has a cluster of meanings that alter slightly depending on the situation in which it is used. The teacher counts on the toban to do their duties, just as the toban count on the class to cooperate with them, and in turn the children in the class count on the toban as leaders.

Once these rituals are taken care of, the two toban face each other and engage in "jankenpon" which we are familiar with as the "rock-paper-scissors" game, the winner of which gets to serve vitamin pills while the loser is stuck with providing the stickers for the children. For some mysterious reason of which we are not yet aware, children prefer to serve vitamins. When the winner is announced, the class applauds the victorious vitamin server. The teacher then comforts the child who has been relegated to the substandard role of sticker provider, saying, "Maybe next time you will get to serve the vitamins." A short time later the mystery of why children covet the job of vitamin server is resolved when the teacher, following our query, explains to us that they prefer to serve the vitamins because they are sweet and chewy, a perfectly valid reason indeed. As one toban serves the vitamins, he is wandering aimlessly around the classroom, making sweeping motions with one arm that indicates that he is a pilot, and that the pill bottle is an airplane circling the classroom. The children make it known in no uncertain terms that he should return to his duties of serving the pills, yet this toban/vitamin pill pilot continues to navigate the classroom, taking many detours and looking at toys displayed on the shelves. Finally, the other toban who has finished her less glamorous job of passing out stickers as quickly as possible, comes to the less professional toban and insists that he finish performing his duties. At this time, this toban/vitamin pill pilot comes to the second author and offers his product, and she graciously accepts. Before she has had adequate time to contemplate taking these pills, he has returned and says "Open wide!" making sure that she has in fact swallowed the pills. Fortunately she is able to gulp down the pills just before being caught with them lodged in her mouth.

By the time the children finish their morning greetings and songs, it is approximately 10:40 a.m., and the teacher announces the classroom activities for the day. This particular day the children are instructed to draw pictures of their own choosing. The teacher asks the children to take out their drawing books and crayons from their shelves. When the teacher finishes her announcement, she turns her back to the children and begins organizing her materials. There is a minor storm of children flying around the classroom getting ready for the activity: some are bouncing on the floor while others are talking and wrestling simultaneously, however, they all manage to get back to their tables by the time the teacher faces the class to instruct the children to begin their drawings.

During the drawing activity, there is a great deal of talking, running in place and in circles, getting up to visit others at different tables, and even visiting children in other classrooms. Although the teacher is well aware of what is happening, she says nothing to discourage their meanderings. These children's behavior may not seem appropriate to those unfamiliar with a Japanese preschool classroom, but, because educators aim to nurture a child-like child who is energetic, social, and active, they allow high levels of noise or chaos in the classrooms. Such a child is considered to be kind, cooperative, and moral, yet highly energetic (Lewis, 1986; Shigaki, 1983; Tobin, Wu, & Davidson, 1989). When the teacher steps out of the classroom for a while, the children vividly demonstrate what could be referred to as developmentally appropriate chaos. It is at this time that the toban come to the front of the classroom, chanting, "Zip up your lips, put your hands on your laps, and get quiet." The children follow the toban and begin chanting the same thing, "Zip up your lips, put your hands on your laps, and get quiet!" The children who are scattered around the classroom, stop in the middle of their activities, perk up their ears, and while in the process of returning to their tables, begin chanting along with the toban, "Zip up your lips, put your hands on your laps, and get quiet!" By the time the chant is repeated for the third time, everyone is seated, and when the teacher returns, she praises the orders for quiet and the efforts made by the toban and their charges.

The drawing activity lasts until 11:30 a.m., at which time the teacher begins playing the piano signaling cleanup time. Cleanup time goes smoothly as none of the children resist in helping with this chore; this is probably because even cleanup can be turned into a playful activity. There are two boys, who run at top speed, fall and then slide across the floor from one side of the room to the other, and in the process, find trash on the floor to pick up and put in the receptacle. After cleanup, the toban start preparing for lunch by washing their tables with wet cloths, while the other children wash their hands and take their lunch boxes from their bags. None of the children are required to line up to go wash their hands, yet everything goes smoothly.

It is fascinating to see the fact that children at this kindergarten usually did not line up to go to the bathroom, to go outside, or to wash their hands, yet everyone appeared to manage these tasks without the teacher's supervision. These observations are supported by Nagasaki, Kaneda, Taylor, Watanabe, and Goshiki (2002) who found that Japanese kindergarten teachers generally do not ask children to form a line when engaging in such activities, whereas their American counterparts are more likely to do so. When we shared our observations with teachers at the kindergarten in Kawasaki City, one teacher shared her thoughts:

I do this case by case. Since the children in my class are five years old, they know the rules and can conduct themselves calmly. Going to the bathroom is no problem with my students, and they should have freedom to do that. But, I do remind them of rules before they go outside for their safety.

Another thoughtful teacher's comments reflected an importance issue of lining up:

It depends on what we do. If everyone at our school is meeting in the hallway, for safety reasons I ask them to do so. However, if we are just going outside to observe flowers and bugs, it's not necessary for them to line up, because they need a lot of freedom to explore. I think lining up is important for children's safety, but if we place too much emphasis on getting children in line, their interests, anticipations, and desires to engage in activities can diminish.

In many kindergartens, teachers letting children regulate themselves often takes precedence over staying within the lines (Izumi-Taylor & Taylor, 2009).

By 11:50 a.m. every table is adorned with the children's obento (lunch boxes) all laid out in an orderly fashion. When the colorfully designed cloth wrapper securing each lunch box has been unfolded to serve as a placemat, the lunch box is placed along with chopsticks, a fork, a spoon, and a drinking cup in the appropriate locations upon the cloth. Lunches have been brought from home in plastic or aluminum boxes decorated with cartoon characters. Food has been prepared in such a way as to appeal to the eye as well as to the palette: carrots are sculpted into the shape of flowers, and dessert, usually consisting of fresh fruit, includes apples cut into the shape of bunny ears. An example of a lunch consists of codfish cut into small bite-size pieces, buttered sautéed spinach, cooked carrots cut into butterfly shapes, cherry tomatoes with lettuce, and quartered boiled eggs. Food items are fit into the box neatly and precisely in the fashion of a jigsaw puzzle, and Simons (1987) also described Japanese lunch boxes as culinary jigsaw puzzles. It is interesting to note the children at such a young age are serving green tea (lukewarm for their safety).

When everyone is ready, a ritual begins with the teacher sitting at the piano and playing the lunchtime song. The song indicates the children's appreciation of their parents' preparation of the food, as well as encouragement to eat all the food that has been provided so the children can grow strong and healthy. Here is the lunch song:

We hear the bell for lunch.

We wash our hands with good manners.

Let's greet our teacher.

Then we will eat lunch. We are happy.

After the song, everyone chants in unison the formal announcement for beginning the meal: "Dear father and mother, thank you for the delicious lunch. I will eat slowly, will chew my lunch well, and will not leave or spill anything. Thank you for the food, I am going to eat now." In acknowledging the children's chant, the teacher says, "Please eat your food." It is fascinated to observe that no children have touched their food until the preliminary ritual has been completed. It is then that the children commence eating along with their teacher who has brought her own lunch. According to Lichtman and Taylor (1993), the serving of meals is an important ritual in Japanese schools just as it is in all levels of Japanese society, and the level of effort involved in the preparation of food by the children's parents indicates that the meal is of great importance.

By 12:40 p.m., the children begin chanting the word "Gochisosamadeshita" that translates, "Thank you for the food, it was delicious." Between 12:40 and 1:40 p.m., the children have free time to play inside the classroom except for those who are not finished eating. This free time includes art activities, play dough, books, blocks, manipulative toys, and card games. During this time, it is amusing to see some children wandering around the school building as well as visiting the teachers' lounge and the director's office with no objections from those in charge. As a matter of fact, one boy wanders into the director's office during class, and the director asks, "Are you supposed to be here?" The boy enthusiastically answers, "Yes!" This answer must be correct, because the director says nothing and simply walks away. By 1:40 p.m., smocks are hung up in their cubbies, and the children put back their school uniforms in preparation for going home. The teacher plays the goodbye song, and everyone joins in singing, again in decibels sufficient to nearly cause one's ears to bleed. The good-bye song is:

We have finished today's play.

Let's all go home together.

We will come to school tomorrow.

Let's all play together again.

"Goodbye" to the teachers.

"Goodbye" to everybody.

Once the song is completed, the children all bow to the teacher and say, "Sensei sayonara" (Teacher, goodbye). They then bow to each other and say, "Minasan, sayonara" (Everyone, good-bye). By 1:50 p.m. all children who are ready to go home have gathered in the hall. While waiting to be picked up by their parents, other family members, or the school van, the children sing songs and play games with the teachers.

During the observations, it is amazing to see how the children are allowed to wander in and out of the classrooms freely at all times, and these visits include other classrooms and the teachers' lounge. The teachers make no effort to prevent these excursions but leave it up to the classmates to instruct the wanderers to return to where they belong. It is also intriguing to observe how teachers use ritual songs and chants to lead the children in transitioning to new activities, and there is always plenty of time allowed for the transitions to take place. There are no verbal requests for cleanup; instead, music is used to indicate cleanup time, and this is why all teachers must know how to play piano in order to teach in early childhood settings. There are no complaints from the children about cleaning up their classrooms. Although cleaning up appears to be chaotic, by the time this tumultuous storm of activity has passed, pristine order is left in its wake (Izumi-Taylor & Taylor, 2009).

BACKGROUND

The Traditional Japanese View of the Child and of Early Childhood Education

It is important to understand the context from which current practice has developed in order to understand the use of technology in Japanese Early Childhood Programs. The philosophical cultural norms directly influence the application and acceptance of technology in educational settings. Japanese early childhood education and its use of technology are based on cultural traditions of the Japanese society. Understanding this perspective will enable readers to see the development and role of technology in Japanese educational systems.

The Japanese educational guidelines (The Ministry of Education, Culture, Sports, Science, and Technology, 2000) state that the basic ideal of kindergarten education is to understand the nature of children and to educate them accordingly. In furtherance of this ideal, section 2 states that children learn through play, that play is their voluntary activity and that such an activity creates the foundation for a balance between mind and body. It is during early childhood when children develop their foundation of life upon which all else will be built, and with parental involvement, early childhood education seeks to provide children with what the Japanese refer to as the power of living (the basic foundation of their feelings, desires, and attitudes). And since the main focus of Japanese early childhood education is to guide children to develop basic human attributes rather than to teach them academics, the guidelines also set forth the following five objectives:

1. Teach children basic habits and attitudes necessary for developing healthy, safe and happy lives, and develop foundations for healthy minds and bodies.
2. Help children to love and trust people, develop their independence, and promote

cooperation and good morals.

3. Develop children's interests in and feelings toward nature and their surroundings, and nurture their ability to contemplate.

4. Develop children's interests in spontaneous verbal expression, their listening and speaking skills, and their understanding of language in their everyday lives.

5. Cultivate in children sensitivity and creativity through various experiences (Translated from the Ministry of Education, Culture, Sports, Science, and Technology, 2000).

Cultural Influences on Educational Epistemology

Japan is composed of a majority of Japanese people, a minority of Ainu people and Riukyu people, as well as other minority groups. The minority groups assimilated into Japan approximately three to four hundred years ago, and the view of the child in Japan is dominated by that of the majority group. Because Japan was an agrarian society, many mixed-aged children played together while adults worked in the fields. The Japanese people tended to value a group or a community life, and such values were reflected in children's play which focused on cooperative engagement rather than individual play. This tradition carries over to the educational environment and is evident in the early childhood programs.

Japanese religious beliefs also influence the societal view of childhood. Japanese primitive religions were based on the idea of more than one God, and children were considered to possess a divine nature (Yamamura, 1986). The Japanese perceived children as mediums of the Gods who "played an important part in local religious festivals when the gods were supplicated" (Yamamura, 1986, p. 34). Because of this supposed divine nature, children are viewed as possessing a natural tendency to play; thus, adults need not control this inherent tendency. Likewise, there exists no notion that adults need to provide children with play activities. This traditional Japanese religious background can be better understood by examining the founder of Japanese early childhood education, Shozo Kurahashi, who was influenced by Frobel (Sakamoto, 1976). His philosophy centered on child initiated play activities and on the importance of guiding children's development based on their everyday lives. Although Kurahashi was influenced by Frobel's ideas about education, his philosophy did not support the idea of children belonging to God. The Western idea of children being God's children was not easily within his grasp. Rather children were born divine, free to explore and grow.

Based upon Kurahashi's principles of education, the Japanese did not see play as good or bad nor as influencing children's later lives. To the Japanese play is play, and it has nothing to do with preparation for later life or for child development. These ideas are reflected in some poems in "Imayo" (an old book of poems published around 1180). To illustrate, "Children are born to play, and adults feel it in their hearts when they hear children's voices while playing." As is noted in this poem, the Japanese believe that children should initiate their play and that adults should promote such initiative in children but should not instruct them how to play.

What is children's play to the Japanese, and how do they support their development through play? Japanese early childhood education is focused on the notion of constructivism that is defined as learners constructing their knowledge through exploring the environment (Taylor, 2004). Japanese early childhood curricula are formalized within specific guidelines that mandate play-centered programs. Early childhood educational settings are less structured, and children spend more than twice as much time involved in play than American children (Bacon & Ichikawa, 1988). Because of the belief that play should be play itself, traditional preschools/kindergartens offer relaxed, nonacademic programs in the context of group-oriented environments (Izumi-Taylor, 2006).

To find the meaning of play among early childhood teachers in Japan and the US, Taylor, Rogers, Dodd, Kaneda, Nagasaki, Watanabe, and Goshiki (2004) have examined the meaning of play to both American and Japanese preschool and kindergarten teachers. Taylor et al. (2004) have found that these teachers "used the rhetoric that is congruent with the current zeitgeist of developmentally appropriate early education" (p. 311), and that their perceptions of play were clearly related to their cultures. To illustrate, Japanese children's play was perceived by teachers in Japan to reflect the power of living (Taylor et al., 2004), while the play of American children was considered by teachers in the United States as a means to promote learning and development. They also have found that Japanese children engaged in more unstructured play than did their American counterparts, and that both American and Japanese teachers noted that the effects of play on children consisted of cognitive, social, emotional, and physical development. When asked to describe their notions of adult play, both nations' teachers wrote that adults play for enjoyment. Japanese teachers further elaborated by defining playfulness as the state of one's heart (spirit, mind, lightheartedness), whereas their American counterparts described it as fun feelings.

When asked to discuss the meaning of play, none of Japanese teachers related play to academic learning, but rather they "emphasized that play embodies the essence of living and promotes children's social and emotional development," (Taylor et al., 2004, p. 26). They considered play to be one positive way for children to learn to interact with each other. One teacher's comment summarizes this notion of play thusly: "Play is a must and provides us with the power of living through optimism and initiative" (p. 315). As has been indicated earlier, the power of living is one goal of early childhood education set forth by the Ministry of Education, Culture, Sports, Science, and Technology (2000). It includes the basic foundation of children's feelings, desires, and at-

titudes, and it should be nurtured in group-oriented environments. When teachers nurture children's power through play, then they can grow up to become empathic, receptive, and open-hearted people (Taylor et al., 2004). To Japanese such people are mature, sensitive, and anticipative of others' needs, and selfishness is perceived by the Japanese to be a sign of immaturity.

To fully understand the strong emphasis on the role of play in Japanese early childhood education, the parent handout created by the first author is helpful (Taylor, 2006):

What kind of children do you want to raise? Do you want your children to be good at writing kanji (the most difficult type of writing) or do you want them to be good at arithmetic? It is natural for parents to hope such things, isn't it? However, let's think about this. Do you think that because children are good at kanji or math during kindergarten years, they will become happy adults? Even if they have such abilities and are able to learn everything, if we keep forcing them to use rote memory, they might grow up to without experiencing the joy and excitement of learning and of discovery. Children who are told what to do all the time will not know the joy of discovery and will grow up without initiative. Such children are unable to find their own values and are unable to pursue anything until they are told to by adults.

Children's job is to play. Through play, they discover things they did not know before, and then they are happy and amazed at their findings. Thus, children will know the joy of discovery and will develop the volition to engage in anything in which they are interested. Children's desire to learn springs from their interests, so we provide them with opportunities and appropriate environments in order to promote their interests. However, it is not just about free play, as total freedom without guidance leads children to become bullies. In order to avoid this situation, we provide a curriculum that facilitates the development of the power of living and of moral hearts through teachers' guidance.

Based on our belief that children learn for play, we provide developmentally appropriate materials and activities in which children are interested. We especially provide children with outdoor play, arts, crafts, and computer play, but these activities are not for the purpose of studying academics, but rather for enjoyment. Through play children develop agility, the power of persisting till the very end, the power of living, the joy of expression, and the fun of thinking and planning. These experiences will become children's sources of power of living. (pp. 27-28)

ISSUES, CONTROVERSIES AND PROBLEMS

Japanese adults have historically valued children's play as such and have not related it to education. Such values can be seen in the way early childhood educators' focus on play which respects children's role as inventor of play activities. Through their initiative in play, children can learn appropriate skills and can gain knowledge; thus, the role of the adult is to support children and to provide an environment that encourages expansion of their play. According to the National Curriculum Standards for Kindergarteners published by the Ministry of Education, Culture, Sports, Science, and Technology (2000), play is the "voluntary activities of children, is an important aspect of learning which cultivates the (sic) foundation of balanced mind and body development (p. 1)." In order to provide such play to children, the standards also note the following:

...the environment should be created with the intention of ensuring voluntary activities among children, based on an understanding and anticipation of the individual actions of each child.

Teachers should therefore create a physical and psychological environment in view of the importance of the relationship between a child and other people and things. Teachers should also play various roles in response to the situations of an (sic) individual child's activities and should strive for making activities more enriching. (p. 1)

From this perspective, Japanese early childhood education concentrates on the importance of play and focuses on providing appropriate environments for children rather than on direct instructions.

The heuristic system emphasizes the following points:

1. The aim of Japanese early childhood education is based on the approach that through play, teachers observe children's development and support them. In this sense, teachers trust children's initiative and ability to develop and grow.

2. Since Japanese early childhood education supports children's self-initiated play, it does not perceive play as a planned a developmental factor. Instead, the aim of development is focused on children's natural initiative in play. Play leads development. Japanese early childhood educators do not offer children play activities just because they might promote children's language development or cognitive development, but they present such activities to children based on their observations of their play, and these activities must support children's play. Play develops the whole child, socially, emotionally, cognitively and physically in a natural progression based on the child's play experiences. The Japanese philosophy does not view play as a narrow venue for structured lessons developed by the teacher. The teacher does develop a rich environment and supports a variety of play experiences to address children's interest.

3. Japanese early childhood education focuses on the importance of children's cooperative play. This idea of a cooperative culture among the Japanese originates from the fact that in order to cultivate crops on limited land area, people had to work together. The Japanese early childhood education philosophy integrated the western ideology of the importance of individualism and structured play activities for a time but found that when they changed the focus of their approach key ideas of their traditional values disappeared from the children's behavior. The integrated approach devalued human relationships which was contrary to the Japanese philosophy. It is believed that this resulted in a trend of people not caring about others which increased crimes committed by young people thus contributing to the moral decay of society. Revision of the Japanese Standards is in progress to reflect the more traditional values of Japanese tradition learning. In order to rebuild the Japanese society, educational systems have begun to revise their standards which emphasize the importance of cooperation, group-oriented education, and group harmony, a more altruistic approach to support children's development. New standards will include the importance of cooperative play. This approach nurtures individual development through group-oriented environments. This altruistic approach better reflects traditional cultural values.

4. Finally, Japanese early childhood educators do not formally engage children in writing and mathematics activities until the children have initiated interest in concepts. It is believed that such activities should come from children, should be naturally nurtured through play, and the role of the educator is to support child-initiated play activities This constructivist approach is accepted across all areas of child development.

5. The National Curriculum Standards for Kindergartens (2000) clearly supports this philosophy as indicated in the following statement:

Children should be encouraged to place importance on their experiences based on the necessities of their own lives, as that interest, curiosity and feelings of understanding the concept of quantity and numbers, and written words can be fostered. (p.5)

This transfers to the use of technology with young children. These ideas are important because the interest in technology must come from the child through play activities. The teacher's role is to closely observe and analyze children's play interactions and provide the environment to support this interest. The teacher must have a strong background in technology and all areas in order to recognize the child's thinking and provide appropriate experiences and materials. While subtle, the teacher's organization of the environment is key to technology interest.

SOCIALIZATION SKILLS

One of the most important goals of Japanese early childhood education is socialization of children based on cultural values. This goal is achieved when educators provide children with integrated guidance and suitable experiences in a group-oriented environment through play (Izumi-Taylor, 2006; Taylor, 2004). The focus of successful socialization emphasizes the use of group-oriented environments and play. In as much as educators value children's everyday activities in a group-oriented environment, the National Curriculum Standards for Kindergartens (2000) articulate the importance of group-oriented environment as follows:

Given that the voluntary activities of children are enhanced and enriched through relationships with others and that children recognized the necessity of each other through such relationships, teachers should foster in children the ability to relate with others while forming a group in which each member of the group is valued. (p. 4)

By creating these environments, teachers help children to love and trust people around them as well as to develop independence, cooperation, and good morals (Taylor, 2004). To develop warm human relationships, establishing a community spirit, altruism, is important. In this sense, Japanese teachers believe that "during the early childhood years, children need to learn to connect with one another and to build a willingness and capacity to live harmoniously in a group" (Izumi-Taylor, 2008b, p. 76). Early childhood education programs heavily emphasize the importance of creating a community spirit to nurture children's interpersonal skills in group-oriented environments. The main goal of developing such communities is for children to learn mutual respect and to build healthy interpersonal relationships (DeVries, Zan, Hildebrant, Edmiaston, & Sales, 2002). Japanese educators develop respectful interpersonal relationships by offering ample play activities based on children's interests and invite their contributions. The Japanese teacher allows children to interact and solve their problems through their thinking rather than a dictated approach to relationships. Encouraging such relationships leads to children's emotional involvement with peers (Lewis, 1995), and in turn, teachers can promote children's positive emotions toward each other, including kindness, empathy, cooperation, sympathy, obligation, and a sense of responsibility (Taylor, Ogawa, & Wilson, 2002). The primary goal of nurturing such emotions in children is to develop their autonomy which is defined as making one's own decisions by considering the needs and wishes of others (Branscombe, Castle, Dorsey, Surbeck, & Taylor, 2003). "Autonomous children show initiative,

empathy, cooperation, and problem-solving skills" (Izumi-Taylor, 2008b, p. 76).

Just as Japanese educators promote children's positive emotions in their efforts to create a community spirit, American educators (Damon 1988; Turiel, 1998) report that such focus can encourage children's morality. To establish a community spirit, Japanese teachers offer children many opportunities to create their own rules for the group in order for them to feel ownership of the rules. Teachers encourage children to have group meetings to discuss the issues that are important to them, to elicit children's opinions in making group decisions that concern them and to help children develop their sense of responsibility by delegating authority to them. It is equally important to accept children as they are so they may develop their own identity as active and important members of the group.

Japanese educators perceive play as a salient mode for children to develop and learn in group-oriented environments (Izumi-Taylor, Rogers, & Samuelsson, 2007; Izumi-Taylor, 2006, Taylor, 2004). Children encounter authentic learning opportunities when they initiate their play activities based on their own interests. Through play children are able to become acquired with those around them and to experience the joy of being with others. In a similar view, the National Curriculum Standards for Kindergartens (2000) conclude that, through their play experiences, children can think for themselves, can become curious about their environments, and keep appropriate relationships with them, as well as develop understanding of the rules and codes of such environments. Through play children discover things in their environments that they did not know about before, and they experience joy in their discoveries. At the same time, children can learn about the conduct and rules of play appropriate to their society. Children should learn their roles in the environment and about their relationships with others "in the order of necessity in the context of play and daily life" (Muto, 2004, p. 3).

By creating group-oriented settings and offering opportunities for children to play with others, Japanese educators nurture children's socialization skills. The use of technology in a group setting is based on the cultural beliefs that with a little support from their teachers children are remarkable spiritual beings who can develop their self-regulating skills. Therefore, the use of technology in early childhood settings is based on the notion that appropriate technology can "provide children with authentic and playful learning experiences, and that technology can increase children's connection to one another, promoting a willingness to work with others harmoniously in a group-oriented environment" (Izumi-Taylor, 2008b, p. 10).

CHANGES IN THE USE OF TECHNOLOGY IN JAPANESE EARLY CHILDHOOD SETTINGS

Traditional societal values influence the use of technology in Japanese Early Childhod Programs. Early childhood education professionals tend to hesitate to implement new skill-related technology or newly developed developmental psychology as well as brain development research in the classroom. This perception may be in part related to Shozo Kurahashi, who is a major influence on Japanese pedagogical applications in Early Childhood. Kurahashi, considered to be the best early childhood educator in Japanese history, has been the guide for early childhood programs and his disciples/students have followed his educational principles to the letterand are hesitant to change his teachings. His strong influence on Early Childhood philosophy in Japan has impacted the use of technology. One kindergarten director states, "You have been studying computers for young children, but Kurahashi never talked about the use of computers in the classroom." It is puzzling what this person meant by this because Kurahashi has been dead since 1955, and he had

never discussed the use of computers. It is well known that Japanese early childhood educators have intensely focused on the early childhood education philosophy described by Kurahashi. In his search for the best care and education for young children, he traveled around Europe to collect new toys, researched them, and wrote a book on toys, entitled, Gangu kyoikehen (1935). According to the book, he believed that in order to nurture children's development, educators should study and implement not only traditional toys but also the newest toys and machines in the classroom. This point is often overlooked by his disciples who associate technology with computers. However, his followers did not agree with this point of view.

The Japanese view of early childhood education is inclined to focus on the importance of child-initiated play, and because of this, educators avoid the idea of "teaching children something." This influences the use of computers which were introduced as business tools and are seen as contradictory to play philosophy. The Japanese cultural idea of internalized and self-initiated learning resists direct introduction of computers as accepted in American education. The idea that if one is not computer literate, one will not be able to compete in a global society is not well accepted. In the United Sates it is believed that "because of this rapid expansion of technology and its early influences on young lives, early childhood educators themselves need opportunities to experience and to explore technology-based education" (Izumi-Taylor, Sluss, & Turner, 2007, p. 6), but many early childhood educators are uncomfortable implementing technology-related activities in the classroom. Japanese educators may perceive computers as "direct teaching machines", and based on this refuse to use them. The idea that computers can be used for many educational applications is just now starting to be accepted by educators. In spite of cultural perceptions among Japanese early childhood educators, there has been some implementation of computers in classrooms.

One example of successful implementation from the early 1980's, includes mathematics software. The first author tried mathematics software in a classroom of young children to build pre-allgebraic concepts. The activities built understanding of number relationships. For example, in the problem:

$$\circ + \square = 7$$

children can make 7 by inserting combinations of two numbers into ○ and □. The numerals can include the following combinations: 1, 6; 2, 5; 3, 4; and so on. This software was designed to promote children's awareness of how to combine two numbers to arrive at a certain number. As a result of this experiment, it was found that this software was more flexible than regular arithmetic activities.

In the mid 1990's a few early childhood educators started implementing computers in the classroom. Implementation was varied but the goal of using computers was to enhance children's conceptual understanding... One example was that some educators used the revised version of LOGO, software developed by Papert (1993) Children were able to use LOGO as "computational materials as an expressive medium" (Papert, 1993, p. 4). For example, some Japanese educators took their children to the zoo and later on offered them an activity using LOGO to animate children's drawings of animals. However, this particular use of computers was limited, and computers were still considered to be special equipment, not a natural part of the environment. Teachers allowed limited use for special activities and only in the computer classroom. The perception that computer use was not supportive of child-initiated play inherent in Japanese early childhood education was still evident. If educators are to utilize computers they need to view technology as an integral element of the classroom environment, and allow children easy access at all times (Izumi-Taylor, Sluss, & Lovelace, 2006).

More recently, technology use has increased in the classroom as more early childhood educators reflect on their use of computers and begin to reject the idea of computers as "special occasional tool" in education. Japanese educators have begun to perceive computers as children's play materials. Many teachers provide opportunities for children to draw computer pictures during play activities moving the focus away from teacher directed to children initiated use. This use of computers is aligned with the goal of Japanese early childhood education. These implementations of computer use set the stage for early childhood education programs by actively applying such technology in the classroom; however, some software has still not received the complete approval of all teachers. Some are concerned that it is too easy for children to draw and since it is erasable, it discourages children's active involvement in drawing. It is true that software with a low level of challenge could discourage children's active involvement. Dependant on the teacher's guidance, such software can be used to support active involvement. Teachers can encourage children who might be intimidated by computers. The teacher is the key to software use in the classroom and is only limited by their imagination and technology understanding.

Another important use of technology is communication. Rather than the idea of global competition the idea of global communication is a key reason for computers in classrooms. Japanese children often enjoy exchanging letters and playing mail carriers. As an extension of such play, children use emails to communicate with each other and experience both the pros and cons of emails. They enjoy instantaneous arrival of their messages in the next door classroom; children run to the classroom next door to see their messages arrive. This supports their play and interest.

Considering technology to be a method of communication is nothing new to the Japanese. As Izumi-Taylor (2009) has examined pre-service teachers' perceptions of technology in early childhood educational settings in Japan and the

United States, she has found that only Japanese pre-service teachers have responded that technology improves communication, and none of their American counterparts have indicated such opinions. Also, these Japanese pre-service teachers have considered technology to be a good way of communicating with others. These observations are supported by Sakamoto's study (1995) stating that Japanese view technology as communication device and that it was developed as one tool for human beings to communicate. Such communication devices include websites, cell phones, email, TV, radio, etc.

CURRENT AND FUTURE USE OF TECHNOLOGY

In this section the first author will introduce his current implementation of and ideas about the use of technology in the early childhood settings: using computers as toys, play environments, hubs, and digital pictorial dictionaries. Each issue will be discussed as current applications and the vision of future use of technology in educational environments.

Using Computers as Toys

As the first author indicated before, the notion of using computers as one of children's toys aligns with that of Japanese early childhood educators. Some educators have been successfully putting this into practice. Nevertheless, in order to expand and support children's play through technology, educators need to improve existing software and to develop different versions.

It is true that some software can expand children's play, and children can find enjoyment in using the software. Take drawing software, for example, after a child draws a picture, it can be used as a template, and the picture can be used for others to add to or elaborate upon; thus, promoting children's collaboration skills. Therefore, the no-

tion of a computer as a toy will continue for a long time to come, and educators will offer it as part of play. Such a notion is similar to that of others in the Untied States (Van Hoorn, Nourot, Scales, & Alward, 2007) who maintain that technology such as computers should be applied as tools to support children's play.

Using Computers as Play Environments

Using computers as play environments might be the best way to implement technology in early childhood education in Japan. It means that we consider a computer as a hub which is closely related to the common notion of an airline hub. For example, a pilot with ideas comes to the airport, refuels, is serviced, and is ready to fly. The processes involve the ideas of children plugging their ideas into computers, expanding and integrating them, gaining new ideas, and applying them to their play. Through these processes, educators guide and support children's activities related to their everyday lives and play.

Children's everyday activities are multidimensional. Children's outdoor play, sand and water play, nature walks, and manipulative toy activities can be regarded as cooperative, physical, and imaginative play. However, each type of play tends to be independent of each other, and usually each type of play does not connect to the other. Play in which children find bugs outdoors usually does not connect to play in which children create a story. While teachers could lead children to write their stories about bugs, Japanese educators are adamant about respecting children's initiative in play and not interfering in their play. On the other hand, if educators value comprehensive play and comprehensive approaches in teaching as stated in the National Curriculum Standards for Kindergartens (2000), teachers need to think of ways to integrate play activities. When children participate in comprehensive integrated activities children connect different experiences that stay in their hearts, and such psychological experiences should be interrelated to each other in order to fully support children's whole development and learning.

To connect different play activity to other activities, the notion of the computer as a hub is useful. If educators naturally unite each activity, children's experiences can be richer. Think of children's information going through computers in the following manner:

a. Insert information: one activity → information received: one activity
b. Insert information: one activity → information received: multiple activities
c. Insert information: multiple activities → information received: one activity
d. Insert information: multiple activities → information received: multiple activities

Also, consider the following as well:

p. Insert information: one's own information → information received: one's own activity
q. Insert information: one's own information → information received: others' activities
r. Insert information: others' information → information received: one's own activity
s. Insert information: others' information → information received: others' activities

Through the processes of obtaining information through computers, children can work on a-q or c- r to gain the information. When they are engaging in multiple activities, children can also experience c-p, and q.

Examples of Using a Computer as a Hub

The following two examples can be useful in understanding the concept of the computer as a hub: playing a store and the creation of digital pictorial map dictionary. Additionally, we will include one example of how schools can share the information with parents and family members of children through computers. Each example will be described accordingly.

Playing Store

Children enjoy pretending to sell and buy items at a store. Suppose children in one classroom wanted to be sellers and they wanted their next door classmates to be buyers.

The children who are sellers can use a video camera to make their own commercials about their store, can save them on a computer, and offer their commercials to their next door classmates through LAN (Local Area Network). This type of activity is a-p, q, as indicated above. Information received is part of their own pretend store activity and at the same time, the next door classmates' participation in such play. This type of activity might motivate children in other classrooms to play and to make their own commercials to show through the internet.

The Creation of a Digital Pictorial Map Dictionary

Children enjoy finding different items in schools, value such items, and want to treasure them. Also, they like their own special places in schools and keep them close to their hearts. Through the use of technology, if children photograph or videotape such items and places, insert them in the school's map on a computer which was prepared by the teacher, then, children can create their own digital pictorial map dictionary. In doing so, children have their own space to store their information, can show it to others, and can view others' information. For these reasons, this activity involves a-p, q, r types of play. Also, if children are inspired by the digital pictorial map dictionary, they might draw pictures of flowers or bugs that they found and write stories about them. Then, this activity will be a-p, q, r, and b types of play. It may lead to a different activity in which children find the names of flowers and of bugs using the pictorial dictionary books.

Another example is videotaping children's shadows regularly and saving the lengths of shadows on a computer. By engaging in such an activity, children might observe different seasons, the sun's positions, and changes in weather. This activity could lead to a new activity and that would be a-p, q, r, and c. These are only few examples, and creative teachers can put into practice different ideas through the use of computers, and in turn, they can inspire children's new play ideas. Teachers can videotape children's different play activities and show them to the entire school. In viewing such play activities, children can share them and can quiz each other regarding their play. Future uses of computers as creative communication hubs have much potential for play applications.

Sharing Information with Parents and Family Members

Involving parents and family members in children's school lives is a vital part of Japanese early childhood education. As stated in The National Curriculum Standards for Kindergartens: "Education during early childhood is extremely important in cultivating the foundation of lifelong character building, while working in cooperation with the home" (p. 1), teachers must communicate with parents and others involved in children's lives. In using the concept of a computer as a hub, teachers can share information with parents and others. Many schools use blogs to give information to parents, but if parents are also able to share their information and comments with others, then, the computer is used as a hub. In the first author's kindergarten, in addition to blogs, he offers an online space entitled, "Saving Places for Parents Information" where parents can share nice places for children and parents to play and visit, such as parks and restaurants; parents can view how to

make lunch boxes for their children; and parents are able to share other relevant information with each other.

In summary, to employ the concept of a computer as a hub requires certain skills, but in the future computers will be improved in such a way that children can operate them as hubs without much help from their teachers. It is the first author's hope that the use of technology is based on the Japanese early childhood education goals, and it should support such goals. Educators must strive to use technology to enhance children's initiative in play and social skills. This allows teachers to use their creativity when developing technology experiences.

SUMMARY

We will offer our recommendations for educators based on our experiences and observations of Japanese early childhood education and technology in relation to socialization of young children. Such recommendations are cultural in nature and the practices of Japanese educators are focused on the belief that children are truly active and powerful learners who should initiate their play and learning. With a little support and encouragement from them, teachers trust that children can learn to initiate and self-regulate their play and learning.

1. Provide children easy access to technology in group-oriented environments at all times.
2. Allow children's initiative in engaging in technology-related activities.
3. Offer technology to children in a group-oriented environment where children can help each other.
4. Encourage children to support each other in order to accomplish their goals while playing with computers (Izumi-Taylor, 2008).
5. Consider technology as a tool that supports, enhances, and expands children's play.

6. Implement the idea of using computers as hubs in order to connect children's individual play activities to others.

7. Involve children's parents and family members in school activities by giving them easy access to communicate through the use of technology.

8. Create online spaces where children's parents and family members can exchange their information.

9. Learn to support children's technology-related activities by becoming technology literate by understanding the use of play and technology to promote children's social skills.

10. Consider that fact that technology and play can be used to "nurture children's social and emotional development, not just for the development of their academic skills" (Izumi-Taylor, 2008, p. 13).

SOME QUESTIONS FOR REFLECTIVE PRACTITIONERS:

1. The main focus of Japanese early childhood education is to guide children in developing culturally valued human characteristics (such as social skills, empathy, cooperation skills, etc.) rather than teaching them academics. What role could technology play in this approach to early childhood education?

2. The Japanese idea that children's play is just play and not related to education is unusual. How does your cultural view of play influence your teaching?

3. Play is the media from which children in Japan learn about cultural social values. If technology becomes more highly valued in this country how might the early childhood environments change?

4. The idea that technology can be used as a play environment for young children opens many possibilities for classroom use. How could you create a technology play environment in your classroom? What types of technology might you provide to build on the children's play?

5. Japan, along with Taiwan and China are countries that consistently score high on international comparisons in mathematics and science ratings. The United States consistently scores statistically significantly lower than these countries. How might their approach to early education influence this?

6. What differences do you see in the Japanese and Taiwanese approach to early childhood experiences with technology?

7. What parallels do you see between Shozo Kurahashi and Piaget in regards to early learning?

8. What are the similarities among different countries approach to early childhood education and technology? How can thinking about these perceptions help you develop your personal approach to technology use in your classroom?

9. Do you agree with the idea that technology should be viewed as a toy? Why or why not?

10. It is interesting that the Japanese early childhood programs were structured in a similar manner to those in the United States but recent thinking is moving their approach back to a more cultural value system. Why do you think this has happened?

11. What ideas from the Japanese approach to early childhood education could you use in your classroom?

12. What do you think a typical Japanese classroom would look like after reading this chapter? How would it be similar and different from your classroom?

REFERENCES

Bacon, W., & Ichikawa, V. (1988). Maternal expectations, classroom experiences, and achievement among kindergartners in the United States and Japan. *Human Development, 31*, 378–383.

Better than people. (2005, December 24th). *The Economist* (pp. 58-59).

Damon, W. (1988). *The moral child.* New York: Free Press.

DeVries, R., Zan, B., Hildebrant, R., Edmiaston, R., & Sales, C. (2002). *Developing constructivist early childhood curriculum.* New York: Teachers College Press.

Hey, big-spender. (2005, December 5th). *The Economist* (pp. 60-61).

Iikura, H. (2007). *Nihonjinno shikitari* [Japanese customs]. Tokyo, Japan: Seishun Shupansha.

Izumi-Taylor, S. (2006). Play of Japanese preschoolers in constructivist environments. *Play-Rights, 27*(1), 24–29.

Izumi-Taylor, S. (2008a). Play and technology in group-oriented Japanese early childhood educational settings. *He Kupu, 1*(4), 9–15.

Izumi-Taylor, S. (2008b). Sunao (cooperative) children: How Japanese teachers Nurture autonomy. *Young Children, 63*(3), 76–79.

Izumi-Taylor, S. (2009). *Pre-service teachers' perceptions of teaching technology To young children in Japan and the United States.* Unpublished manuscript.

Izumi-Taylor, S., Rogers, C., & Samuelsson, I. (2007). *Teachers' perspectives on play in Japan, the US, and Sweden.* Paper presented at the annual meeting of the International Play Association/ the Association of Study of Play Conference. Rochester, NY.

Izumi-Taylor, S., Sluss, D., & Lovelace, A. (2006). Nurturing children's love of learning through play and technology. *He Kupu, 1*(1), 35–46.

Izumi-Taylor, S., Sluss, D., & Turner, S. (2007). Three views of learning experiences using technology-enhanced teaching: How online video conferencing sessions can promote students' construction of knowledge. *He Kupu, 1*(2), 6–48.

Izumi-Taylor, S., & Taylor, J. W. (2009). I am the boss of me! *An intuitive approach to constructivism in Japanese childhood education.* Unpublished manuscript.

Kurahashi, S. (1935). *Gangu kyoikuhen* [Education with toys]. Tokyo, Japan: Yuzankaku.

Levin, T., & Wadmany, R. (2008). Teachers' views on factors affecting effective integration of information technology in the classroom: Developmental scenery. *Journal of Technology and Teacher Education, 16*(2), 233–263.

Lewis, C. (1986). Children's social development in Japan. In H. Stevenson, H. Azuma, & K. Hakuta (Eds.), *Child development and education in Japan* (pp. 186-200). New York: W. H. Freeman and Company.

Lewis, C. (1995). *Educating hearts and minds.* New York: Cambridge University Press.

Lichtman, M. (2006). *Qualitative research in education: A user's guide.* Thousands Oaks, CA: Sage Publications.

Lichtman, M., & Taylor, S. I. (1993). *Conducting and reporting case studies.* ([). East Lansing, ML: National Center for Research on Teacher Learning.]. *Report No. TM, 019,* 956.

Ministry of Education. Culture, Sports, Science, and Technology. (2000).

Muto, T. (Ed.). (2004). *Early childhood education handbook.* Tokyo, Japan: Yoshimi Kohsan.

Nagasaki, I., Kaneda, T., Taylor, S. I., Watanabe, Y., & Goshiki, T. (2002). How the quality of early childhood education affects the social development of American and Japanese children. *Research Bulletin of Tokoha Junior College, 33,* 123–134.

National Curriculum Standards for Kindergarten. Retrieved from http://www.mext.go.jp/a_menu/ shotou/youji/english/youryou/ mokuji.htm

Papert, S. (1993). Situating constructionism. In I. Harel & S. Papert. (Eds.). *Constructionism.* (pp. 1- 12). Norwood, NJ: Ablex Publishing Corporation.

Prairie, A. (2005). *Inquiry into math, science, and technology for young children.* Clifton Park, NY: Thomson Delmar Learning.

Sakamoto, A. (1995). *Moricimidiajidainokodomotachi* [Children in the era of multi-media]. Tokyo, Japan: Sanchou Shupan.

Sakamoto, H. (1976). *Kurhashi Shozo sonohitoto shisou* [Kuahashi Shozo, the person and his thoughts]. Tokyo, Japan: furuberusha.

Shigaki, I. (1983). Child care practices in Japan and the United States: How do they reflect cultural values in young children? *Young Children, 38*(4), 13–24.

Shinji, R. (1996). Nuyojino seiriteki hatsutatsu [Young children's physical development]. In M. Takauchi (Ed.), *Shoji hoken jushu* [Health practices for young children] (pp. 27-49). Osaka, Japan: Hoiku Shpansha.

Simons, C. (1987, March). They get by with a lot of help from their kyoiku mamas. *Smithsonian,* 44–53.

Taylor, S. I. (2004). Let it be: Japanese preschoolers rule the classroom. *Young Children, 59*(5), 20–25.

Taylor, S. I., Ogawa, T., & Wilson, J. (2002). Moral development of Japanese children. *International Journal of Early Childhood, 43*(3), 12–18.

Taylor, S. I., Rogers, C., Dodd, A., Kaneda, T., Nagasaki, I., Watanabe, Y., & Goshiki, T. (2004). The meaning of play: A cross-cultural study of American and Japanese teachers' perspective on play. *Journal of Early Childhood Teacher Education, 24,* 311–321. doi:10.1080/1090102040240411

Tobin, J., Wu, D., & Davidson, D. (1989). *Preschool in three cultures.* New Haven: Yale University Press.

Turiel, E. (1998). The development of morality. In W. Damon, & N. Eisenberg. (Eds.), *Handbook of child psychology, 3,* (5th ed.) (pp. 863-932). New York, NY: John Wiley.

Van Hoorn, J., Nourot, P., Scales, B., & Alward, K. (2007). *Play at the center of curriculum* (4th ed.). Upper saddle River, NJ: Pearson Merrill Prentice Hall.

Yamamura, Y. (1986). The child in Japanese society. In H. Stevens, H. Azuma, & K. Hakuta (Eds.), *Child development and education in Japan* (pp. 28-34). New York, NY: W. H. Freeman and Company.

Chapter 4
Technology and Preschool Education in Mexico
A Country in Transformation

Jorge López
University of Texas at El Paso, USA

María Eugenia López
Centro de Desarrollo Infantil, Cd. Juárez, Chih., México

ABSTRACT

The last nine years have seen major change in the Mexican educational system as sweeping reforms across all levels have been implemented. In particular the early years of education have become the focus of legislation to increase quality, open access, and improve curriculum. How technology shaped these sweeping reform efforts will change the future of Mexico in a global community. Early childhood education must support the use of technology if the population is to move into a techno-society.

INTRODUCTION

In other chapters you have read about preschools, teachers and technology in New Zealand, Taiwan, and Japan. This chapter will focus first on Mexico and then briefly on the border regions which connect the United States to Mexico. Given global trends that indicate that the world's predominant growth populations are largely non-Anglo students, we can expect that tomorrow's schools will need more teacher experts who can cross all borders that separate groups, whether the borders are geographic, physical, linguistic or cultural. One of the strengths of the digital generation is they are global

with no borders to bind the education, business and communication systems. As most countries of the world become more economically dependent on the global money market it is important for all countries to prepare their populations for technology use. Universally higher levels of education for larger numbers of students are being demanded of educational systems that were designed decades or centuries ago to meet very different requirements (Darling-Hammond, 1996). While challenges remain such as training for teachers (Stevens et al, 1997), glimpses of hope are provided as different factions call out for education for all, especially in areas of meeting early childhood needs.

The first author of this chapter has worked in the field of physics for several years. My degrees

DOI: 10.4018/978-1-60566-784-3.ch004

include a B.S., M.S. and PhD in Physics. I have done Postdoc work at the Niels Bohr Institute, Copenhagen Denmark and the Lawrence Berkeley Lab in Berkeley, California. At this point you may be wondering if this chapter will be filled with equations and you may be questioning the reason a Physicist would be writing a chapter connecting young children and anything. While working at the University of Texas at El Paso I developed an interest in how students learn. During my experiences it became my belief that the early years are the most important for development of thinking. Through the funding of the National Science Foundation (NSF) I had the opportunity to develop science activities for preschool children and became involved in the Ysleta Preschool Center. This experience has changed the direction of my work. Since then my belief has been confirmed that these age groups and teachers are crucial to the future of the globalization of all cultures. Within this population lie the answers to how we can connect and support successful learning for all children. I now write children's books, develop science activities, and work with grants for teacher training and international understanding of culture on early childhood learning. My co-author always knew the importance of early childhood and was the Regional Coordinator of the Centros de Desarrollo Infantil in Cd. Juarez. Her many years of experience with young children in Mexico provides the practitioner component for the development of this chapter. Between us we have tried to approach this chapter to address university and practitioner concerns about technology and young children in Mexico.

Mexico has been referred to as a "developing country" in many reports and articles. This term comes from a Western analysis of economic development. This may mislead readers as Mexico had been developed in many areas for centuries. We have a rich cultural history, the country of Mayas and Aztecs, of civilizations that were considered highly technical and advanced. There is still a large indigenous population in our country. There are 62 indigenous towns in Mexico, where one of the 80 languages and their variants is spoken. This diverse cultural heritage influenced how education has developed. The impact of technology has changed the economic system in Mexico. In 2009 Wikipedia listed Mexico as the country with the 13th largest gross domestic product. The change has been rapid and the educational systems struggle to keep up with the technology needs of our citizens.

As a practicing scientist for many years I have become concerned about the future of science and science education. The economic system is important but even more important is the future of science education which depends on the inclusion and investigation of diverse populations and how best to develop and utilize these resources in school environments. Cumulative research over the last five decades shows that children's development can be modified and enhanced by the quality of their early environments and experiences. Research provides strong evidence that early childhood care and education programs boost children's physical health and well-being, their cognitive and language skills, their social emotional skills and their enrolment in primary school (UNESCO 2006).

Technology is and has always been vital to the development of science. Long before the general population used the internet to communicate the science community shared research and ideas through technology and on a global basis. Computer simulations are increasingly used in experiments to explore and develop science research. As the world becomes more technology dependent there is a clear need to insure all children have the best possible educational preparation in technology. We can no longer separate communities or narrowly identify groups of people based on ethnicity if we are to meet the needs of a global community. Because early childhood cognitive and socio-emotional development strongly predict later school enrollment and life success, we cannot afford to ignore the importance of technology in these early educational programs. If educators are to give all children the potential to become scientifically literate efforts to introduce children to essential experiences of science inquiry and technology must begin at an early age (Lind, 2004).

In the first section we will give a brief overview of technology in Mexico and then the history of early childhood education in Mexico, which includes some information about current programs. The next section will describe the components of the reform efforts which include a plan for universal pre-school, enhanced quality programs, policy changes and curriculum reform. We will discuss how technology influences and supports reform efforts. We include some of the issues, problems and controversies concerning technology use in Mexico and some of the working solutions. Finally we will share our vision of technology and early childhood in Mexico. We hope the readers will develop a better understanding of issues surrounding the use and acceptance of technology in Mexican educational systems.

TECHNOLOGY IN MEXICO

Within the last two decades, the Mexican economy has expanded to become the ninth largest in the world (UNESCO, 2006). The industrial sector has been the driving force behind much of this progress. Through the National Development Plan for 2001-2006, the government launched the Program for the Competitiveness of the Electronics and Hi-tech Industries (PCIEAT). The program's aim is to put the country in the top five electronics manufacturers in the world through a variety of strategies, including: developing local providers of electrical and electronic components, promoting the transition from analogue to digital technology, creating marketable technology nationally, and increasing investment in the sector. Business, academia, and the government are collaborating on the initiative, which counts the development of

the domestic market, the strengthening of the local IT industry, the provision of technological education, the establishment of a solid legal framework, and the promotion of exports and FDI among its key goals. The drive for digitalization is seen as crucial to create a stronger internal market for software and related services, which will in turn make Mexico more competitive internationally.

The national e-Mexico initiative is further raising awareness of the power of technology and fostering the development of the internal ICT market. Led by the Ministry for Communications and Transport, its main objective is to create widespread online access to information, to encourage rapid community development, particularly among marginalized communities. According to an article in the New York Times (2008) employers are being encouraged to digitalize their day-to-day processes, from ordering to accounting. The government and state enterprises are also increasingly going digital and are tending to buy software and solutions from local suppliers.

Some of the smaller Mexican software providers are beginning to form alliances so that they can compete for large-scale projects. "Although multi-national companies are, on the one hand, competition, they are also stimulating Mexico's technological evolution by setting up software and program development sites there," says Mr. Bernal Arce (2008)." Parts of the country do not have access to and the use of cutting edge technologies because there is no market for the private sector to invest in them," says Jorge Alvarez Hoth (2008), Under-Secretary for Communications. "We are providing incentives so that the private sector finds it attractive to invest where those technologies are not present."

Mexico is one of the Latin American countries that do not impose censorship of internet use. Mexico has approximately 25 million Internet users and continues to increase the demand for broadband Internet services. Mexico is the country with the most internet users in Latin America, and in August 2005 Cisco Systems, the industry leader in Internet backbone routing equipment, said "they see Mexico and other Latin American countries as the focal point for growth in coming years, with Mexico receiving the biggest chunk of their investments, identifying it as a hypergrowth market for equipment suppliers." Additionally looking at the historical growth for the period from 2001 to 2005 we see broadband Internet jump from 0.1 subscribers per hundred population to 2.2 subscribers per hundred population, a growth of 2200% in just 5 years (http://en.wikipedia.org/wiki/Internet_in_Mexico). As Mexico continues to move toward a more technological state it is vital that the schools keep up by preparing the children of Mexico for global economy. Mexico is considered the hope for Latin American in industry and technology. These issues have influenced the educational system to rethink their policies and approach to education.

BACKGROUND

At the present time, Mexico ranks eleventh among the most populated nations in the world, with about 100 million inhabitants. The demographic analysis carried out in 2000 by the Consejo Nacional de Población (Conapo) [National Council on Population] makes it possible to anticipate two tendencies that will influence the demand for educational services over the next few decades: i) the reduction in the population under fifteen years of age and the increase in the population at a working age, between 15 and 64, as well as of adults over 65; and ii) the increase in the number of small towns, spread across the national territory (SEP, 2003b).

From 1970 to the present, the birth rate has dropped markedly, so that the proportion of the group at preschool age has fallen from 13.6 million in 1995 to 12.9 million in 2000. However, the demand for this educational service will increase as a result of the national act that makes pre-school education for children of three, four and five years of age obligatory. Also, the population at an age to attend primary education (6 to 11) also began to fall gradually in the year 2000, so that it is estimated that the maximum figure reached in 2001 of 13.7 million will decline by more than two million over the next fourteen years to reach 11.2 million in 2015, which implies a reduction in demand of 18% during that period among the population at an age to study primary school (Conapo, 2003).

The government of the Mexican Republic is made up of the Legislative, Executive and Judicial powers, and legally it is governed by the Political Constitution of the United Mexican States, enacted in 1917, that has been reformed with respect to some of its articles over nearly nine decades, to give it greater validity. The Federal Executive Power, through the Secretaría de Educación Pública (SEP) [Department of Public Education], is responsible for educational administration; the General Education Law and the State Laws represent the legal basis for its application and development. The Third Article of the Constitution is one of the distinctive stamps of the educational system and its essence resides in the fact that the education offered by the State on Mexican territory is national, lay, free of charge, and obligatory. Nowadays it is obligatory for the entire population of the country to study pre-school, primary and secondary (junior high) education. Until 1992, most of the processes related to the issue of education were centralized in the national authority, a situation that was modified soon after issuing, that year, an agreement between federal and state authorities called the Acuerdo para la Modernización de la Educación Básica y Normal [Agreement for Modernizing Basic and Normal Education], which mainly resulted in educational decentralization. Since then, federal and state authorities have shared responsibilities in the operation of the Sistema Educativo Nacional (SEN) [National Educational System].

Mexico today is undergoing profound transformations and it is a nation with great diversity, where extreme situations coexist, in both socioeconomic and demographic terms; it is a nation that recognizes the importance and impact of the educational function, in the country's present and future development, so that a great deal of attention needs to be paid to the field of education. Located geographically in North America, it forms a Federal Republic, made up of 32 federative entities (states and a federal district). According to 2003 figures, the Mexican population is 104.2 million (Conapo, 2003), 20% of whom are concentrated in the metropolitan area made up of the Federal District, which is the country's capital, and the metropolitan municipalities of the State of Mexico.

While the Mexican population is becoming mainly urban this growth of the cities creates a process of dispersion of the rural settlements. It is estimated that a third of the settlements of fewer than 500 inhabitants are located outside of the area of urban influence and far from a highway, and that more than 77% of the towns with fewer than 1,000 inhabitants show high and very high degrees of marginalization, which, in turn, is related to geographical conditions that hamper access to these communities and represents an obstacle to providing them with the goods and services necessary for their development. Attention to the educational demand of dispersed groups of population requires differentiated educational modes in order to guarantee opportunities for education (SEP, 2000a).

Finally, a topic that we must not neglect to mention is that of the indigenous population in our country. According to the General Population and Housing Census in 2000, this population comes to over 8 million native people distributed throughout the country's 32 states, most of them settled in 24 states. There are 62 indigenous towns, where one of the 80 languages and their variants is spoken. The indigenous population from 0 to 14 years of age in the country comes to over two and a half million people. Services of indigenous education are provided in 24 states in this country in order to guarantee that the students reach the goals of the national basic education, are able to express themselves in oral and written Spanish and in their mother tongue, and know and value their own culture. (http://sep.gob.mx/wb2/sep/sep_4413_informacion_basica_g).

MEXICAN EDUCATION

This section will help the reader understand the evolution of preschool in Mexico which directly influences impact, acceptance and use of technology in early childhood programs. Formal attention to children in the preschool years in Mexico began in the late 19th century. Similar to program development in many countries Mexico divided their approach between programs that focused on the education of young children as the primary purpose and those that focused on care, mainly within a welfare context. These were seen as two different issues in education which required different approaches to program development. These two different goals influenced the types of experiences children have and services provided.

For seven decades, from 1921, the Mexican education system was centralized under the authority of the Ministry of Public Education (Secretaría de Educación Pública - SEP). However, in 1992, the National Agreement for the Modernization of Basic Education brought constitutional reforms and in 1993, a new education law established the framework for the reorganization of the education system. The main policy reforms under the new law include decentralization, by which the government transfers most responsibilities for basic education and teacher education to its 31 states; extension of compulsory schooling; expansion of the preschool system; curricular reform; and increased emphasis on compensatory programs to improve education in disadvantaged communities (Salas Garza, 1998). Teacher in-service training programs also have received increased attention, as the government recognized the needs of teachers to update and refresh their skills.

Table 1. Proportion of students, teachers, and schools, by type of support 2002-2003 school year

	Students	Teachers	Schools
Public	88%	82%	89%
Private	12%	18%	11%

Source: DGPPP-SEP, 2003.

Despite improvements in education in Mexico over the last century, such as a rise in the adult literacy rate to over 90% and steady increases in enrollment in all levels of education (SEP, 1999), the system still faces challenges such as high rates of failure and drop-out. In the mid-1990s, only about 60% of the students who enrolled in primary school completed that level and only 88% of those continued on to lower secondary school (Gadel, 1997). As education reforms and new programs in rural and indigenous areas take further hold, the Mexican government hopes to continue to see improvements in meeting its goal for all citizens to have access to and to successfully complete basic education (US Department of Education, 2003) (Table 1).

Three organizations considered notable by the UNICEF Innocenti Research Centre (2007), set up during the nineteen nineties influenced the changes to early childhood program practice. One mechanism is the National Commission for Monitoring and Evaluating the National Program of Action to Benefit Children (the Commission). Set up in 1990 after Mexico signed the Convention on the Rights of the Child, the Commission is tasked with monitoring the country's commitment to the World Summit for Children. Led from the health sector, the Commission drew high-level membership from almost all key ministries in the government including bodies responsible for food, water and security. The Commission's biggest achievement was the development of a National Plan and State Plans for improving children's well-being. But, underscoring disadvantage of politically supported mechanisms, the Commission was dismantled with the change of govern-ment in Mexico in 2000, giving way to another presidential mechanism, the National Council for Children and Adolescents.

Another notable mechanism is the Informal Working Group to Define Indicators of Well-Being for Children under Six Years of Age, which was set up on the advice of the international development agencies operating in the country. The members, drawn from the education, health and family development sectors, were low-ranking officials. Although the success of this mechanism remains to be proven, it shows that focusing on specific tasks is workable in an informal mechanism. And the third notable and successful mechanism is the National Coordination and Technical Committee of the Program Opportunities in Mexico. Located within the Secretary of Social Development, the Committee was set up in 1997 to coordinate different sectors and deliver an integrated social assistance program, concerned with education, social assistance and health and nutrition, to extremely poor families. Its membership is composed of representatives of the social, education, health and treasury ministries. Having jointly set the rules of operation and approved initiatives, the Committee helped deliver the multi-sectored program successfully to the target populations.

ISSUES, CONTROVERSIES, PROBLEMS AND POSSIBLE SOLUTIONS

A recent study by Mexico's National Institute for Educational Evaluation (INEE) reveals that the number of private preschools in Mexico jumped

116% from 2000 to 2005, while the number of private elementary schools increased 15% during the same time period. Conversely, the number of public primary schools (and teaching staff) decreased nationwide by 2% from 2000 to 2005, according to the INEE (2007). In some regions, closures of public preschools and reductions in their teaching staff were even more dramatic. In Guanajuato state, for instance, the number of public preschools and teachers that served indigenous communities dropped 67% and 44%, respectively, from 2000-2005. However, overall student enrollment in Guanajuato's indigenous preschools increased by 1% during the five-year period examined. This trend is attributed to the inclusion of English and technology in private school curriculum (Felix, 2007). This may influence the enrollment and goals of the reform for public schools of Mexico.

Illiteracy among the population from 15 to 19 years of age is less than 2.9%, and the average schooling for the group from 20 to 29 is ninth grade, which is equal to finishing secondary (junior high). More than 92% of children between 6 and 14 attended school, and 9 out of every 10 teenagers in our country have completed primary school by the age of 15. These figures reflect the expansion of the coverage of educational services and the improvement of the terminal efficiency rates. The SEN has had to face great challenges. It is necessary to point out, first of all, the population growth, from 13.6 million people in 1900 to nearly 100 million in the year 2000. At the beginning of the 20th century, Mexico was a country where three-quarters of the population inhabited small towns and settlements, far from the urban centers. It is estimated that in 1921, the year in which the Department of Public Education was founded, illiteracy affected nearly 70% of the country's adult population, and the lack of teachers and schools made access to education very limited, for which reason the average schooling was one year (SEP, 2001a). In 1930, the educational system attended to 1.4 million students and 20 years later the

registration had increased to more than twice as many. By the second half of the 20th century, the population had quadrupled and the great expansion and diversification of educational services began. Owing in great measure to the dynamics of population growth, the SEN had concentrated on extending the coverage. Now, having overcome such basic problems as providing widespread access to primary education and reducing illiteracy, the SEN faces, among other challenges, a more complex one that consists in making it possible for all children and teenagers to study basic education and to successfully finish this fundamental part of their studies (SEP, 2001c).

Other major challenges for the level of the basic education will be to attend to the demand of the age group from 3 to 5, resulting from the implementation of the obligatory nature of preschool education, and to train the number of teachers that are required by the increase in demand, as well as to strengthen secondary education, because it constitutes a necessary step for people to enter upper intermediate and higher levels of education. At the moment, the greatest integration question pending in Mexico is the merging of Early Education for 0-3-year-olds with Preschool Education for 4-6year-olds. The development of an integrated curriculum could be a milestone achievement that would eventually provide a firm pedagogical framework with which different sectors could work harmoniously, without necessarily the help of a coordination mechanism. The state is developing a comprehensive curriculum for children 0-6 years old.

CURRENT REFORM EFFORTS

In recognition of the value of providing early learning opportunities, many nations have expanded early childhood care and education in recent years. Mexico is a unique case in which expansion of early childhood care and education has occurred in the past 5 years, as have initiatives to improve quality and revise the national curriculum for preschoolers. The preschool expansion included a mandate for all parents in Mexico to send their preschool-aged children (3, 4 and 5 years old) to preschool, with target dates of 2004, 2005 and 2008 for 100% coverage of 5-year-olds, 4-year-olds and 3-year-olds, respectively. The quality improvement initiative was part of a larger program providing supplemental funds to select preschools and schools in Mexican public education system. Finally, the curricular reform instituted a new preschool curriculum to be implemented nationwide for all programs across the 3- to 5-year-old age range.

CHANGES IN EDUCATIONAL POLICY

Social Commitment to Quality in Education

The Social Commitment to Quality in Education is an agreement made in 2002 among representatives of different sectors, educational institutions, and society. Its nature lies in creating a consensus and agreement regarding the measures that are intended to improve the quality of education, which will allow these sectors to monitor them and check they are carried out. The importance of this initiative is the joining of different sectors in a tacit recognition of their responsibility in achieving educational quality.

The priorities of the Social Commitment, for whose implementation different commissions have been formed, are the following: the shared responsibility of the sectors, the importance of social participation, the application of contents and focuses constantly being revised, and the conviction that the school is and should be the nucleus of the educational project, which in turn will be in keeping with the needs of the context. Another of its priorities is to consider the school the place where strategies are generated for the teaching-learning process and the constant updating of teachers.

National Institute for the Evaluation of Education (INEE)

The National Institute for the Evaluation of Education (INEE) was created in 2002 by the SEP as a means to weigh the results of the National Educational System with rigorous and reliable mechanisms, disseminate them, and use them in improving the quality of teaching and learning. To achieve this, the INEE works with three types of indicators: the quality of the national educational system and of the state subsystems, learning tests, and the evaluation of schools. It is the responsibility of the SEP to issue guidelines for the evaluations, as well as to assess the results of the Educational System. It is the responsibility of the INEE to make precise diagnoses of the educational situation that would make it possible to establish viable goals and design appropriate strategies for improvement, to create and operate a system of indicators for evaluating the processes related to learning and the teaching function, to promote the culture of evaluation and disseminate its results, to develop training measures, to carry out and encourage educational research, as well as to coordinate international projects in which Mexico would participate and represent it before international organisms.

During the first year of operation of the INEE, the following results stand out:

- Analysis of the results of the national progress tests in reading and mathematics (called National Standards) applied by the SEP at the end of the 2002-2003 school year.
- Analysis of the test results of the Latin American Laboratory of Evaluation of the Quality of Education of 1997.
- Two studies on the tests of the TIMSS (Trends International Mathematics and Science Study) applied in Mexico in 1995 and 2000.
- Different analyses of the results of the application of reading and mathematics tests

in 1998 and 2002.

As for the PISA tests (Program for International Student Assessment) of the Organization for Economic Co-operation and Development (OECD), the INEE will make a thorough analysis during 2004. The results expressed yearly in the first report of the INEE on the evaluation of the SEN with respect to basic education may be consulted through the following website: http://capacitacion.ilce.edu.mx/inee/estadisticas.htm

COMPENSATORY PROGRAMS

The National Educational System faces many challenges through the different levels of attention and coverage of teaching services, as well as compensatory and welfare-type programs. Since 1992 national programs have been developed that are aimed at counteracting the lack of equity in the population groups with greater educational backwardness. Some examples of these programs are:

- **Program to Combat Backwardness in Initial and Basic Education**. The purposes of these programs are to reduce the dropout rate, increase attendance, and improve progress at school. To this end measures are being taken to improve the conditions of teachers and schools in initial and basic education by means of didactic resources, training of teachers and administrators, recognition of teaching performance, support for school supervision, infrastructure and equipment, participation of parents in supporting the school administration and institutional strengthening. In the 2002-2003 school year, the program benefited 4.5 million students by providing packages of school supplies; 40,000 schools and over 122,000 teachers were given consultancy;

more than 13,000 teachers benefited from the incentive for teaching performance; economic support was given to parent associations in 12,000 kindergartens and 47,000 primary schools; the infrastructure was strengthened through the construction of classrooms; and 500,000 parents were trained to order to improve the initial education of their children in the form of home study. (del Refugio Guevera, M. & Gonzalez, L.E. 2004).

- **Community Education**. Through this program, services in preschool and primary education are offered to children of small mestizo and indigenous rural towns, with populations ranging from less than 100 up to some 500 inhabitants. In 2002-2003, around 128,000 students were provided with community preschool services, and over 141,000 students with community primary education.

- **National Program for the Development of Indigenous Peoples**. Through this model, services in bilingual pre-school and primary education were offered for children who speak an indigenous language. During the 2002-2003 school year, nearly 1,150,000 students were attended to. Text books were printed in 55 variants of 33 indigenous languages.

- **Opportunities Human Development Program**. By assigning scholarships, this program supports school access and regular attendance for students under 18 years of age who study from the third grade of primary education to the final grade of senior high school. It also provides school supplies to scholarship holders who are studying in primary grades. In 2002-2003 nearly 4 million students in primary and secondary schools were benefited. This program constitutes one of the Federal Government's most important initiatives in supporting the inclusion, continuance, and progress in school of children and teenagers in conditions of extreme poverty.

- **National Program to Strengthen Special Education and Educational Inclusion**. The objective of the National Program to Strengthen Special Education and Educational Inclusion is to guarantee an educational attention of quality for children and teenagers with special educational needs, giving priority to those who have some disability. These students are integrated into the basic educational establishments - kindergarten, primary and secondary schools -applying specific methods, techniques and materials. During the 2002-2003 school year, more than 420,000 students were attended to with this program. Since 1993's education law – the integration of children with special needs has been mandated. But a national program and monitoring system was not instituted until 2001. Integration is the aim of the program.

- **Schools of Quality Program**. The aim of this program is to enhance the capacity of school organization by incorporating into basic education schools a model of self-management based on eight basic principles: freedom in decision-making, shared leadership, team work, flexible teaching practices depending on the diversity of the students, participative planning, and evaluation for continuing improvement, responsible social participation, and accountability(http://www.escuelasdecalidad.net/).

The Programa de Escuelas de Calidad (PEC) is a quality improvement initiative directed toward public schools providing educación básica, focusing on school management. The voluntary PEC program aims to increase school autonomy and performance by encouraging collaborative work among parents, teachers and school authorities, by improving planning and pedagogical processes and by providing modest resources. To qualify for the program, schools must carry out a diagnostic evaluation and present a School Strategic Transformation Plan. Funds for the program are provided by the Mexican government, the World Bank and other sources (World Bank 2005). Grants are provided for up to 5 years to each qualifying school, subject to annual review. Federal funding is expected to be matched by states, in a 3 (federal) to 1 (state) ratio.

The PEC program has, as one central goal, increasing parent and community involvement in school management. It seeks to do this principally by including parents in decision-making and monitoring; for example, parents are expected to engage actively in the planning of quality improvement, and to verify purchases and contracts made to the participating school. In addition, the program mandates evaluation, both at the school level (ongoing monitoring of the School Strategic Transformation Plan) and nationally, through evaluations that incorporate student assessments and a national information system. Thus, although the program increases school-level autonomy, it also includes an accountability and evaluation component that requires reporting on whether goals set in planning exercises were met and, at primary and secondary levels (not preschools) includes student-level assessments of educational progress.

The PEC program was first extended on a large scale to preschools in the 2003-2004 school year, after it had become established in the two prior years in primary and secondary schools. In the 2004-2005 year, there were a total of 4,096 PEC preschools. This represents about 5 per cent of the total set of preschools in Mexico. The vast majority of PEC preschools are of the general type, with about 10 per cent of the indigenous type. Note that the PEC program does not extend coverage; rather, the program focuses on improving quality in existing preschools.

CURRICULUM CHANGES

In primary education, there is a core curriculum. However, the implementation of the curriculum may vary across the country, as the government has tried to tailor the core curriculum to address the ethnic and cultural diversity of students and the special needs of Mexico's indigenous population and students living in remote areas (Husén and Postlethwaite, 1994). The school calendar is 200 days in length and daily class time is between four and four and a half hours (SEP, 1999). Within primary education, there are seven subjects that form the core curriculum: Spanish, mathematics, history, geography, civic education, health, and environmental education. Approximately 45% of class time is devoted to Spanish in the first two grades. In grades three to six, about 30% of class time is in this subject (SEP, 1999). Textbooks are prepared by the central government and distributed free of charge to all primary education students. In 1993, SEP undertook to revise all primary education textbooks in order to bring them abreast of new curricula, a process that was to be completed in 1999. SEP prepares the free textbooks, and other educational resources, in both Spanish and native languages. In fact, in 1998, over 1 million textbooks were distributed in 33 native languages and 52 dialects (SEP, 1999).

Now that new mandates encompass the early years of education is anticipated that these programs will follow a similar pattern of development as the primary grades. The next section discusses the proposed and new expectations for preschool. We have added our ideas about how technology should be included in these changes.

PEDAGOGICAL PRINCIPLES OF MEXICAN REFORM IN PRESCHOOL EDUCATION

The following three groups of pedagogical principles guide the curriculum reform in early childhood education. Specifically, they provide a common framework to guide teacher practice.

These principles help teachers identify the conditions under which practice is effective. It is important to emphasize the centrality of reflective practice to this reform effect – it guides not only the development of activities, but also the way in which a teacher individualizes instruction to meet the needs of children (UNICEF 2007).

Pedagogical Principle I

The first set of principles concern children's development and learning processes. There are four assumptions:

- Children will arrive at primary school with knowledge base and the capacity to develop further knowledge
- The primary role of the teacher is to promote and sustain children's motivation to learn'
- Children learn through peer interaction
- Play promotes development and learning

This social connection is said to manifest effectively because young children respond to each other using: symbols; naïve language and nonverbal communication; practice self-narrating; and thinking in metaphors. Peer groups support the power of negotiation that is not accessible in families or classrooms because of the authoritarian nature of the hierarchical system. It was Maria Montessori who said: "Our schools show that children of the same age and different ages influence one another (Montessori, 1967, p. 226). Denham et al. (2003) and Dunn, Cutting, & Demetriou (2000) have researched preschool children's social competence in relationship to cognitive development; both studies indicate that environmental influences resulting from peer interactions advance social competence and cognitive development. In addition, they conclude that peer influences are particularly vulnerable to affect and dispositional traits in preschool children. Freeman & Somerindyke (2001) studied peer interactions of preschool children during a computer exercise using a Vygotskian constructivist framework. They concluded that the computer center could effectively encourage supportive scaffolding interactions among children as they work side-by-side to achieve the goals. This implies that computers support social and peer interaction in preschool classrooms.

Pedagogical Principle II

The second group of principles concerns diversity and equity. There are three assumptions:

- School should offer opportunities regardless of cultural background
- All teachers, schools and parents should work to promote the inclusion of children with disabilities
- Schools should be regarded as a place for socialization and learning and therefore must promote equity across gender and race

This principle is vital to the acceptance of the global environment. The large percentage of diverse populations in Mexico demands understanding and education for all children. The inclusion concept is similar to programs implemented in Texas and some parts of the United States. In chapter 6 of this book you will find many ways that technology can be used to insure special needs students have the opportunity to participate in educational environments. Cultural expectations of gender roles are evident in science and technology professions. If we are to overcome these stereotypes we must work intentionally to insure equity of technology learning and use.

Pedagogical Principle III

The third group of principles concerns school as an intervention. There are three assumptions:

- The school and classroom climate should promote children's trust and the ability to learn
- Individualized instruction is critical for schooling to have positive results
- Collaboration between teachers and family members promotes children's development

Parts of this principle make Mexico a unique reform effort as it addresses the ideas of trust and belief systems. Bandura (1988; 1986, 1987); Schunk (1995); Parajes & Miller, (1995) and more recently Tschannen-Moran and Woolfolk Hoy (2003) strongly support the influence of self-efficacy or one's belief in their ability to perform a task successfully as an influencing variable in education. The next chapter gives more information about this thinking. Other new research on children's epistemological beliefs could be another factor in early childhood development. Chapter 10 discusses the new research about epistemology.

School as an intervention to all aspects of the child's learning is an important idea. Mexico supports the support of the affection dimensions to learning which would include trust relationships among peers, caregivers and teachers. This supports the work of Bakhtin's (1895-1975) Public Square approach to interaction. This guides educators to think of the interplays of time and space that influences the socio-cultural-economic-political and demographic implications of the contexts in which our schools operate. Technology would clearly support individualized instruction in the preschool classrooms as new and better software is developed to address learning needs. Family collaboration is developing as another technology based educational tool. Chapter 8 discusses ways

Table 2. Child competencies from the curricular reform (UNICEF, 2007)

Formative Fields	Aspects in which they are organized
Social and personal development Language and communication Mathematical Thinking Exploration and knowledge of the world Art expression and appreciation Physical development and health	Personal identity and autonomy. Interpersonal relationships. Oral language. Written language. Number. Form, space, and media. The natural world. Culture and social life. Musical expression and appreciation. Corporal expression and dance appreciation. Plastic expression and appreciation. Dramatic expression and theatrical appreciation. Coordination, strength, and equilibrium. Health promotion.

technology can involve families through on-line communication.

The Mexican preschool curriculum is most similar to the High/Scope curriculum in the U.S., though it takes a broader approach in some developmental domains and clearly emphasizes some similar competencies as other well known learning approaches such as experiential learning.

By emphasizing children's competencies, this reform not only recognizes that children come to school with a range of skills and experiences, but it also places the child at the center of the learning process. In doing so, educators are required to develop tools and strategies to promote development across domains and experiences. However, these competencies will be realized only when educators have a clear understanding of the program, when comprehensive work occurs in the classroom setting, and when educators critically analyze and share their experiences in the classroom with their colleagues. The early childhood reform has an open character, meaning that teachers are able to adapt the content and methodologies they use to respond to the needs of the particular populations they serve. It is worth noting that in contrast to other early childhood programs like Reggio Emilia (Cadwell, 2003), the theory underlying the national curriculum reform in Mexico is focused on the classroom

and center. Specifically, the reform efforts in Mexico tend to take a more setting level-approach to children's learning as opposed to the broader approach involving numerous stakeholders (e.g., children, teachers, parents and the public) taken by Reggio Emilia.

The reformed Mexican curriculum is based on a detailed set of child competencies, rather than a set of predetermined activities, and therefore has a child-centered character. There are six domains of competencies, with many component behaviors that illustrate that domain. The curricula and pedagogical guidelines are meant to emphasize the child's holistic development (Table 2).

The "Programa de Educacion Preescolar 2004" does not include direct mandates for the introduction of educational technology; this however takes place at different levels in individual schools. The teacher plays a critically important role in determining how to best meet the individual needs of students. In contrast to the prior curriculum, the current one has an open character, in which teachers adapt the content and methods they use to respond to the needs of the particular populations of families they serve. It is also more explicitly responsive to cultural diversity and the needs of local communities, in emphasizing teachers' involvement with their communities. During the Fox administration technology was introduced to the latter years of elementary school and the middle school, but not to pre-K. As Mexico continues to reform policies and standards for pre-K education it is expected that technology will be included.

PRESCHOOLS IN MEXICO

Traditional preschool caters to children between the ages of three and five and is generally provided in three grades. Preschool is provided free and it has been mandated that all children ages 3-5 attend. New mandates have added the 0-3 age range to public preschool. In general, preschools operate along age cohort lines, and open for 3 or 4 hours daily, five days a week. Some preschools offer a morning and an afternoon session. A special subset of preschools are labeled "mixed pre-schools" (jardínes mixtos) because they combine a regular preschool session with care during a day-long program. Obligatory "basic education" in Mexico includes preschool, primary school and lower secondary school, covering the period from age 3 to age 15. The Law of Obligatory Pre-schooling, November, 2002, backed strongly by the National Teacher's Union (SNTE), not only makes it obligatory for the State to provide pre-school education services for children 3 to 6 years of age when that is demanded, but also makes it obligatory for parents to see that their children attend a public or private pre-school (OCED, 2006).

Children from 0-3 years

Educación inicial, or child care with an educational purpose, caters for about 3% of children 0-3 years, mostly in the Federal District and other large administrative centres. Programs are generally divided into programs of direct (centre-based services for young children) or indirect attention (targeted at parents and families). Programs of direct attention reach the fewest children (about 30% of the total), and then, in majority, the children of women holding a recognized job, often within

the state sector. Small programs organized by DIF and SEDESOL attempt to address the needs of children of working women without social security. Public preschool includes several systems. These types of preschool are administered directly by the Secretaria de Educación Pública (SEP):

- general (general), CENDI, or Centros de Desarrollo Infantil: In CENDIs, care is provided for children from 45 days up to 4 years of age. CENDIs are generally well regulated, with good resources and favorable child-staff ratios. In general, they use a curriculum elaborated by SEP, but as they are located predominantly within and staffed from the health and social security sectors, they tend to pursue a health/protective approach, although today with a growing emphasis on child development.
- indigenous (indigena): About 8% of the population (8 381 752 people) is classified as "indigenous", distributed among 64 ethnic groups. Of these, 1 233 455 are children under 5 who live in families where an indigenous language is spoken. Enrolment rates for indigenous groups are considerably lower than for urban middle-class or non-indigenous groups (OECD 2003). The economic and educational circumstances in these families are much poorer than the national average. The indigenous pre-school program is administered by a special division within the SEP, and a new program of inter-cultural education is also exploring ways to attend better to these groups. A variety of other programs also exist for particular populations including indigenous children, those in small rural communities, children of migrant workers, children of women working in the informal sector, mothers in prisons, etc., but outreach is small compared to the number of children and families concerned.

Table 3. 2003 Pre-school education

Pre-school education	Children	Teachers	Schools
	3,635, 903	163, 282	74, 758

Source: DGPPP-SEP, 2003.

- community preschools operated by CONAFE (Consejo Nacional de Fomento Educativo). The CONAFE system of education aims to reduce educational inequities in Mexico by providing support to the most disadvantaged schools and populations (Garza, 2005). Its aim is therefore explicitly compensatory, when compared to the general preschool system. Multiple indicators of poverty are used to select schools for CONAFE support. The program provides professional development of teachers, audiovisual technology, curricular materials, and improvements to school infrastructure. Local preschools are run by parents and community leaders. Teachers are mostly without prior formal experience in teaching, and are provided scholarships for their tuition in schools of education. In return, they live in the communities of CONAFE preschools, teaching as well as providing social services and educational assistance directly to parents in homes. CONAFE was in fact using a competencia-based system of curriculum before the curricular reform of 2003-2004. It is worth noting that socioeconomic disadvantages that accumulate over the first five years of life significantly diminish access to ECCE program for many nations' most vulnerable children (UNESCO 2006).

Among these types the general or CENDI type of preschool serves the largest number of preschool-aged children in Mexico. General preschools may be located in urban or rural areas. The CENDIs, which are almost exclusively urban, provide services mainly for children ages zero to 48 months, with some centers adding care and education for older children. The IMSS, or Mexican Institute for Social Security, administers several types of ECCE, including some of the CENDIs, child care and preschool for children of IMSS employees and child care preschool for children of working mothers in the formal sector (eligible for social security).

Pre-K Education in Mexico and Ciudad Juárez (María Eugenia López, 2009)

The nature of the reform places responsibility on teachers to find ways to support the new curriculum. This results in a wide variance among programs. This section describes the program environments and the efforts of teachers in Juarez to meet the new reform requirements. Juarez in on the border of the United States and with El Paso is the largest metro-plex on the border. Like many of the border cities Juarez has a high illiteracy and dropout rate.

As a teacher in Mexico, I am aware of the many changes in the country's economic development and the importance of technology in education. Our schools have gone from schools in poverty to schools preparing children for a digital future. It is very exciting to see my country grow in a competitive economic presence in the world. There is a large variation among schools across Mexico. I can only describe the efforts we are making in Juarez to insure our children are ready to move into the ever demanding need for technology . Following is some specific information about how our system is organized and where Juarez fits into our national preschool programs.

Early childhood education in Mexico is mostly federally supported. There are four main institutions in Juarez:

- Instituto Mexicano del Seguro Social (IMSS).
  - Maintains its own 1562 nurseries in Mexico attending 228,503 children between newborn and up to 4 years of age (see breakdown by States here: www.imss.gob.mx/prestaciones/guarderias/númeroguarderiasrm.htm)
  - Private nurseries adhered to IMSS' program. There are approximately 38 in Ciudad Juárez.
- Secretaria de Desarrollo Social (SEDESOL). Subcontracts individuals to set up nurseries as own businesses. http://www.sedesol.gob.mx/index/index.php?sec=802311
- Secretaria de Educación Pública (SEP).
  - Centro de Desarrollo Infantil (CENDI). Supported by the Secretary of Education, the CENDI program maintains and runs over 100 nurseries across Mexico, with 10 in the State of Chihuahua and 2 in Ciudad Juarez.
  - Private nurseries adhered to SEP's program
- Instituto de Seguridad y Servicios Sociales para los Trabajadores del estado (ISSSTE).
  - Maintains its own nurseries using SEP's "Programa de educación inicial"
  - Subcontracts private individuals to set up private nurseries under SEP's program

Additionally, in Ciudad Juárez there is one municipal nursery (Eva Sámano de Echeverría"), and about 50 private nurseries, which – in principle- must adhere to one of the official educational programs, but in reality, many do not.

One major change in our preschool programs in Mexico is a move from the division of social and educational programs. The pre-K programs are divided in two distinct categories in Juarez:

1. Programa de Educacion Inicial (SEP). Established in the late 1990s and under current renovation, it is applied with children between 0 and 3 years of age.
2. Programa de Educacion Preescolar 2004 (SEP). Based on research performed in Mexico and on theoretical fundamentals. Applicable for kids between ages of 3 and 6 years of age (in Mexico preK education in levels 2 and 3 -from 4 to 6 years of age- is now mandatory). Currently, assessment plans are being developed.

Information on the reform work in Juarez may be accessed on the following web sites:

- http://intrauia.iberopuebla.edu.mx/repository2/312/o1275/PROGRAMA%20DE%20EDUCACION%20PREESCOLAR%202004.pps
- http://www.escuelasenaccion.org/conocimiento/archivos/EDUCACION%20PREESCOLAR.%20CONTRUCCION%20COLECTIVA.ppt.

The following section includes information from the Centro de Desarrollo Infantil in Juarez. This section gives an overview of how technology is used in these programs.

In my program we have just installed new computer centers in our classrooms. This picture shows two of our children in front of our new computers. They are discussing two books and if these stories will be on the computer. This is very different from 10 years ago when there were no computers for children in the classroom. My children are very proud to have computers in their room and my parents want their children to learn about technology so they can become better educated. The reform in education is moving rapidly here. It is hard for our teachers to learn all they need to know about computers and plan for technology use. I do use different forms of technology in my programs.

At one of the Ciudad Juárez CENDIs, for instance, there are computers, projectors, TV sets, printers, copy machines, fax, internet and other devices which are used in the daily educational activities. This equipment was obtained through personal efforts of the educators and thanks to a donation from a private school. All schools do not have this equipment. In this center there was a high level of computer use at home so the parents wanted it to be used in the school. Our typical preschool class size is 40 and approximately 35 out of these children have a personal home computer.

At this point computers are primarily used for computer educational games with our children. Some of the topics mandated by curriculum reform here are available to support our new curriculum. One such site is "Pipo" (http://www.pipoclub.com/) which is for Pre-K Level 3 (5-and 6- year old children). It is used to implement some topics of the "Programa de Educacion Preescolar 2004" which includes geography, math, human body, animals, nature, etc. This site is primarily a skill development site. The children work on this program individually but with the number of children in our classes this means each child only gets two turns a week.

We also have a projector that children use with the computers. We sometimes assign homework that requires the children to work with their families to take pictures to support "didactic situations". One example was a project entitled, *How do we improve the neighborhood park?* The children took pictures with their parents of the park, came up with ideas for improvement, wrote down the ideas and submitted their photos on USB memory sticks or CDs. These pictures were then shown in class to complete the lesson. We also have the children make videos at home and at school and show them during class time to either sing along

with or have children tell their stories about activities. The use of these videos with children's songs is a favorite of the class.

We also use technology when we show movies, about once a month. Our centers do have internet access but the children's use is limited at this point. While we consider ourselves on the way to reforming technology use and education in our programs we also know that there are many others who do not have the equipment or training to implement these ideas. Some schools have no technology and other schools have more and better equipment. Technology use depends on the type of school and the teachers. Until the government mandates technology as part of the curriculum it will have little chance of infiltrating all of our schools. Funding is always a problem and as new technology is developed this access issue will become more evident.

ADDITIONAL ISSUES, CONTROVERSIES AND PROBLEMS

Gender Cultural Issues

Technological innovations have generally not been readily available to females in traditional societies especially when these innovations challenge or imply changes to long held customary designations of professions along gender lines(West, 2000). The Mexican culture still follows the traditional gender roles of the mother in the home and the father working to support the family. Until recently females were not encouraged to move into fields like science and technology. It is necessary to understand that social, cultural, economic, and political factors define how computers are perceived, utilized, and dispersed, and experienced in traditional societies. Since Mexico is a country of great diversity with large groups of indigenous populations this wide cultural variety impacts how technology is used. An understanding of computer technology and its socio-cultural, political, and economic consequences in developing nations may shed some light on impediments for females as they venture into this traditional, cultural, gender-biased world of technology. Since the economic spurt had been so dramatic in Mexico the gender roles are forced to change to accommodate growing educational demands. There are socio-cultural, political, and economic consequences with which these cultures need to grapple.

Introduction, exposure, and equal access to technology, precisely computers to young children in their early education will assist in diminishing gender preferences and bias toward professions defined along gender lines. Technology-driven curricula that affirm equal education and participation from the formative stages will effectively make computers routine in the lives of both males and females perceptions and attitudes would gradually change, allowing for gender equity in computers and computer technology (West, 2002). Realities of modern global interdependence in such areas as commerce and education, and a need for experts in technology may determine strategic directions for educational curricula in developing countries.

Access

As within the United States there is a large gap among socioeconomic classes which influences access to technology. The quality improvement initiative affected a relatively small number of preschools. In addition, the preschools that received quality improvement funds in the first 2 years of the program were relatively larger and had more resources to begin with than other preschools. The national curricular reform was created after a comprehensive process of obtaining input from teachers, directors and early education officials from across all the Mexican states. This process resulted in the implementation of an open curriculum based on comprehensive notions of the multiple domains of competencies in early childhood development. The curriculum requires high

levels of teacher initiative and reflective practice (Yoshikawa, McCartney, Myers, Bub, Ramos, & Knaul, 2007). Technology use is determined by individual schools and teachers. This increases the gap among programs. Disparities in resources for basic education are evident between urban and rural areas (US Department of Education, 2003). The nature of the new reform in all areas, including early childhood education, place the curricular responsibility on the teachers which intensifies the difference among programs. The implementation of the curriculum may vary across the country, as the government has tried to tailor the core curriculum to address the ethnic and cultural diversity of students and the special needs of Mexico's indigenous population and students living in remote areas (Husén and Postlethwaite, 1994). This respect for different cultural beliefs is admired but also causes some groups of people to remain in the traditional environment which often ignores technology. It would seem that the use of technology would hold the answer to educating the rural populations of Mexico but funding remains an issue for these areas. There are still some remote areas where there are no highways and the only way into a village is through the use of an all-terrain vehicle or walking. This increases the probability of limited access to technology.

The Teacher Training Gap between Education and Demands of the Growing Economy: Funding and Adequate Resources May be Lacking in Transition Countries

"The fact of the matter is that the neediest states, even when they act in good faith, lack adequate resources to ensure that institutions, services, facilities, and staff are available to children and families" (Ensalaco & Majka, 2005, p. 16). Governments often lack financial resources to support institutions that provide training for teachers. The quality of training can affect the quality of learning environments, teacher-child interactions, resources, and school readiness.

Primary school teachers are now required to have college degrees (Gadel, 1997). In upper secondary school, most teachers have a four-year degree. Educators in institutions of higher education also have a four-year degree, although some institutions require a master's degree, as well. Technology is included in teacher education but the growing demand for a techno-literate population is growing faster than the changes to teacher preparation. As Mexico continues to increase their technological resources the training of teachers must keep up in order to prepare citizens that are capable of succeeding in the new economic world. Early childhood has changed from a social services focus to an academic focus which demands technology integration and education. The pace of change in universities is painfully slow as all policies go through a long and tedious review system. If universities are to prepare teachers for the challenges of technology education then new approaches to teacher training are needed.

The standard for recruiting teachers varies among the states. Some states require a competitive examination before appointment, whereas other states base their decisions solely on candidates' qualifications and performance. In remote regions, teacher qualifications may be lower, and some practicing teachers may not have adequate pedagogical training. The requirements for indigenous education are culturally sensitive, partially because instruction and textbooks are in native languages and dialects. However, how these programs will address the changes in technology is not specified.

Border Issues

While the United States and Mexico are considered different countries they share a common 2,000-mile-long border area where the socio-economic dynamics of two interacting cultures have a strong influence on the educational resources for young children. The border regions are a mix of two cultures, many languages and many traditions and therefore have become almost a separate educational culture. Is it usually an easy task to separate national identities in countries that are geographically linked. This is not the case on the borderland between Mexico and the United States. There are more than 800,000 people crisscrossing this area legally every day, some walking, more driving, not to mention the 4,600 or so who jump the fence and get caught a few minutes or hours later. This unique environment brings concerns about the discrepancy between two countries standards and educational expectations. The Mexican population speaks predominantly Spanish in the border area so language compounds the educational issues.

There are 800,000 children living along the California-Mexico border alone. These "border kids" reflect the region's diversity and offer a glimpse into the state's dynamic cultural future. Half of all children living along the border are in an immigrant family—households with at least one parent born abroad. Of the border kids in immigrant families, 81% are U.S. citizens. Children in immigrant families often face similar challenges as those faced by low-income children, including below-average health outcomes and academic performance. Immigrant parents often have to deal with the added challenges of limited English proficiency and different cultural norms as they work to provide their children with the resources and opportunities they need to succeed.

New academic standards in the United States, which outline learning achievement expectations, are required in border as well as all other states. Significant variation in test score performance exists among ethnic groups, however, both along the border and statewide. Support educational programs such as pre-kindergarten and effective practices in K-12 to accelerate the time it takes for English Learners to master English and be redesignated as Fluent English Proficient. These issues along with limited access to technology are not addressed by either country.

The Secure Fence Act authorizes the construction of at least two layers of reinforced fencing in high-crossing and high-risk sections along the border. This includes around the border town of Tecate, Calif., and a huge expanse stretching from Calexico, Calif., to Douglas, Ariz., which is virtually the entire length of Arizona's border with Mexico. Another section would stretch over most of the southern border of New Mexico. An additional section will wind through Texas, from Del Rio to Eagle Pass, and from Laredo to Brownsville. The Department of Homeland Security were required to install an intricate network of surveillance cameras on the Arizona border on orbefore May 30, 2007. The barrier will leave around 1,300 miles of border uncovered. The entire fence was scheduled to be completed by the end of 2008.

As we begin the 21st century, one of the most prominent features of our time is globalization, which has led to a greater sense of interconnectedness than ever known before. While this has led to tremendous advances on many fronts, society continues to face great challenges with regard to poverty, human rights, education, health care, and violence across the globe (Lutterman-Aguilar, 2000). How this fence will impact the relations between Mexico and the United States is a question that effects all aspects of education and economy.

SUMMARY

Technology has forced a major change in the Mexican economy. This change, from a "developing country" into a techno-transformation country, has demanded educational reform in early childhood and across the continuum of education. The system of early education has many agencies and layers that address the different needs of the Mexican population. This is like other countries you have read about as technology has and is leading the educational reform in early childhood. Technol-

ogy standards are required in primary through secondary education and will soon follow in early childhood. Presently the implementation of technology varies according to the type of program and the teachers working in the programs. The rapid change has left early childhood behind in technology training for teachers and classroom equipment. Some teachers have taken the initiative to provide technology in their programs. As Mexico continues to climb the economic global ladder of competition it is expected that all programs will include technology use and training.

VISION

The last 9 years have indicated that Mexico is fast becoming a competitor in the global technology arena. The reform efforts support change in educational policy and practice. We think Mexico will surpass many of the other preschool educational systems in technology use once the issues of rural access are solved.

SOME QUESTIONS FOR REFLECTIVE PRACTITIONERS

1. Mexico has a diverse population that includes indigenous groups, many languages, and socio-economic status. In an attempt to meet the needs of all groups of people the Mexican government has implemented different forms of early childhood programs. How does this approach compare to your country? What are the similarities ?
2. The current reform places a lot of responsibility on the teachers to develop delivery approaches to early childhood programs. How does this compare to the program in which you are currently working?
3. The rapid demands of technology have demanded cultural and societal changes in Mexico. After reading this chapter what

would you describe as the major cultural values of Mexican early education?

4. How would you insure that all areas of Mexico receive equal technology access?

5. Compare you curriculum to the newly revised Mexican plans. What could you identify as common, global issues in early childhood curriculum?

6. The changes in educational policy to address the needs of the Mexican population provide an overview of the reform efforts. What policies does you country support for early childhood education?

7. What types of social programs do your schools provide for teachers and children of young children?

8. After reading what María Eugenia López describes as her program use of technology compare and contrast your use of technology in your program with hers.

9. Do you believe there are gender issues in your country concerning technology? Describe some of your experiences to support your answer.

10. The border issues have been controversial across both countries. How would you approach these issues in your classroom? When a child from Mexico enrolls in your program what will you do to insure objective interactions?

REFERENCES

ANUIES. (2001). Anuario Estadístico 2000. Población escolar de posgrado, México.

ANUIES. (2003). *Mercado laboral de profesionistas en México. Diagnóstico* (1990-2000), México, ANUIES(Biblioteca de la educación superior. Serie Investigaciones. Arnaut, A. (1998). Historia de una profesión. *Los maestros de educación primaria en México*, 1887-1994, México, SEP (Biblioteca del normalista).

Arnaut, A. (2003). Sistema de Formación de Maestros en México. Continuidad, reforma y cambio en educación 2001. Revista mexicana de educación, año IX, núm. 102, nueva época, noviembre, México.

Bandura, A. (1986). *Social foundations of thought and action: A social cognitive theory.* Upper Saddle River, New Jersey: Prentice-Hall.

Bandura, A. (1988). Perceived self-efficacy: Exercise of control through self-belief. In J. P. Dauwalder, M. Perrez, & V. Hobi (Eds.), *Annual series of Euporean research in behavior therapy, 2*, 27-59. Lisse, The Netherlands: Swets & Zeitlander.

Bandura, A. (1993). Perceived self-efficacy in cognitive development and functioning. *Educational Psychologist, 28*(2), 117–148. doi:10.1207/s15326985ep2802_3

Bandura, A. (1997). *Self-efficacy: The exercise of control.* New York: Freeman.

Bayardo-Moreno, M. G. (2003). *El posgrado para profesores de educación básica*, México, SEP(Cuadernos de discusión, 5).

Calderoni, J. (June 1998). Telesecundaria: Using TV to Bring Education to Rural Mexico. *World Bank Human Development Network: Education Group-Education and Technology Team.*

Calvo-Pontón, B., et al. (2002), Tendencias en supervisión escolar. *La supervisión escolar de la educación primaria en México: prácticas, desafíos y reformas*, México, UNESCO/Instituto Internacional de Planeamiento de la Educación.

Castañeda-Salgado, A., et al. (2003). *La UPN y la formación de maestros de educación básica*, México, SEP (Cuadernos de discusión, 15).

Cervantes-Galván, E. (2003). *Los desafíos de la educación en México. ¿Calidad en la escuela*, México, FUNDAP.

Conapo (2002). *Proyecciones de la población de México 2000-2050*, México, Conapo (Prospectiva demográfica).

Conapo (2003). *Informe de Ejecución del Programa de Acción de la Conferencia Internacional sobre la Población y el Desarrollo 1994-2003*. México, México.

Congreso de la Unión. (2002). *Título Sexto del trabajo y de la Previsión Social*, Artículo 123, Fracción XX", en Constitución Política de los Estados Unidos Mexicanos, México, Porrúa.

Coordinación General de Actualización y Capacitación para Maestros en Servicio. (2003), Centros de Maestros. Un acercamiento a su situación actual, México, SEP (Cuadernos de discusión, 14). DGI-SEP (s/f), Direcciones generales de la SEP. Dirección General de Educación Indígena. *Información básica*, México, en: http://sep.gob. mx/wb2/sep/sep_4413_informacion_basica_g.

del Refugio Guevera, M., & Gonzalez, L. E. (2004). Country background for Mexico. *Attracting, Developing and Retaining Effective Teachers*. Organization for Economic Cooperation and Development (OECD).

del Rufugo, M., & Gonzalez, L. E. (2004). *Country Background Report. Attracting, developing and retaining effective teacher*s. Franciso Deceano, National Coordinator. OECD.

Denham, S. A., Blair, K. A., DeMulder, E., Levitas, J., Sawyer, K., Auerbach-Major, S., & Queenan, P. (2003). Preschool emotional competence: Pathway to social competence. *Child Development*, *74*(1), 238–256. doi:10.1111/1467-8624.00533

DGPPP-SEP. (2003), Estadística Básica del Sistema Educativo Nacional. *Inicio de cursos 1970 a 2002*, México.

Dunn, J., Cutting, A. L., & Demetriou, H. (2000). Moral sensibility, understanding others, and children's friendship interactions in the preschool period. *The British Journal of Developmental Psychology*, *18*(2), 159–177. doi:10.1348/026151000165625

Educación Primaria, Plan 1997. (2002b). *Lineamientos Académicos para Organizar el Proceso de Titulación*. Licenciatura en Educación Secundaria, Plan 1999, México.

Educación Primaria, Plan 1997. (2002c). *Lineamientos para la Organización del Trabajo Académico durante Séptimo y Octavo Semestres*. Licenciatura en Educación Primaria, Plan 1997, México.

Educación Primaria, Plan 1997. (2002d). *Plan de Estudios 2002*. Licenciatura en Educación Física, México.

Educación Primaria, Plan 1997. (2002e). *Plan de Estudios 1997*. Licenciatura en Educación Primaria, México.

Educación Primaria, Plan 1997. (2002f). *Programa Nacional de Fortalecimiento de la Educación Especial y de la Integración Educativa*, México.

Educación Primaria, Plan 1997. (2003a). *Documento base, México, SEP* (Cuadernos de discusión, 1).

Educación Primaria, Plan 1997. (2003b). *Informe de Labores 2002-2003*, México.

Educación Primaria, Plan 1997. (2003c). *Lineamientos Académicos para Organizar el Proceso de Titulación*. Licenciatura en Educación Primaria, Plan 1997, México.

Educación Primaria, Plan 1997. (2003d). *Principales cifras y avances del sector educativo reportadas en el tercer informe de gobierno*, México.

Educación Primaria, Plan 1997. (2004a). *El seguimiento y la evaluación de las prácticas docentes: una estrategia para la reflexión y la mejora en las escuelas normales,* México, SEP (Serie Evaluación interna, 1).

Educación Primaria, Plan 1997. (2004b). *Documento Rector*, México, SEP (Política nacional para la formación y el desarrollo profesional de los maestros de educación básica) (en prensa). SG (1993), "Acuerdo Secretarial 179. Instructivo general para su aplicación", en *Diario Oficial de laFederación*.

Ensalaco, M., & Majka, L. C. (2000). Acuerdo Secretarial 252. In *Diario Oficial de la Federación*, México.

Ensalaco, M., & Majka, L. C. (2002a). Decreto por el que se adiciona el Artículo 3º, en su párrafo primero y el Artículo 31 de la Constitución Política de los Estado Unidos Mexicanos. In *Diario Oficial de la Federación*, México.

Ensalaco, M., & Majka, L. C. (2002b). Decreto por el que se reforma el artículo 25 de la Ley General de Educación. In *Diario Oficial de la Federación*, México.

Ensalaco, M., & Majka, L. C. (2005). *Children's Human Rights*. Lanham, Maryland: Rowman & Littlefield Publishers, Inc.

Felix, G. (2007, February 28). Mexican education. In *El Diario de Juarez*.

Freeman, N., & Somerindyke, J. (2001). *Social play at the computer: preschoolers scaffold and support peers computer competence Information Technology in Childhood Education Annual.* [Online]. Available USCA Library System Directory Discus. http://web3.infotrac.galegroup.com.

Furlan, A., et al. (2003). Investigaciones sobre disciplina e indisciplina. In J. M. Piña et al. (coords.), Acciones, actores y prácticas educativas. Libro 2, México, Grupo Ideograma (La investigación educativa en México 1992-2004).

Gadel, J. (1997). Education. Available at: http://www.tulane.edu/~rouxbee/children/mexico1.html (Reviewed 27 December 2008).

Husén, T., & Postlethwaite, N. (Eds.). (1994). *The International Encyclopedia of Education* (2nd ed.). Oxford: Pergamon Press.

INEE. (2004). *Informe Anual 2003*, México, en http://capacitacion.ilce.edu.mx/inee/estadisticas.htm. (Accessed November 2008).

Klien, A. (2000). *Culturally Consonant Education: An analysis of techniques that are academically empowering for children of immigrant and guest workers.* A paper presented at the International Congress on Challenges to Education. Mexico City - Aug. 30-Sept. 1, 2000.

Lutterman-Aguilar, A. (2000). *Challenges Faced by Academic Programs Abroad: Breaking Stereotypes & Promoting Intercultural Awareness.* A paper presented at the International Congress on Challenges to Education. Mexico City - Aug. 30-Sept. 1, 2000.

Merrill, T. L., & Miró, R. (Eds.). (June 1996). Mexico: a country study. In *Education: Section 7 of Chapter 2. Federal Research Division: Library of Congress*. Available at: http://lcweb2.loc.gov/frd/cs/cshome.html. (Reviewed 25 November 2008).

Montessori, M. (1967). *The absorbent mind.* NY: Dell.

Myers, R. Yoshikawa, H., McCartney, K., Bub, K.L., Lugo-Gil, J., Ramos, M., Knaul, F., & UNICEF Innocenti Research Centre (2007). *Early childhood education in Mexico: expansion, quality improvement, and curricular reform*, Innocenti Working Papers:inwopa07/40, UNICEF Innocenti Research Centre.

Ortiz Jiménez, M. (2003). *Carrera Magisterial. Un proyecto de desarrollo profesional*, México, SEP (Cuadernos de discusión, 12).

Pajares, F. (1996a). Self-efficacy beliefs and mathematical problem solving of gifted students. *Contemporary Educational Psychology, 21*(4), 325–344.doi:10.1006/ceps.1996.0025

Pajares, F. (1996b). Self-efficacy beliefs in achievement settings. *Review of Educational Research*, (66): 543–578.

Pajares, F., & Graham, L. (1999). Self-efficacy, motivation constructs, and mathematics performance of entering middle school students. *Contemporary Educational Psychology, 24*(2), 124–139.doi:10.1006/ceps.1998.0991

Salas Garza, E. (May 1998). *Mexico-Basic Education Development Project*. Washington, D.C.: The World Bank.

Sandoval Flores, E. (2002). *La trama de la escuela secundaria: institución, relaciones y saberes*, México, UPN.

Santibáñez, L. (2002). Están mal pagados los maestros en México? Estimado de los salaries relativos del magisterio. In *Revista Latino americana de Estudios Educativos, 33*(2), México, Centro de Estudios Educativos.

Savín Castro, M. A. (2003). *Escuelas normales: propuestas para la reforma integral*, México, SEP (Cuadernos de discusión, 13).

Schunk, D. H. (1995). Self-efficacy and education and instruction. In J.E. Maddux (Ed.), *Self-Efficacy, Adaptation, and Adjustment: Theory, Research, and Application* (pp.281-303). New York: Plenum Press.

Secretaría de Educación Pública (SEP) (1999). *Profile of Education in Mexico* (2nd ed). Mexico City: SEP.

Section for Early Childhood and Inclusive Education Division of Basic Education, Education Sector. (2003, December 19-21). *Early Childhood Care and Education in E-9 Countries: Status and Outlook*. A report for the Fifth E-9 Ministerial Meeting. Cairo: Egypt.

SEP (2004). Balance del proceso de la Reforma Integral de la Educación Secundaria.

SEP/Heurística Educativa. (2003). Evaluación cualitativa del Programa Escuelas de Calidad. *Reunión para el estudio del reporte descriptivo de la línea de base de la evaluación cualitativa del PEC*, México.

Socha, D. E. (1997). *Perspectives on the Mexican Education System: Prejudices, Problems, Possibilities*. Fulbright-Hays Summer Seminar Abroad.

Tschannen-Moran, M., & Woolfolk Hoy, A. (2003). *Teacher efficacy: Capturing an elusive construct*. Teaching and Teacher Education. http://www.unesco.org/

United Nations Educational, Scientific and Cultural Organization (UNESCO) (2006). *Address by Mr Koïchiro Matsuura, Director-General of UNESCO, on the theme of education, the university and cultural diversity Universidad Nacional Autónoma de México*.

US Department of Education. (2003). *Early Childhood Education in Developing Countries*. Education Around the World: Mexico. http://www.ed.gov/offices/OUS/PES/int_mexico.html

Zorrilla Fierro, M., & Lorenza Villa, L. (2003). *Políticas educativas. La investigación educative en México. 1992-2002*. Libro 8, México, Grupo Ideograma (La investigación educativa en México, 1992-2004).

Chapter 5
Technology and its Role in Teacher Education

Zelda McMurtry
Arkansas State University, USA

Candice Burkett
University of Memphis, USA

ABSTRACT

This chapter discusses technology and its role in teacher education. In order for technology to reach the early childhood classroom, it must first reach the classroom of the teacher education programs. The effect of self-efficacy on preschool teachers use and understanding of technology may influence their instructional applications. Early childhood faculty come from the same career pool as early childhood teachers and may share the same beliefs that practitioners have concerning technology. Teacher education programs have a responsibility to produce professionals who are literate in technology tools and applications.

INTRODUCTION

Technology, for this chapter will be defined as, "the application of tools and information to make products and solve problems" (Morrison, 2007, p. 371). The authors will discuss how technology is used as tools for teacher training and some of the expectations schools in the United States have for new teachers entering the career market. There are usually an assortment of technology tools found in an early childhood classroom, such as televisions, computers and digital cameras. As a teacher in an

DOI: 10.4018/978-1-60566-784-3.ch005

early childhood classroom, it is vital to take into account the great range of technology tools that could be essential to the development of young children today (Morrison, 2007). While some of these tools are used for direct instruction, there are also a variety of technology tools teachers need to perform their roles as classroom managers.

Educators who prepare teachers of young children must become techno proficient to help their students enter the new age of digital competency. Teachers must also be prepared to use technology in their classrooms as schools become computer competent. New expectations for skills that teachers need to perform their jobs are developing as more efficient methods of communication and management become available. Technology that was once considered to be "cutting edge" a few years ago is now found either to be commonplace or obsolete. Therefore, it is imperative that teacher education programs keep up with the high demands of the technological world. Gates (2007) states, "technology integration is much more than placing a computer into a classroom and giving the teacher some software to use. It is a systematic process that requires time and commitment from principals, teachers, students and parents" (p. 21). The Colleges of Education must take responsibility for teacher preparation in technology use if children are to be given the necessary tools to succeed in today's world. This chapter explores some ways that technology is being used in university teacher training programs and how university faculty are preparing teachers to move into jobs that demand technology.

This chapter has been a collaborative effort between a faculty member in a college of education and a student of education who is a research assistant in psychology. The faculty member learned to use technology after she had matured which is typical of many teachers in the United States. She models the use of technology in a Curriculum Development course she teaches at her university and describes how she prepares future teachers for their jobs. Like most students entering a university, the education student grew up in the digital world using computers and other technology since early childhood. She brings the thinking of psychology and education to this chapter. She has experienced technology in her educational experiences in schools in different states. They have had very different background experiences with technology in teaching and learning. Of particular interest is the thinking behind technology teaching from the personal experiences the university faculty member. Her writing gives insight into how teacher educators perceive what is important when teaching technology. She gives examples she uses in her courses and ideas she believes

are important to teacher training. This allows the reader to see how education faculty develop their thinking about teaching technology. To provide a broader view of technology the education student relates ideas she has seen in schools and other courses. Together they provide an overview of the how educators in the United States understand the role of technology in teacher training.

The first section of this chapter discusses background information regarding the general use of technology in teacher education. The focal point of this section is the need for teacher education programs to graduate teachers who are competent in technology. As the level of technology increases in the classroom, the level of technology must also increase in teacher education programs. The National Standards and expectations of the professional organizations for teacher training are included in this section. Colleges of Education have been challenged to prepare teachers to come to schools knowledgeable and competent about technology applications. This requires faculty to also become competent in technology use.

The next section of this chapter focuses on technological tools used in the classroom of today. This part is organized around four areas of technology applications that are related to professional responsibilities and includes specific tools. This section discusses tools for instructional presentation, assessment, accountability and communication that teachers are expected to use in their teaching jobs. These tools include specific applications like PowerPoint presentations, document cameras, digital cameras, SMART boards, spreadsheets, electronic portfolios, web pages and on-line communities. The discussions of each of the aforementioned technologies include a definition of each technology and relevant uses in the classroom.

The following section of this chapter explores some of the most common barriers to teacher technology use in the classroom. These barriers are relative to Colleges of Education and their courses for teacher training and teachers entering their professional careers. The use of technology connects all levels of teaching from pre-school to university classes when viewed as tools for teaching. We have also included possible solutions to overcome these barriers. If Colleges of Education are to prepare teachers to meet the technology standards as defined by professional organizations, university faculty must model applications as they teach.

The final section addresses the possible influence of self-efficacy on early childhood teachers and the use of technology. The association of technology to science, mathematics and engineering related fields may be a factor that influences early childhood teachers' instructional decisions. It is well documented that preschool teachers often select this area of teaching because of their lack of confidence in their abilities to teach science and mathematics. Faculty in early childhood education in Colleges of Education comes from the same educational group as practitioners. Consequently the acceptance of technology at the university level may share some of the same belief barriers as we see in schools.

BACKGROUND

NAEYC

While at one time the members of National Association for the Education of Young Children (NAEYC) were resistive to technology use in early childhood classrooms, they amended their position statement in 1996 to recognize and address the importance of technology. The revised official position statement of the National Association for the Education of Young Children regarding Technology and Young Children (ages 3-8) has seven main points. These points are as follows:

1.   The NAEYC believes that in any given situation, a professional judgment by the teacher is required to determine if a specific use of

technology is age appropriate, individually appropriate, and culturally appropriate.
2.   Used appropriately, technology can enhance children's cognitive and social abilities.
3.   Appropriate technology is integrated into the regular learning environment and used as one of many options to support children's learning.
4.   Early childhood educators should promote equitable access to technology for all children and their families. Children with special needs should have increased access when this is helpful.
5.   The power of technology to influence children's learning and development requires that attention be paid to eliminating stereotyping of any group and eliminating exposure to violence, especially as a problem-solving strategy.
6.   Teachers, in collaboration with parents, should advocate for more appropriate technology applications for all children.
7.   The appropriate use of technology has many implications for early childhood professional development (Adapted from NAEYC, 1996).

NAEYC is accepted as the leading professional organization for educators of young children in the United States. Their positions statements are the guiding standards for professionals in the field and establish the benchmarks for teacher training. When NAEYC included technology in its position statement, it changed the thinking about teacher preparation for early childhood programs. NAEYC's support for technology clearly indicates that the time had come for educators to rethink how they teach across all levels of education.

The National Council for Accreditation of Teacher Education (NCATE), in an effort to emphasize the need for teacher educators to address the importance of producing teacher education graduates who can effectively integrate technology into the classroom curricula, has developed technology standards. These standards state that a prospective teacher should be educated in "the use of computer and other technologies in instruction, assessment, and professional productivity" (NCATE, 2000). In collaboration with NCATE, the International Society for Technology and Education (ISTE) established guidelines for NCATE accreditation of educational computing and technological competencies for programs in teacher education (ISTE, 1992). These standards set new expectations for Colleges of Education and their use and teaching of technology.

The National Council for Accreditation of Teacher Education (NCATE, http://www.ncate.org/) is the official body for accrediting teacher preparation programs. The International Society for Technology in Education (ISTE) is the professional education organization responsible for recommending guidelines for accreditation to NCATE for programs in educational computing and technology teacher preparation.

TECHNOLOGY IN TEACHER EDUCATION

Teacher educators in teacher education institutions are finding themselves under pressure to provide pre-service teachers with courses where the use of technology is modeled on a consistent and usable basis. They are expected to incorporate technology into their courses and demonstrate how their students can use technology in early childhood classrooms (Epper & Bates, 2001). Educators are expected to teach with technology not about technology (Duhaney, 2001). This changing view of teacher educators has challenged Colleges of Education not only to train teachers to become techno proficient but their faculty must also use technology tools in an appropriate manner. Preparing pre-service teachers to be "technology-proficient teachers" is now a goal of many teacher education programs (Kariuki & Duran, 2004, p. 431). Most teacher education

programs require at least one educational computer skill course in their curricula. Traditionally, these courses are taught as "mini-workshops" with the students learning a particular software package and then being assigned to develop a product using a specified software. This approach was, at one time, considered sufficient for teacher training. As technology becomes more accepted in educational environments, the level of technology proficiency teachers are expected to acquire increases from single program use to multiple applications. Teacher educators working to meet NAEYC and NCATE standards must rethink how they use technology when preparing teachers.

When teacher educators analyze their own perspectives about technology in the classroom, they seem to fall into a predictable range of perceptions of appropriate use.

On one end of the continuum is the technophile, the teacher who has embraced technology to the fullest. On the other end of the continuum is the technophobe, the teacher who is convinced that technology is something to fear. Walker and White (2002) introduced the term "technorealism" to indicate a middle of the road philosophy regarding technology. Technorealism, as it falls in the middle, calls for technology to be recognized as a tool for learning. Bill Gates (2007) said, "Technology is just a tool. In terms of getting the kids working together and motivating them, the teacher is the most important." This implies the responsibility of teacher training programs is to prepare confident and competent teachers. Teachers cannot allow their personal opinions to guide their use of technology in classrooms. Fisher (2000) advocated that the creating of an appropriate learning setting is the responsibility of the teacher. The teacher must model the authentic application of the technology rather than focusing on the technology itself. While the most current technology will not replace a skilled, competent teacher educator, the new vision of competency includes use of technology. The technology skills of the faculty play a major role in how much pre-service teachers benefit from technology. The marriage of teachers and technology is still an evolving relationship.

Instructional Tools: Content Delivery

This section will discuss some uses of technology that teacher trainers model in their courses as presentation tools for teaching. It includes personal experiences from the university faculty's courses and the pre-service teacher's experiences in schools where technology was being used for instruction. These tools are presently used in teacher training and will more than likely be obsolete and replaced by better programs soon. The important part of this section is looking at the thinking about how trainers of teachers help their students prepare for accepting technology. This gives us insight into approaches to using and teaching about technology.

PowerPoint Presentations

PowerPoint presentations have become commonplace in teacher education classrooms. This tool has replaced the overhead projector as a visual aid for teaching. The software that comes with PowerPoint allows for addition of videos, art, and colorful templates which gives the teacher an opportunity to vary slide makeup. PowerPoint, like the overhead projector, will more than likely be replaced as new technologies evolve. The following is writing is from the personal experience of one faculty member as she developed her abilities to analyze content delivery using this tool. It is important to examine how faculty members develop their thinking about technology tools and their relation to content delivery. This process of discovering how to adapt tools to learning should provide insight into how they can adapt their teaching to use technology tools.

PowerPoint presentations when used to lecture can become boring if the teacher relies on the built-in templates for every presentation. Winn

(2003) wrote about this very concern. I felt like the proverbial light had come on after reading his article, *Avoiding Death by PowerPoint.* I used my Curriculum Development class as a testing ground. I typically used PowerPoint presentations developed by using the built-in template bullet-points. To test the effectiveness of Winn's premise, I designed a completely new presentation starting with a blank slide each time. I focused on a main point trying to be very concise with words. Then, I went online to search for clip art or photos to enhance the idea of each slide. At the conclusion of class, which had seemed to have far more discussion and interest from the students than usual, I explained what I was attempting to do. Several students commented that it had, indeed, made the class more interesting and easier for class discussion. I will extend this idea by requiring students to "build from scratch" assigned PowerPoint presentations not only for this class but for each of my classes in the future.

Winn recommends five rules for designing meaningful PowerPoint presentations. He advocated avoiding "the text based 'bullet' slides," design a slide with the goal of facilitating discussion, it is okay for slides to entertain, avoid using the same background, graphics, and text format on each slide, and take advantage of going online to find meaningful images to use" (2003, p.115). The goal of a PowerPoint presentation should be to make students think in an interesting, even entertaining, way. I tried to follow these ideas as I developed my presentations.

Faculty need to understand that tools like PowerPoint are not the big idea of using technology, but a way to deliver content. One idea here is how to engage students in conversation, not just how to make slides interesting. By varying the visual supports faculty can better stimulate conversation from students.

Document Cameras

Like all technology cameras have evolved into more user friendly tools for teaching. The following ideas are how the faculty explained the possible applications of a tool like this to her students. She was trying to help teachers start thinking about multiple applications of cameras in classrooms. These ideas were an attempt to stimulate teachers to explore possible applications of two types of cameras in their classrooms.

Document cameras are another way to present content in courses. Using and modeling the use of the document camera is a technology that is beneficial to both teacher education classes and to school classrooms. The document camera, also referred to as a visual presenter, is a small camera mounted on a stand which is connected to a projector, usually an LCD projector (Carmona, 1996). This tool projects materials on a screen and can be attached to equipment such as a computer or a television to show examples of visual aids. While the document camera can do the some of the things an overhead projector can, it is more than an overhead projector (Brooks-Young, 2007). The document camera can project 3-Dimensional objects, as small as a tack or as large as a book and maintains the dimensionality of the material. It can be used to project pictures, maps, and text while showing the original document in its real form. The entire class has a "front row seat" when objects, texts, or pictures are projected.

The document camera has numerous uses in the classroom. Teachers can show new material whether an object, a picture, or a text. It can provide a close-up look at small items such as a penny, a flower, leaves, an insect, or a small picture. There is no need to pass 3 dimensional objects around because all can see clearly at the same time when projected by the camera. However, when previously projected 3-D objects are passed around, students are better acquainted with the details to observe. The document camera can be used throughout the day. During a read aloud

session, the camera can project the book onto a wall turning it into a big book for all to see. It makes the pictures or illustrations come alive when projected. It can also turn one chapter book into a class set. When projected, all students can read it at the same time.

This technology is particularly beneficial for teaching math. Because the document camera provides an in-depth look from a distance, teachers can model math concepts step by step with manipulatives, or zoom in on very small units such as marks on rulers or thermometers, or demonstrate how to use a compass. During a study of money, coins can be projected. Details that are almost impossible to see with the naked eye are very visible when projected. When using pattern blocks, the blocks can be seen from all sides. Students, both pre-service students and children in classrooms, can use the document camera to display their work and explain their thought processes when working with math concepts and manipulatives.

The science class is also an opportunity for enhanced instruction using the document camera. There is no more having to gather around so all can try to see during a demonstration or experiment. Students can have a "close up" look from their seats during experiments. Communication with a large group is improved as all can see because the document camera allows close up, detailed observations by the entire class. A blank sheet of paper or a blank transparency can be placed on the working surface and then used as a writing surface with the results projected. This makes it useful when modeling, thinking aloud or writing. It can be used to project a blank piece of lined paper onto a white board to provide lines for the teacher or the students to use to keep their writing straight and neat. Students can use the document camera to display and explain their work or projects.

The document camera can be useful when giving instructions. Workbook pages or worksheets can be enlarged and projected to aid in explaining the directions. It can also be used effectively to explain directions for how to do assigned work, or for reading directions or teaching games. The document camera can serve as a countdown timer helping to keep students focused by placing a timer on the working surface. All children can see the remaining time as the timer "counts down" the time remaining.

Digital Cameras

This is the instructional information the education faculty provides her students concerning digital cameras. These are the issues she considers important for teachers to know about these tool and some suggestions for use in classrooms.

Another camera that is particularly useful for teacher educators to use and model is the digital camera. Using digital cameras can give students hands-on access to learning. A digital camera that uses a floppy disk adds the capability of each student photographer having a disk to store photos. This eliminates the need to download the photos onto a computer between users to keep work separate. If teachers make a dedicated effort to teach all students how to use the camera, having a disk for each student makes the hands-on experience more valuable for each student. During the teaching about how to use the digital camera, the teacher educator should inform the pre-service teachers who use the camera that it is not just about taking pictures but is about using the camera as a tool to help explore and understand other subjects. In using such tools, safety issues need to be addressed emphasizing the importance of always using the wrist strap or the neck strap to eliminate the danger of the camera being dropped. This is an area of concern for both adults and children. If the camera does not have a strap, one can be made from ribbon or decorative cord.

In addition to physically handling the camera safely, students need to be taught to use good manners when taking pictures. Reminders about how to respect others is important. After instructing and modeling how to use the camera, then give time to practice, first with close supervision and then on their own. Photo release requirements differ among schools. Each teacher/pre-service teacher is expected to know the guidelines for the school and to follow them explicitly.

The digital camera is useful in all grades. Teach every student in the class to use the digital camera. Using the digital camera gives students the opportunity to become more involved with a subject and to learn to observe carefully and purposefully. The students will decide what they will photograph. In the beginning, kindergartners may need help making decisions about the purpose or choice of what to photograph. Students learn to reason and plan what pictures to take and why those pictures are needed. They learn, with teacher guidance, to be selective in making choices. The digital camera is useful in teacher education classes as well as public school classrooms because the pictures are immediately available to print or to save for use in other projects such as PowerPoint presentations, web pages, electronic books, posters, signs, reports, banners, certificates, or to add to word-processed documents. Digital pictures can be used for any project in lieu of clip art making the final project more personal. Authentic uses in the classroom are limited only by imagination. Pictures of students can be used for seating charts, taking attendance, lunch count, star of the week, faces on special events characters, of each student using the digital camera, screensaver for computers in the room, to personalize awards, and photographs of class bulletin boards especially interactive bulletin boards.

The digital camera enables learning to be integrated across curricula. Take a virtual field trip before the actual field trip to be better prepared for the learning that will take place on the field trip. Take pictures during the field trip and then use both sets of pictures to re-enforce the learning that took place during the trip. Compiling a book of the event can be a class project. Scavenger hunts provide a hands-on opportunity for students to search for assigned items, take a picture to document it was found, and then compile a presentation to demonstrate the learning that took place. The presentation could be a poster, a book, a PowerPoint presentation or any medium of choice. All subject areas can be addressed using digital scavenger hunts.

The digital camera provides an authentic way to show natural processes such as, seeds sprouting, blossoms opening, food spoiling, shadows lengthening, or any "growing/growth" project. Students can be assigned to find pictures to illustrate things that are hot, or cold. They can take pictures of specific body parts such as arms, shoulders, legs and knees. They can be assigned to take pictures of eyes only, or hands only to be used to identify classmates. These series of pictures can be used in the types of final projects already discussed.

Students can look for geometric patterns both in nature and in man-made items. This type of search provides a valid focus on the continuing need to decide, select, compare, search, and even reevaluate decisions. Another useful assignment is to have students find real-life examples of symmetry. These and other photos could be developed into games using everyday math concepts. Digital scavenger hunts require students to search for objects, colors, or shapes meeting specific criteria. This information can be printed and bound into a booklet for future use in the classroom or used for a bulletin board. Take a picture of each student, or better yet, let the students take pictures of each other, print a copy of each picture then, when polling students to form data on a graph, each student places his picture in the proper spot on the graph. If pictures are laminated, they can be used over and over.

Literacy activities can take on new meaning when incorporating the digital camera. Illustrate the steps in a sequence of events or in projects using before and after pictures along with student drawings to compare what students actually observed and reproduced in their own drawings. The pictures can be printed on flash cards for sequencing enrichment. Alphabet books can be made by taking pictures of children holding the object or children forming letters with their bodies. Again, this is an assignment that student photographers can design, plan, implement, and complete. This idea can be extended by having students write an "all about me" book and find pictures to take to illustrate the book, or write a bio poem and illustrate with digital pictures. Students can be assigned to search for images to represent synonyms, antonyms, homonyms, homophones and other vocabulary such as emotions.

Classrooms with weekly job assignments can add photographer to the list. The photographer's job is to take a picture of at least one example of "learning in action" noticed during the week adding one or two sentences to describe the action in the photo. This could become a regular item in a weekly class newsletter to parents and family members.

A search on the Internet using any search engine will provide many, many more ideas for using digital cameras in the classroom. I have restricted the discussion to ideas I have used or fellow teachers, friends of mine, have used.

SMART Boards

The next sections address tools that the education student has used in her coursework and seen in schools for content presentation. The use of SMART boards in the classroom is becoming an increasingly popular instructional trend. The SMART board is an interactive whiteboard that has a touch-sensitive display that connects to a computer and a digital projector, projecting the image from the computer to the whiteboard. Computer applications can be controlled directly from the screen. In addition, we can use the SMART board to write and store notes using digital ink. This is particularly useful for lessons or topics that may span more than one day or week. Children can write or draw on the SMART board and project their drawings for sharing or discussion. Documents prepared on computers can be projected on a SMART board and the system allows for multiple windows of information to be opened at one time.

Perhaps the most interesting use of the SMART board is internet accessibility. We can interact with any website in the classroom through the SMART board. There are a number of interactive websites designed to enhance student learning that could prove valuable when brought into the classroom. It can also be beneficial to use the internet accessibility of the SMART board to conduct internet searches and display a variety of videos or other multi-media tools. This includes webcam accessibility which could be used for communication with other childhood programs and preview field trips.

The use of the SMART board in the classroom makes engaging a variety of learning styles easy. It is ideal for visual learners, who can see colorful and moveable images on the interactive display. Tactile learners also benefit from the use of the SMART board because they can interact directly with letters, numbers, words, and pictures by drawing or writing on screens. The SMART board is also beneficial to auditory learners because they can be immersed in multimedia experiences (SMART, 2008). University students retain their modalities of learning so applications of a SMART board in university classes would address adult learning in a similar manner.

Assessment Tools

Spreadsheets

Spreadsheet systems are an invaluable tool used in most school districts and early childhood programs. These systems are used often for the clerical functions in the school, such as class rosters, attendance, grading, and various forms of performance indicators such as test scores. Teachers can use the information stored in these systems as a tool to analyze teaching and student achievement as it relates to curriculum planning (Hammond, et al., 2005). Therefore, it is vital that

teacher education programs produce teachers who are not only fluent in the use of these spreadsheet systems, but also teachers who are fluent in how to apply the information stored in these systems. According to Hammond, et al. (2005), "Teachers must have knowledge of what changes they might make in how they organize and deliver instruction to strengthen student learning for individual students, groups of students who are underperforming, or the entire class or school" (p. 200). The proper information stored in the spreadsheet combined with the proper analysis of said information can lead to necessary change in curriculum and teaching methods. Chapter 6 has more detailed information about assessment systems for teachers of young children.

Electronic Portfolios

Preparing a portfolio in teacher education has been a prominent component of numerous programs. In today's technology driven environment, many universities are striving to find ways to assess student work in a way more consistent with the performance based focus resulting from the technology emphasis (NCATE, 2000). The advent of the electronic portfolio has provided a way to aid students in developing an understanding of their growth and learning with student selected artifacts accompanied by reflecting that leads to the rationale of the selected artifact (Barrett, 2000). An electronic portfolio, sometimes referred to as an efolio, eportfolio, digital portfolio, or web portfolio, is more than a digital scrapbook. It is a powerful tool that is used as a form of assessment (Bartlett, 2002). A significant part of the power is derived from its ability to demonstrate growth over time (Barrett, 2000).

The Education faculty shares her experiences with electronic portfolios. I am a teacher in a teacher education department of a state university that has adopted the use of a commercial program, LiveText©, for our students to use to prepare an electronic portfolio. LiveText© is marketed by

College LiveText edu solutions™ and provides a way for colleges and universities to develop, manage, and assess program and student achievements using an electronic portfolio system. Portfolios prepared using LiveText© are stored online thus providing easy access for students. Planning is an important aspect of developing an electronic portfolio. Our students can begin the planning early because LiveText© allows the teacher education department to set up specific objectives for the assignments included in the portfolio. Templates have been added to help students work with the portfolio program. Therefore, the students are able to develop lesson plans in LiveText© and add the additional items that they develop for the project. We feel our students benefit by the clearly set standards and expectations. Our department has also provided links to state frameworks to aid students in connecting frameworks to lesson plans and activities. Certainly, a benefit of an electronic portfolio is the convenience of having everything in one location rather than in boxes, binders, numerous computer sites, and portable storage devices.

Usually, when an individual designs an electronic portfolio, the first decision to make is what audience will be the target. For our students, this decision has been made for them. The primary audience is the course instructor. It becomes the student's job to collect artifacts and to reflect on his/her role in the portfolio. An artifact is defined as anything physical or tangible that demonstrates the student's efforts, progress, and achievements toward a course objective. The reflection usually starts as the student develops a rationale for the artifact selected. The rationale is expected to show the learning produced by the artifact. In teacher education, many times student artifacts consist of paper documents they have prepared, such as lesson plans; however, electronic portfolios provide an avenue for adding graphics, audio or video to the portfolio. My students strive to interject their personality into their work. The use of digital cameras and scanners has aided students in

creating meaningful portfolios. Using hyperlinks to link the viewer directly to another document or website has also added an opportunity for students to expand the depth of their portfolios.

Students in our program spend many weeks of the first semester of their senior year in elementary schools in field placements, and they spend the second semester in internship. These placements are used for students to complete assignments that are also required to be included in their electronic portfolios. The students develop and teach a three-day science investigation, write and teach a social studies unit and complete a reading case study on a child during their field placement. When working with a child during the completion of a reading case study, the audio portions of the child reading at the beginning of the study, during the study, and at the completion of the study can be linked to the electronic portfolio providing additional documentation of the progress the student made with the child. Videos of the child and the student working with literacy activities can be linked to the portfolio.

During internship, the students develop, write, and teach a three week integrated instruction plan, formerly referred to as a unit. They also prepare an action plan, and an advocacy project. With the electronic portfolio, my students are not restricted to paper documents and one-dimensional pictures. As they create lesson plans and activities with objectives tied to specific state frameworks that will engage their students in a variety of learning experiences, they can use hyperlinks to link those activities to their lesson plans. These activities may include the use of various web sites, videos, web based games, or additional student created documents. As my students plan and design these assignments, the convenience of being able to attach their work in a variety of ways allows the students to find creative ways to accomplish their assigned tasks. During their work with the children using the lessons and activities they have developed, the pre-service student can include the work of the children either by scanning in completed work or by videoing the children at work and linking the video to the portfolio.

My university also requires graduating seniors to create a "Learning to Teach, Teaching to Learn" portfolio. This portfolio is a composite of artifacts developed by the students during their enrollment in teacher education. The students select two artifacts that they feel demonstrate their achievements in each of the eight conceptual frameworks emphasized by the university during the teacher education program. The eight conceptual frameworks include communication skills, professionalism, curriculum, teaching models, classroom management, assessment, reflective teaching, and subject matter (Teacher intern handbook, 2006). This portfolio provides a showcase to display student growth over time in these important frameworks. The artifacts for this portfolio are taken from the portfolios created during their coursework. The students are again reflecting and developing the rationale for the selection of items to showcase their development in these areas.

Our teacher education department takes advantage of the capability of the LiveText© system to gather aggregated data for NCATE assessments. A variety of reports are available to the instructors and to the department. These reports reflect the results of data gleaned from the assessments of each section of the portfolios. The department developed the rubrics used to assess the assignments in the portfolio.

Web

One of the greatest benefits of technology in teacher education is the level of accessible accountability it provides. According to the No Child Left Behind Act (NCLB, 2001), schools are now required to post their ranking on standardized comparisons on the Internet so that everyone can access the information. It is mandatory that school districts have web pages that provide performance data available to the public. This provides a higher

level of accountability information than has been achieved prior to the use of this technology. Teachers are expected to collect data and either send to a central web master or post for public access. The information allows teacher to compare results from other states, cities, schools, and districts. This analysis helps teachers determine how their students are performing when compared to students from similar backgrounds and environments. This system helps teachers self-assess their teaching and document their work. Teacher education programs need to prepare teachers to use this information in a productive manner to inform their teaching.

Communication

Parent/Family Communication

Technology in the classroom has opened the door to parent-teacher communications. The Internet is one of the most valuable tools for keeping parents informed and involved with their child's education. Many parents and family members have access to e-mail, which offers a quick and convenient form of communication. E-mail also provides a great way to circulate regular classroom newsletters. In addition to class news, e-mail is an excellent way to update parents and family members on the progress and needs of individual students. However, it is important to remember that some parents will not have Internet access. It is vital to accommodate the needs of these parents and make the same information available to them in the most appropriate format.

Classroom web pages are a simple and advantageous way to keep parents and the community current on classroom activities and student progress (Morrison, 2006). A web page is a great place to list any on-going projects in the classroom, post photographs of classroom activities and list any homework that may be assigned. This can also be an ideal place to showcase both classroom and individual achievements, upload videos of student activity and provide links to websites that may be beneficial to student development. Most schools now have their web sites available for public access. As this communication aspect increases teachers prepare their individual class web sites and allow children to designate what information they want published.

Professional Communication

Though teachers spend their days surrounded by other people, teaching is often considered to be an isolated profession. Despite the efforts of many school districts, teachers remain largely responsible for their own professional development. It is imperative that teachers find a place where they can find encouragement, inspiration and support. This is especially important during the first years in the classroom. The Internet provides an ideal setting for teacher to teacher communication. Websites, such as Tapped In©, provide an environment for teachers to chat with others about a wide variety of topics. This can be an excellent way to share ideas and gain support from other educators. The United States Department of Education has supported the Tapped In© site as a mentoring program for teachers at all levels of experience. This and other sites allow teachers to form a global community for discussion of problems and solutions that peers recommend. The information often helps teachers to see that most educational issues are national or even international which develops a support system. The voices of practitioners are a powerful tool for beginning teachers and the chat rooms allow open communication, free from fear of administrative judgment.

ISSUES, CONTROVERSIES AND, PROBLEMS

Research suggests that as availability to technology has grown, so has the number of students and teachers who use the computer with growing frequency (Levin et al., 1998). However, it is interesting to note that the introduction of computers and the Internet has not drastically changed how teachers teach or how students learn (NCES, 2000). The use of technology in the classroom can take learning to a new, previously unattainable, level. However, technology can only take students as far as the early childhood teacher allows. It is for this reason that educators must use their professional judgment on developmentally appropriate ways to integrate technology into their classroom (Morrison, 2007). Morrison identifies three main barriers to the implementation of technology use in the classroom. They are as follows:

- Teachers' personal acceptance of technology
- Confidence that technology has a positive influence on children
- Indecision about how to use technology in early childhood programs and classrooms (Morrison, 2007)

It is the responsibility of the developing teacher to work to overcome these personal barriers and is the responsibility of teacher education programs to support pre-service teachers in this endeavor. The first step in this process is to accept technology and learn the best ways to use it. In order to do this, teachers need to be aware of the potential benefits of technology use in the classroom. It is important to collaborate with other teachers, parents and members of the community during this phase of technology awareness (Morrison, 2007). Little research has been done to determine the best approach to help pre-service teachers overcome their understanding of technology in their future classrooms. It is, however, accepted that teacher trainers will have a major role in the acceptance of technology in the classroom.

There are many resources available to assist teachers' decisions about what technology to use in the classroom. It is often beneficial to consult with other teachers during this phase of technology awareness. It is also important to spend time researching appropriate software and technology to use in the classroom. A key point to remember is that "the more interactive the software, the more the child is able to manipulate what happens when the program is used" (Morrison, 2007, p. 386). These ideas must be communicated and developed through coursework for pre-service teachers. The faculty itself can be a barrier not only to integrating technology into the university classroom, but a barrier to the process of learning for the pre-service teacher. A lack of clear vision for appropriate technology use appears to exist in many faculties today (Finley & Hartman, 2004). Lack of technology training continues to be a negative factor in many teacher education programs. The one-time training or expectations of self-training on technology leads to a feeling of inadequate preparation for pre-service teachers (Finley & Hartman, 2004; Fisher, 2000; Milbrath & Kinzie, 2000). Many teacher educators are novice technology users while many of their students are coming to universities with a high level of technology comfort levels.

Pre-service teachers may enter classrooms without the advantage of seeing technology applications used or without being expected to use them in their own classrooms. Teacher educators need to focus on the functional aspect of technology as they integrate it in their teaching. The focal point needs to be on specific content objectives not just the "bells and whistles" aspect of technology. Finley and Hartman (2004) advocated ongoing professional development not only to learn to integrate technology into teacher education courses, but to provide opportunities for pre-service teachers to incorporate it in their teaching. Positive attitudes about computers and technology are important components for teacher educators as they serve as role models for pre-service teachers. A lack of positive attitude has been labeled as "computer anxiety" and delayed greater use of technology in the classrooms according to Milbrath and Kinzie (2000, p. 375).

Walker and White (2002) posed the question whether IT stands for Informational Technology or Instructional Technology. Schooling has never been just about "disseminating" information (p. 65). Computers can help with disseminating information. The Internet is a way to get information cheaper and faster, however, computers cannot "construct meaning" (Walker & White, 2002, p. 67). Just because the information is cheaper and faster does not mean that there is an improvement in education. To achieve improvement in education with the use of technology will require incorporating authentic, everyday uses for the classroom. This demands that education courses help pre-service teachers learn how to use these tools to construct knowledge while developing skill in using technology. This two pronged task is vital if teachers are to be ready to step into schools techno-proficient.

SOLUTIONS AND RECOMMENDATIONS

In order for technology to reach the early childhood classroom, it must first reach the classroom of the teacher education programs. Teacher education programs have a responsibility to produce professionals who are literate in technical matters. According to Hammond, et al. (2005), "Teachers, and the school districts that employ them, should have the expectation that when teachers arrive on the job they already know how to use general desktop productivity tools, including word processing, spreadsheets, and other applications like general search tools, in ways that are linked to the practice of teaching" (p. 199). Balance is needed in exploring the role of technology in teacher education.

According to the National Center for Education Statistics, research is clear that teachers who feel better prepared to use technology are more likely to use it in the classroom (NCES, 2000). Therefore, it is imperative that teacher education programs make it a priority to better prepare pre-service teachers for the technologically advanced classroom. Teacher education programs today must graduate teachers who are prepared and confident in their use of technology in order to pass that confidence on to the classroom. Teachers must first familiarize themselves with available and new technology before they can use technology to transform the classroom (Gates, 2007). Teacher educators must rise to the task by learning technology skills, integrating technology into their teaching, and find ways in which knowledge can be constructed and supported through technology.

SELF-EFFICACY

We know that the teachers of young children share some common beliefs about their academic and teaching abilities. Traditional thinking about early childhood educators preparation focuses on social and emotional development with little support for academic disciplines like mathematics and science. Anecdotally we have observed faculty from ECE teacher programs often express their aversion to mathematics and science by not requiring courses in these fields in program development. "They don't need math and science" is a statement that is commonly heard from university faculty. We know that:

- Teachers least likely to be educated in mathematics and science are the ones most likely to be in early childcare settings (Johnson, 1999).
- Early Childhood teachers generally prefer to teach reading and other language-oriented skills. Mathematics and science or both are considered difficult subjects-ones they feel unable to teach (Copley & Padron, 1999).
- These teachers often express an aversion to mathematics and science and are concerned

about their abilities to instruct in these areas (Johnson, 1999).
- Mathematics and science or both are considered difficult subjects-ones they feel unable to teach (Copley & Padron, 2004).

Because technology is often grouped with science, mathematics, and engineering in the minds of teachers we think the same aversion influences are present. This avoidance of technology could come from their self efficacy beliefs about themselves and their ability to use and teach technology. The influence of teacher's beliefs can impact their use of technology.

The first part of this chapter discussed different applications of technology in the training of early childhood teachers. It gave us insight into how a typical early childhood faulty member understands technology and it uses in the classroom. Now we would like to look at some of the possible influences on teacher learning that impact technology use. Bandura and Schunk (1981) explain self-efficacy as "People's judgment of their capabilities to organize and execute courses of action required to attain design types of performance" (p. 391). They also found that people's performance is better predicted by their beliefs about their capabilities than about what they are able to do. Schunk (1995) further defines self-efficacy in the learning process as students' judgments about their cognitive capabilities to accomplish a specific academic task or obtain specific goals. Self-efficacy is one's self-judgments of personal capabilities to initiate and successfully perform specified tasks at designated levels, expend greater effort and persevere in the face of adversity (Bandura, 1988; 1986, 1987; Parajes & Miller, 1995). Bandura suggests that one of the most important aspects of self-efficacy is the person's perception of *self-regulatory efficacy*. In other words, students will learn better if they believe that they are good at managing their thinking strategies in a productive manner.

If students are able to perform a task successfully, then their self-efficacy can be raised. In contrast, if students are not able to perform a task, then students may believe that they do not have the skills to do the task which, in turn, lowers their self-efficacy. While it is important to enhance the self-efficacy of the learners themselves, self-efficacy theory also has important implications for other agents in the instructional process (Ashton, 1984; Ashton & Webb, 1986). Henson, (2001) argues that teachers' self-efficacy beliefs have been repeatedly associated with positive teaching behaviors and student outcomes but such beliefs will likely be contingent on development of strong theoretical models and effective instrumentation to assess theoretical constructs.

Consistent with the general formulation of self-efficacy, Tschannen-Moran and Woolfolk Hoy (2003) defined teacher efficacy as a teacher's "judgment of his or her capabilities to bring about desired outcomes of student engagement and learning, even among those students who may be difficult or unmotivated." For example, Gibson and Dembo (1984) have found that teachers who have a high sense of instructional efficacy devote more instructional time to academic learning, give students more and better help when they need it, and are more likely to praise students for their successful accomplishments. Likewise, Woolfolk and Hoy (1990) have found that teachers with a low sense of self-efficacy are likely to employ a set of "custodial" strategies that focus on extrinsic inducements and negative sanctions (which are likely to be ineffective), whereas teachers with higher self-efficacy are more likely to employ strategies that support their students' intrinsic motivation and encourage the students to direct their own learning. Custodial strategies could be the defining term for many of the activities that teachers and faculty select as teaching strategies which are often strongly teacher directed. The teacher or faculty's own insecurity in their ability and understanding influences the decision to use lower level memorized lessons to support their

teaching or even worse keeps them from using and teaching technology all together.

When teachers of young children set goals for learning they may be influenced by beliefs about their own capabilities rather than what their children need to learn to succeed in the ever demanding academic environment. Personal goal setting is influenced by their self-appraisal of capabilities. The stronger the perceived self-efficacy, the higher the goals or challenges people set for themselves and the firmer is their commitment to them (Bandura, 1991). It becomes quite clear that ability is not a fixed attribute residing in one's behavioral repertoire. Rather it is a generative capability in which cognitive, social, motivational, and behavioral skills must be organized and effectively orchestrated to serve numerous purposes (Bandura, 1993).

Because efficacy judgments are said to be most accurate at reasonable degrees of specificity (Bandura, 1997; Pajares, 1996), teacher efficacy items should be task specific. It is possible that related tasks eventually find themselves clustered together in a factor. However, it is also possible, and almost completely ignored in the teacher efficacy literature, that these factors cluster into more parsimonious general factors. Recent work suggests that teacher efficacy can be conceptualized as a one-factor construct. This could explain the data concerning early childhood teachers choice of reading and language related activities over technology and related fields.

Finally, Bandura (1997) points out that different schools and departments are likely to have varied perceptions of their collective self-efficacy. School staff members who collectively judge themselves as having high self-efficacy are likely to provide an environment that will promote similar feelings and high levels of productivity among their students. This thinking aligns with university faculty as well as school program teachers. Until university faculty involved with training of early childhood teachers become more confident in their abilities to use and understand technology their competence levels will not increase. This will directly influence the technology development of their students which in turn can affect their use and understanding of technology in ECE classrooms.

FUTURE TRENDS

It is difficult to predict the future trends of the role of technology in teacher education. It is; however, clear that the future will have even greater technological demands than the present. The glass that is viewed by one as half-empty is the same glass viewed by another as half-full. Those on both sides of the technology issue could do well to compare it to the invention of the wheel in the Stone Age. Just as the world was changed by the invention of the wheel, we have been changed and are continuing to be changed by technology. As technology is continually updated and improved, the technology aspect of the teacher education programs must also continually update and improve. The new role of technology in the planning of curriculum is substantial. Proficiency with the newest technologies is a "societal goal" for curriculum. Also, technology allows access to a vast amount of information that was once inaccessible for both teachers and students. Furthermore, technology can allow greater opportunities for reflection and improvement for students as well as teachers (Hammond, et al., 2005).

CONCLUSION

In summary, in this chapter we have discussed the need for teacher educators to consistently model authentic uses of technology in their classrooms while expecting pre-service students to develop and implement technology in the early childhood classroom. Technology goes beyond instruction as more schools adopt software for record keeping and communication purposes. The role

of self-efficacy may be a determining factor in teacher and faculty use. The modeling done by teacher educators is important for imprinting and supporting the idea of teaching with technology rather than teaching about technology. Teacher trainers must use and accept technology tools in order to help teachers meet the new demands of school environments.

It is time for technology to have a prominent place in teacher education. Students graduating from today's teacher education programs need not only to understand how to incorporate technology into their classrooms on a daily basis, but have firsthand experience teaching with technology.

SOME QUESTIONS FOR REFLECTIVE PRACTITIONERS:

1. What role will standards about teachers and technology play in your classroom?
2. Do you think the use of PowerPoint presentations help teachers learn or are they a modern overhead projector? Explain your thinking.
3. Is technology a fad in teacher training? Why or why not?
4. What types of technology did you observe when you were enrolled in your program degree courses? Have you used any of these in your teaching? If yes, how did you use these tools?
5. The use of SMART boards in the classroom is becoming an increasingly popular instructional trend. What instructional advantages do you see with this tool? What problems do you anticipate with SMART boards or similar tools?
6. What types of assessment tools have you used that are technology based? Do these types of tools facilitate of hinder your assessment? Explain your thinking.
7. Technology in the classroom has opened the door to parent-teacher communications. The

Internet is one of the most valuable tools for keeping parents informed and involved with their child's education. How will you use technology in your class to communicate with parents?

8. Though teachers spend their days surrounded by other people, teaching is often considered to be an isolated profession. Despite the efforts of many school districts, teachers remain largely responsible for their own professional development. How could technology be used to develop a support system for you and your colleagues?

9. Morrison identifies three main barriers to the implementation of technology use in the classroom. They are as follows:

    ◦ Teachers' personal acceptance of technology

    ◦ Confidence that technology has a positive influence on children

    ◦ Indecision about how to use technology in early childhood programs and classrooms (Morrison, 2007)

    ◦ How will you overcome these barriers in your classroom?

10. What advice would you give to teacher trainers to insure they provide appropriate information to students and teachers?

11. According to the National Center for Education Statistics, research is clear that teachers who feel better prepared to use technology are more likely to use it in the classroom (NCES, 2000). What kinds of experiences would help you develop a level of comfort using technology?

12. How does self-efficacy relate to use of technology in classrooms?

REFERENCES

Ashton, P. (1984). Teacher efficacy: A motivational paradigm for effective teacher education. *Journal of Teacher Education, 35*(5), 28–32. doi:10.1177/002248718403500507

Ashton & Webb. (1986) *Making a Difference: Teacher Efficacy and Student Achievement.* Monogram. White Plains, NY: Longman.

Bandura, A. (1977). Self-efficacy: Toward a unifying theory of behavioral change. *Psychological Review, 84,* 191–215.doi:10.1037/0033-295X.84.2.191

Bandura, A. (1986). *Social foundations of thought and action: A social cognitive theory.* Upper Saddle River, New Jersey: Prentice-Hall.

Bandura, A. (1988). Perceived self-efficacy: Exercise of control through self-belief. In J. P. Dauwalder, M. Perrez, & V. Hobi (Eds.), *Annual series of Euporean research in behavior therapy, 2,* 27-59. Lisse, The Netherlands: Swets & Zeitlander.

Bandura, A. (1991). Self-regulation of motivation through anticipatory and self- regulatory mechanisms. In R. A. Dienstbier (Ed.), *Perspectives on motivation: Nebraska symposium on motivation, 38,* 69-164. Lincoln: University of Nebraska Press.

Bandura, A. (1993). Perceived self-efficacy in cognitive development and functioning. *Educational Psychologist, 28*(2), 117–148. doi:10.1207/s15326985ep2802_3

Bandura, A. (1997). *Self-efficacy: The exercise of control.* New York: Freeman.

Bandura, A., & Schunk, D. H. (1981). Cultivating competence, self-efficacy, and intrinsic interest through proximal self-motivation. *Journal of Personality and Social Psychology, 41,* 586–598. doi:10.1037/0022-3514.41.3.586

Barrett, H. (2000). *Electronic teaching portfolios: Multimedia skills + portfolio development = powerful professional development.* Paper presented at the Society for Technology and Teacher Education (SITE) conference, San Diego, CA. Available online: http://transition.alaska.edu/www/portfolios/site2000.html.

Bartlett, A. (2002). Preparing preservice teachers to implement performance assessment and technology through electronic portfolios. *Action in Teacher Education, 24*(1), 90–97.

Bartlett, A., & Sherry, A. C. (2006). Two views of electronic portfolios in teacher education: Non-technology undergraduate and technology graduate students. *International Journal of Instructional Media, 33*(3), 245–252.

Brooks-Young, S. (2007). Are document cameras the next big thing? *T.H.E. Journal, 34*(6), 20–23.

Carmona, J. (1996). Presentation devices extend reach of information to entire groups. *T.H.E. Journal, 23*(6), 12–15.

Duhaney, D. C. (2001). Teacher education: Preparing teachers to integrate technology. *International Journal of Instructional Media, 28*(1), 23–33.

Epper, R. M., & Bates, A. W. (2001). *Teaching faculty how to use technology: Best practices from leading institutions.* Westport, CT: Oryx Press.

Finley, L., & Hartman, D. (2004). Institutional change and resistance: Teachers preparatory faculty and technology integration. *Journal of Technology and Teacher Education, 12*(3), 319–330.

Fisher, M. (2000). Technology, pedagogy and education. *Journal of Information Technology for Teacher Education, 9*(1), 109–123.

Gates, N. C. (2007). Technology integration for the savvy teacher. *Journal of the Tennessee Association for the Education of Young Children,* 21-22.

Gibson, S., & Dembo, M. (1984). Teacher efficacy: A construct validation. *Journal of Educational Psychology, 76,* 569–582. doi:10.1037/0022-0663.76.4.569

Goddard, R. D., Hoy, W. K., & Woolfolk Hoy, A. (2000). Collective teacher efficacy: Its meaning, measure, and impact on student achievement. *American Educational Research Journal, 37,* 479–507.

Hammond, L. D., et al. (2005). Educational goals and purposes: developing a curricular vision for teaching. In Linda Darling-Hammond and John Bransford (Eds.), *Preparing teachers for a changing world, what teachers should learn and be able to do* (pp.169-200). San Francisco, CA: Jossey-Bass.

Henson, R. K. (2001). *Teacher Self-Efficacy: Substantive Implications and Measurement Dilemmas.* 1337Invited keynote address given at the annual meeting of the Educational Research Exchange. Texas A&M University, College Station, Texas.

International Society for Technology and Education (ISTE) Accreditation Committee. (1992). *Curriculum guidelines for accreditation of educational computing and technology programs.* Eugene: ISTE.

Kariuki, M., & Duran, M. (2004). Using anchored instruction to teach preservice teachers to integrate technology in the curriculum. *Journal of Technology and Teacher Education, 12*(3), 431–450.

Levin, D., Stephens, M., Kirshstein, R., & Birman, B. (1998). *Toward assessing the effectiveness of using technology in K-12 education.* U.S. Department of Education. Washington, DC: Office of Educational Research and Improvement.

Maddox, C., & Cummings, R. (2004). Fad, fashion and the weak role of theory and research in information technology in education. *Journal of Technology and Teacher Education, 12*(4), 511–528.

Milbrath, Y. L., & Kinzie, M. B. (2000). Computer technology training for prospective teachers: Computer attitudes and perceived self-efficacy. *Journal of Technology and Teacher Education, 8*(4), 373–384.

Morrison, G. S. (2006). *Fundamentals of early childhood education* (4th ed.). Columbus, OH: Pearson Merrill Prentice Hall.

Morrison, G. S. (2007). *Early childhood education today* (10th ed.). Columbus, OH: Pearson Merrill Prentice Hall.

National Association for the Education of Young Children (NAEYC). (1996). *Technology and young children – ages 3 through 8: a position statement of the National Association for the Education of Young Children.*

National Center for Education Statistics (NCES). (2000). *Teachers' tools for the 21st century: a report on teachers' use of technology.* Washington, DC: U.S. Department of Education.

National Council for Accreditation of Teacher Education (NCATE). (2000) *NCATE Standards: Unit standards.* Washington: NCATE. Also available at: http://www.ncate.org/2000/pressrelease.htm

National Council for Accreditation of Teacher Education (NCATE). (2000). *Program standards for elementary teacher preparation.* Washington: NCATE. Also available at: http://www.ncate.org/standard/elemstds/pdf.

Pajares, F. (1996a). Self-efficacy beliefs and mathematical problem solving of gifted students. *Contemporary Educational Psychology, 21*(4), 325–344. doi:10.1006/ceps.1996.0025

Pajares, F. (1996b). Self-efficacy beliefs in achievement settings. *Review of Educational Research,* (66): 543–578.

Pajares, F., & Graham, L. (1999). Self-efficacy, motivation constructs, and mathematics performance of entering middle school students. *Contemporary Educational Psychology, 24*(2), 124–139. doi:10.1006/ceps.1998.0991

Schunk, D. H. (1984). Self-efficacy perspective on achievement behavior. *Educational Psychologist, 19*(1), 48–59.

Schunk, D. H. (1987). Peer models and children's behavior change. *Review of Educational Research, 57*(2), 149–174.

Schunk, D. H. (1995). Self-efficacy and education and instruction. In J.E. Maddux (Ed.) *Self-Efficacy, Adaptation, and Adjustment: Theory, Research, and Application* (pp.281-303). New York: Plenum Press.

Schunk, D.H., & Hanson, A. R. (1985). Peer models: Influence on children's self-efficacy and achievement. *Journal of Educational Psychology, 77*(3): 313–322. doi:10.1037/0022-0663.77.3.313

Schunk, D. H., Hanson, A. R., & Cox, P. D. (1987). Peer-model attributes and children's achievement behaviors. *Journal of Educational Psychology, 79*(1): 54–61. doi:10.1037/0022-0663.79.1.54

SMART Technologies. (2008). http://www2.smarttech.com/st/en-US/Products/SMART+Boards/.

Teacher intern handbook. (2006). State University, AR: Arkansas State University.

Tschannen-Moran, M., & Woolfolk Hoy, A. (2003). Teacher efficacy: Capturing an elusive construct. Teaching and Teacher Education.

Tschannen-Moran, M., Woolfolk Hoy, A., & Hoy, W. K. (1998). Teacher efficacy: Its meaning and measure. *Review of Educational Research, 68,* 202–248.

Walker, T., & White, C. (2002). Technorealism: The rhetoric and reality of technology in teacher education. *Journal of Technology and Teacher Education, 10*(1), 63–71.

Winn, J. (2003, July). Avoiding death by power-point. *Journal of Professional Issues in Engineering Education and Practice*, 116–118.

Chapter 6
Using Assistive Technology
Enabling All Children to Feel Capable and Connected in the Early Childhood Classroom

Rene Crow
University of Central Arkansas, USA

ABSTRACT

This chapter explores how technology is used with young children with special needs in the United States. It also discusses the legal issues and mandates and the reality of how teachers and schools are dealing with children with special needs in early childhood settings. Information resources and how assistive technology fits into developmentally appropriate practice is included in this discussion.

INTRODUCTION

This chapter investigates the value of assistive technology by first addressing its definition of law and the legislative history of assistive technology to enrich the lives of children with special needs, and then describes the benefits of technology in all areas of development, including cognitive, language, physical and social domains of development. The final part of the chapter investigates the use of assistive technology in the early childhood classroom and in the home, and offers guidance to teachers and families of children with special needs to assist them in learning to access technology tools that can be great assets to the inclusion of their children in

early childhood classrooms and throughout their communities.

As an early childhood special education teacher, I found that technology is not only a great equalizer, but also a great motivator for young children with special needs. For most people, it is success that breeds success. When children experience success with the use of a device that enables them to do more than they could do without it, they find within themselves the desire to try again and achieve even more. They feel like contributing, capable members of the overall school community and family, an idea supported by those who promote social and emotional learning for young children (Albert, 1996; Bailey, 2001; Cooper, 2005) and it is my belief as a special educator that there is no greater motivator available to teachers than to empower

DOI: 10.4018/978-1-60566-784-3.ch006

children in this way. More recently in my career, I have worked passionately as a teacher educator, preparing eager men and women to meet the needs of the early childhood students in their care, and I continually impress upon those teacher candidates the importance of assisting all children in feeling like vital members of the classroom and overall school communities. During the last decade, technology has become a buzz word in education. Accreditation boards scan syllabi and lesson plans to see where technology is being implemented, and entire courses are devoted to ensuring that students leave their teacher education programs prepared to incorporate technology into their teaching goals. While this is all appropriate and understandable, if the underlying theme of using technology to enable *ALL* children to experience success is overlooked, a very valuable asset of technology in education is missed. This chapter sets out to address this essential element of the technology in education issue.

BACKGROUND

Children, regardless of their levels of functioning in cognitive, social, emotional, language, and/or physical domains, have the desire to belong and to feel significant (Nelsen, 1996). Like no other time in our educational system's history have educators been better able to support this desire in children with special needs. Not only do educators have the law working on the behalf of children who struggle, the increased availability of technology in classrooms, even in classrooms for young children, supports the efforts of teachers and students in enabling all children to feel capable and connected (Albert, 1996) to their peers in the early childhood classroom environment and beyond.

With assistive technology, the ability of young children to experience success through access to the general curriculum and to contribute to the overall functioning of the school community is heightened in a way that goes beyond meeting the academic goals outlined on the child's Individualized Education Plan (IEP). With the aid of technology, not only can children gain access to the curriculum and succeed in mastering measurable goals outlined therein, they can genuinely be valuable, contributing members of the school community, thus enriching their social and emotional competence in ways that are not as easily measured but perhaps most important to overall growth and satisfaction.

ASSISTIVE TECHNOLOGY

Definition and Special Education Law

Special education services are provided to young children in educational settings under the Individuals with Disabilities Education Improvement Act of 2004 (PL 108-446). Originally named the Education for All Handicapped Children Act (PL 94-142), this legislation has been amended and reauthorized three times with the most recent reauthorization being in 2004. One of the major revisions of the law occurred in 1997, when Congress mandated that every Individual Educational Plan (IEP) team must consider assistive technology when planning the educational program of an individual with a disability. Assistive technology was originally defined in the Assistive Technology Act of 1988. The 1988 version of the act was amended in 1998, and the original definition of assistive technology has become standard definition in all subsequent federal legislation and regulations legislation affecting children with special needs (Alliance for Technology Access, 2004), including the Individuals with Disabilities Education Improvement Act of 2004. Assistive technology is legally defined in two parts. First, an assistive technology device is defined as "any item, piece of equipment, or product system, whether acquired commercially off the shelf, modified, or customized, that is used to increase, maintain, or improve the functional capabilities of a child with a disability" (20 USC, 1400, SECTION 602(1), 2004). A companion to this definition is that of an assistive technology service, which is defined as "any service that directly assists a child with a disability in the selection, acquisition or use of an assistive technology device" (20 USC, 1400, SECTION 602(2), 2004). Services must include a) evaluating an individual's assistive technology; b) purchasing, leasing, or providing for acquisition of devices; c) selecting, designing, adapting, maintaining, repairing, or replacing devices; d) coordinating therapies, interventions, or services; e) providing training and technical assistance for the individual and/or family; and f) providing training and technical assistance for professionals. In short, school districts are responsible for helping children with disabilities select, acquire, and learn to use assistive technology devices (Olson, Platt, & Dieker, 2008).

Another term crucial to understanding the law as it applies to integrating technology for the benefit of young children in the early childhood classroom is *universal design*. When the Individuals with Disabilities Education was reauthorized in 2004, the definition from the Assistive Technology Act of 1998 was added to the law, defining universal design as "A concept or philosophy for designing and delivering products and services that are usable by people with the widest range of functional capabilities." The concept of universal design for learning was actually adapted from architecture, where buildings are designed with diverse users in mind. While meeting the needs of people with disabilities, the accommodations actually are beneficial to the population at large (Hardman, Drew, & Egan, 2008). For instance, curb cuts were originally designed for wheelchair access, but the adaptation has proved helpful for a much wider group, including people using baby strollers and children and adults riding bicycles or skateboards (Edyburn, 2003). Another example of universal design as related to technology includes

changes to personal computers that were originally made to assist persons with disabilities. One such change occurred when computer manufacturers began relocating the power switch of the computer from the traditional location in the back of the computer to the keyboard or on the front of the computer. While this change did in fact enable persons with disabilities to more independently use the computer, it also offered a convenience to all computer users (Alliance for Technology Access, 2004).

One attraction of the universal design for learning with specific ties to the use of technologies is described by Polloway, Patton, & Serna (2008), in that the design "capitalizes on new technologies and electronic resources" (p. 14). Universal design for learning calls for considering the needs of students with special needs along a continuum of learning related differences, and that developing curricula and materials that attend to the needs of students with disabilities increases usability for everyone, not just the students with special needs (Rose & Meyer, 2000; Meyer & Rose, 2000).

A summary of legislation affecting children with disabilities as it relates to assistive technology is included in Table 1.

BENEFITS OF TECHNOLOGY

Numerous benefits of technology exist for young children with disabilities, not only in academic achievement, but in more complex cognitive, language, and social domains, as well. Some of the benefits of technology pertaining to various aspects of development are discussed below.

Cognitive Development

Judge and Lahm (1998) remind us that if play is the work of children, and many early childhood educators agree that it is, then it is beneficial to enhance play through the use of assistive technology for the young child with disabilities. Without

Table 1. Assistive Technology Legislation: A Chronology

Name of Legislation	Year Passed	Basic Tenets of the Law
Technology Related Assistance Act for Individuals with Disabilities	1988	Provided funding for each state to develop a responsive system for providing residents with assistive technology devices and services. Was amended in 1994; also called Tech Act.
Americans with Disabilities Act	1990	Introduced concept of "reasonable accommodations" as a responsibility of employers to consider and use appropriate technologies and accommodations to enable persons with disabilities to complete work related tasks. Also mandated accessible transportation systems, buildings and programs and communication systems for people with disabilities.
Individuals with Disabilities Education Act	1990	Renamed Education for All Handicapped Children Act; ensured a free and appropriate public education for all children with disabilities in the least restrictive environment. Children with disabilities must be provided supplementary services that permit them to benefit from their education, including assistive technology services.
Individuals with Disabilities Education Act Reauthorization	1997	Every IEP team must consider assistive technology when planning the educational program of an individual with a disability.
Assistive Technology Act	1998	The amended version of the earlier Tech Act of 1988. Provides funds to assist states in developing consumer-responsive access to assistive technology, technology services, and information.
Individuals with Disabilities Education Improvement Act	2004	Reauthorized IDEA; continued basic tenets of that law including FAPE and LRE. Added the definition for universal design from the Assistive Technology Act of 1998. Provided that students who are blind or have print disabilities have access to print instructional materials in accessible format, free of charge.

it, children with special needs are often on the sidelines watching the play of others rather than engaging in play itself. Wershing & Symington (1998) comment that while children with disabilities often have limited opportunities to explore their worlds through play, such experiences are just as important to them as it for children who are typically developing, and the use of assistive technology can offer a scaffold for their development in various domains of development that would not be possible without the devices. Judge (1998) asserts that assistive technology is a tool for playing, allowing children with disabilities the opportunity to explore and discover their worlds in ways that they could not without the assistive devices and services to enhance their play.

Toys and props that are part of early childhood classrooms become the "tools of play" (Hamm, Mistrett, & Ruffino, 2006) for children, and the selection of toys for children with disabilities requires additional considerations. In selecting toys for typically developing children, families and teachers can rely on toy manufacturers' input on the package of the toy; for children with developmental or physical delays, this information is often inappropriate. For parents of children with disabilities as well as for parents without disabilities, a number one concern regarding toy selection concerns safety. In addition, parents and teachers of children with and without disabilities must also consider which toys children are most likely to enjoy and use. A study by Hamm, Mistrett, & Ruffino (2006) indicated that in selecting toys, parents of children with disabilities most often included those that are easily activated and respond with lights, sounds and moving parts, with fewer selections of symbolic toys like books or play sets. This supports former research (Munoz, 1986) that suggested an emphasis on the part of parents of children with special needs on motor activity during play over exploratory play. Implications of this research suggest that due to the importance of symbolic play in the cognitive development of young children (Piaget, 1962), parents of children with challenges need training in the value of symbolic play and help in learning how to engage their child in pretend play. Important to consider in guiding children in this type of play are earmarks of Piaget's cognitive theory: assimilation, accommodation, and equilibrium. According to Piaget, when children encounter a new concept, they must first assimilate the new information into their existing cognitive structures, or match new information to something similar in their experience. In doing so, they accommodate for the new information by adjusting what they already knew about the concept to include the new idea. In successfully doing so, they reach equilibrium. To apply Piaget's ideas to guiding children with disabilities to a better understanding of symbolism, it is important to use toys that are symbolic of experiences that the children for whom they are intended are familiar. A toy that would support this notion would be a baby doll, as described above, rather than a toy dinosaur. As children are learning to play symbolically, toys that are more authentic and concrete will be more easily understood than those highly representational. To illustrate, a stuffed puppy that is furry and looks realistic might be easier to use symbolically than an action hero figure, and a tea set that looks like dishes the child has used in his or her experience might be more easily understood than the symbolic use of toy blocks.

The use of simple switches can help young children explore the concept of cause and effect, but higher level cognitive concepts can be enhanced through assistive technology, as well. Using technology to enable children to make choices from an array of possible responses is a way of moving children from the simple cause and effect response to a higher level of thinking (Judge & Lahm, 1998).

Computer technology can be helpful in promoting cognitive development of young children. Judge & Lahm (1998) correctly note that computers are "nonjudgmental and infinitely patient, allowing children to explore or practice at their own pace, and never tire of repeating the same activity or story" (p. 27). While computer software programs once emphasized drill and practice for academic skills, more developmentally appropriate software is available and utilized today. Still, Haugland (2005) asserts that less than 20% of software and web sites available are developmentally appropriate. Software that is highly interactive and which offers more child control is considered to be developmentally appropriate. Rather than serving as electronic worksheets, Haugland (2005) suggests that open ended, exploratory software is more appropriate for use by young children and leads to greater developmental gains (Haugland, 1992).

Language Development

One of the most obvious ways that assistive technology is used to promote language development is through the use of augmentative and alternative communication devices. Augmentative communication systems are "communication systems that involve adapting existing vocal or gestural abilities into meaningful communication; teaching manual signing, static symbols, or icons; and using manual or electronic communication devices" (Hardman, p. 335). Children with limited verbal skills can use picture boards or high tech communication devices to express their wants and needs, thus leading to an understanding of the value of language. Other visual supports are extremely helpful to children with language difficulties, as is often the case for children with autism, developmental delays, speech and language disorders, and hearing impairments. "Visual supports can attract and hold attention, thus enabling the student to focus on the message, reduce anxiety, make abstract concepts more concrete, help prompt the student, and help the student to express his or her thoughts" (Rao & Gagie, 2006). One such visual support is a *visual schedule*. Visual schedules are cues that outline the schedule of a child's day, both in and out of school, to aid them in organizing their completion of activities and feeling some control over the environment. Visual schedules can be made using computer software like Boardmaker, or simply handwritten or hand drawn by teachers, depending upon the needs of the child. For children using the language of Boardmaker in other facets of their day, it might be helpful to carry through with the same images on a visual schedule. For children who need more concrete representations, teachers often find that taking photographs of the classroom setting and activities is more helpful than using clip art images to include in the visual schedule.

Other examples of visual cues for children with language impairments include labels on shelves outlining the toys that are to be replaced there; classroom rules posted in pictures, or better yet, in photographs of children in the classroom engaged in positive behaviors; and tape added to the floor indicating where children are to sit at circle time.

Another assistive technology support which promotes emergent literacy and language development is the "talking book." Both commercial and teacher-made "talking books" are supporting emergent literacy by filling in the gap for many children whose language is impaired and/or whose literature experience in the home is limited (Weikle & Hadadian, 2003). Talking books can be purchased or teacher made by scanning in familiar books and using computer software to add audio. Standard software such as PowerPoint and PowerTalk can be inexpensively used to make talking books. Fostering language development through the use of assistive technology is best accomplished through a team approach wherein the classroom teacher works to extend the therapy begun by a child's speech and language pathologist to the natural setting of the classroom (Skau & Cascella, 2006). Such assistive technology could include sign language, wherein the classroom teacher would commit to

learning a number of signs that are relevant in the classroom, picture communication boards, and communication output devices. The key is for children to use the technology supports across settings in similar ways.

Physical Development

For children whose motor abilities are limited, adaptations through assistive technology can accommodate their environments. One way such accommodations can be made is through the use of switches to operate battery operated toys. Various types of switches can be added to many toys that can be activated by touch, light pressure, pneumatic pressure from a sip or a puff, squeeze, or movement of a body part with a light mounted on it (Judge & Lahm, 1998).

An obvious benefit of assistive technology for children with gross motor development deficits and delays is in reference to aids in mobility. When children are more able to explore their environments as they would without mobility limitations, they experience their worlds more like children whose physical development is typical. Petty (1994) notes that the use of powered mobility reduces the risk of further delays in development by providing important experiences for young children. Though powered mobility options are not appropriate for all children, they can sometimes provide great benefits to young children who have the skills and support their use.

Other types of mobility aids include walkers, which offer supervision and support in walking. King & Sussman (1998) describe various types of walkers, beginning with the most common: standard *front-wheeled walkers,* which are walkers that children push, which are helpful for children with visual impairments or orthopedic disabilities; *reverse pull-type walkers* which are more appropriate for people who have mild or moderate cerebral palsy, spina bifida with fair hip and leg strength, or who use leg braces; *ring walkers* which have chest support and four wheels, more appropriate for people with poor trunk control and who cannot stand independently but enjoy being upright and moving; and *gait trainers*, which are specialized supports for the child who is working on gait training and who needs maximal support that a traditional walker cannot provide.

Standers are "positioning devices that allow users to stand upright and which provide weight-bearing through the legs to keep bones strong, stretch tight muscles, promote normal bodily functions like digestion and respiration, and for socialization with peers in an educational setting" (King & Sussman, 1998, p. 74). Various types of standers are available and are described by King & Sussman (1998). The most common type of stander is the *standing frame* for children with good neck control and fair trunk control. The *supine stander* offers support at the side of the head and straps at the trunk, knees and feet. The *prone stander* provides more support than the standard standing frame but less than the supine stander, and the *mobile stander* allows the user to move around in an upright position. Finally, the *sit to stand stander* has a wheelchair base that gradually moves the child from a sitting to a standing position.

Many low-tech assistive devices can be helpful to assist young children with fine motor deficits. These include adaptive scissors, pencil grips, slanted boards/clipboards, slanted easels, jumbo letter and number stamps, adaptive pencils and crayons, adaptive eating aids, mouth sticks to press keys on a keyboard, and keyguards for computer keyboards (http://www.ncrel.org/sdrs/areas/issues/methods/technlgy/te7assist.htm). Keyguards are plates that lie over standard keyboards to isolate keys. Keyguards are helpful to people who have poor fine-motor control and need to depress keys with a pointing device (Ulman, 2005). High tech assistive devices include adaptive computer keyboards and track balls or joysticks that replace the typical computer mouse. Touch screens can be especially helpful for young children, particularly those with poor

motor control (Hutinger & Johanson, 1998). Touch screens have touch-sensitive sensors that attach to the computer monitor, allowing for direct access to choices on the monitor (Ulman, 20005).Other high tech helps include eye controlled computer-input devices, onscreen keyboards, voice input or output devices and word completion utilities (http://www.ncrel.org/sdrs/areas/issues/methods/technlgy/te7assist.htm).

Assistive technology devices to aid students who are visually impaired include large print books, books on tape, Braille aids such as translation software that inputs text so that it can be printed in Braille, stereo headphones, lighting contrasts, calculators with large keys or large display, talking calculators, computer with speech output, and glare reduction screens. Various assistive devices are helpful for persons who are hearing impaired, as well, including hearing aids, signaling devices, photographs, communication boards, electronic books, and audio-voice amplification devices for teachers (http://www.ncrel.org/sdrs/areas/issues/methods/technlgy/te7assist.htm). People who are hearing impaired also greatly benefit from the use of computers and the internet to gain access to information about the world, as well as tele-communication devices such as text telephones which "send, receive, and print messages through thousands of stations across the United States" (Hardman, p. 411).

Social Development

Numerous studies have supported the use of technology for promoting social development in young children, including young children with disabilities. Once an area of concern for early childhood educators, it has been well established that rather than impede social development, computer usage can actually serve as a catalyst for social interaction (Clements & Sarama, 2002). One study by Muller & Perlmutter (1985) reported that children spent nine times as much time talking to peers while on the computer than while doing puzzles. In a study by Spiegel-McGill et al (1989), preschoolers' participation in computer activities sparked social interaction between typically developing children and children with identified disabilities. Howard, Greyrose, Kehr, Espinosa, & Beckwith (1996) found that when the use of age appropriate software and teacher facilitated activities with preschoolers with moderate to severe disabilities was compared, the preschoolers' behavior with the computer activities "demonstrated more active waiting, less solitary play, more turn taking, more attention to communication and more positive affect" (p. 43). Researchers have reported that social interaction is affected by the physical environment of computer placement. Placing two seats in front of the computer and one at the side for the teacher can encourage positive social interaction, and it is also suggested two computers be placed side by side for optimal social effectiveness (Judge, 2001; Clements & Sarama, 2002). In addition, placing computers in a central location is helpful in that it allows children to pause and participate in the activity at the computer.

The availability of digital photography, both video and still camera, provides teachers of young children with social and emotional challenges with an easy resource to provide visual supports for promoting positive behaviors. Crow (2007) supports the development of Interactive Behavior Picture Stories, wherein teachers use authentic digital photographs to create behavior stories that concretely and playfully engage children with behavioral challenges in learning new social skills. Similar to social stories which were developed by Carol Gray for children with autism, Interactive Behavior Picture Stories are more appropriate for young children and for children with cognitive developmental disabilities in that they offer more concrete representations through photographs and have a hands-on quality. One Interactive Behavior Picture Story created by Crow seeks to teach young children to share toys and materials. Not only is the child who is exposed to the text in the story learning the text through hearing the auditory

text, he or she practices the skills introduced in the text in interactive ways. On one page of the story, the child uses a magnet (attached to the end of a craft stick) to move a magnetic ball back and forth from a photograph of himself on one side of the page to a photograph of a peer on the other side of the page. On a separate page in the story, he sets a movable timer to allow for turn taking, a concept introduced in the story.

Another social asset to assistive technology goes beyond benefiting the child with special needs. Exposure to the success of their peers with disabilities through assistive technology is of benefit to children who are typically developing, in that they come away from time spent with peers who overcome struggles with a better appreciation for the unique qualities of people and an authentic understanding of how modifications and accommodations can bring out the potential in all people. Becky Bailey (2001) stresses the importance of developing a school family, or classroom community of learners. Similarly, Ruth Charney (2002) describes the crucial significance of encouraging children to feel connected in the classroom, to truly internalize the concept that it matters whether or not they come to school and that they are missed when they are not there.

Clearly, assistive technology devices can lead to increased social interaction. When children are better able to communicate with augmentative communication devices, move about to secure favorite objects, explore their environment, and place themselves in closer proximity to their peers, social interaction and autonomy leading to a more positive self esteem is undoubtedly increased.

USING TECHNOLOGY TOOLS IN THE CLASSROOM

A study by Lesar (1998) indicated that 68% of early childhood special educators surveyed felt unprepared in the use of assistive technology. With the breakneck speed at which technology has continued to grow since that time, and since the law now requires that assistive technology be considered in the planning for children with disabilities, understanding the myriad technology tools and services available and how to implement them in the classroom is essential for teachers of young children today.

Assistive tools and services for technology are diverse, as are the children for whom they are intended. Some devices are considered low tech devices, while others are categorized as high tech devices. Low tech devices are discriminated from high tech devices in their definitions as described by Judge (2006). She defines low tech devices as "passive or simple, with few moving parts" (p. 20) and high tech devices as "more expensive, complex, and often having electronic components" (p. 20). When low tech items can be used, teachers often prefer them due to their availability, ease of use, and low cost.

Various components of a child's school day are typical in early childhood classrooms. Judge & Lahm (1998) offer assistive technology suggestions to enhance the learning experiences across the curriculum for young children with disabilities, and Judge (2001) emphasizes the integration of computer technology across the curriculum. These suggestions are in keeping with the position of the National Association for the Education of Young Children (1996) with regard to the use of technology in early childhood classrooms. The NAEYC position statement indicates that "appropriate technology is integrated into the regular learning environment and used as one of many options to support children's learning" (p. 2).

A frequent component of the typical early childhood classroom day is circle time. Common activities in circle time are to share items of interest with one another, attend to daily news and announcements, and participation in calendar time, and singing and movement activities. Assistive technology can be helpful in many of these language-intensive circumstances. From high tech devices like augmentative communication

devices to more low tech devices such as choice making boards, children with disabilities can fully participate when teachers use ingenuity and determination to enable all children to participate in circle time activities.

Another common activity in an early childhood classroom includes snack time. Again, using augmentative communication devices can be of assistance to young children who have language deficits, allowing them to communicate their wants and needs. Prosthetic devices and aids like sipper cups and adaptable utensils can enable some children to be more independent in feeding themselves.

Free choice center time is another common occurrence in the early childhood classroom. The addition of a computer center can be a great enhancement to the choices for children with disabilities, in that they often have fewer barriers to play there than at other centers. In setting up a computer center, Judge (2001) cautions early childhood teachers to take care in choosing developmentally appropriate software. Evaluation forms such as the Haugland/Shade Software Developmental Scale (Haugland & Wright, 1997) can be helpful in evaluating software. Software that is interactive and open-ended has been found to result in more developmental gains than software that is essentially for drill and practice (Haugland, 1992). In setting up an effective computer center, not only is it critical to consider expenses with regard to computer hardware, but it is also important to carefully use expenditures to purchase good quality, interactive software that can be used at more than one developmental level (Hutinger & Johanson, 1998).

In addition to the computer center, other learning centers can be enriched with assistive devices to enable young children to more fully participate in them. The study discussed earlier by Hamm, Mistrett, & Ruffino (2006) indicates that young children with disabilities are often limited in their use and access to toys to support symbolic play and dramatic play. Placement and deliberate modeling of symbolic toys in the dramatic play center that are usable by children with disabilities is one way to accommodate for their special needs throughout the classroom. Simple access is not sufficient, however. Teachers must commit to engage with children in the modeling of how to use such toys, and rely upon peer modeling and support to encourage such play, as well. Teachers may find it helpful to use toys that have both symbolic and cause and effect qualities to help scaffold growth from reliance on motor play to include symbolic play. For instance, baby dolls that can be activated by touch to cry or move can be used to draw interest, allowing teachers to model the symbolic use of the toy, such as cradling, wrapping in a blanket, or rocking.

Judge (2006) suggests that one solution to current difficulties in the process for access, funding, and training for assistive technology devices is in the preparation of an assistive technology toolkit. After surveying early childhood special educators, she determined many assistive technology devices that were preferred by the educators surveyed, many of which were low tech devices. Some of the most preferred devices identified are listed below: visual schedules, picture communication systems, Boardmaker software, touch screens, picture symbol boards, adaptive seating, positioning devices, and adaptive keyboards. Judge suggests that if toolkits with such items included were made available to teachers in inclusive classrooms, the difficulties with access and training would be minimized.

DETERMINING APPROPRIATE TECHNOLOGY

In order to match the needs of young children with the plethora of assistive technology devices and services, it is critical that a team approach be used, beginning with a thorough assessment. Technology needs are not constant; they change over time (Alliance for Technology Access, 2004;

Hess, Gutierrez, Peters, & Cerreta, 2005). It is important that families of children to receive the supports and services be included in the assessment process, and IDEA supports this inclusion. With regard to young children, the Individualized Family Service Plan as outlined by IDEA supports the notion of families being integral to every phase of early intervention, beginning with initial assessment and following through to intervention and monitoring of effectiveness.

Judge (1998) offers strategies for obtaining assistive technology that lead to their effective use that ultimately benefits the young child in need of assistive devices and services. Included in her suggestions are a) Match the device to child and family needs, strengths and resources; b) Gather all the information possible about the device; c) Obtain a comprehensive evaluation that uses a team approach; d) Borrow assistive devices for a trial period before purchasing them; e) Seek out funding sources; f) Provide adequate training in using the device for the child, family, and professionals involved.

FAMILY NEEDS, STRENGTHS, AND RESOURCES

Families should be interviewed and consulted regarding their long term as well as short term goals for the child in choosing assistive technology equipment. The team should consider the child's current level of functioning in making decisions about appropriate assistive technology that is a good fit for the child, taking into account the child's gross and fine motor abilities, cognitive skills, and communication skills, as this is important information in choosing assistive technology that is usable and beneficial to the individual child (Judge & Parette, 1998). Equally important is consideration of features of the assistive technology devices being considered, such as potential to increase performance levels, durability, compatibility with other devices, safety features, and repair considerations (Judge & Parette, 1998).

Goode (2005) reminded educators to consider how the culture, ethnicity, and socioeconomic backgrounds of families impact their decisions regarding the desire to obtain and use assistive technology devices. Studies have highlighted how specific cultural backgrounds often influence family attitudes (Hourcade, Parette, & Huer, 1997; Judge, Parette, 1998; Parette, 1997; Parette & Petch-Hogan) and how professionals must show sensitivity to families in making recommendations. For instance, while Caucasian families tend to be more accepting of assistive technology for their children with disabilities, many African-American families are not comfortable with the public attention drawn by the use of it. Native American and Asian families sometimes value dependence to a larger degree than Caucasian families, which leads to a difference in acceptability of assistive technology. Finally, families of low socioeconomic backgrounds have urgent issues with providing daily needs, making it difficult to participate in meetings important to the successful usability of assistive technology devices and services (Goode, 2005).

Parette & McMahan (2002) describe family concerns that often arise at initial assessment meetings and subsequent sessions in the process of providing assistive technology devices and services for young children. They suggest three questions (pp. 57-60) that teams should ask of families in planning for assistive technology: a) What are the family's expectations for child independence; b) To what extent does the family want the child accepted by others; c) What are the family's expectations regarding immediacy of benefits; and d) What are family resource commitments to the implementation of assistive technology? These are all crucial questions in meeting IEP team goals, because asking them can help IEP teams respond in ways that better lead to success in assistive technology effectiveness. To illustrate, teams should commit to celebrating small successes with families who express a high expectation of immediate benefits to assistive technology. They can benefit from help with organizing their time and outlining how they will commit to the training and use of assistive techniques (p. 58). Similarly, families without resources to commit to the process will need a lot of guidance in the acquisition of devices, including devices on loan. These families will need counseling regarding the timeline that is normally required for funding devices (p. 59).

INFORMATION GATHERING

Many good resources are available that can offer guidance in making good decisions regarding the availability of assistive technology. Table 2 outlines some reputable sources that can be helpful to teachers and families in matching the needs of individual children with various types of assistive technology devices and services.

ISSUES, CONTROVERSIES, AND PROBLEMS

Comprehensive Evaluation

A full evaluation using a transdisciplinary team approach that includes the family is necessary to adequately and ethically choose appropriate assistive technology devices and services for individual children. Ulman (2005) offers specific guidance for teachers to use in documenting evidence for the IEP team to consider: watch the study carefully to determine what things he or she is unable to do; listen to the student to find out what they would like to do but are unable to do, and about their needs and preferences; identify the goals for the child. It is also important to consider the child's strengths when trying to determine what type of technology is appropriate for children with special needs, because this information can be helpful in determining which types of technology are more

Table 2. Assistive technology resources related to technology and children with disabilities

Name of Organization	Contact Information	Description of Services
Alliance for Technology Access	www.ataccess.org	Works in partnership with technology vendors, families, professionals, and persons with disabilities.
Assistive Technology Centers or Resource Programs	Contact various State Depts of Education	Offer loan programs, evaluations, and training.
Closing the Gap	www.closingthegap.com	Offers workshops, consultations, annual international conference, and annual resource directory that is a guide to purchasing computer related products and services.
Council for Exceptional Children – Division of Technology and Media	www.tamcec.org	A division of the Council for Exceptional Children whose mission is to support individuals with disabilities through the selection, acquisition, and use of technology. Publishes peer-reviewed *Journal of Special Education Technology* highlighting empirical studies and information regarding assistive technology.
National Assistive Technology Technical Assistance Partnership (NATTAP)	www.resna.org	A cooperative agreement between U.S. Dept of Education and Rehabilitation Engineering and Assistive Technology Society of North America (RESNA). Offers information regarding assistive technology including individual contact information for all state assistive technology programs.

likely to work and promote a positive response from the child.

Testing Equipment

Loan programs for families and schools to try out equipment are often available through agencies serving those populations through funding from the Technology Act and other sources. It is helpful to take advantage of this service, since equipment and services can be expensive. Implementing the use of a device on a trial basis sometimes can mean avoiding investing in equipment that either will not work well or does not meet the interests and goals of the child.

Funding

Through the Tech Act of 1998, each state and U.S. territory received funding to provide assistive technology devices and services to people who need them. Limited knowledge on the part of teachers and parents regarding how to access services, as well as ineffective training in using the devices, can lead to an underuse of available resources and abandonment of the devices and services once they are received. The section below is intended to offer guidance to teachers and families of young children with disabilities in learning to access needed technological services and devices.

Many states offer technological access centers which can be located by contacting state departments of education. In some states, technological resources are available through Alliance for Technology Access (ATA) Centers. Some states offer funding programs such as low interest loans, equipment borrowing programs, and equipment exchanges (http://www.abledata.com/abledata_docs/funding.htm).

When assistive devices and services are needed in order for a child to receive a free and appropriate public education, the Individuals with Disabilities Education Improvement Act (2004) requires that school districts provide the funding for such needed devices and services. In order to qualify for such funding, the assistive technology must be needed in order to accomplish academic and educational goals.

Other sources of funding could include private insurance, workers' compensation, disability insurance, Medicaid, Medicare, or other state or local agencies. Medicaid is a national program which provides medical assistance for the poor, including people with disabilities. If durable medical equipment is considered to be medically necessary, then Medicaid will purchase, rent or lease it. In order to be medically necessary, the equipment "must be prescribed by a physician, related to a medical condition, expected to provide therapeutic benefit, and restore or approximate normal function of a body part" (Alliance for Technology Access, p. 112-113). Various state and local agencies often provide assistive technology assistance, such as agencies for the blind or visually impaired, agencies for the hearing impaired, and agencies serving people who are developmentally delayed.

Medicare is similar to Medicaid in that it is a federally funded program, and that it will sometimes purchase assistive equipment devices "when they are prescribed by a physician, supplied by a Medicare provider, and medically necessary" (p. 113).

Ulman (2005) encourages IEP teams to, in the spirit of the least restrictive environment aspect of IDEA, "select the least restrictive assistive technology adaptation" (p. 123) when choosing devices to support children with disabilities. This means choosing the adaptation that is as close to what children without disabilities are using, which typically is also the least expensive, easiest to learn to use, to repair, and to replace.

Training

Adequate training in the use of the assistive technology device is critical to its effectiveness. Without adequate training, abandonment of the device is common. To illustrate, several studies suggest that the use of augmentative communication devices by preschoolers is not effective for many of the children using them, partly due to the ineffective level of training received by the child and other stakeholders (Judge & Lahm, 1998). Access to technological devices is not enough; young children need "frequent examples

of interactive use of the augmentative alternative communication [system] in natural settings" (p. 36), such as play based activities naturally occurring in the classroom.

In order to keep up with ongoing demands of technology, adequate training for teachers and other service providers is critical. The integration of technology across the curriculum takes genuine commitment of a teacher's time, effort, and sometimes even a change in belief (Clements, 2004), and it is crucial that those interested in meeting the needs of children with assistive technology needs are support in what can be a frustrating and confusing endeavor.

CONCLUSION

Time spent in the early childhood classroom is precious for all children. Each child's contribution is important and valuable to the overall functioning of the school community, and as Male (2003) so aptly stated, for the child with disabilities "time is more precious and more limited; technology may be the only way an idea or need can be expressed" (p. 5). Assistive technology is far reaching; not only does it include access to computer technology, a wide variety of other assistive devices and services enhance the development of young children with disabilities in all areas of development, including cognitive development, language support, physical development and mobility, and perhaps most importantly, social and emotional competence. In order to feel connected to the classroom community, all children need to genuinely be involved in the activities, conversations, and discovery taking place there. Assisting every child to become competent and connected (Albert, 1996) is helpful not only to the child with disabilities, but to their typically developing peers, as well, as all children have much to share and teach one another. In classrooms that promote unity and acceptance for everyone, teachers are committed to providing the supports that are needed for *all* children to grow and contribute to the overall classroom community. When teachers can be instrumental in modeling and passing on the attitude of inclusion that goes beyond the physical presence of children with disabilities in the early childhood classroom to include genuine involvement in the school family, they have given to the children in their care a great gift that will be life changing for all.

SOME QUESTIONS FOR REFLECTIVE PRACTITIONERS

1. Much controversy surrounds the rights of special needs children in the classroom. One issues deals with the rights of the few verses the rights of the many. It is sometimes perceived by parents that money spent on assistive technology in classrooms takes money away from the general population of children. How can this issue be addressed with the parents in your classroom?

2. Should the government mandate the approach to working with special needs children? Why or why not?

3. How will these laws be implemented in your classroom to insure you are in compliance with all regulations? How can technology help teachers meet the accountability laws and standards?

4. Assistive technology is expensive. Should parents of special needs children pay for assistive technology? Should school districts pay for the needed technology? Who should be accountable for the funding needed for these tools and why?

5. It is believed that assistive technology helps special needs children increase cognitive development. This is contradictory to many early childhood educators beliefs about the effect of technology on cognitive growth. How could these two opposing beliefs influence the use of technology in classrooms?

6. One of the most obvious ways that assistive technology is used to promote language development is through the use of augmentative and alternative communication devices. Should these tools be limited to only special needs children? How might these tools help other children develop language skills?

7. Should the classroom teacher be responsible for monitoring and assistive technology for physical needs children? How can one person manage a classroom full of children and still insure physical needs children are given the opportunity to participate in instructional activities that enhance physical development?

8. How could you structure your classroom environment to ensure social development is supported for special needs children?

9. Should early childhood degrees include increased special education coursework or should these professionals earn two degrees? What kinds of training should early childhood teachers receive in order to best deal with special needs children in their classrooms?

10. How will you, as a teacher, address cultural differences among your parents concerning assistive technology?

11. It is important that you explore your attitudes towards special needs children. What obstacles to your teaching do you anticipate from having assistive technology in your classroom?

12. What benefits to your teaching do you see from having assistive technology in your classroom?

REFERENCES

Albert, L. (1996). *Cooperative discipline*. Shoreview, MN: AGS Publishing.

Alliance for Technology Access. (2004). *Computer resources for people with disabilities: A guide to assistive technologies, tools and resources for people of all ages.* (4th ed.) Alameda, CA: Hunter House, Inc.

Americans with Disabilities Act of 1990, 42 U.S.C.A. 12101.

Bailey, B. A. (2001). *Conscious discipline: Seven basic skills for brain smart classroom management.* (Rev. Ed.) Oviedo, FL: Loving Guidance.

Charney, R. (2002). *Teaching children to care: Classroom management for ethical and academic growth.* (Rev. ed.). Greenfield, MA: Northeast Foundation for Children.

Clements, D. H. (2004). Young children and technology. In K.M. Paciorek & J.H. Munro (Eds.) *Annual Editions: Early Childhood Education* (24th ed.). Guilford, CT: McGraw-Hill.

Clements, D. H., & Sarama, J. (2002). The role of technology in early childhood learning. *Teaching Children Mathematics, 8*(6), 340–346.

Cooper, M. (2005). *Bound and determined to help children with learning disabilities succeed.* Weston, MA: Learning Disabilities Worldwide.

Crow, R. (2007). *You ought to be in pictures: Using behavior picture stories with preschoolers with challenging behaviors.* Paper presented at Annual Conference of the Southern Early Childhood Association, Jacksonville, Florida

Edyburn, D. L. (2003). *What every teacher should know about assistive technology.* Allyn and Bacon Smart Series. Boston, MA: Allyn and Bacon.

Goode, S. (2006). Assistive technology and diversity issues. *Topics in Early Childhood Special Education, 26*(1), 51–54. doi:10.1177/02711214 060260010501

Gray, C. (2000). *The new social story book.* Arlington, TX: Future Horizons.

Hamm, E. M., Mistrett, S. G., & Ruffino, A. G. (2006). Play outcomes and satisfaction with toys and technology of young children with special needs. *Journal of Special Education Technology, 21*(1), 29–34.

Hardman, M. J., Drew, C. J., & Egan, M. W. (2008). *Human exceptionality: School, community and family.* (5th ed.) Boston, MA: Houghton Mifflin.

Haugland, S. (1992). The effect of computer software on preschool children's developmental gains. *Journal of Computing in Childhood Education, 3*(1), 15–30.

Haugland, S., & Wright, J. (1997). *Young children and technology: A world of discovery.* New York: Allyn & Bacon.

Haugland, S. W. (2005). Selecting or upgrading software and web sites in the classroom. *Early Childhood Education Journal, 32*(5), 329–340. doi:10.1007/s10643-005-4401-9

Hess, J., Gutierrez, A. M., Peters, J., & Cerreta, A. (2005). *Family information guide to assistive technology.* Washington, D.C.: United States Department of Education Office of Special Education Programs (OSEP).

Hourcade, J. J., Parette, H. P., & Huer, M. B. (1997). Family and cultural alert! Considerations in assistive technology assessment. *Exceptional Children, 30*(1), 40–44.

Howard, J., Greyrose, E., Kehr, K., Espinosa, M., & Beckwith, L. (1996). Teacher- facilitated microcomputer activities: Enhancing social play and affect in young children with disabilities. *Journal of Special Education Technology, 13*(1), 37–47.

Hutinger, P., & Johanson, J. (1998). Software for young children. In S.L. Judge & H.P. Parette (Eds.), *Assistive technology for young children with disabilities* (pp. 76- 126). Cambridge, MA: Brookline Books.

Individuals with Disabilities Education Improvement Act of 2004, Pub. L. No. 108-446, 118, STAT. 2647 (2006).

Judge, S. (2006). Constructing an assistive technology toolkit for young children: Views from the field. *Journal of Special Education Technology*, *21*(4), 17–24.

Judge, S. L. (1998). Providing access to assistive technology for young children and families. In S.L. Judge & H.P. Parette (Eds.), *Assistive technology for young children with disabilities* (pp. 1-15). Cambridge, MA: Brookline Books.

Judge, S. L., & Lahm, E. A. (1998). Assistive technology applications for play, mobility, communication, and learning for young children with disabilities. In S.L. Judge & H.P. Parette (Eds.), *Assistive technology for young children with disabilities* (pp. 16-44). Cambridge, MA: Brookline Books.

Judge, S. L., & Parette, H. P. (1998). Assistive technology decision-making strategies. In S.L. mJudge & H.P. Parette (Eds.), *Assistive technology for young children with disabilities* (pp.127-147). Cambridge, MA: Brookline Books.

Judge, S. L., & Parette, H. P. (1998). Family-centered assistive technology decision making in infant-toddler intervention. *The Transdisciplinary Journal*, *8*(2), 185–206.

Lesar, S. (1998). Use of assistive technology with young children with disabilities: Current status and training needs. *Journal of Early Intervention*, *21*, 146–159. doi:10.1177/105381519802100207

Male, M. (2003). *Technology for inclusion: Meeting the special needs of all students*. Boston, MA: Allyn & Bacon.

Meyer, A., & Rose, D. H. (2000). Universal design for individual differences (2000). *Educational Leadership*, *58*(3), 39–43.

Munoz, J. P. (1986). The significance of fostering play development in handicapped children. In *Play: A skill for life* (pp. 1-12). Rockville, MD: American Occupational Therapy Association.

National Association for the Education of Young Children. (1996). *Technology and young children – Ages 3 through 8: A position statement of the National Association for the Education of Young Children*. Washington, D.C.: NAEYC.

Nelsen, J. (1996). *Positive discipline*. New York: Ballantine Books.

Olson, J. L., Platt, J. C., & Dieker, L. A. (2008). *Teaching children and adolescents with special needs*. (5th ed.) Upper Saddle River, NJ: Pearson.

Parette, H. P. (1997). Family-centered practice and computers for children with disabilities. *Early Childhood Education Journal*, *25*(1), 53–55. doi:10.1023/A:1025690032730

Parette, H. P., & Petch-Hogan, B. (2000). Approaching families: Facilitating culturally/linguistically diverse family involvement. *Exceptional Children*, *33*(2), 4–10.

Parette, P., & McMahan, G. A. (2002). What should we expect of assistive technology? Being sensitive to family goals. *Teaching Exceptional Children*, *35*(1), 56–61.

Piaget, J. (1962). *Play, dreams, and imitation in childhood*. New York: Norton.

Polloway, E. A., Patton, J. R., & Serna, L. (2008). *Strategies for teaching learners with special needs*. (9th ed.). Upper Saddle River: New Jersey.

Rao, S. M., & Gagie, B. (2006). Learning through seeing and doing: Visual supports for children with autism. *Teaching Exceptional Children*, *38*(6), 26–33.

Rose, D., & Meyer, A. (2000). Universal design for learning. *Journal of Special Education Technology, 15*(1), 67–70.

Skau, L., & Cascella, P. W. (2006). Using assistive technology to foster speech and language skills at home and in preschool. *Teaching Exceptional Children, 38*(6), 12–17.

Spiegel-McGill, P., Zippiroli, S., & Mistrett, S. (1989). Microcomputers as social facilitators in integrated preschools. *Journal of Early Intervention, 13*(3), 249–260. doi:10.1177/105381518901300306

Technology Related Assistance for Individuals with Disabilities Act of 1998. 20 U.S.C. 1401[1].

Ulman, J. G. (2005). *Making technology work for learners with special needs: Practical skills for teachers.* Boston, MA: Allyn and Bacon.

Weikle, B., & Hadadian, A. (2003). Can assistive technology help us to not leave any child behind? *Preventing School Failure, 47*(4), 181–194.

Wershing, A., & Symington, L. (1998). Learning and growing with assistive technology. Judge & H.P. Parette (Eds.), *Assistive technology for young children with disabilities* (pp. 45-75). Cambridge, MA: Brookline Books.

Chapter 7
Applications of Technology for Instruction and Assessment with Young Children

Lee Allen
University of Memphis, USA

Sally Blake
University of Memphis, USA

ABSTRACT

This chapter discusses the roles of technology in instruction and assessment of young children. The influx of technology in schools and homes has been rapid and wide spread. Most children today have seen or used a computer or other technological tool before they enter school. As the student-to-computer ratio has improved from 60-to-1 in 1983 (OTA, 1988) to an average 4-to-1 nationwide in 2007 (Nagel, 2007) the question is no longer whether computers can assist in early childhood learning in general, but rather how computers can and should be used and to what end (Johnson, 1998; Cuban, 2001).

INTRODUCTION

This chapter has been a collaborative effort between two authors whose expertise are Instructional Technology (IT) and Early Childhood (EC). This team provides perspectives from both fields. The IT author is faculty in an IT program and has many years of experience in schools. The Early Childhood contributor was a kindergarten teacher for seventeen years before returning to earn a terminal degree in Curriculum and Instruction with a focus on early childhood mathematics and science. She was a self-confessed "techno phobe" or someone

who was resistive to technology (computer) use in general and more specifically in an Early Childhood Educational Environment. In this chapter we will explore current use of different forms of technology in early childhood classrooms and discuss some of the problems we have encountered in technology use with a focus on computers. We will discuss three main issues associated with instruction and assessment with young children: developmentally appropriate use of computers, instructional use of computers and equity issues.

The first section of this chapter will be an overview of technology instruction and assessment through the lenses of two distinct purposes: Use of technology in assessments and assessing children's

DOI: 10.4018/978-1-60566-784-3.ch007

use of technology. The questions that arise from this focus are the following:

- What are the roles of technology in instruction and assessment of young children?
- How can teachers of young children use technology for instruction and assessment of individuals and programs?

The next section of this chapter will explore some issues and problems with technology use for instruction and assessment in Early Childhood programs. These issues are impacting the use of technology in the United States classrooms and have a direct relationship to the acceptance of educational technology. In this section we have also included possible solutions or information to help educators better understand how to address these problems.

The culture of learning is dramatically different for children today. There was a time when teachers and textbooks were the gatekeepers of knowledge, but now much of the world's knowledge is accessible to any student who can turn on a computer and log on to the internet. (Renzulli, 2007).

The digital age…is changing the nature of knowledge and even the meaning itself. We are entering the age where to understand something is to see how it isn't what it is…Information Communication Technologies (ICT) are best seen in terms of how one might, in a given educational community, engage in problem solving for more effective teaching and learning in ways that are enhanced by ever-evolving tools of the digital age. (Brogden & Couros, 2007, p.34)

Technological artifacts are products of an economy, a force for economic growth, and a large part of everyday life. Technological innovations affect, and are affected by, a society's cultural traditions. Newer technologies such as laptop computers, cell phones, digital cameras, and PDAs, along with new communication vehicles such as blogging, wikis, and interactive role-playing virtual environments are changing the classroom environment both physically and conceptually. Schools are approaching near-universal access to the Internet via wireless routing and increasing the use of teaching tools as conduits for Web-based research and encouraging the development of higher order thinking skills. The transformation of intellectual inquiry brought about by the presence of computers and other information technologies in preschool settings is changing the thinking in regard to the role and importance of technology in early childhood education.

With the increased emphasis on assessment accountability in U.S. education today, it is not surprising to find that there is increasing interest in determining how technologies can be used to improve and assess teaching and learning. Educational assessments serve a variety of purposes and yield different kinds of results. Sometimes computer technology is used as a diagnostic function, as in the identification of children with special needs. At other times, technology is used to research young children's thinking as in brain research and cognitive reactions studies. Computer based content assessments are beginning to be utilized in many Early Childhood programs such as Head Start. For example, a now common method of assessing kindergarten students' reading skills and comprehension levels is the use of programs that require students to interact with a computer interface as the software records the students' responses. Instructional use often includes use of software programs that require children to match and identify different objects. While these programs are becoming common in school environments we have to ask is this quasi-robotic approach to instruction and assessment really an example of the effective use of the technological tools available to educators today?

BACKGROUND

Use of Technology in Early Childhood Learning: Web Interfaces and Cognitive Development

Due to the proliferation of computers in early childhood learning environments since the 1990s, recent studies have focused on the use of computers and other technologies with increasingly younger subjects. The research has centered primarily on what impact, if any, can be attributed to the regular exposure of young children to computer or Web-based programs and other technologies (Haugland, 2000). From developmental concerns (Chang, 2001) to the benefits of toddlers interacting with specific computer software (Ellis & Blashki, 2004), an increasing number of studies are assisting researchers and early childhood professionals in gathering information on how younger children learn by using technology either as a component of or catalyst for learning, or as a tool used in measuring learning (Haugland, 1997).

As the use of the Internet/World Wide Web becomes an intrinsic component of the educational environment questions arise as to the propriety of specific websites as resources for children, especially younger children. Many parents and teachers likely would not have a problem with a child accessing Disney.com or using Google to search for online resources. But how many are aware that an innocent and perhaps inadvertent click on an advertising pop-up appearing on the website could lead to an adult-oriented website with content utterly inappropriate for children of any age, as well as many adults? Educational institutions, along with commercial Internet providers, are accommodating such fears by providing filtering software to catch such online transgressions. In addition, an entire cottage industry has arisen to provide child-oriented websites with content that, while entertaining enough to hold a toddler's attention span, propose to offer some instructional or educational value (Kearsley, 2000).

Harbeck and Sherman (1999) provided guidelines for website designers in keeping with appropriate developmental benchmarks. Among these, the concepts of usability and navigability for younger learners are key issues, along with the recommendation that an adult appropriately guide the child's interactions with the website. This finding resembles the debates created by the introduction of television in another era, yet is somewhat mitigated by the fact that passive viewing cannot be exactly replicated due to the interactive nature of the World Wide Web. The aspect of visual and tactile interaction with a computer screen presents its own set of problems for the learner; as per Mayer and Moreno (2003), a "challenge for designers of multimedia instruction is the potential for cognitive overload, in which the learner's intended cognitive processing exceeds the learner's *available cognitive capacity*" (p. 24). This would appear to present an obvious factor to consider when involving young children with interactive websites for the purpose of learning. Indeed, a study in the use of computers by young children demonstrated that parental involvement is directly related to the children's cognitive development (McCarrick et al, 2007). In a more recent study by some of these same researchers, the results obtained suggested that computer use by children enrolled in a Head Start program in Detroit, MI could be positively correlated with certain aspects of cognitive development (Fish et al, 2008). However, the results of the study also suggested that the use of the computer in the children's home exerted a positive influence on the children's overall cognitive development, again raising the issue of defining variables in this type of research.

Similarly, a recent study involving the use of digital video cameras mounted on or near the computer screen (commonly referred to as Web cams) with students age 5-8 again demonstrated that adult interaction with the young learner greatly enhanced the positive aspects of the Web cam technology, which can be used as both an interactive assessment tool as well as an exploratory vehicle for children engaging with others at a distance, facilitated by the technology (Hastie, Chen, & Kuo,2007).

Technology and Early Childhood: Special Needs

The use of technology with learners who have special needs is most often associated with assistive technology (AT), which has been defined in the Technology Related Assistance to Individuals with Disabilities act of 1988 as "any item, piece of equipment, or product system whether acquired commercially off the shelf, modified, or customized, that is used to increase, maintain, or improve functional capabilities of individuals with disabilities." The adaptation of assistive technologies to accommodate younger children's special needs, along with the associated cognitive development issues, is central to understanding how such technologies can be most successfully implemented to achieve maximum benefit for the young learner.

The types of technologies that can be considered as "assistive" range from simple on/off switches indicating simple responses to complicated hardware systems that allow the learner to interact via computer-generated voice synthesis processes. There are other, less readily identifiable types of learning tools for children, in addition to those designed for teachers' use that can be placed in the category of assistive technology. As per Behrmann (1998), "this is true for individual children with disabilities whose disability has a primary impact on academic performance (e.g., learning disabilities) or functional performance (e.g., multiple physical and visual disabilities)" (p. 83). Once again, the definition of a type of technology cannot always be exclusively relegated into a single classification; just as teaching and learning itself is often best accomplished by individualizing instruction based on specific, circumstantial, and situational needs. Providing a comprehensive as-

sessment of technologies specifically designed to be used with young special needs learners requires that the technologies discussed be those that are readily identified as serving the purpose of assistive technology as defined by the American with Disabilities Act (ADA) and the Individuals with Disabilities Act (IDEA), with an emphasis on special education.

Experts in the field of early childhood special education have stated that determining what type of assistive technology is appropriate for a young child is best performed by a team effort that includes the parents as well as educators and other professionals with expertise in assistive technology for special needs children (Robinson, 2007; Hutinger, Robinson & Schneider, 2004). The UNUM Provident insurance company developed an Assistive Technology Decision Tree (1999) and the accompanying Steps to Evaluate Assistive Technology Solutions as a means to assist individuals and employers in determining how best to match assistive technologies with physical or developmental needs. Although primarily targeting the workplace environment in accommodating disabilities of employees, the recommended steps can be adapted to almost any situation where a special need can be matched with an assistive device or technology, because the root of the decision tree lies in correctly diagnosing the problem or difficulty first, and then identifying the potential AT solution. The steps therefore provide a useful guide in diagnosing a need and the corresponding AT required. In summary, the six essential steps in the process (slightly modified for the purposes identified) are progressive in nature and identified in the following:

1. Identify and define the special needs that require addressing (e.g., fine or gross motor control, attention span, etc.) and recognize that the special need is not the issue in and of itself. The issue arises due to the conflict between the traditional methods of accomplishing tasks and what is required to

accomplish the same task by a learner with special needs. This discernment can resolve the question as to whether the tasks can be accomplished by means other than those used by most children.

2. Modify the task itself. AT should not be the deemed as the automatic solution unless all other factors are considered beforehand, such as whether visual cues can enhance audible ones.

3. Modify the environment. If the environment in which the task is to be accomplished can be altered slightly (e.g., addition of handrails, external support, etc.) then such solutions should be investigated.

4. Identify if hardware or software is already available that can be applied. Often, existing solutions can be adapted or only slightly modified to accommodate a special need without additional equipment (i.e., many software companies such as Microsoft and Apple incorporate voice recognition into their operating systems).

5. Research commonly available specialized software or hardware. Specially-designed keyboard and mouse configurations and touch-sensitive screens, along with highly advanced voice recognition software are available readily via suppliers of computer peripherals and software packages.

6. Locate providers of specialized solutions that can be adapted or modified to assist the special needs learner. Often, commercial providers of AT devices, hardware, and software will work directly with a potential client in insuring that a product will meet or can be modified sufficiently to accommodate the special needs. (Adapted from UNUM Provident, 1999)

As is shown from the sequential nature of the steps in assessing how best to address a special needs learner via AT or other, there are several avenues for those assisting the learner aside from

immediately resorting to highly specialized, and often costly, solutions. In addition, the executive director for the Division for Early Childhood of the Council for Exceptional Children, states:

We must consider the level of technology necessary for the child to fully participate, what technology is best suited to the child's needs and abilities, and what can reasonably be used in the environment given available space and resources. Before investing in sophisticated, high-tech devices, we should explore less intrusive yet effective low-tech alternatives" (Mulligan, 2003, p.50); and "Even the most sophisticated device won't help unless it matches the child's abilities and the demands of the environment. (Ibid., p.51)

The assessment and evaluation of what assistive technologies can best be used in effectively supporting young learners with special needs is thus dependent on multiple variables; all of which can and should be addressed *prior* to initiating the decision process in determining what, if any, AT should be applied in assisting the learner. Chapter 6 has more detailed information about how assistive technology is used with young children.

Practical Applications of Technology in Early Childhood

Toward the end of matching young learners to appropriate technologies, the study conducted by Hutinger and Johnson (2000) concluded that "technology applications alone are not enough to ensure that children engage in the most appropriate technology experiences" (p.171). The researchers further pointed out that a lack of support services provided on a continuing basis would result in only short term results, and that surrounding variables such as teacher, staff, and parental training and participation are all key elements in continuing success for technology implementations. Such findings are consistent with practically all analyses of technology-induced changes in curriculum delivery (Kerr, 1996; Zhao et al, 2001; Barron et al, 2003; Trinkle, 2005), with the teacher's technological proficiency playing a primary role in successfully implementing technology in the classroom, regardless of age group or grade level.

In using technology with the youngest of learners, practitioners in the classroom have found that technology has found uses in enhancing learning in four major modes of instructional delivery: teacher-directed instruction, using the Internet for research, independent learning on either stand-alone computers, or integrated learning systems, and in cooperative learning (Schwalje, 2001). It is in the area of cooperative learning that most advocates of constructivist teaching and learning have found common ground with the advocates of instructional technology: it has been found that in using technology, cooperative learning "fosters the development of leadership, teamwork, and group pride" and that children "learned to communicate, plan together, make decisions, consult, share responsibilities, and teach each other" (*Ibid.*, p.41).

In assessing young learners' uses of technology, researchers have found it is probable that a child's first encounter with computers and other technologies will occur in the early childhood education setting, e.g., pre-school, or in some cases, instructionally-oriented day care settings, with the first interactions likely involving such "input devices" as the computer mouse, ball or joystick controller, touch screen, touch pad, or keyboard (Wood et al, 2004). In the 2004 study, Woods et al concluded that

Clearly, other factors also are important in predicting children's successful use of the input devices. It will be important to consider other context-specific factors (such as motivation and attention) and cognitive factors (such as working memory) that might impact on their ability to use the different input devices. In summary, although each of the devices may have its own merits, the

mouse and the EZ ball may prove to be the least expensive and most accessible devices to have available to introduce computer technology in the ECE setting. (p.279)

Again, as in evaluating the use of the Web, computer interfaces, and assistive technology with young learners, "other factors" or environmental variables enter the overall picture when assessing the use of computer input devices; which are, after all, forms of interfacing with a computer or other types of technology. One common theme is found in identifying the developmentally appropriate stage that is often considered as a factor when introducing younger children to technologies. A study by Li and Atkins (2004) suggested that no relationship exists "between computer accessibility and visual motor or gross motor skills among the participating children" (p. 1721). The researchers also found that the frequency of access and availability of technologies in the home did not confirm such a relationship. The data in the study thus did not suggest a causal relationship between computer experience and visual motor or gross motor skills among the participating children, essentially confounding the notion that use of technologies are intrinsically linked with cognitive development, either as indicators or in enhancing skills and learning. However, in the same study, the researchers did find that "children who had access to a computer performed better on school readiness and cognitive development, suggesting that computer access before or during the preschool years is associated with the development of preschool concepts and cognition" (p. 1721).

The finding only adds to the existing questions as to the appropriate purpose, rather than the timing, of using technology with children, and to the significance of the variable of home access to computers and technologies. Such questions drive the continuous search for new meaning and new purposes of incorporating in our children's lives, whether via education or in everyday experiences. Commercially available digital toys for toddlers and baby activity centers, complete with interactive lights and sound, abound, while census numbers indicate that approximately 25% of the U.S. population has access to a computer at home, and many more have access to a computer and Internet at work or in libraries, community centers etc.(McNeely, 2005). The search for the appropriate use of technology and its incorporation into the developmental and learning processes of young children will continue to fascinate and perplex early childhood researchers, teachers, and parents alike, as the known boundaries of the technological frontiers continue to expand into the 21st century.

Individual Student and Group Instruction and Assessment

The nature of children's growth, development, and learning is fast paced, episodic and marked by enormous variability (Johnson, 1998). One assessment instrument cannot by itself, capture the complexity of a child's understanding. Evaluation should be based on multiple forms of evidence from many sources. Through use of technology children make choices, voice ideas, and perform various activities involving technology. In early childhood settings children might demonstrate their ideas and interest through their conversations, their questions, their interactions, and the work produced or artifacts. This is the evidence of learning that teachers rely upon when assessing the value of activity as meaningful for children's learning. The richer the instructional environment, the broader the potential range of evidence for assessing learning (Bredekamp and Rosegrant, 1995).

Young children's thinking reflects both development and experiential factors. Children need time to revisit interesting ideas, opportunities to ask the same question repeatedly in new and different ways. Computer programs should support this approach to thinking. The development of

thought is not linear or necessarily sequential but rather marked by detours and explorations (Chittenden and Jones, 1998). The children's ongoing behaviors and their work fall under the teacher's everyday observations, records, and evaluations. The goal of assessment is to collect records that reflect the child's developmental progress (Brendekamp & Rosegrant, 1995). This requires a series of artifacts that reflect what the child can do and the thinking process that develops. Artifacts can and should be developed through technology. Technology can allow for a broader array of assessment tools for use in classrooms.

As the use of technology increases, new and varied instruction and assessment issues arise. A recent statement of principles and recommendations for early childhood assessment, prepared by the advisory group for the National Education Goals Panel accentuates the importance of differentiating purposes of assessment (Shepard et al, 1997); to summarize, the *purposes* should determine the content of the assessment. Misuse of tests and other instruments in early childhood may stem from the confusion of purpose. It is important for teachers to identify their goals and align them with technology. We recommend the following steps for teachers as they develop their applications of technology for instruction and assessment.

Teachers Steps in use of Technology:

1. Develop an Assessment Framework
2. Clearly define your project or goal
3. Evaluate all references (internet sites)
4. Identify resources needed (time teacher or mentor assistance)
5. Balance resources (technology and non-technology)
6. Formative assessment of work and adjust project according to your findings

Evaluation of the appropriate use of technology requires an active role from the teacher or childcare professional. Technology integration is much more than placing a computer into a classroom and giving the teacher some software to use. It is a systematic process that requires time and commitment from principals, teachers, students, and parent. (Gates, 2007). Just having computers in the class does not insure appropriate development of computer skills.

The National Association for the Education of Young Children (NAEYC) identifies the role of the teacher as the gate keeper or technology guide (Brendekamp, 2004). The teacher must make value judgments in any given situation as to the appropriateness, age, individual and cultural appropriateness are the components a professional is charged to monitor. The concern is how to identify and define each of these areas. NAEYC suggest the approach teachers use to select books and assessment tools for their classroom. NAEYC further recommends computer use to support development and learning that are accepted parts of the curriculum. This means teachers must become computer confident in order to develop assessments that address children's needs.

ISSUES, CONTROVERSIES AND PROBLEMS

When considering the use of technology with young children, one issue is raised more often than not: what is the purpose of using technology with young learners, since so many non-technological resources are available? The question requires that one review the developmental goals and milestones that researchers have identified as core components in childhood: social and emotional development; language development; physical well-being and motor development; cognition and general knowledge; and developing approaches to learning (Kagan, Moore, & Bredekamp, 1995). These developmental goals should be considered when technologies are appropriately introduced according to the developmental stage of the learner. According to a report released by the Northwest

Regional Educational Laboratory (NWREL), use of technology should rely on the needs of the young learner, the focus of the learning opportunities, and whether the technologies will enhance learning opportunities and experiences for the child (Van Scoter, Ellis, & Railsback, 2001). As with other considerations in early childhood education, the age and developmental stage of the learner should be taken into account when considering use of technologies. According to the NWREL researchers the two primary questions to be asked when considering young learners' use of technologies are: Is the technology developmentally appropriate and consistent with the child's developmental stage; and, critically, what *benefit* will the child derive from the use of the technology. (*Ibid.*, p. 14)

Childhood Development: Developmentally Appropriate Practice

Many early childhood professionals in the United States still believe that computers are not appropriate for young children (Alliance of Children, 2007). They argue that there is little evidence to support that computers in schools have improved learning at this point in time. In fact these anti-technology supporters provide a strong argument as to the potential harm of computer use in education. Let's explore their thinking and see if we can find ways to address these issues. "The national drive to computerize schools, from kindergarten up, emphasizes only one of many human capabilities, one that naturally develops quite late-analytic, abstract thinking_aims to jump start prematurely" (Cordes & Miller,1999, p. 19).

It is true that research in child development over the past 60 years has supported the idea that abstract thinking is only found in older children as they mature. This has been accepted in our country and is primarily based on the work of Piaget. The term "Developmentally Appropriate" has become a catch phrase that educators use to defend, justify, and condemn educational practice in early childhood programs. Developmentally appropriate activities are important to support children's growth and development. The concern is what once was accepted during the fifties and sixties may not apply to the changing social environment of a global community. New breakthroughs in research have begun to challenge some of our old notions of children's capabilities.

Three reports from the National Academies address different aspects of education for very young children from a variety of prospects (National Research Council, NRC, 2005). *From Neurons to Neighborhoods: The Science of Early Childhood Development* (National Research Council and Institute of Medicine, 2000) provides a detailed look at the many factors that influence development in very young children. *Eager To Learn: Education Our Preschoolers* (NRC, 2001a) describes the current status of the programs in which young children are educated, setting that description in the context of recent contributions from the field of cognitive science. *Adding It Up: Helping Children Learn Mathematics* (NRC, 2001) closely examines mathematics learning and describes its facets. Each of these reports contributes to an evolving base of evidence that the early learning programs to which students are exposed are extremely important (NRC, 2005). With increased recognition of the intellectual capacities of young children (three- and four-year-olds), as well as a growing understanding of how these capacities develop can be fostered, has come a growing recognition that early childhood education, in both formal and informal settings, may not be helping children maximize their cognitive capacities (NRC, 2005). Other studies by Rochel Gelman and her colleagues have found ways to engage young children in complex scientific thinking using a coherent program that is sustained over extended periods of time. The program is designed as collaboration among researchers and early childhood educators, and it is based on research indicating that young children are capable of

building progressively on knowledge they gain in a particular domain (Gelman & Brenneman, 2004). The key finding from Gelman's work is that children may be capable of scientific thinking far more complex than most casual observers might expect, and than scholars such as Piaget had considered possible.

The introduction of new technologies in education is often cited as being indicative of shallow trendiness and fad mongering. Lamentation continues over the apparent loss of basic mathematical and language skills due to hand-held calculators and word processing software, respectively. One of the first organizations to be recognized as proudly anti-technology for children, the Alliance For Childhood, provides reports to the media based on research indicating questionable practices in the classroom where computers were used. In particular, the research was often used to target the use of technology by younger children, typically in the earliest pre-school and elementary grades. Since it is not at all uncommon to find computers and software created for- and being used by- preschool children and kindergartners in classrooms, the Alliance and other groups with similar agendas quickly found what they believed to be an ethical dilemma: how young was *too* young to have students use computers at school?

In a report titled "Fool's Gold: A Critical Look at Computers in Childhood" by the Alliance for Childhood (1999), an international group of educators, physicians, and others who are concerned about the current environment for children identify concerns about computer use with young children in general which relate to instruction and assessment. Editors Cordes and Miller take a strong stand against computer use with young children, as technology in American classrooms is regarded as a contributing factor for repetitive stress injuries, attention deficit disorder, and even obesity while diverting resources from other priorities identified in the report. Among the many specific concerns raised regarding computer instruction with young children are threats to physical development and health. They believe that young children are at greater risk of injury because their bones, tendons, nerves, muscles and soft tissue are growing, and that computers will contribute to childhood obesity due to the sedentary and passive nature of human-computer interaction. Social and emotional developments are predicted to be damaged due to lack of social interactions with humans. They claim that the decreasing face-to-face interaction with humans will damage societal interactions causing an increase in crime and decrease in empathy. An increased use of computers for instruction may create an imbalance among the traditional components of child development which early childhood professionals believe are necessary for mental health. Claims that intellectual and creative development will be damaged by use of computers with young children are supported in this report. This report paints an ominous picture of negative effects in all areas of child development and implies that technology use for instruction and assessment may actually hurt children's development. A question exemplifying the Alliance's concerns and stance is, "Must five-year-olds be trained on computers today to get the high-paying jobs of tomorrow?" which is later answered by the assertion that "the technology in schools today will be obsolete long before five-year-olds graduate;" the central focal point of their stance is encapsulated in the following pronouncement: "Those who place their faith in technology to solve the problems of education should look more deeply into the needs of children" (Cordes & Miller, 1999, p.4).

This primary ethical concern for the Alliance for Childhood and their adherents is what truly constitutes "the needs of children." From their standpoint, young children should not be surrounded by only virtual tools and environments - a real world exists around them. To direct more effort, and consume more time, in synthetic, artificial environments instead of learning about the natural world is contradictory to what they have identified as supporting sound practices and time-tested theories of early childhood learning (Gelernter, 1994). Again the argument holds validity but we ascertain that a balance of virtual tools and real world experiences is needed to prepare children for the digital communication age. It seems unlikely that any educational program for young children would rely on virtual experiences as an exclusive approach to working with students. Rather the use of virtual environments should be used to supplement and support learning as many opportunities are available through web access that would not be practical through real world experiences.

Reports such as "Fool's Gold" influence the thinking of many educators and build on the techno-phobic fear of the general population. These types of publications are usually written in a manner that appears to be supported by professionals. A closer examination of these prophecies of doom reveals that there is no research to support the statements or claims. The research cited as support documentation is general and rarely applies directly to the issues but address possible problems with technology use. Any technology has potential problems when abused. The key is the teacher and their understanding of how to supplement learning through technology that supports real world experiences. The teacher controls the applications of the real and virtual environment for instruction.

The opposition to the Alliance for Childhood makes equally convincing arguments, as evidenced by the following excerpt from the Department of Education's e-Learning Report published only a year later, in 2000: "All students will benefit from enhanced learning opportunities afforded by new and emerging communications and information technologies...emerging technologies will allow us to develop new content to address evolving conceptions of the skills and knowledge needed to succeed in today's global society" (p. 54). This side of the argument holds validity as more applications of technology for instruction become available and accepted. Refusing to introduce young children in the United States to computers could very well put them at a disadvantage globally. Developing computer skills is like any other form of learning requiring practice and a good self-efficacy in ability to successfully use technology. Beginning use of technology is often superficial as one acquires the basic skills of technical use before moving on to higher order applications. As young children move through the continuum of their educational experiences it would seem logical that they would need to be skillful and secure in computer use in order to benefit from instruction. Students with poor computer skills are at a distinct disadvantage in a modern classroom as they spent time just acclimating to technology use while their more proficient peers spend their time engaged in higher order applications. If information is power that educators would want to help children develop necessary skills to access information. At the very least technology provides numerous opportunities for improved global communication which open opportunities of learning for children.

Controversy surrounding this issues is strong and members of each group believe their thinking is "the best" approach for working with young children. On one thing we should all be able to agree: we acknowledge that there needs to be more research about computer use in educational settings. We must also acknowledge that the applications of technology are hard to generalize due to the fast paced development of new technology. However, it is unlikely that computers can be blamed for all physical and societal problems our children face. Historically new technologies have been met with a fear factor. You may remember when video tapes were introduced to the educational arena. The educational community knew these tapes would replace the human teachers in schools. While this thinking seems ludicrous in this day and age it was a very real fear a few decades ago. While it is true that robots and computers have replaced humans in some jobs, the choice was ours. Technology is not an entity which controls humans but a tool that we control.

Equity Issues

Computer access for children has increased but there still remains a gap of access among the socioeconomic groups in the United States. This "digital divide" is evident in two ways; access to computer equipment and use of computers for instruction. Becker (2000) stated that only about 22% of children in families with incomes of less than $20,000 had access to home computers compared to 91% of those in families with incomes of more than $75,000. Becker further found that lower income students are directed to use computers in schools for repetitive practice while upper-income students are allowed more sophisticated, intellectual complex applications. Forty percent (10.5 million) of children 6 and under are from low income families (identified by income and number of family members) and another twenty percent (5 million) more come from poor families (poverty level income qualifiers) in the United States (Dodge-Hall & Chau, 2007). The population of low-income children is increasing which places more children at risk of limited access to computers. This issue is further compounded by funding formulas in schools where many states base school money on community income or tax-base levels. Schools in low income areas receive less funding than schools in high income areas. Further the No Child Left Behind ([NCLB], 2002) allots school funding on test success. The low income schools consistently have lower test scores than the higher-income schools. (Education Trust, 2004) All of these factors impact schools' use of technology for instruction and assessment.

In the third in a series of reports from the National Telecommunications and Information Administration (1999), the digital divide is defined as the "divide between those with access to new technologies and those without" and "the divide is now one of America's leading economic and civil rights issues." The report went on to state that low-income persons, minorities, the less educated and children of single parent households are among the groups that lack access to information resources. As the 72.5% "technology deprivation" rate for those families identified as low-income cited in the report suggested, computers and Internet access are not available in all homes. Information Administration, 1999) Schools can assist in leveling the playing field by providing the infrastructure and equipment in the classroom, narrowing the digital divide by allowing technology to be accessible to all segments of society. According to the above referenced NTIA report, "information tools, such as personal computers and the Internet are increasingly critical to economic success and personal advancement." One needs only to look at the number of companies that allow job applications to be submitted via the web, colleges that provide information and courses to students online and the exponential growth of e-commerce to see how disparities exist for those who lack access. Public and private education can assist in leveling the playing field by utilizing technology to support the growing needs of students and staff, providing access to global resources, and preparing them for the expectations of a technological society.

The creation and implementation of the so-called E-Rate in 1996, allowing schools and libraries to receive large discounts on telecommunications infrastructure and services to allow "universal access" to the then-newly welcomed "Information Highway" provided additional incentive for schools to increase the technological capacity in the classroom (Wayne, Zucker & Powell, 2002). However, the issue of equity in the distribution of technology is difficult to resolve. It does support the important role that teachers in early childhood programs can play in order to insure *all* children have the opportunity to learn about computers. The public school system in the United States has been challenged to solve many societal problems. This is in part because this institution does have access to a large percentage of the population in our country. The American public education system has been accused of not fulfilling all of its responsibilities for decades.

Rather than blame the federal government, the community, or the family for social and moral problems, the nation blames schools for not educating youngsters and failing to keep youth off the streets. It seems unrealistic to expect teachers to address these issues without a strong infrastructure and support system. If teachers and schools are to be held responsible for the inequity of computer access in the United States it might be time to rethink how teachers are trained and how resources are allotted to schools. Computer communication has the potential to really make educational access equal for all students.

FUTURE TRENDS

It is difficult to predict where technology will move the educational community. Traditionally education has been used to transmit culture, establish societal expectations, and assess what each community values and defines as important learning. Instruction has been based on what different cultures believe young children should know to acculturate in environments that were border bound by political ideologies. Technology has erased these borders by allowing communication across cultural environments starting with the telegraph, telephone and now computer applications. Scientists have long worked in a global community through computers to improve their research without traditional cultural restrictions. Educators of young children now have the opportunity to do the same. The applications for Culturally Appropriate interactions are only limited by our fears and thinking.

We believe that computers are and will be important tools for educators of young children. As the communication applications of technology increase we think that classrooms will change their traditional boundaries of each class within four walls. Teaching could become collaborative efforts among international early childhood professionals. Instructional and assessment practice will

Table 1.

Age	Child's Behavior
Toddlers	Clicking various options to see what will happen next.
Pre-school (3-4-year olds)	Developing confidence in computer explorations. Play enactments. Exploration.
Pre-school-primary	Make choices about computer experiences. Creative projects
Kindergarten and primary	Directed activities to match learning objectives. Creative projects and problem investigation.
Primary and older	Action-oriented problem investigation. Find and focus on creative exploration of personal interest for in-depth exploration. Working with groups on the internet. Advanced-level thinking.

develop an international standard of excellence. This will change the nature and design of early childhood programs. Since computers are not location bound they will be the tools that allow early childhood educators to prepare children to understand and work for a global community. Educators have access to the best approaches to instruction through computer communication. Children will have access to knowledge from all cultures and can develop their potential to compete in a global economy.

We think that computer and technology understanding will become a part of the developmental process of children's growth. Table 1 identifies what we consider possible developmental stages for computer use with children in early childhood programs.

As the variety of technology grows the questions about the appropriate use with young children increases. Technology is a fact and is not going away in the global society. We need to determine how technology can improve learning and how to best prepare our children to use computers. Computer technology has moved faster than most technologies earning world wide acceptance and use. The pace has caught early childhood educators unprepared for classroom applications. How we accept and use this technology will determine the effectiveness for instruction and assessment.

Access to computers and the Internet is necessary for children and teachers to grow up with the information gathering, analytical, and written and graphical communications skills that will constitute "being educated" in the 21st century (Becker, 2000).

CONCLUSION

We hope we have written some ideas to help teachers think about uses of and issues about technology for instruction and assessment with young children. Clearly technology is something that can enhance educational opportunities for children of all ages. As newer and better technology develops it is the role of the educator of young children to determine the appropriate use in their classroom. In order to give all children the opportunity to compete in a global economy technology has become a key to unlock gates of access. The educator has the responsibility to become technology competent and learn to discriminate appropriate from inappropriate applications. We have to keep an open mind about how the knowledge of child development is and could change as society and culture change. The child of today is in many ways very different from the children Piaget worked with and studied. We must also realize how these changes influence the school environment to better address the needs of the modern child.

Technology does hold the potential to bring equal information opportunity to all children regardless of socioeconomic conditions if access is made available. However technology surpasses just socioeconomic status to encompass cultural differences. The potential for sharing knowledge, collaborative projects, and teachers working towards common goals could become global through computer use.

SOME QUESTIONS FOR REFLECTIVE PRACTITIONERS

Practitioners have identified four major modes of instructional delivery that they consider appropriate for classroom use. Think of an activity for your class that would fit under each of these four categories.

1. Teacher-directed instruction
2. Internet research
3. Independent learning
4. Cooperative learning
5. What are the roles of technology in instruction and assessment of young children?
6. How can teachers of young children use technology for instruction and assessment of individuals and programs?
7. When did you first use a computer? What did you think about computers when you first started using one? How have your perceptions changed in the last five years?
8. What types of technology-based children's work might you collect for assessment purposes in your classroom?
9. How will you organize your assessment to insure you have a balance of technology and non-technology documentation?
10. Does technology threaten a child's development? In what ways? Is your thinking supported by research or is it opinion? How will you find good research about child development and technology?
11. How will you address the technology equity gap among the children in your class?
12. What are some of the benefits of technology instruction and assessment that would evident in your work?

REFERENCES

Barron, A. E., Kemker, K., Harmes, C., & Kalaydjian, K. (2003). Large-scale research study on technology in K-12 schools: Technology integration as it relates to the National Technology Standards. *Journal of Research on Technology in Education, 35*(4), 489–507.

Becker, H. J. (2000). Who's wired and who's not: Children's access to and use of computer technology. *Children and Computer Technology, 10*(2), 44–75.

Behrmann, M. (1988). Assistive technology for young children in special education. In C. Dede (Ed.), *Learning with Technology. 1998 ASCD Yearbook* (pp. 73-93). Alexandria, Virginia: Association for Supervision and Curriculum Development.

Brendekamp, S., & Rosegrant, T. (Eds.). (1995). Reaching potentials: Transforming early childhood curriculum and assessment. (Vol. 2). Washington, DC: National Association for the Education of Young Children.

Brogden, L. M., & Couros, A. (2007). Toward a philosophy of technology and education. *The Delta Kappa Gamma Bulletin, 2*(73). Retrieved May 1, 2008, from http://vnweb.hwwilsonweb.com.proxy.lib.odu.edu/hww/results/getResults.jhtml?_DARG S=/hww/results/results_common.jhtml.7#record_6

Cardelle-Elawar, M., & Wetzel, K. (1995). Students and computers as partners in developing students' problem solving skills. *Journal of Research on Computing in Education, 29*(4), 378–401.

Chang, N. (2001). Is it Developmentally Inappropriate to Have Children Work Alone at the Computer? [Norfolk, VA: AACE.]. *Information Technology in Childhood Education Annual, 2001*(1), 247–265.

Chittenden, E., & Jones, J. (1998). *Science assessment in early childhood programs. Dialogue on early childhood science, mathematics, and technology education.* Washington, DC: Project 2061, American Association for the Advancement of Science.

Clements, D. (1998). *Young children and technology. Dialogue on early childhood science, mathematics, and technology education.* Washington, DC: Project 2061, American Association for the Advancement of Science.

Clements, D. H. (1994). The uniqueness of the computer as a learning tool: Insights from research and practice. In J. L. Wright & D.D. Shade (Eds.), *Young Children: Active Learners in a Technological Age.* Washington, DC: NAEYC. ED 380 242.

Cordes, C., & Miller, E. (Eds.). (1999). *Fool's Gold: A Critical Look at Computers in Childhood. Alliance For Childhood.* Retrieved July 11, 2008 from http://www.allianceforchildhood.net/projects/ computers/computers_reports_fools_gold_download.htm

Cuban, L. (2001). *Oversold and underused: Computers in the classroom.* Cambridge, MA: Harvard University Press.

Dodge-Hall, A., & Chau, M. (2007). *Basic facts about low-income families: Birth to age six.* National Center for Children in Poverty. Washington, DC: Columbia University. Mailman School of Public Health.

Education Trust. (2004). Measured Progress. Achievement rises and gaps narrow, but too slowly. Washington, DC: Author.

Ellis, K., & Blashki, K. (2004). Toddler techies: A study of young children's interaction with computers. [Norfolk, VA: AACE.]. *Information Technology in Childhood Education Annual, 2004*(1), 77–96.

Ferdig, R. E. (2006). Assessing technologies for teaching and learning: understanding the importance of technological pedagogical content knowledge. *British Journal of Educational Technology, 37*(5), 749–760. doi:10.1111/j.1467-8535.2006.00559.x

Fish, A. M., Li, X., McCarrick, K., Butler, S. T., Stanton, B., & Brumitt, G. A. (2008). Early Childhood Computer Experience and Cognitive Development among Urban Low-Income Preschoolers. *Journal of Educational Computing Research, 38*(1), 97–113. doi:10.2190/EC.38.1.e

Gates, N. G. (2007). Technology integration for the savvy teacher. Tennessee's Children (pp. 21-23).

Gelernter, D. (1994, September 19-26). Unplugged: The myth of computers in the classroom. *The New Republic* (pp. 14-15).

Gelman, R., & Brenneman (2004). Mathematic and science cognitive development. In *Mathematical and Scientific Development in Early Childhood: A Workshop Summary.* National Academies Press.

Harbeck, J. D., & Sherman, T. M. (1999). Seven principles for designing developmentally appropriate web sites for young children. *Educational Technology, 39*(4), 39–44.

Hastie, M., Chen, N.-S., & Kuo, Y.-H. (2007). Instructional Design for Best Practice in the Synchronous Cyber Classroom. *Educational Technology & Society, 10*(4), 281–294.

Haugland, S. W. (1997). How teachers use computers in early childhood classrooms. *Journal of Computing in Childhood Education, 8*(1), 3–14.

Haugland, S. W. (2000). Early childhood classrooms in the 21st century: Using computers to maximize learning. *Young Children, 55*(1), 12–18.

Hutinger, P., Robinson, L., & Schneider, C. (2004). *Early Childhood Technology Integrated Instructional System (EC-TIIS) Phase 1: A final report*. Macomb, IL: Center for Best Practices in Early Childhood, Western Illinois University. (ERIC Document Reproduction Service No. ED 489166).

Hutinger, P. L., & Johnson, J. (2000). Implementing and maintaining an effective early childhood comprehensive technology system. *Topics in Early Childhood Special Education, 20*(3), 159–173. doi:10.1177/027112140002000305

IDEA. (1997). H.R. 5 Public Law 105-17. U.S.C. Sections 1400-1485 (also known as P.L.94-142). Washington, DC. Johnson, J. (1998*). Perspectives: The dialogue on Early Childhood science, mathematics, an technology education*. Washington, DC: Project 2061, American Association for the Advancement of Science.

Kagan, S. L., Moore, E., & Bredekamp, S. (1995). Reconsidering children's early development and learning: Toward common views and vocabulary. National Education Goals Panel, Goal 1. Technical Planning Group Report, 95-03. Washington, DC: National Education Goals Panel. (ERIC Document Reproduction Service No. ED 391 576).

Kearsley, G. (2000). *Online education: learning and teaching in cyberspace*. Belmont, CA: Wadsworth Publishing

Kerr, S. T. (1996). Toward a sociology of educational technology. In D.H. Jonassen (Ed.), *Handbook of research for educational communications and technology* (pp. 143-169). New York: Simon & Schuster.

Li, X., & Atkins, M. S. (2004). Early Childhood Computer Experience and Cognitive and Motor Development. *Pediatrics, 113*(6), 1715–1722. doi:10.1542/peds.113.6.1715

Lindstrand, P. (2001). Parents of children with disabilities evaluate the importance of the computer in child development. *JSET E. Journal, 16*(2).

Mayer, R. E., & Moreno, R. (2003). Nine ways to reduce cognitive load in multimedia learning. In E.M. Wills, R.H. Bruning, C.A. Horn, & L.M. PytlikZillig (Eds.), *Web-based learning: What do we know? Where do we go?* Greenwich, CT: Information Age Publishing.

McCarrick, K., Li, X., Fish, A., Holtrop, T., Bhavnagri, N.P., Stanton, B., Brumitt, G.A., Butler, S., & Partridge, T. (2007). *Parental involvement in young children's computer use and cognitive development, 10*(2), 67-82. NHSA Dialog: A Research-to-Practice Journal for the Early Intervention Field.

McNeely, B. (2005). Using technology as a learning tool, not just the cool new thing. In D.G. Oblinger & J.L. Oblinger (Eds.), *Educating the Net Generation* (pp. 4.1-4.10). Washington, DC: Educause.

Mulligan, S. A. (2003). Assistive technology: Supporting the participation of children with disabilities. *YC Young Children, 58*(6), 50–51.

Nagel, D. (2007, February 2007). Groups respond to proposed EETT Cuts. *T.H.E. Journal*. Retrieved June 6, 2008 from: http://thejournal.com/articles/20166.\

National Association for the Education of Young Children. Position Statement Office of Technology Assessment (1988, September). *Power on! New tools for teaching and learning* (p. 7). Washington DC: U.S. Government Printing Office, OTA-SET-379.

National Research Council. (2000). *From neurons to neighborhoods: The science of early childhood development.* Committee on Integrating Science of Early Childhood Development. In J.P. Shonkoff & D.A. Phillips (Eds.), *Board on Children, Youth, and Families, Commission on Behavioral and Social Science and Education.* Washington, DC: National Academy Press.

National Research Council. (2001). *Adding it up: Helping children learn mathematics.* Mathematics Learning Study Committee. J. Kilpatrick, J. Swafford, & B. Findell (Eds.), *Center for Education, Division of Behavioral and Social Sciences and Education.* Washington, D.C: National Academy Press.

National Research Council. (2001a). *Eager to learn: Educating out preschooler.* Committee on Early Childhood Pedagogy. B.T. Bowman, M.S. Donovan, & M.S. Burns (Eds.), *Commission on Behavioral and Social Science Education.* Washington, DC: National Academy Press.

National Research Council. (2005). *Mathematical and scientific development in early childhood.* Washington, DC: The National Academies Press. Text Citation: (NRC, 2005).

No, C. L. B. (2002). (NCLB) Act of 2001, Pub. L. No. 107-110, § 115 . *Stat,* 1425.

Papert, S. (2007). *Technology in the schools: To support the system or render it obsolete.* Report supported by the Milken Family Foundation.

Popham, W. J. (2008). *Classroom assessment: What teachers need to know* (5th Ed.). Boston: Allyn and Bacon.

Renzulli, J.S. (2007). The Renzulli learning system: Assessing and developing children's interest. *Duke Gifted Letter for Parents of Gifted Children, 7*(3) Spring

Robinson, L. (2007, March). *FCTD Newsletter.* The Family Center on Technology and Disability. Retrieved June 24, 2008 from http://www.fctd.info/resources/newsletters/displayNewsletter.php?newsletterID=10045

Schwalje, C. (2001). Empowering our youngest learners. *Principal, 80*(5), 40–41.

Shepard, L., Kagan, S. L., & Wurtz, E. (1997). *Principles and recommendations for early childhood assessments.* Unpublished Draft. Washington, DC: National Educational Goals Panel.

Technology-Related Assistance for Individuals with Disabilities Act of 1988 (Tech Act) (P.L. 100-407, 102 Stat. 1044, 29 U.S.C. §§ 2201 *et seq.*). *Id.* § 705(3) and (4).

Trinkle, D. A. (2005). The 361° Model for transforming teaching and learning with technology. *EDUCAUSE Quarterly, 28*(4), 18–25.

United States Department of Commerce. (1999). *Falling through the net: Defining the digital divide.* Washington, DC: U.S. Dept. of Commerce, National Telecommunications and Information Administration.

United States Department of Education. (2000, December). *E-Learning: Putting a world-class education at the fingertips of all children.* The National Educational Technology Plan. Darby, PA: Diane Publishing.

UNUM Provident Insurance Company. (1999). *Assistive Technology Decision Tree.* Retrieved June 21, 2008 from http://www.microsoft.com/enable/download/default.aspx#righttech

U.S. Department of Justice. (2005). *A guide to disability rights laws.* Washington, DC: Civil Rights Division. U.S. Department of Justice.

Van Scoter, J., Ellis, D., & Railsback, J. (2001). *Technology in early childhood education: Finding the balance*. Portland, OR: Northwest Regional Educational Laboratory.

Wartella, E. A., & Jennings, N. (2000). *Children and computers: New technology-old concerns*. Children and Computer Technology. Fall.

Wayne, A., Zucker, A., & Powell, T. (2002). *So what about the "digital divide" in K-12 schools? Educational technology and equity in U.S. K-12 schools*. Menlo Park, CA: SRI International.

Wood, E., Willoughby, T., Schmidt, A., Porter, L., Specht, J., & Gilbert, J. (2004). Assessing the Use of Input Devices for Teachers and Children In Early Childhood Education Programs. *Information Technology in Childhood Education Annual,* (1), 261-280. AACE.

Wortham, S. C. (2008). *Assessment in Early Childhood Education*. Columbus, OH: Pearson Merrill Prentice Hall.

Zhao, Y., Byers, J., Mishra, P., Topper, A., Chen, H., & Enfield, M. (2001). What do they know? A comprehensive portrait of exemplary technology-using teachers. *Journal of Computing in Teacher Education, 17*(2), 25–37.

Chapter 8
Promoting Family Involvement through Using Technology

Vivian Gunn Morris
University of Memphis, USA

Satomi Izumi-Taylor
University of Memphis, USA

Cheri Lewis Smith
University of Memphis and Harding Academy, USA

Denise Winsor
University of Memphis, USA

ABSTRACT

In this chapter the authors have provided an overview of some of the ideas about families and technology use in early childhood programs. The four authors are university faculty and provide their thinking and some experiences with family involvement and teacher training. The chapter is framed with the idea that families are the first teachers of children and play a major role in learning. There is a special introductory section written by Denise Winsor, who piloted the Family Builders and Family Preservation grants in the 1980's. Winsor provides insight into the role of family in early childhood education. The next section explores technology that is used to facilitate family involvement and building family involvement through technology. The authors briefly discuss some of the issues, problems and solutions to technology within family relationships and the role you might play as a professional. They try to address the advantages and disadvantages of family/school communication approaches to developing technology relationships with caregivers. They have included some real world examples from practitioners and how they help our students conceptualize technology use with families. The last section includes helpful advice for families concerning appropriate use of technology with their child. The authors hope this chapter helps you think about the role of families in your classroom and how technology can work for the development of stronger relationships as well as academic support.

DOI: 10.4018/978-1-60566-784-3.ch008

INTRODUCTION

Discussions about early childhood education and development cannot be justified without the inclusion of parental and family involvement (Winsor & Blake, 2008). In ecological systems approach (Bronfenbrenner, 1978) and according to Vygotsky, humans develop externally as a result of interactions with others, and we are products of the cultures in which we are reared (1978). Likewise, Bronfenbrenner, who was a co-founder of Head Start Programs in the United States believed that the immediate classroom environment is a *microsystem* (i.e., family, peers, teachers); a *mesosystem* is that which directly links to the immediate classroom environment (i.e., a child's home environment); an *exosystem* is that which indirectly links but may affect the immediate classroom environment (i.e., a parent's work, relationship, financial situation); and a *macrosystem* is the much larger cultural context that can impact the classroom environment. Given that preschool education is often times the gate keeper between a child's first formal educational experience and perhaps the end of nurturing pedagogy as they exit the tender care of their parents, it is essential that in early childhood models of education the parent(s) is an essential and vital component. In order for a teacher to have a successful relationship with a child there needs to be a relationship between the parent and the teacher. Similar to running a relay race, the runners who exchange the baton must have a strong connection between them; much time, energy, and practice goes into executing the exchange to be flawless. Preschool teachers get the first opportunity to prepare young children to be lifelong learners, but this includes educating parents, too.

John Dewey believed that parents are the central component of a child's growth and development. For decades there has been an ongoing controversy between the influences of nature versus nurture, this research is grounded using multiple theoretical approaches that heavily supports the nurture theory, which is strongly supported by most developmental researchers, particularly in areas that are concerned with the influences of parents. There are difficulties involved in researching parents and very young children (i.e., parent accessibility, children's language development, valid measures to reliably evaluate); therefore, most of the parent-child research in education usually involves social and emotional factors or play. There are several studies that have found that, parent's beliefs influence child rearing (Okagaki & Sternberg, 1993; Segal, 1985; Stevenson et al., 1990) but limited research exists on how parents' beliefs influence academic performance in early childhood education. Just as education has changed in the past half-a-century, so has parenting and the role of parents. Eisenberg, Cumberland, and Spinard (1998) studied parents' emotional expressiveness and found that children tend to express their emotions more freely when parents expose their children to emotional vulnerability. The important idea here is that children learn first from their family, and this knowledge and understanding get carried over into the classroom. Senge (2000) found that parents can often be the most resistive towards adjusting to their child entering school because they lose control of what their child's learning. In this study, parents had strong beliefs about what and how their children should be taught and justified this belief based on: (a) an association with their own positive or negative experiences and (b) how it connected to their belief within a large family and social dynamic (e.g., how their child compares to the neighbors child, what to tell the grandparents, and will their child be able to get into a competitive college).

It should be clarified that the relationship between the parent and child is reciprocal in nature, that is, the impact is not solely from the parent to the child in a linear course of action. As children begin to develop the cognitive, social, and emotional changes, in turn, influence the parental interactions with them; depending on the parent's beliefs and experiences this shift can be positive or negative for the child. Children play a central role in their parents' actions and interactions; after parents define the criteria they believe to be acceptable for their children to succeed in life, they set goals and expectations for the children and others involved in their lives. However, the child's success begins to signify or represent a portion of the parent's self-worth, the degree to which this happens varies according to the parenting style (Burchinal, Peisner-Feinberg, Pianta, & Howes, 2002; Castro, Bryant, & Peisner-Feinberg, 2004) and context of the family (Denham, Mitchell-Copeland, Strandberg, Auerbach, & Blair, 1997; Minuchin, 1974; Walker, Wilkins, Dallaire, Sandler, & Hoover-Dempsey, 2005). All of these studies have found that the role of parents and gaining knowledge about the family dynamics can impact academic performance, emotional competence, social development, behavior, and motivation. Clearly the family will have a strong influence on technology as well as all areas of child learning.

Whitehurst and Lonigan (2002) stated, the period from birth to kindergarten is the "emergent literacy stage" of reading and writing in which children acquire a large variety of pre-literacy skills that are positively correlated with later success in reading (Burgess, Hecht, & Lonigan, 2002; Lonigan, 2006). A meta-analysis, (Scarborough & Dobrich, 1994) suggests parent-child shared reading demonstrated that parents involved in their children's literacy development, children are actively engaged, have better language skills, and excel at giving explanations and making predictions. It seems logical that these ideas would transfer to technology.

IMPORTANCE OF FAMILY INVOLVEMENT

Dr. Winsor's introduction indicates that the relationship between family and student learning is complex and multifaceted. When parents and family members know how to be involved in their children's everyday activities in school, they are more likely to support their children's performance. Family involvement can be defined as parents and relatives participating in their children's education and development based on the assertion that parents are the most influential people in children's lives (Morrison, 2007). Henderson and Mapp (2002) summarize research studies related to the benefits of family involvement in the education of children. They report that when families are involved in the education of their children, they are more likely to:

- Earn higher grades and test scores, and enroll in higher-level programs.
- Be promoted, pass their classes, and earn credits.
- Attend school regularly.
- Have better social skills, show improved behavior, and adapted well to school.
- Graduate and go on to postsecondary education (p. 7).

Strong family involvement is important and necessary in building better schools.

Chaboudy and Jameson (2001) also summarize the positive benefits of family involvement in the education of children. Regardless of the economic, racial, or cultural background of the family, when parents are actively involved in their children's education, many positive things happen: student achievement improves, students attend school more consistently, dropout rates go down, and there is a pronounced decrease in school delinquency. With the new technology available to teachers and students, it is likely that this knowledge can be used with families.

Epstein (2007) developed a comprehensive plan or six ways for involving families and other community stakeholders in the educational lives of children including:

- Parenting
- Communicating
- Volunteering
- Learning at home
- Decision making
- Collaborating with the community

Although educators know the importance of family involvement, it is sometimes difficult to create a school culture where there is true partnership with families in the education of their children. Practical implementation sometimes gets lost as schedules get busier and school and home life become more hectic. Technology is one way to support communication in a fast, efficient manner. Communication between teachers and families must be intentional, with systems in place to make collaboration easily initiated and managed. The types of family involvement recommended by Epstein were developed prior to the wide use of computers and the Internet in the homes of most families. However, many of the six strategies advocated by Epstein (2007) can be facilitated via other technology sources in addition to telephone and television.

Generally, parents today voice their opinion that their children need to be computer literate in order to cope with "the demands of the 21st century" (Swaminathan & Wright, 2003, p. 145). For these reasons, this chapter includes ways for early childhood educators to get family members involved in their children's school lives through the use of technology. Technology refers to the application of science to create products or to solve problems, including computers, fax machines, cell phones, digital cameras, overhead projectors, PowerPoint, tape recorders, video cameras, TV, VCRs, electronic or digital devices, etc. Bouffard (2008) reports that while Internet technology represents an opportunity for increasing communication between families and schools, it is generally underutilized for this purpose. Several new innovations, in addition to some of the more common uses of technology, are being used by

schools in the United States in an attempt to capitalize on the efficiency of technology for family involvement including electronic communication, web sites and blogs, and student information systems (SIS).

Since the focus of this chapter is on family involvement through the use of technology, we will discuss the importance of family involvement, building family involvement through technology, recent technologies used to facilitate family involvement, and the ways to promote such involvement. We also present pros and cons of family involvement using technology, as well as our questions for teachers.

SUPPORT FOR FAMILY INVOLVEMENT

According to the position statement by the National Association for the Education of Young Children (NAEYC), "establishing reciprocal relationships with families" (1997, p. 22) is one of the best ways to care for and to educate young children. "Early childhood teachers work with in collaborative partnerships with families, establishing and maintaining regular, frequent two-way communication with children's parents" (NAEYC, 1997, p. 22). When teachers and parents communicate with each other, everyone who is involved in children's lives share knowledge of them and understand their development and learning, and family involvement can occur.

The importance of family involvement in children's development and learning has been documented since children whose parents or relatives are involved in their school lives are more positive about their schools, have better attendance, and exhibit better homework performance than children whose family members are less involved (Epstein, 2000). Such parents tend to have self-confidence in child rearing, to have knowledge of child development, and to have good understanding of their homes as important environments that promote their children's learning and development (Bessell, Sinagub, Lee, & Schumm, 2003; Eldridge, 2001). When parents and teachers work together, they can support children's positive growth and learning (Copple & Bredekamp, 2006; File, 2001). Additionally, family involvement benefits children, parents, family members, teachers, and administrators (Eldridge, 2001; Kaufman, 2001; Swaminathan & Wright, 2003). However, many teachers do not possess the training, skills, knowledge, dispositions, or attitudes to work effectively with those who are involved in children's lives (Eldridge, 2001; Morris & Taylor, 1998). Many teachers as well as others who are involved in children's lives recognize the importance of family involvement, but "there is still a significant lack of family involvement in schools" (Kieff & Wellhousen, 2000, p. 19).

RECENT TECHNOLOGIES USED TO FACILITATE FAMILY COMMUNICATION

Electronic Communication

Note writing has long been used as the most common form of parent communication. Teachers write notes to communicate a need or a problem, and ideally, to give praise to a student for a job well done. With the entrance of email, sending a note, an electronic note, has become fast and efficient (Chaboudy & Jameson, 2001). One note can be sent to a variety of recipients at once, including separate family members, the principal, and the student himself if appropriate. This system is also efficient in that it provides documentation of the communications. Updates about school events and general information can also be sent through e-mail instead of paper newsletters.

Although email is an inexpensive and effective way to communicate with parents and the community, it is important to follow the constantly changing laws relating to privacy, spam, and email communication in general. Care should also be taken when communicating sensitive or confidential information with parents via email. Teachers should avoid discussing volatile subjects or discipline issues that would be more appropriate for discussion by phone or in person (Morrison, 2009).

Web Sites and Blogs

School or class Web sites can be an effective tool for posting useful information for families (Bouffard, 2008). Basic announcements, such as upcoming tests, projects, conferences, field trips, and special events can be posted as a reminder to parents. Class rules can be posted, procedures and course objectives explained, and other helpful information for parents can be easily accessed on a class Web site. A Web site is especially useful for posting information that does not have to be changed daily or weekly but that will be helpful to parents throughout the year.

Another use for a Web site would be to provide forms that are used repeatedly in the class, such as reading logs, math facts, or maps (Chaboudy & Jameson, 2001). Parents could have immediate access to the forms without having to ask the teacher for extra copies. This would be especially helpful for families where children stay at different houses during the week. A Web site could provide support and access to more nontraditional families.

Pictures of special events could also be posted on the Web so that parents could log on and see their children's field trip or special event shortly after it takes place. See chapter 3 written by Tetsuya Ogawa and Satomi Izumi-Taylor in this book for more information regarding how Japanese preschools promote family involvement by using their own log to inform parents and family members about their school events. Both schools and parents use logs to communicate with each other, and parents can communicate with other parents.

This window into the child's school day might make parents feel as though they are involved even if they are not the home room parent or chaperone. They can then use those pictures to communicate about that event with their child, which increases positive communication between the parent and child as well. Some schools like the Barbara K. Lipman Early Childhood School and Research Institute post child activity pictures weekly for parental viewing. This keeps parents informed of class activities and documents work in this school. The teachers write brief narratives about the working projects which help parents understand the importance of early childhood developmental activities. Parents can also post related pictures on this site.

Other opportunities for communicating within a class website, according to Chaboudy and Jameson (2001), include a secure chat room, student Web pages, and a bulletin board. A secure chat room allows students to chat with each other in a safe online environment. They can also collaborate with other students to discuss current topics of study. Students can create his or her own Web page and present information about themselves and their families. Students can also use the bulletin board for communication. Sometimes students will write concerns on a bulletin board that they would not say to the teacher in person.

Links to other helpful Web sites can be placed on the class Web site. Students and parents are able to explore them without leaving the security of the class Web site. Family members feel more comfortable knowing that teachers have previewed the sites and that they are safe and helpful for their children (Morrison, 2009).

Some teachers are creating blogs instead of building their own Web sites or putting pages on a school's site (Ray, 2006). Teachers post lesson plans, write about daily happenings, and share pictures of class activities. Blogs could also provide a forum for parent discussion and input, which would need to be monitored closely by the teacher, but would give parents and the teacher a

forum for two way communication. Parents would not simply have access to information, but they could respond and comment as well.

Student Information Systems

Student information systems (SIS) are giving parents more and more access to their children's academic life. Parents can check the internet any time of the day or night to check on their child's attendance, grades, and general activities. Student information systems, such as Edline or Power-School among others, give parents constant access to their child's progress. The students have the same access also. Since using student information systems, many schools are reporting a decline in discipline reports, higher test scores, and better attendance (Bird, 2006).

One of the requirements of No Child Left Behind is the parent's right to information about academic content. Before student information systems were used, schools often depended on students to provide information to the parents about school life, such as homework assignments and daily grades. Now parents of students of all ages can have specific information, unabridged, on a daily basis from the SIS. These systems are especially helpful to parents of older students, since parental involvement in schools tends to decrease as children grow older (Ramirez, 2001).

BUILDING FAMILY INVOLVEMENT THROUGH TECHNOLOGY

According to its position statement of technology (1996) published by the National Association for the Education of Young Children (NAEYC), teachers need to collaborate with families to choose appropriate technology for young children as well as to "promote equitable access to technology for all children and their families" (p. 13). One study done by Bers, New, and Boudreau (2004) examines how parents and children explore technology together. The authors conducted many workshop sessions for children and their parents in order for them to have the opportunity to experience "a technology-rich environment with diverse expertise and interests" (p. 4). Parents and children created a technology-enhanced representation of their shared interests. Many of their interactions changed the family dynamics by using technology to enhance their understanding of their religious and cultural heritage. Teachers could conduct these types of workshops in the school.

The main goal of the use of technology is to foster communication between parents and teachers. Various educators and researchers acknowledge that technology can improve parent/family involvement (Bessell et al., 2003; Hernandez & Leung, 2004; Huseth, 2001; Lewis, 2003; Nelms, 2002; Ramirez, 2001; Tobolka, 2006). According to Hernandez and Leung (2004), when used appropriately, technology, such as the Internet, can offer tremendous possibilities to promote more meaningful family involvement for parents and teachers. Likewise, Gennarelli (2004) uses digital cameras to communicate with children's parents about their activities at school. Morrison (2007) suggests different ways for teachers to promote family involvement using technology including "…email as new ways to exchange information and to get help assistance; school websites; teacher and classroom websites; and phone conferencing" (p. 390). Robinson (2003) implements technology to create interactive storybooks for toddlers and to involve the family in making such books that "come alive with a parent's voice, a family pet's photo, a video clip of siblings playing with the pet, and simple text" (p. 43). Other teachers create their own websites with students' everyday activity pictures in the classrooms, and others provide online instructional systems to assist students and parents in learning technology (Morrison, 2007). Young and Behounek (2006) provide kindergarten children with opportunities to create their own PowerPoint presentations for parent-teacher conferences. Because their children

lead such conferences using technology, all of the parents have enjoyed and recommended these types of conferences. Another teacher connects with not only parents and family members but also with extended families and families who live apart from their children through technology as alternate forms of communication (Ray & Shelton, 2004). Grandparents and siblings can enjoy children's pictures of school activities and their notes using technology. Phone calls, emails, and recorded messages can also facilitate communication between parents/families and teachers (Kaczmarek, 2007).

ISSUES: CONTROVERSIES, PROBLEMS AND SOLUTIONS

As with all innovations technology comes with its own set of controversies and problems. We outline three main concerns from our experiences with parents, families, and children. These concerns influence how teachers and families may perceive technology. We also offer possible solutions to these problems and hope that the readers will extend the solutions to fit their individual classrooms.

The Digital Generation Gap

It is well known that family members may face difficulties in understanding their children's use of the media because of the rapid progression of technology (Jordan, 2008). Children seem to learn about technology faster than their parents. It is not unusual for parents and family members to ask their children to fix or program their computers, cell phones, and the television remote controls. This can create a communication gap between parents and children. Often children see their parents as "outdated" or not "with it" and this thinking is often reflected through negative interactions. Parents or caregivers may perceive this as a show of "disrespect" from their children.

It is recommended that adults empower themselves for technology literacy. Working with children to learn new technology can bring mutual respect and create quality learning time together. One approach to this is through interaction with educational programs. Morrison (2007) explains that technology has changed the way educators teach as well as the way children learn. In this sense, such changes influence parental roles as well. Technology can provide parents and family members the opportunity to participate in, support, and supervise their children's learning. When teachers provide web sites that support learning families can work together on assignments or tutorials. Teachers who post pictures of weekly student activities allow families to participate vicariously in student learning. Another way is through more and easier access to communication using technology. Tobolka (2006) finds that "electronic communication improves students' interest in their coursework and provides their parents with more knowledge about daily class activities" (p. 26). This notion of communication supports that of Keyser's stating that written communication can give family members and teachers diverse opportunities to communicate, and that such communication styles are more comfortable than talking in person (2006). Teachers need to encourage parents to use technology for communication.

Other forms of communication include telephone and web hotlines that can be used to "support children and parents with homework and to monitor latchkey children" (Morrison, 2007, p. 502). Gestwicki (2007) has described how one teacher comforted an anxious mother by text-messaging her infant's daily activities. To connect home, school, and community, master teachers in Chicago have created a virtual Pre-K which is "an interactive educational resource in English and Spanish that bridges classroom learning with hands-on home activities and community experiences (Narvaez, Feldman, & Theriot, 2006, p. 52). Webcams used in classrooms can allow parents to visit their child's classroom in real time.

Equity Issues

Not all families have access to computers, parents and teachers may not be able to communicate with them through the use of technology. Such a lack of access to technology is called "the digital divide" (Attewell, Suazo-Garcia, & Battle, 2003, p. 277) which refers to the current trend indicating unequal access to computer technology that divides families with technology and families without it. Unequal access to computer technology creates problems since families without technology are excluded from social and economic life in our society. In this sense, children's and their families' access to technology is related to family incomes (Becker, 2000; Bouffard, 2008; Children and Computer, 2000; Chen, 2000). In order to increase equity in use of technology, it is important to provide the needed training and access through school activities for family members and other caregivers as well as for teachers (Chen, 2000).

Schools that are beginning to implement technology programs for parent involvement must map out a plan for how they will get parents to use them. Schools should not assume that students and parents have access to technology at home. Teachers need to make an effort during the first week of school to determine if students have access to telephones, computers and the Internet. Sometimes a phone call during the first week, before there are any problems, is the best way to gather needed information and make a positive first connection. The main office of the school is a useful resource for finding current telephone numbers. Information can then be gathered as to what technology resources a family has at their disposal (Ramirez, 2001).

Schools need to be proactive when implementing communication with technology. Parents may need to be trained in how to access the information on the Internet. Parents could be surveyed to find times that would be good for them to receive the training. If the majority of parents are available on Saturdays, then training sessions could be on a Saturday instead of a weekday. In other words, the schools should make an effort to meet the parents' needs for training and access.

Some schools are using the school library as a resource for parents who need help and access (Farmer, 2002). Because school librarians usually works with the entire school community, they are in a good position to help facilitate parental involvement. The librarian can serve as a technology resource person for the school and helps train the parents to use the technology. Another idea is to open the school's computer lab to the parents. Parents can come and use the school's lab if they do not have computer access elsewhere. The school can make parents feel welcome by sending them personal invitations to use the school as a technology resource. The schools could also offer courses in technology for parents, especially courses that parents might have requested (Ramirez, 2001).

As technology is integrated into a school culture, students could be the biggest assets in training teachers, parents, and others who are involved in children's lives. Most students are computer natives, and are more than happy to share their knowledge with others. Some technology corporations are promoting Family Technology Nights nationwide that teach parents and students first-hand how technology can be used to bridge the school and home. In addition, the corporations that are sponsoring these events donate software and other products to the schools. It is a fun way for parents to learn about new technology alongside their children.

Open Access

While there are many benefits in using technology to enhance teaching and learning in both the school and home environments, many parents are concerned about the negative potential to their children as well (Lipper & Lazarus, 2000). Parents are particularly concerned about children's access to pornography and children disclosing personal information that may put them or other family members in danger. As a result of these concerns and of the often over commercialization of Internet sites, parents must learn how to monitor children's use of the Internet for both time spent online and the access to web sites.

Parents and others who are involved in children's lives need to know how to limit the amount of time children spend with computers and closely supervise the content of programs, games, software, and the Web (Children and Computer Technology, 2000). For these reasons, parents and family members need to become computer literate to oversee and to understand the kinds of computer-related activities in which their children are engaged.

Lipper and Lazarus (2000) emphasize the importance of all caregivers having the knowledge and skills required to safely monitor the use of technology by young children. They state that:

In the most fundamental way, parents and other direct caregivers—such as grandparents, other family members, and care workers—are able to teach their children safety rules, set appropriate limits for a child based on age and disposition, and tailor strategies that a child benefits from time spent with new media in the home. (p. 175)

NAEYC (1996) recommends that teachers must work closely with parents as advocates for appropriate technology related activities for young children. "Working together, parents and teachers are a large consumer group wielding greater influence on the development of technology for young children" (NAEYC, 1996, p. 14).

Schools that succeed in engaging families from very diverse backgrounds share three key practices. They:

- *focus on building trusting collaborative relationships among teachers, families, and community members.*
- *Recognize, respect, and address families' needs, as well as class and cultural difference.*
- *Embrace a philosophy of partnership where power and responsibility are shared.* (Henderson & Mapp, 2002, p. 7)

Lipper and Lazarus (2000) offer some good advice related to promoting family involvement through using technology. They state that:

At this crucial stage in the development of computer technology, parent involvement is essential to secure what is best for your children in a digital age. History demonstrates that media are developed in ways that are beneficial to children only when there is vigorous and sustained pressure from parents. We must support parents' vital role in shaping the evolution of more quality content in the new media that will surround our children for many years to come. (pp. 177-178)

As teachers, you can help families think about what types of technology would be appropriate for educational purposes. Families often need direction and welcome your input when done in a respectful manner. As an educator, you need to make sure you are supporting the families' cultural values when you approach technology. A simple technology questionnaire could be sent home. (See appendix B)

SUMMARY

It is well documented that parents or caregivers play an important role in the educational success of their children. As technology continues to develop and change, it alters the role of parents and children's access to information and the potential for communication. How technology is used by children places an added responsibility on parents. The parent now must monitor technology use and teach children to discriminate between appropriate and inappropriate information sources. While technology opens many doors to families, it must also be closely watched to insure children maintain the families' moral and ethical beliefs.

A technology gap emerges as technology use increases. There is a big difference between generations concerning understanding and use of technology. Teachers can help bridge the gap between family and child through modeling and introducing appropriate technology to parents and family members. Teachers can help provide opportunities for parents and family members to learn about and use technology.

As mentioned in previous chapters, there remains the issue of equal access to technology. Schools can and should play an important role in providing access to technology for all families regardless of socioeconomic status. Some schools offer classes, allow parents to use libraries and computer labs, and some schools have a laptop checkout system for families. This issue needs attention if we are to ensure all children have the same experiences and access to technology.

VISION

Clearly technology has become and will stay an issue in all facets of modern life. We are just learning the many benefits of its' use and applications in education and all forms of communication. While it is hard to predict the direction technology will take, we believe future use will increase and that it will become a major contributor to the educational success of children of all ages. As we move toward a Global Economy, the idea of family expands to include groups of people who can contribute to the educational success for children outside the traditional definitions.

SOME QUESTIONS FOR REFLECTIVE PRACTITIONERS

1. What ways do you involve your parents in school activities?
2. Could you integrate technology into your already existing parent relationships? How?
3. How could you best educate parents on technology to support their child's education? List ways you could train parents.
4. Many children now come to school from nontraditional families and caregivers come in all age groups. How can you communicate with the primary caregivers using technology and what types of communications would be appropriate?
5. What types of web based information might help the families of your students?
6. How could your school ensure equal access for all children and families?
7. How can you help families learn how to monitor computer time and access?
8. How can you build trusting collaborative relationships among teachers, families, and community members that enhance technology?
9. How can you support parents' vital role in shaping the evolution of more quality content in the new media that will surround our children?
10. How will you recognize, respect, and address families' needs, as well as class and cultural difference through technology use?

REFERENCES

Attewell, P., Suazo-Garcia, & Battle, J. (2003). Computers and young children: Social benefit or social problems? *Social Forces, 82*(1), 277–296. doi:10.1353/sof.2003.0075

Becker, H. (2000). Who's wired and who's not: Children's access to and use of computer Computer. *The Future of Children, 10*(2), 44–75. doi:10.2307/1602689

Bers, M., New, B., & Boudreau, L. (2004). Teaching and learning when no one is expert: Children and parents explore technology. *Early Childhood Research and Practice, 6*(2). Retrieved April 16, 2008. http://ecrp.uniuc.edu/v62n2/bers.html

Bessell, A., Sinagub, J., Lee, O., & Schumm, J. (2003). Engaging families with technology. *T.H.E. Journal, 31*(5), 7–13.

Bird, K. (2006, February 1). How do you spell parental involvement? S-I-S: student information systems are engaging parents, benefiting kids, and finally winning over teachers, too. *Technological Horizons in Education Journal.* Retrieved October 5, 2008 from http://www. highbeam.com

Bouffard, S. (2008, July). Tapping into technology: The Role of the Internet in family-school communication. *Family Involvement Research Digests: Harvard Family Research Projects.* Retrieved July 30, 2008 from http://www.hfrp.org/family-involvement/fine-family-involvement-network-of-educators/fine-newsletter-archive/july-fine-newsletter-the-role-of-technology-in-family-involvement.

Chaboudy, R., & Jameson, P. (2001, September 1). Connecting families and schools through technology. *The Book Report.* Retrieved October 5, 2008 from http://www.highbeam.com/doc/1G1-96306627.html

Chen, M. (2000, Fall/Winter). Five commentaries: Looking to the future. *The future of children, Children and Computer Technology, 10*(2), 168-171. Retrieved August 6, 2008 from http://www.futureofchildren.org.

Children and Computer Technology. (2001). Analysis and Recommendations. *The Future of Children, 10*(2), 4–30. doi:10.2307/1602687

Copple, C., & Bredekamp, S. (2006). *Basics of developmentally appropriate practice: An introduction for teachers of children 3 to 6.* Washington, DC: The National Association for the Education of Young Children.

Eldridge, D. (2001). Parent Involvement: It's worth the effort. *Young Children, 56*(4), 65–69.

Epstein, J. (2000). *School and family partnerships: Preparing educators and improving schools.* Boulder, CO: Westview.

Epstein, J. (2007). Families, schools, and community partnerships. In D. Koralek (Ed.), *Spotlight on young children and families* (p. 37). Washington: National Association for the Education of Young Children.

Farmer, L. (2002, January 1). Teaming parents with technology. *The Book Report.* Retrieved October 5, 2008 from http://www.highbeam.com/doc/1G183077440.html

File, N. (2001). Family-professional partnerships: Practice that matches philosophy. *Young Children, 56*(4), 70–74.

Gestwicki, C. (2007). *Home, school, and community relations* (6th ed.). Clifton Park, NY: Thomson Delmar Learning.

Henderson, A. T., & Mapp, K. L. (2002). *A new wave of evidence: The impact of School, family, and community connections on student achievement.* Austin, TX: Southwest Education Educational Development Laboratory. Retrieved August 21, 2008 from: http://www.sedl.org/connections/resources/evidence.pdf.

Hernandez, S., & Leung, B. (2004). Using the Internet to boost parent-teacher relationships. *Kappa Delta Pi Record, 40*(3), 136–138.

Huseth, M. (2001). The school-home connection. *Learning and Leading with Technology, 29*(2), 6–17.

Jordan, A. (2008). Children's media policy. *The Future of Children, 18*(1), 235–249. doi:10.1353/foc.0.0003

Kaczmarek, L. (2007). A team approach: Supporting families of children with disabilities in inclusive programs. *Spotlight on Young Children and Families* (pp. 28-36).

Kaufman, H. (2001). Skills for working with all families. *Young Children, 56*(4), 81–83.

Keyser, J. (2006). *From parents to parents: Building a family-centered early childhood program.* St. Paul: MN. Redleaf Press.

Kieff, J., & Wellhousen, K. (2000). Planning family involvement in early childhood programs. *Young Children, 55*(3), 18–25.

Lewis, A. (2003). Using communications technology and parental involvement to improve homework completion and quality. *Action Research Exchange, 2*(1).

Lipper, L. A., & Lazarus, W. (2000). Five commentaries: Looking to the future. *The Future of Children, Children and Computer Technology, 10*(2), 175-178. Retrieved August 6, 2008 from http://www.futureofchildren.org.

Morris, V. G., & Taylor, S. I. (1998). Alleviating barriers to family involvement in education: The role of teacher education. *Teaching and Teacher Education, 14*(2), 219–231. doi:10.1016/S0742-051X(97)00037-1

Morrison, G. (2007). *Early childhood education today* (10th ed). Upper Saddle River, NJ: Pearson Merrill Prentice Hall.

Morrison, G. (2009). *Early Childhood Education Today.* Upper Saddle River, NJ: Pearson.

Narvaez, A., Feldman, J., & Theriot, C. (2006). Virtual pre-k: Connecting home, school, and community. *Young Children, 61*(1), 52–53.

National Association for the Education of Young Children. (1997). *Developmentally appropriate practice in early childhood programs serving children from birth through age 8.* Washington, DC: National Association for the Education of Young Children. Retrieved April 14, 2008, http://naeyc.org/about/positions/pdf/PSDAP98.PDF

Nelms, E. (2002). The effects of a teacher-created web page on parent communication: An action research study. *Action Research Exchange, 1*(2).

Position Statement, NAEYC: Technology and Young Children-Ages Three Through Eight. (1996). *Young Children,51*(6), 11-16.

Ramirez, F. (2001, September/October). Technology and parental involvement. *The Clearing House.* Retrieved October 5, 2008 from http://www.highbeam.com

Ray, J. (2006). Welcome to the blogosphere: The educational use of blogs (aka edublogs). *Kappa Delta Pi Record, 42*(4), 175–177.

Ray, J., & Shelton, D. (2004). Connecting with families through technology. *Young Children,* 30–31.

Robinson, L. (2003). Technology as a scaffold for emergent literacy: Interactive storybooks for toddlers. *Young Children, 58*(6), 42–48.

Swaminathan, S., & Wright, J. (2003). Educational Tech in the early to primary years. In J. Isenberg & M. Jalongo (Eds.), *Major trends & issues in ECE.* (pp. 136-146). NY: Teachers College Press.

Tobolka, D. (2006). Connecting teachers and parents through the Internet. *Tech Directions, 66*(5), 24–26.

Vygotsky, L. S. (1978). *Mind in society.* Cambridge, MA: Harvard Universal Press.

Young, D., & Behounek, L. (2006). Kindergarteners use PowerPoint to lead their own parent-teacher conferences . *Young Children, 61*(2), 24–26.

Chapter 9

Technology Integration in Early Childhood and Primary Classrooms
Access, Use & Pedagogy Remain Critical Components to Success

Michael M. Grant
University of Memphis, USA

Clif Mims
University of Memphis, USA

ABSTRACT

Calls for increased use of technology in early childhood and primary classrooms have not gone unanswered. However, recent research findings report little technology integration with computers continuing to be unavailable. This descriptive study looked to explore to what extent and in what ways technology is integrated into early childhood and primary classrooms. Findings corroborate previous dated research that trivial technology is being used. Technology use, computer access and styles of pedagogy remain critical in the debate to whether teachers will integrate computers for teaching and learning.

INTRODUCTION

In a recent special edition of the *Early Education and Development* journal dedicated to technology integration, guest editors Wang and Hoot (2006) argued that

Early childhood educators are now moving away from asking the simple question of whether tech-nology is developmentally appropriate for young children. Rather, they are more concerned with how [information and communication technology] can be effectively used to facilitate children's learning and development. (p. 317)

It would seem the value of using technology to support teaching and learning for young children has been reconciled.

Over a decade ago, the National Association for the Education of Young Children (NAEYC)

DOI: 10.4018/978-1-60566-784-3.ch009

adopted a position statement regarding the use of technology in the education of young children. This statement has since not been modified or replaced (NAEYC, 1996). Their prescience highlighted the increasing ubiquity of computers and information and communication technologies. NAEYC's (1996) statement also cautioned that "computers supplement and ... not replace highly valued early childhood activities and materials" (p.1). The obvious concern and assumption were that computers would become pervasive enough so that it would supplant other meaningful instructional methods. The authors, in fact, warn educators to "weigh the costs of technology with the costs of other learning materials and program resources to arrive at an appropriate balance for their classrooms" (NAEYC, 1996, p.1). Again, the assumption was that computer technologies may overshadow tactile learning. However, is the reverse also true? Has a balance been struck between traditional forms of learning and technology integrated instruction? Have computer technologies become integral to learning? The conclusions appear to be less clear.

Smeets (2005) called for technology-supported learning environments in early childhood and primary education that align with the tenets of NAEYC. He argued that for technology to be best used to support student learning, then the environments must (a) embed authenticity, (b) emphasize knowledge construction, (c) use open-ended learning, (d) include student cooperation and collaboration and (e) integrate mixed ability levels and differentiated instruction where appropriate and possible. Smeets criticized schools for emphasizing "traditional, skill-based [information and communication technology] use" (p. 345), reporting that teachers made little use of technology to advance learning. Few teachers, but particularly males, were most likely to implement constructivist environments, where technology could be used in the most meaningful ways.

Possibly the strongest advocate for technology integration in *all* classrooms has been the

International Society for Technology in Education (ISTE). In 1998, ISTE launched the National Educational Technology Standards for Students (NETS-S). In 2007, a significant revision to these standards reflected changes in technologies, security and ethics, individuals' skills and contemporary teaching and learning. In parallel, the 2000 National Educational Technology Standards for Teachers (NETS-T) were approved. In 2008, a similar revision to the NETS-T resulted in a greater emphasis on learning and creativity, assessment, authentic work, and ethics. These calls for meaningful technology integration have not gone unanswered.

Examples of Technology Integration and Use

There are numerous contemporary examples of innovative uses of computers and other technologies in early childhood and primary classrooms, such as with language and writing development, problem solving and drawing. For example, Couse and Chen (2008) considered the appropriateness of tablet computers for three- to six-year old children with drawing and technological independence. Ching, Wang, Shih and Kedem (2006) explored how kindergarten and first-grade students created and reflected upon digital photograph journals. Integrated learning systems, like those investigated by Paterson, Henry, O'Quin, Ceprano and Blue (2003) and Bauserman, Cassady, Smith and Stroud (2005), continued to produce inconsistent and mixed results with regard to their utility, implementations and teacher facilitation. Voogt and McKenney (2007) researched a more constructivist system to support language and literacy development. Finally, comprehensive programs, such as the Key Instructional Design Strategies (KIDS) project (Knezek & Christensen, 2007), have incorporated extensive teacher professional development in addition to hardware, software and instructional modules.

Outside of schools and formal learning institutions, the uses of technology are quite staggering. Specific to using the Internet, the Corporation for Public Broadcasting's ([CPB], 2002) report "Connected to the Future: A Report on Children's Internet Use" found that the largest group of new Internet users from 2000-2002 were children aged two to five. Second was children aged six to eight. In 2000, 6% of two- to five-year-olds were online. In 2002, the number jumped to 35%. Similarly, in 2000, 27% of six- to eight-year-olds were using the Internet, while in 2002, the proportion was 60%. The amount of time children are spending online is not inconsequential. CPB went on to report that six- to eight-year-olds were on the average spending 2.7 hours per week using the Internet for exploration (e.g., surfing, searching), education (e.g., learning, homework, research) and games.

Challenges Describing the Technology Integration Landscape

Few large scale studies have examined technology integration in early childhood and primary classrooms. Moreover, few studies provide the generalizability and corroboration necessary to fully depict technology integration in general. Norris, Sullivan, Poirot and Soloway (2003) reported survey data from approximately 3,700 teachers across four geographically diverse states. In general, they report that teachers' uses of computers and the Internet were "disappointingly spare," (p. 22) and access to technology was equally bleak. Teachers in middle and high schools were much more likely to use computer technology in their classrooms than elementary schools. Poignantly, Norris et al. report "by far the most significant predictor of technology use is the number of classroom computers" (p. 22). This was echoed in Smeets (2005) results, where "the availability of a sufficient number of computers contributed most to the probability of" integrating technology for higher order thinking.

Similarly, O'Dwyer, Russell and Bebell (2004)

analyzed survey data from approximately 1,500 elementary teachers in kindergarten through sixth grade in Massachusetts. When technology was used, it was most often used by teachers to prepare for class. Student uses of technology to create products were the lowest. Thus, the type of instructional methods called for by Smeets (2005) above occurred least often. However, O'Dwyer et al. reported that the more constructivist the teacher's beliefs, the more technology use was reported. Finally, they report "the strongest positive predictor of whether a teacher will use technology to deliver instruction, have their students use technology during class and have their students create products is a teacher's belief about the positive impacts of technology integration" (p.15).

Becker's (2006) study included data from 40 states and over 70,000 students from a 2000 National Assessment of Educational Progress mathematics database of fourth graders and a 1998 survey from the Miliken Exchange on Educational Technology. Almost 60% of the students reported never or hardly ever using a computer with math. In addition, Becker found that 80% of the variance of whether computers were used was attributable to differences within a school. He went on to suggest that these differences were most attributable to teacher characteristics and whether teachers may employ more constructivist strategies, which echoes O'Dwyer et al.'s (2004) findings. Moreover, Becker found that computers in classrooms did increase the probability for use, which corroborates Norris et al.'s (2003) results as well.

Using data from the Early Childhood Longitudinal Study sponsored by the U.S. Department of Education, Judge, Puckett and Bell (2006) considered longitudinal data from over 8,000 children in third grade. They reported that access to computers is improving, but there are still too few computers to meet a five to one student-to-computer ratio in classrooms. They also reported that low-achieving readers from all economic groups did not receive gains from increased computer times. This may connect with findings from Paterson et al. (2003) regarding ineffective use of integrated learning systems. Therefore, these longitudinal results are providing a clearer picture of technology access and use, but we are still left with little data about the types of instructional activities with computers that are taking place inside classrooms and computer labs.

Research Question

The purpose of this research was to examine the current state of technology integration and describe access, instructional activities and use. The primary research question was to what degree and in what ways have teachers integrated technology with instruction in early childhood and primary grades? Some of the strongest, most sophisticated and largest investigations of technology integration (e.g., Becker, 2006; Norris, Sullivan, Poirot & Soloway, 2003; O'Dwyer, Russell & Bebell, 2004) have used data sets restricted by discipline (e.g, mathematics), state (e.g., Massachusetts) or currency (e.g., 1998-2002). In addition, these studies relied on self-report data from teachers, students and administrators. More robustly, Judge, Puckett and Bell's (2006) longitudinal data offered a broader perspective, collecting frequency data from parent interviews and administrator questionnaires. As noted above, however, we were unable to examine the instructional methods and subject areas to determine whether technology integration is or is not occurring. As a whole, these data provided indications of technology integration, but they are insufficient in providing a complete picture. The current research was an attempt to corroborate or refute the existing findings with observational data.

METHOD

Design and Data

This was a descriptive study reporting classroom observational data collected by external trained observers. We aggregated an extant set of data from the Center for Research in Educational Policy (CREP) at The University of Memphis. The data were collected during Fall 2005 through Spring 2007, aggregating two years of classroom observations (i.e., 2005-2006 & 2006-2007) for kindergarten through fifth grades. Data were originally collected as part of formative evaluations conducted by CREP for individual schools and school districts.

Across the two years of data, five states were represented, encompassing 81 individual schools and 316 summaries of school classroom observations. Each summary reported represents approximately 10-12 individual classrooms within a school, totaling approximately 3,100 classroom visits. The schools represented were diverse in their population densities (e.g., urban, suburban, rural) and populations served (e.g., high proportions of free and reduced lunches, low proportions of free and reduced lunches). All of the schools, however, were interested in change and school reform hence the desire for an external formative evaluation. Also, all of the schools were interested in documenting technology integration, which included an observation instrument to do so. Table 1 shows the data collection distribution.

Instrumentation

Data from two instruments were used: (1) the Survey of Computer Use and (2) the School Observation Measure. Descriptions of the instruments are explicated in the following sections.

Table 1. Distribution of classroom observations

2005 - 2006			
	States	Number of Schools	Number of Observations
	Kentucky	40	116
	Michigan	7	7
	Tennessee	19	94
	Texas	3	12
2006-2007			
	Kentucky	23	61
	Florida	9	26
Totals	5	81*	316

* Note: 20 of the Kentucky schools reported in 2006-2007 were duplicates from 2005-2006. As a result the total number of schools is 81.

Survey of Computer Use

The Survey of Computer Use (SCU©) examined the availability of and student use of technology and software applications (Lowther & Ross, 1999). The SCU was completed as part of the 15-minute observation with each SOM. Four primary types of data were recorded: (a) computer capacity and currency, (b) configuration, (c) student computer ability and (b) student activities while using computers. Computer capacity and currency was defined as the age and type of computers available for student use and whether or not Internet access was available. Configuration referred to the number of students working at each computer (e.g., alone, in pairs, in small groups). Student computer ability was assessed by recording the number of students who were computer literate (e.g., easily used software features/menus, saved or printed documents) and the number of students who easily used the keyboard to enter text or numerical information. Student use of computers was focused on the types of computer-mediated activities, subject areas of activities, and software being used. The computer activities were divided into three categories based on the type of software tool (a) production tools (word processing, databases, spreadsheets, draw/paint/graphics, presentation authoring, concept mapping, plan-

ning), (b) Internet/research tools (Internet browser, CD reference materials, communications) and (c) educational software (drill-practice/tutorial, problem solving, process tools). This section ends by identifying the content subject area of each computer activity (i.e., language arts, mathematics, social studies, science, other). Like the SOM, the computer activities and software being used are summarized and recorded using a five-point rubric that ranges from (0) Not Observed to (5) Extensively Observed. The final section of the SCU was an "overall rubric" designed to assess the degree in four levels to which the activity reflects "meaningful use" of computers as a tool to enhance learning (1=low-level use of computers, 2=somewhat meaningful, 3=meaningful, 4=very meaningful).

The reliability of the SCU was determined in a study involving pairs of trained observers conducting SCU observations in 42 targeted visits to classrooms that were schedule to have students using technology. Results from the study revealed that overall the paired observers selected the identical SCU response on 86% of the items with all other responses being only one rating apart. When looking at subcategories of the SCU, the percentage of times that paired observers selected the same responses was as follows: (a) computer capacity and currency, 83%; (b) configuration,

95%; (c) student computer ability, 70%; (d) student activities while using computers, 92%; (e) subject areas of computer activities, 88%; and (f) overall rubric rating meaningfulness of computer activities, 88% (Lowther & Ross, 1999).

School Observation Measure

The School Observation Measure (SOM©) examined the frequency of usage of 24 instructional strategies, including traditional practices (e.g., direct instruction and independent seatwork) and alternative, predominately student-centered methods associated with educational reforms (e.g., cooperative learning, project-based learning, inquiry, discussion, using technology as a learning tool) (Ross, Smith, & Alberg, 1999). The strategies were identified through surveys and discussions involving policy makers, researchers, administrators, and teachers, as those most useful in providing indicators of schools' instructional philosophies and implementations of commonly used reform designs (Ross, Smith, Alberg, & Lowther, 2001).

The observer examined classroom events and activities descriptively, not judgmentally. Notes were taken relative to the use or nonuse of 24 target strategies. Observation forms were completed every 15 minutes, and then the observer changed classrooms. This process continued for approximately 3 hours, resulting in approximately 10-12 classroom observations. At the conclusion of the visit, the observer summarized the frequency with which each of the 24 strategies was observed across all classes in general on a data summary form. The frequency was recorded via a 5-point rubric that ranges from (0) Not observed to (4) Extensively. The same 5-point scale was used to summarize how frequently high academically focused class time and high student interest/attention were observed.

To ensure the reliability of data, observers received a manual providing operational definition of terms, examples and explanations of the target strategies, and a description of procedures for completing the instrument. After receiving the manual and instruction in a group session, each observer participated in sufficient practice exercises to ensure that his or her data are comparable with those of experienced observers (i.e., the trainers). In a 2004 reliability study reported by Sterbinsky, Ross and Burk, observer ratings were within one category for 96% of the multiclass observations.

FINDINGS

Data for both years were aggregated. Descriptive statistics were calculated for both instruments, where None=0 through Extensively=4. Results from each measure are detailed in the sections below.

SCU

Summary tables with all SCU results are shown in Tables 2, 3, 4, 5, and 6. Observations using the SCU documented that almost 70% (66.8%) of all classrooms had at least two computers. Surprisingly, over 30% (31.6%) had at least five computers or more. At least 50% (50.3%) of the computers were observed to up to date and almost all (98.7%) of the computers were observed to be connected to the Internet. During the majority of the classroom visits (62.8%), on the average 50% or less of the class were using computers. When computers were used, overwhelmingly, students used computers alone (74.8%). In fact, just over 10% (12.1%) of the time, students were using the computer collaboratively. Computer literacy skills were consistently observed to be moderately or very good (73.2%), while keyboarding skills were observed to be moderately or very good almost 50% of the time (46.6%). The configurations of computers most often observed were desktop computers (80.1%). Laptop computers were observed about 30% (27.3%) of the time, while personal

Table 2. SCU computer configurations descriptive statistics

Classrooms most frequently had the following number of computes or digital tools	0	1	2-4	5-10	11 or more
Frequency	0.0	1.6	66.8	19.6	12.0
Classrooms computers were most frequently:	Up-to-date	Aging but Adequate	Outdated/limited capacity	No computers were observed	
Frequency	50.3	37.3	12.3	0.0	
Classroom Computers were most frequently	Connected to the Internet	Not connected to the Internet	No computers were observed		
Frequency	98.7	0.9	0.3		
Classrooms computers or digital tools were most frequently used	Few (less than 10%) students	Some (about 10-50%) students	Most (about 51-90%) students	Nearly all (91-100%)	Students did not use computers
Frequency	29.8	33.0	11.1	13.7	12.4
Students most frequently worked with computers or digital tools	Alone	In Pairs	In small groups	Students did not use computers	
Frequency	74.8	10.5	1.6	13.1	
Student Student computer literacy skills were most frequently:	Poor	Moderate	Very Good	Not observed	
Frequency	2.2	45.5	27.7	24.2	
Student keyboarding skills were most frequently:	Poor	Moderate	Very good	Not Observed	
Frequency	8.6	33.3	13.3	44.4	

digital assistants and graphing calculators were almost never observed. Information processors, such as AlphaSmarts tablets, were observed about 7% (6.6%) of the time.

On the average, all production tools and Internet tools were rarely observed to the be used in classrooms ($M <= 1$). When observed, combining rarely through extensively frequencies, word

Table 3. SCU Types of Computers and Devices Descriptive Statistics

	Mean	SD	Percent None	Percent Rarely	Percent Occasionally	Percent Frequently	Percent Extensively
Desktop Computers	2.05	1.48	19.9	20.3	19.0	17.4	23.1
Laptop Computers	0.62	1.22	72.7	9.8	7.0	4.8	5.4
Personal Digital Assistants (PDAs)	0.04	0.52	98.7	0.6	0.3	0.0	0.0
Graphing Calculators	0.03	0.57	99.4	0.3	0.0	0.0	0.0
Information Processors (e.g., AlphaSmarts)	0.14	0.76	93.4	2.5	3.2	0.6	0.0
Digital Accessories (e.g., camera, scanner, probes)	0.23	0.92	88.6	6.0	2.8	1.3	0.9

Table 4. SCU Software Descriptive Statistics

Production Tools	Mean	SD	Percent None	Percent Rarely	Percent Occasionally	Percent Frequently	Percent Extensively
Word Processor	0.76	1.30	62.1	15.9	12.7	5.4	3.5
Database	0.08	0.84	98.1	0.3	0.6	0.6	0.0
Spreadsheet	0.12	0.94	95.5	2.2	0.3	1.6	0.0
Draw/Paint/Graphics/Photo-Imaging	0.29	1.09	84.0	8.6	5.8	1.0	0.3
Presentation	0.42	1.28	80.3	8.9	6.1	2.2	2.2
Authoring	0.18	1.14	93.6	2.6	1.6	1.6	0.3
Concept Mapping	0.21	1.17	89.5	5.7	4.1	0.3	0.0
Planning	0.11	1.18	98.1	0.3	0.0	1.3	0.0
Other Production tools	0.20	1.28	91.4	3.8	3.5	1.0	0.0
Internet/Research Tools	**Mean**	**SD**	**Percent None**	**Percent Rarely**	**Percent Occasionally**	**Percent Frequently**	**Percent Extensively**
Internet Browser	0.84	1.21	58.9	16.1	11.7	8.2	5.1
CD Reference	0.08	0.36	95.2	1.9	2.9	0.0	0.0
Communications	0.06	0.34	96.8	1.3	1.3	0.6	0.0
Other Internet/ Research Tools	0.11	0.48	94.2	2.6	1.9	1.0	0.0
Educational Software	**Mean**	**SD**	**Percent None**	**Percent Rarely**	**Percent Occasionally**	**Percent Rarely**	**Percent Frequently**
Drill/Practice/Tutorial	1.05	1.18	46.0	20.0	20.6	9.5	3.8
Problem Solving	0.24	0.66	85.6	7.1	4.8	2.6	0.0
Process Tools	0.15	0.57	92.3	1.9	4.2	1.3	0.3
Other Educational Software	0.24	0.74	87.4	4.9	4.5	2.6	0.6
Testing Software	**Mean**	**SD**	**Percent None**	**Percent Rarely**	**Percent Occasionally**	**Percent Frequently**	**Percent Extensively**
Individualized/ Tracked	0.76	1.15	59.8	19.0	11.7	4.1	5.4
Generic	0.05	0.30	96.8	1.3	1.9	0.0	0.0
Other testing software	0.10	0.55	95.8	1.3	0.6	1.3	1.0

processors (37.9%) and Internet browser (41.1%) were observed most often. Drill and practice/ tutorial software was observed on the average between rarely and occasionally (M=1.05), and it was observed 54% of the time. Individualized/ tracked software was on the average rarely ob-

Table 5. SCU Subject Areas of Computer Activities Descriptive Statistics

	Language Arts	Mathematics	Science	Social Studies	Other	None
Production Tools	30.34	7.52	9.47	9.71	3.64	39.32
Internet/ Research Tools	20.29	9.18	12.32	12.80	2.90	42.51
Educational Software	33.56	24.54	6.02	5.09	1.39	29.40
Testing Software	34.87	8.65	2.59	2.31	1.73	49.86

Table 6. SCU Overall Meaningful Use of Computers Descriptive Statistics

	Mean	SD	Percent None	Percent Rarely	Percent Occasionally	Percent Frequently	Percent Extensively
Low Level use of Computers	1.00	1.28	49.8	24.1	10.9	6.8	8.4
Somewhat meaningful use for computers	0.86	1.00	48.4	24.5	21.0	4.5	1.6
Meaningful use for computers	1.00	1.21	51.9	15.3	15.3	15.6	1.9
Very meaningful use of computers	0.51	1.02	74.8	10.3	6.8	5.2	2.9

served (M=0.76), but it was observed 40.2% of the time. Notably, in comparison to all software types, drill and practice/tutorial software was on the average observed most often in a school with a mean=1.05 (between Rarely and Occasionally) and in 54% of the observations as compared to the next three highest software uses of Internet browser (41.1%), individualized/tracked (40.2) and word processing (37.9). Internet browser and drill and practice software were observed 13.3% of the time. All categories of software were observed most often in language arts classrooms, while the largest category of software observed in mathematics class was educational software.

On the average, all levels of quality for computer uses were rarely seen (M<=1). Somewhat meaningful uses of computers were observed from rarely to extensively 51.6% of the time just surpassing low level uses of computers (50.2%) and meaningful uses of computers (48.1%). Very meaningful uses of computers were only observed one quarter (25.2%) of the time.

SOM

A summary table with all descriptive statistics is located below in Table 7. Three instructional strategies were observed on the average at least occasionally with M>=2.0. Combining the frequencies of Rarely through Extensively, direct instruction (M=2.87) was observed in 98.4% of the visits. Likewise, independent seatwork (M=2.25)

was observed in 97.2% of the classroom visits, and teacher acting as a coach/facilitator (M=2.16) was observed in 90.5% of the visits. Thirteen of the 24 strategies identified on the SOM were most observed rarely or less (M<=1.0). In rank order of means, these strategies are listed below.

1. Team teaching (M=0.99)
2. Ability groups (M=0.91)
3. Student discussion (M=0.91)
4. Individual tutoring (M=0.81)
5. Sustained writing (M=0.78)
6. Integration of subject areas (M=0.63)
7. Independent inquiry (M=0.59)
8. Project-based learning (M=0.56)
9. Multi-age grouping (M=0.56)
10. Systematic individual instruction (M=0.53)
11. Performance assessment (M=0.53)
12. Student self assessment (M=0.37)
13. Parent/community involvement in learning activities (M=0.53)

Observers recorded the two items for technology integration on the SOM on the average as between rare and occasional use. Combining the frequencies of Rarely through Extensively, computer for instructional delivery (M=1.24) was observed in almost 70% (68.4%) of the visits. Similarly, technology as a learning tool or resource (M=1.12) was observed approximately 60% (59.5%) of the time.

Table 7. SOM Descriptive Statistics

Instructional Orientation	Mean	SD	Percent None	Percent Rarely	Percent Occasionally	Percent Frequently	Percent Extensively
Direct Instruction Lecture	2.87	0.98	1.6	9.2	18.4	42.1	28.8
Team Teaching	0.99	1.00	38.9	33.2	18.7	7.9	1.3
Cooperative/ Collaborative Learning	1.07	1.03	36.7	31.3	21.8	8.5	1.6
Individual tutoring (teacher, peer, aide, adult volunteer)	0.81	1.01	51.3	25.0	16.8	5.1	1.9
Classroom Organization	Mean	SD	Percent None	Percent Rarely	Percent Occasionally	Percent Frequently	Percent Extensively
Ability Groups	0.91	1.18	52.8	19.6	15.8	7.0	4.7
Multi-Age Grouping	0.56	1.04	70.6	13.9	7.9	4.1	3.5
Work centers (for individuals or groups)	1.37	1.12	26.6	31.3	22.8	16.8	2.5
Instructional Strategies	Mean	SD	Percent None	Percent Rarely	Percent Occasionally	Percent Frequently	Percent Extensively
Higher Level instructional feedback (written or verbal) to enhance student learning	1.73	1.18	18.4	24.8	28.6	21.9	6.3
Integration of subject areas (interdisciplinary/thematic units)	0.63	0.94	59.4	26.0	7.9	5.1	1.6
Project-based learning	0.56	0.93	66.2	19.1	8.3	5.1	1.3
Use of higher-level questioning strategies	1.82	1.06	12.7	24.4	36.4	21.8	4.7
Teacher acting as a coach/facilitator	2.16	1.17	9.5	19.9	29.4	27.8	13.3
Parent/community involvement in learning activities	0.32	0.64	75.9	18.4	4.1	1.3	0.3
Technology Use	Mean	SD	Percent None	Percent Rarely	Percent Occasionally	Percent Frequently	Percent Extensively
Computer for instructional delivery	1.24	1.14	31.6	32.3	21.2	10.1	4.7
Technology as a learning tool or resource	1.12	1.17	40.5	25.3	19.0	11.7	3.5
Assessment	Mean	SD	Percent None	Percent Rarely	Percent Occasionally	Percent Frequently	Percent Extensively
Performance Assessment Strategies	0.53	0.91	66.8	21.2	7.3	2.2	2.5
Student self-assessment strategies	0.37	0.80	76.6	15.5	4.1	2.2	1.6
Summary Items	Mean	SD	Percent None	Percent Rarely	Percent Occasionally	Percent Frequently	Percent Extensively
High Academically focused class time	3.23	0.88	1.3	3.5	11.7	38.3	45.3
High level of student attention/interest/ engagement	3.15	0.84	0.9	2.5	15.5	42.4	38.6

On the two summary items, academically focused time and student engagement were both observed on the average between frequently and extensively. Specifically, high academically focused class time (*M*=3.23) was observed 98.7% of the time with 83.6% of the time observed to be frequent or extensive. Similarly, a high level of student attention/interest/engagement (M=3.15) was observed in almost every visit (99.1%) with 81% of the time being frequent or extensive.

DISCUSSION

To answer the primary research question as to what degree and in what ways have teachers integrated technology into early childhood and primary grades, we consider three assertions: (a) technology use, (b) technology access and (c) pedagogy. Each of these is discussed below.

Technology Use

Norris et al. (2003) reported that teachers' use of technology and the Internet was "spare" (p. 22). While their emphasis was on *teachers' use*, they in fact meant *both teachers' use* and *students' use*. Our findings concur that both technology use by the teacher and students were on the average rarely observed. Technology used for instructional delivery was on the average rarely observed (M=1.24, 1=Rarely Observed, 2=Occasionally Observed). Likewise, technology used as a learning tool or resource by students was on the average even more rare (M=1.12). The considerable lack of student use also corroborates O'Dwyer et al.'s (2004) findings that technology as a resource or tool to create learning artifacts was the lowest among all uses of technology.

The current findings also indicate that drill and practice software, Internet browsers and word processing were used most often as software applications. These results continue to substantiate previous well-documented findings by Becker (2001) that games or drill and practice software and word processing are most often observed. That Internet browsers is also one of the most reported applications reflects Clifford's (2008) recent findings that early childhood and primary teachers rate access to the Internet as most inte-

gral to successfully integrating technology into their classrooms. Thus, in general, technology integration continues to be sparse. The types of software used have remained the same except where CD-ROMs for information seeking and references (c.f., Becker, 2001) have been replaced by the Internet.

Technology Access

In addition to reporting technology use as bleak, Norris et al. (2003) and Smeets (2005) asserted that access to technology continued to be a barrier to meaningful technology integration. Judge et al.'s (2006) more recent findings suggest that the student-to-computer ratio is approaching five to one. Because of the categories reported on the SCU (i.e., 0, 1, 2-4, 5-10, 11 or more) it is difficult to discern adequate access. Almost 70% of the observed classrooms had between two and four computers, and another 30% had five or more. Additionally, almost 100% of the classroom computers were observed to be connected to the Internet. Combined with the results from the number of students using a computer and how students worked at computers, these findings suggest that teachers are probably using computer workstations in learning centers typical of early childhood and primary classrooms, where predominately individual students and a small number of pairs use the computers. While not the purpose of the current study, further inferential statistics would be needed to compare whether more computers indicated higher levels of technology integration, which would also provide evidence to compare against Norris et al. and Judge et al.'s results.

Pedagogy

Previous findings (e.g., Becker, 2001; Becker, 2006; Mims et al., 2006; O'Dwyer et al., 2004; Smeets, 2005) have reported that evidence of constructivist pedagogy and epistemologies resulted in higher levels of technology integration. In this vein, the lack of technology integration observed in the current study is corroborated by the dominant instructivist, or teacher-centered, strategies of direct instruction and independent seatwork. While no inferential statistics were conducted, this seems to depict a similar picture with regard to technology integration and pedagogy. In fact, other constructivist strategies, such as student discussions, independent inquiry, project-based learning and performance assessments, were among the least observed strategies. So, the calls (e.g., Bickford et al, 2002; Morrison & Lowther, 2005) for constructivist and student-centered strategies to make the most of technology's potential are warranted.

It seems a balance has not been struck among the important tactile learning, imaginative play and technology integration. These data suggest that direct instruction and independent seatwork, such as worksheets, dominate the instructional landscape. Likewise when technology is used, it is most often drill and practice to promote repetition of skills. The value of technology to support learning has yet to be fully realized.

Wang and Hoot (2006) aggregate three potential reasons why technology integration in early childhood and primary education may be scarce. They argue that:

1. The debate for use of computers with children still stymies teachers' decisions;
2. Teachers feel they are unprepared and lack the confidence to meaningfully integrate technology; and
3. Integrating technology may be an affront to traditional, teacher-centered instruction.

Ertmer (1999) has categorized barriers to technology integration into two categories. *First order*, or extrinsic, barriers are resources and equipment missing or inadequately available, such as poor or missing hardware and software, lack of institutional support and teacher technology skills. These barriers align with the findings by Norris et al. (2003) and Judge et al. (2006) concerning scarce or insufficient access to computers. In contrast, *second order*, or intrinsic, barriers are inherent to teachers' beliefs about teaching and learning. These barriers echo O'Dwyer et al. (2004) and Becker's (2006) findings of increased technology integration when teachers used more constructivist strategies. Second order barriers also reflect previous assertions by Cuban (1986) and Nisan-Nelson (2001) of how teachers reconcile their instructional philosophies and technology's purposes. Wang's and Hoot's potential barriers overlays upon Ertmer's classifications. In fact, Wang and Hoot's barriers only consider the teacher and his/her skills, ignoring any lack of resources and equipment. This is particularly consequential given Norris et al.'s emphatic assertion that lack of computers accounted for the lack of technology integration. Indeed, Judge et al. (2006) recommend more computers are necessary to achieve a five to one student-to-computer ratio.

CONCLUSION

NAEYC's (1996) concern that technology would supplant the rich, tactile and concrete learning experiences in early childhood appears to be unfounded. The findings here suggest very low levels of technology integration in early childhood and primary classrooms. Moreover, when technology is used, it continues to be used for skills-based practice—not in the meaningful methods that require students to create artifacts that represent their knowledge and use critical thinking, or higher order thinking, skills. These uses are incongruous with Smeets' (2005) and ISTE's (2007, 2008) calls for technology integration. If children aged two to five and six to eight are indeed the fastest growing groups of Internet users, some spending upwards of 3 hours online per week as reported in the Corporation for Public Broadcasting's (2002) dated report, then certainly there is an inconsistency with how children are living and learning at home and at school. While we are not advocating that 3 hours online is appropriate for children in early childhood and primary classrooms, the relevancy of how we teach in classrooms and how children learn at home is at the least suspect.

Limitations of this research include the potentially biased sample, since the data were from schools interested in reform, self-evaluation and technology integration. However, given the lack of technology integration observed, it is difficult to believe that the data skewed the results too positively. Additionally, this purpose of this study was descriptive. Future research must consider whether access to more computers and resources enable technology integration. Other research may also consider whether constructivist strategies are indeed correlated with higher levels of technology integration. Finally, longitudinal research may be able to track whether any incremental changes have been made toward increased technology integration.

SOME QUESTIONS FOR REFLECTIVE PRACTITIONERS

1. What role does research like is reported in this chapter play in classroom instruction?
2. Few large scale studies have examined technology integration in early childhood and primary classrooms. Moreover, few studies provide the generalizability and corroboration necessary to fully depict technology integration in general. These statements indicate that while there are a lot of opinions about technology there is limited research about early childhood and primary children's use of technology. How will you analyze articles to determine if they are research-based?
3. When technology is used in K-6 classrooms, it was most often used by teachers to prepare for class. How do you see the role of technology in classrooms? Should it be more teacher or children centered? Why do you think this?
4. Does the information in this report support information you have read in the other chapters of this book? How does this report relate to your understanding of technology and early childhood programs?
5. If your classroom had been included in this study what types of instructional strategies would be reported?
   ○ Number of Computers.
   ○ Percentage of students using computers.
   ○ Types of computers are in your class.
   ○ Use of production and internet tools
   ○ Software used.
   ○ Drill and practice.
   ○ Higher order thinking.
   ○ Group or individual work.
6. The findings of this study concur that both technology use by the teacher and students were on the average rarely observed. Why do you think this was a result of this study?
7. Almost 70% of the observed classrooms had between two and four computers, and another 30% had five or more. Additionally, almost 100% of the classroom computers were observed to be connected to the Internet. However, there was little observed use of these tools. How can you use these tools with your class?
8. The lack of technology integration observed in this study is corroborated by the dominant instructivist, or teacher-centered, strategies of direct instruction and independent seatwork. What will you do to insure your work with your class does not fit into this pattern of behavior?
9. If your school or program does not have a technology budget how will you insure your children have access to these tools? What could you do to acquire technology for your classroom?

10. NAEYC's (1996) concern that technology would supplant the rich, tactile and concrete learning experiences in early childhood appears to be unfounded. Has this study supported this concern or not? What is your evidence to support your answer?

11. If children aged two to five and six to eight are indeed the fastest growing groups of Internet users, some spending upwards of 3 hours online per week as reported in the Corporation for Public Broadcasting's (2002) how will you insure your children learn instructional uses of technology?

12. What teachers say they do and what teachers actually do are often contradictory. With so much conflicting information about technology in classrooms, how will you insure you really implement technology in an appropriate manner?

REFERENCES

Bauserman, K. L., Cassady, J. C., Smith, L. L., & Stroud, J. C. (2005). Kindergarten literacy achievement: The effects of the PLATO integrated learning system. *Reading Research and Instruction, 44*(4), 49–60.

Becker, H. J. (2001, April). *How are teachers using computers in instruction?* Paper presented at the annual meeting of the American Educational Research Association, Seattle, WA.

Becker, J. D. (2006). Digital equity in education: A multilevel examination of differences in and relationships between computer access, computer use and state-level technology policies. *Education Policy Analysis Archives, 15*(3). Retrieved November 24, 2008 from http://epaa.asu.edu/epaa/v15n3/

Bickford, A., Tharp, S., McFarling, P., & Beglau, M. (2002). Finding the right fuel for new engines of learning. *Multimedia Schools, 9*(5), 18–26.

Ching, C. C., Wang, X. C., Shih, M., & Kedem, Y. (2006). Digital photography and journals in a K-1 classroom: Toward meaningful technology integration in early childhood education. *Early Education and Development, 17,* 347–371. doi:10.1207/s15566935eed1703_3

Clifford, A. C., & Grant, M. M. (2008, November). *Teachers: Shaping professionally and becoming technology integrators.* Paper presented at the annual meeting of the Association for Educational Communications and Technology, Orlando, FL.

Corporation for Public Broadcasting. (2002). *Connected to the future: A report on children's Internet use from the Corporation for Public Broadcasting.* Washington, DC: Author.

Couse, L., & Chen, D. (2008). Exploring the potential uses of the Tablet computer as a tool for young children to represent ideas. In K. McFerrin et al. (Eds.), *Proceedings of Society for Information Technology and Teacher Education International Conference 2008* (pp. 3450-3455). Chesapeake, VA: AACE.

Cuban, L. (1986). *Teachers and machines: The classroom use of technology since 1920.* New York: Teachers College Press.

International Society for Technology in Education. (2007). The ISTE national educational technology standards (NETS•S) and performance indicators for students. Eugene, OR: author.

International Society for Technology in Education. (2008). The ISTE national educational technology standards (NETS•T) and performance indicators for teachers. Eugene, OR: author.

Knezek, G., & Christensen, R. (2007). Effect of technology-baed programs on first- and second-grade reading achievement. *Computers in the Schools, 24*(3/4), 23–41.

Lowther, D. L., & Ross, S. M. (1999). *Survey of Computer Use: Reliability analysis.* Memphis, TN: Center for Research in Educational Policy, The University of Memphis.

Mims, C., Polly, D., Shepherd, C. E., & Inan, F. A. (2006). From campus to the field: Examining PT3 projects designed to improve preservice teachers' methods courses and field experiences. *TechTrends, 50*(3), 16–24. doi:10.1007/s11528-006-7599-5

Morrison, G. R., & Lowther, D. L. (2002). *Integrating computer technology in the classroom* (2nd ed.). Upper Saddle River, NJ: Merrill Prentice Hall.

National Association for the Education of Young Children. (1996). *Technology and young children—ages 3 through 8: A position statement of the National Association for the Education of Young Children.* Washington, DC: author.

Nisan-Nelson, P. D. (2001). Technology integration: A case of professional development. *Journal of Technology and Teacher Education, 9*(1), 83–103.

Norris, C., Sullivan, T., Poirot, J., & Soloway, E. (2003). No access, no use, no impact: Snapshot surveys of educational technology in k-12. *Journal of Research on Technology in Education, 36*(1), 15–27.

Paterson, W. A., Henry, J., O'Quin, K., Ceprano, M. A., & Blue, E. V. (2003). Investigating the effectiveness of an integrated learning system on early emergent readers. *Reading Research Quarterly, 38*(2), 172–207. doi:10.1598/RRQ.38.2.2

Ross, S. M., Smith, L. J., & Alberg, M. (1999). *The School Observation Measure.* Memphis, TN: Center for Research in Educational Policy, The University of Memphis.

Smeets, E. (2005). Does ICT contribute to powerful learning environments in primary education? *Computers & Education, 44*, 343–355. doi:10.1016/j.compedu.2004.04.003

Sterbinsky, A., Ross, S. M., & Burke, D. (2004). *Tennessee EdTech Accountability Model (TEAM) reliability study.* Alexandria, VA: The CNA Corporation.

Voogt, J., & McKenney, S. (2007). Using ICT to foster (pre) reading and writing skills in young children. *Computers in the Schools, 24*(3/4), 83–94.

Wang, X. C., & Hoot, J. L. (2006). Introduction: Information and communication technology in early childhood education. *Early Education and Development, 17*(3), 317–322. doi:10.1207/s15566935eed1703_1

Chapter 10

Building Epistemic Awareness in the Early Childhood Classroom
Theory, Methodology, and Technology

Denise L. Winsor
University of Memphis, USA

Sally Blake
University of Memphis, USA

ABSTRACT

It is evident from the information in the previous chapters in this book that there is much to be learned about how technology fits into the world of early childhood education (ECE). This chapter discusses some exciting new thinking about epistemology and how children and teachers learn and how this could relate to technology and all learning with young children and their teachers. The new understanding of preschool education potential demands new approaches to these vital years of schooling if we are to prepare our children to succeed in the increasingly demanding academic environments.

INTRODUCTION

A remarkable convergence of new knowledge about the developing brain, the human genome, and the extent to which early childhood experiences influence later learning, behavior, and health now offers policymakers an exceptional opportunity to change the life prospects of vulnerable young children, says a new report from the Center on the Developing Child at Harvard University "The early childhood years lay the foundation for later economic productivity, responsible citizenship, and a lifetime of sound physical and mental health," says Jack P. Shonkoff,

(2007, p. 2) director of the center and one of the report's principal authors. Early childhood education has long been accepted as important for preparing young children to enter the academic world. Recent reports from the Office of Economic Development (2006) support high-quality preschool education as one of the most promising ways to help strengthen the future economic and fiscal position of our states and nation. There is also growing recognition of the importance of supporting the development of mathematical and scientific knowledge and skills in young children which includes technology. *(*Moon & Schweingruber, 2005*)*

The new understanding of preschool education potential demands new approaches to these

DOI: 10.4018/978-1-60566-784-3.ch010

vital years of schooling if we are to prepare our children to succeed in the increasingly demanding academic environments. Research on the development of cognitive skills related to science, technology, engineering and mathematics has provided fascinating new ideas concerning what young children can do, but very little guidance for adults about how to use this information in caring for young children. Unfortunately, these advances in understanding of children's thinking do not seem to be shaping practice and policy in early childhood. "The tremendous gaps between what is known from developmental research and the usual content of curricula and the nature of practice in early childhood settings may inhibit children's ability to reach their potential (NRC, 2005). Furthermore, when applied research is carried out, it is often not guided by theoretical frameworks and does not draw on research on cognitive development.

The professional challenges that this raises for the early childhood field are formidable. Individuals have to mount new mental structure as well as accumulate relevant data for the structure. It is as if learners have to get to the middle of the lake without a rowboat. The theoretical task is two-fold: to spell out how new mental structures are acquired and to achieve a theory of environment that that supports such learning (Gelman & Brenneman 2004). We believe that Denise's work is a start to understanding how new mental structures are acquired and an approach to possible conceptual change. Because this area of research is new in the field of early childhood education we have provided a review of all current research to build a chain of logic for support if this work. As you read this chapter we have included some direct connections to the relationship between technology and epistemology. As you read the research it is important that you think through the implications for technology and all learning in your classroom.

PERSONAL EPISTEMOLOGY

The study of epistemology (i.e., knowledge) is derived and deeply rooted in the disciplines of philosophy, sociology, and anthropology. For centuries the nature of knowledge has been a profoundly controversial and heavily debated topic, including early childhood. In this chapter, personal epistemology is applied to early childhood development and children's perceptions of early learning. For our purpose, personal epistemology is defined as an individual's *beliefs* about the nature of knowledge and the nature and process of knowing (Hofer & Pintrich, 1997). What are an individual's beliefs about the nature of knowledge and the process of knowing? How do we know what we know? When we are in the process of constructing our knowledge, how do we make decisions about what we believe and whom we believe? Do beliefs about knowledge matter in terms of student learning? The study of personal epistemology focuses on these types of questions. These issues directly relate to how teachers and children learn technology and the decisions they make to use technology. This chapter will share insights how epistemology forms and how you as a teacher make the decisions you make about what technology to teach and how to use technology when teaching. This chapter will help you think about your approaches and conceptual change needed if we are to truly become teachers and users of technology. In addition the author explains the new research field of epistemology in young children which directly influences how they learn, interact, and develop. Although this field of research has struggled to achieve a single definition or a best-fit methodological approach; and embraces multiple conceptualizations of the construct there continues to be a significant amount of progress in the study of personal epistemology.

Personal epistemology has been heavily researched in college students (King & Kitchener, 1994; Perry, 1970; Schommer, 1990) and more recently has focused on development in adolescence (Hofer & Pintrich, 2002). Kuhn & Weinstock (2002) have criticized the field for the absence of research in early childhood epistemological development, however this trend may be shifting with the recent connection between young children's personal epistemology and theory of mind development (Burr & Hofer, 2002; Winsor, 2006). In addition, other researchers have ventured into this unfamiliar area; fourth grade German students (Haerle, 2006); fifth grade science students (Elder, 2002); and comparing elementary students with adolescents and adults (Mansfield & Clinchy, 2002; Kuhn, Cheney, & Weinstock, 2000). The range and variety of literature that exists in personal epistemology research is becoming increasingly more innovative and diverse at a variety of levels including age, gender, culture, subject domains, and measurement instruments.

Even with the considerable amount of theoretical and empirical literature there is little consideration given to researching young children's personal epistemology. In this chapter we propose a more diverse and integrative approach for interpreting the trajectory of young children's epistemic development. It is essential to be clear upfront, it is debated that young children hold beliefs about knowledge and knowing; and it is questioned by many researchers if young children have the cognitive abilities to think about or discuss abstract ideas such as knowledge or beliefs. Therefore, the approach to investigating young children's personal epistemology needs to move along a slightly different course than has traditionally been taken with adults and even adolescents. In addition to the limited investigations into young children's epistemological experiences, another area that will be addressed in this chapter is the lack of technology used to identify epistemological development across the field. Braten (2008) makes two arguments in support of positive influences that may result from incorporating internet technologies as a research methodology for measuring epistemological development. Braten's criticisms are that most research includes a single text and

that the text is primarily in print form. Braten (2008) argues that the impact of epistemological beliefs will be found to be more potent for student learning when the methodologies include multiple sources and when techniques used to identify epistemological development include internet or other technological educational devices.

Although he is criticizing research with adolescents and adults, this may particularly ring true for young children. Especially, due to the high degree of computer games, internet activity, and the technical savvy nature of young children in today's society.

Children's developing epistemologies will be discussed in detail later in this chapter but initially, perhaps, it is beneficial to reframe children's epistemological development. It may be more sustainable to conceive of children's epistemological development as a way to identify how children build beliefs about knowledge and knowing as they develop intrinsically (e.g., cognitively, socially, emotionally) and extrinsically as a result of their complex and multi-dimensional interactions with others and the world around them. This chapter discusses how to look at the child's experiences in a learning environment through a bi-focal lens. That is, as a consumer of knowledge who is an insider possessing awareness of epistemological sensitivities, in much the same way as Vygotsky viewed the intrapsychological (i.e., subject, subjectivity) experiences of children; and as an outsider, by listening to and observing the child's interactions with others or interpsychologically. In much the same way that our vision changes through a bi-focal depending on where we focus; investigating young children's progress in building epistemologies needs to change and adapt to the content, the context, and climate of the environment. A child's interactions with parents, the teacher, and peers play a major role in how children construct knowledge and how they build beliefs about knowledge. The interaction with technology in early childhood environments is instrumental to use and learning of technology.

Early childhood education should emphasize and value children's experiences and perspectives as they cultivate knowledge and the processes of knowing. Early childhood is a rapid and delicate period of development; the beliefs about knowledge and knowing that children build from a very early age inevitably influence nearly every aspect of learning; and later, how they reason, solve problems, and make decisions. Government officials, school administrators, classroom teachers, and parents, as well as researchers and teacher education programs can benefit from understanding the impact of epistemic development. Children are consumers of knowledge in the broadest sense; cognitive theories of learning and sociocultural theories view children as active participants of the learning process. Despite the endless amounts of research on early childhood development; "a remarkably small percentage of the studies specifically address what children do, feel, or think about in school" (LeCompte and Preissle, 1992, p. 819). Regardless of the criticism there appears to little change in thinking about early childhood education and research; Clark, McQuail, and Moss (2003) found limited studies that investigated children younger than six-years-old, in terms of their experiences in a structured or unstructured learning environment.

The purpose of this chapter is three-fold; 1) to discuss personal epistemology and the role it plays in the lives of children ages 2-to-5-years-old (e.g., preschool); 2) to propose a conceptual framework and methodological perspectives that have implications for how parents prepare children for early education and can positively impact student learning; and 3) address classroom practices and instructional techniques that can be influenced by the use of technology and have implications for teacher preparation programs, in-service teachers, and may promote early epistemic ability.

PERSONAL EPISTEMOLOGY: BACKGROUND

Contemporary research in personal epistemology is deeply rooted in Piaget's "genetic epistemology." Perry's (1970), *Scheme of Intellectual and Ethical Development* was created from two longitudinal studies that set out to capture the perceptions of college student's overall development during their college experience rather than academic achievement. This set the momentum for personal epistemological research using similar developmental frameworks for epistemological thinking (Baxter Magolda, 1992; Belensky, Clinchy, Goldberger, & Tarule, 1986; King & Kitchener, 1994; Kuhn, 1991). However, there are other conceptions of personal epistemology that have impacted the thinking within this chapter; epistemological beliefs (Schommer, 1990); epistemological theories (Hofer & Pintrich, 1997); and epistemological resources (Hammer & Elby, 2002). Also, recent research in the field has promoted a Vygotskian perspective which views personal epistemologies as being socially constructed and influenced by one's culture and environment (Bendixen & Rule, 2004; Burr & Hofer, 2002; Haerle, 2006; Hofer & Pintrich, 1997).

Personal epistemology is generally accepted as being comprised of two dimensions concerning beliefs about the nature of knowledge and the process of knowing (Burr & Hofer, 2002). The nature of knowledge includes (1) the simplicity of knowledge (i.e., the relative connectedness of knowledge); and (2) the certainty of knowledge (i.e., the perceived stability of knowledge). The process of knowing includes (1) the source of knowledge (i.e., where knowledge resides, internally or externally); and (2) the justification of knowledge (i.e., how individuals evaluate and warrant knowledge claims). However, in addition to the dimensions of beliefs just described, there is another widely accepted way of conceptualizing epistemological development, that is, in the form of three levels: (1) absolutism (i.e., simple, dichotomous views of knowledge), (2) multiplism (i.e., reasoning is more complex and relativistic), and (3) evaluatism (i.e., views of knowledge focus on evaluation and decision-making among differing views) (Kuhn & Weinstock, 2002). Currently, each way of thinking about epistemological development is distinctly separate.

Most researchers in the field agree on a general trajectory of epistemological development that begins as a type of absolutism, progressing into multiplism, and then finally into evaluativism. Chandler, Hallet, and Sokol (2002) states that this is the same stage progression that appears in most research in personal epistemological development, regardless of who is studied and no matter what the conditions or measure. However, when investigating preschoolers, Burr & Hofer (2002) identified a pre-dualistic or pre-absolutist phase of subjectivity, this phase of subjectivity is thought to be in contrast to multiplistic subjectivity and is in a sense an egocentric subjectivity that occurs prior to an absolutist epistemological stance.

ISSUES, CONTROVERSIES, AND PROBLEMS IN CHILDREN'S PERSONAL EPISTEMOLOGY

In this section the importance of investigating young children is discussed including; developmental issues, research in children's personal epistemology, methodological issues, theory of mind, and the relationship between children's personal epistemology and theory of mind. Research on epistemological development has focused primarily on adolescents and adults and has neglected very young children until recently (Burr & Hofer, 2002; Haerle, 2006, Kuhn & Weinstock, 2006, Winsor, 2006). Originally it was thought that epistemological development began in late adolescence, triggered by the intellectual demands of college (Burr & Hofer, 2002). It is also speculated that researching young children was simply inadvertently overlooked because early

researchers in the field had their interests in higher education and not developmental psychology and therefore studied the age group of most interest to them (Hofer & Pintrich, 1997).

Researching young children addresses the broader issue of engaging in research that closely parallels cognitive development (Hofer, 2001). Development is historically a prominent issue in the personal epistemology of college students but researching young children can be instrumental in identifying periods of epistemic development that have only been hypothesized but never identified. Hofer (2001) proposes that researching young children would contribute toward a "Life-Span" view of personal epistemology (p. 365). Kuhn and Pearsall (2000) states that the development of, epistemological theories are advancing but consistently remains distant from other cognitive developmental research.

Developmental Issues in Children's Personal Epistemology

Piaget's theory. In most accounts early childhood refers to an individual from age two until 7 years-old and according to Piaget (1964) this period of time is called the *preoperational stage of cognitive development.* This stage of development is characterized by the child's ability to use symbols to mentally represent objects that exist in the world and their thinking is egocentric and centrally focused. This is a period of time when children begin to acquire language skill at lightning speed and build knowledge of concepts at an equally fast pace. Piaget believed that much of the way that children think at this stage of development is primitive; however there is some literature that would argue that Piaget underestimated young children and believe that children's ways of thinking are more sophisticated and complex than initially theorized (Flavell & Miller, 1999; Wellman, Cross, & Watson, 2001).

Children in the preoperational phase of development generally lack understanding of the

Principle of Conservation, which demonstrates their inability to focus on more than one event or concept at one time. For example, if a sandwich were cut in four small pieces, a preoperational child would have the tendency to think that the four smaller pieces indicate a larger amount of sandwich than an uncut sandwich because they can only focus on the greater number of pieces; this ability to focus on only one aspect of the situation is called *centration.* Gelman (2000) and Siegler (1998) have found that children in the early preoperational stage of development are capable of succeeding on simpler forms of these tasks that require the same skill. Boden (1980) had similar findings and discovered that the pass rate on many of the tasks depended on the variation of the instructions given to the child.

Irreversibility is another characteristic of a preoperational child. This Piagetian term means that the child cannot manipulate a change of direction in their mind. For example just because a child knows how to walk to the store does not mean that it can be assumed the child could figure out how to walk home in early preoperational development. At this stage it is assumed by Piaget that the child has mastered object permanence; they now know that an object continues to exist even though it may not be directly visible to them at the moment. For example, if mom puts candy behind her back, the candy is still present.

Egocentricity is another main characteristic associated with the preoperational child. Egocentricity refers to the child's beliefs that everyone views things in the same way that they do. Supposedly, children have the inability to view situations and objects from the perspective of another individual. Piaget & Inhelder (1956) in a renowned study placed a child facing in one direction and a doll in the opposite direction, then asked the child to describe the view in the scene (that the doll could not see) from the doll's perspective. Children below age six were more likely to describe the doll's view similar to what they could see, while

it would be apparent to an adult that the child and the doll do not have the same view.

In many areas of cognitive development Piaget's work in viewed as foundational because of his many insights and contributions however; there is research that demonstrates some weaknesses about his theory. Baillargeon, Graber, DeVos, & Black (1990) found that when practical knowledge is assessed, young children are more competent than Piaget originally thought. It could be that we do not consistently capture the sophistication and complexity of preschooler's cognitive abilities because they are more fragile than those of older children and are therefore only present under certain more familiar conditions than they are generally assessed (Gelman, 1979). The heart and sole of Piaget's stage development is more recently being doubted; some researchers question that the broad stages of cognitive development represent the true course of human development.

Personal Epistemology

The lack of research with young children has made way for researchers to speculate conceptually regarding the beginnings of personal epistemological development. Chandler, Hallet, & Sokol (2002) point out that regardless of the age, the participants studied thus far demonstrate similar patterns of thinking and seem to have similar starting points. There are five arguments for this phenomenon and Chandler, Hallet, & Sokol, (2002) propose three of the five: (1) early onset suggests that young children have more sophisticated epistemologies than can be predicted based on studies of college students; (2) recursion is conceptualized as a spiral-like development in which epistemological stages continue to occur and reoccur in a cyclic process, rather than in a linear motion; and (3) suppression which suggests that prior to entering school and during school children's advancing beliefs are discouraged which prompts them to suppress their epistemological development until adulthood.

Two other arguments can be identified in the literature; (4) late onset supports the idea that true epistemological development does not begin until students reach higher academic environments and researchers have been overestimating the ability of young children (Perry, 1970; King & Kitchener, 1994), and (5) domain dependence suggests that early epistemic thinking is dependent on the domain in question. For example, young children may demonstrate multiplistic epistemological perspectives about subjective knowledge (i.e., personal judgments or procedural knowledge) and, on the other hand, not demonstrate objective-type-knowledge (declarative knowledge) until much later (Kuhn & Weinstock, 2002; Mansfield & Clinchy, unpublished). One of these alternatives may be more valid than another but it is much too premature to make this judgment.

Preschool

Addressing developmental issues with young children may require that personal epistemology researchers adopt a more situated perspective and examine more microgentic levels of change (Hofer, 2001). This will be particularly useful at the preschool level because most preschool curricula do not have designated standards, therefore, once researchers begin to study preschool classrooms there will be a vast array of instructional philosophies and strategies that may be informative about how children come to know and understand the nature of knowledge and the process of knowing.

It is also important to point out the *National Center for Education Statistics* and the *Institute of Educational Sciences* at the Department of Education in 2000 indicate that there was a 15% increase in preschool enrollment from 1990 to 2000. Over those same years they indicated that 40% of all 3-year-olds attend preschool, followed by 60% of 4-year-olds, and 92% of 5-year-olds. This increasing trend is consistent across Caucasian, African-American, and Hispanic populations

and showed no correlation between household income and the parents' highest level of education, (National Household Education Survey, NHES, 2000). This is an indication that there is an educational need to gather information about young children in the preschool classroom environment. It is important to investigate young children in a structured learning environment in order to identify patterns during their interactions with others and to understand their epistemic development. Students are entering school younger, demands on teachers are becoming greater, and many states do not require preschool teachers to have specific educational backgrounds. Considering the increase in preschool attendance, developmental factors of personal epistemology could prove to be beneficial for learning and instruction by stimulating the classroom environment (Bendixen & Rule, 2004; Hofer, 2001) or linking personal epistemology with a construct such as situational learning (Schraw & Lehman, 2001).

CURRENT RESEARCH ON CHILDREN'S PERSONAL EPISTEMOLOGY

Haerle (2006) examined fourth-grade children, teacher epistemology, and classroom climate and found that the student's epistemologies were representative of personal theories about knowledge and knowing. He proposed that the findings were identifiable and interrelated according to four dimensions; (1) certainty of knowledge, (2) structure of knowledge, (3) justification of knowledge, and (4) source of knowledge, this is consistent with Hofer & Pintrich (1997). Further, the student's were categorized according to their developmental patterns, absolutism, multiplism, and evaluativism (Kuhn & Weinstock, 2002). Haerle (2006) developed a model that incorporates the findings of the fourth-graders personal epistemologies with the teacher and the classroom climate called *The Educational Model for Personal Epistemology*

Table 1. Epistemic matrix: Integrated understanding of the dimensions of knowledge and the developmental level of epistemological development

	Simple Is knowledge simple or complex?	**Certain** Is knowledge stable or unstable?	**Source** Is knowledge internal or external?	**Justification** How do individuals evaluate knowledge claims?
Absolutist Objective view of knowledge.	I think teachers should focus on facts rather than theories.	If two students are arguing about something, at least one of them must be wrong.	I think children should always listen to their parents.	I am going to do what I want to do because I know what is best for me.
Multiplist Subjective view of knowledge.	Some basics require basic factual knowledge, but other times we need to have a deeper understanding of concepts.	Every student has equally valuable contributions and their opinions should be heard.	At home I listen to my parents, but when I am at school I listen to my teachers because they know what is best for me at that time.	In some situations ignoring a student's behavior is more productive, but other situations require timeout because it is necessary to get them under control more quickly.
Evaluativist Shift of objective and subjective stance when claims are evaluated & warranted.	The more you know about a topic the more there is to know.	The best way to learn about global warming to present several theories & allow the student to decide which is best based on their knowledge & experience.	I think children should be able to question their parent's authority.	Being an effective teacher means that you consider the individual students needs and apply what you have learned from books, experience, & others.

Enhancement (EMPEE). He argues that the student's epistemologies are an essential component in the model and the primary focus of educational enhancement. Haerle (2006) represents another important study that supports the importance of researching children's personal epistemologies for the implications that is presents for education. This study although will focus slightly on the instructional technique of the teacher primarily because it is situated within the classroom context but the main concern is on identifying the ways in which children develop personal epistemological system in relationship to influences and the processes within their learning environment.

Traditionally, personal epistemology investigates either an individual's dimensions of knowledge or developmental levels. Children's epistemological awareness is a complex construct to capture and evaluate. Therefore, we propose that it may not be measurable as strictly dimensions of knowledge of developmental levels, perhaps the two theories need to be integrated as a matrix. Table 1 provides examples of the type of thinking that might occur at each cell of the matrix. For example, a child who is multiplistic in relationship

to their certainty of knowledge would be identified as, *multiplist certain knowledge* (see Table 1, this cell indicates how a child would be thinking and guides how to qualify a child's statements.) Table 1 also provides individual definitions for each of the dimensions and level.

METHODOLOGICAL ISSUES

Measuring young children's epistemological awareness will be challenging if researchers do not make accommodations for their cognitive abilities. This may well explain the discrepancies in the theory of mind literature that illustrates how changing the false-belief task changes the age that children can successful complete the task (Chandler et al., 2002; Gopnik & Meltzoff, 1986; O'Neill, Astington, & Flavell, 1992; Perner, 1991). If researchers have expectations that children need to perform at a higher level than they are developmentally capable, identifying children's personal epistemologies may prove to be emotionally taxing for the child and ineffective for the researcher; however young children should not be underestimated in their ability to perform sophisticated cognitive tasks. King and Kitchener (1994) argue that the research instruments designed to study personal epistemology are geared more toward college students and may be too cognitively challenging for young children.

Personal epistemologies are complex even in adult investigations; therefore, it is reasonable to believe they may be equally as elusive in young children. King & Kitchener (1994) and Kuhn (1991) emphasize measuring personal epistemologies as components of reasoning. The concern with this type of method is that they can vary depending on the nature of the participant, the investigator, and the setting of the investigation. The field of personal epistemology has been critical of measures and frameworks that are too subjective insofar as they can lead the participants to the desired results by focusing on a specific dimension or using a guiding or prompting question. Hofer & Pintrich (1997) concludes that it may be more beneficial to develop a more precise way to measure personal epistemologies as seen with (Baxter Magolda, 1992; King & Kitchener, 1994; Kuhn, 1991). The biggest problem with phenomenological or open-ended types of questions is the low degree of replicability (Hofer & Pintrich, 1997).

Interviews and more qualitative methodologies have led to a deeper understanding of individual's beliefs about knowledge; however, the problem with this type of approach is that it tends to be an issue of time during data collection on the part of the participants and the researcher. This may prove to be a measurement issue in researching young children in general because of the shorter attentions span, but specifically, for this study because it is conducted in the classroom setting. While conducting research within a classroom context the researcher needs to be conscientious of multiple factors that cannot be controlled, in addition to being respectful to the teacher and students. An alternative to structured and unstructured interviews with adults is a paper-and-pencil

questionnaire but this can be problematic with younger children because of their developmental restraints. Not only are they limited in their reading ability but if the questions were to be read to them, the understanding of the Likert scale may be too complex for a young child to understand.

Language development in young children is a gradual process and is found to be a limitation in other areas of cognitive development such as, theory of mind (Wellman & Cross, 2001) and will need to be strongly considered prior to the examination of any cognitive constructs. The language and activities need to be tailored specific to the age group being studied (Poole & Lamb, 1998). Piloting research with young children is recommended (Greig & Taylor, 1999), although piloting research can produce imperative information, it contributes to the time factor.

Researchers are trying new methodologies as they begin to investigate young children's ability to think and express their epistemologies; Winsor (2006, 2008) used whole class instruction which focused on collaborative inquiry among the students; this was a process in which the teacher asked higher-order questions to get the students to build upon each others knowledge and experience. The collaborative inquiry was followed by semi-structure individual debriefing interviews for extrapolation of the child's thinking and experiences in the collaborative inquiry. At the end of each week the child's responses during the collaborative inquiry and the individual interviews; focus groups of three children were conducted to simulate a smaller slower version of the whole class instruction which allowed each child a chance to speak, and associate their personal experiences, in their own words. Tangen (2008) discusses the importance of being especially cognizant of "listening to young children's voices" (p. 158) as a means of adequately understanding their experiences with knowledge in a classroom environment. Tangen (2008) unpacks the ability to hear children's voices as three different experiences: 1) as a research methodology, 2) as a phenomenon (i.e., listening to the child's past experiences, their view of what is happening in the moment, and future perspectives); and 3) as referencing multiple subjects (i.e., the child who is being listen to, the children who are doing the listening, and the interaction between the two). Winsor (2006, 2008) attempted to incorporate the three conceptions of "listening to children's voices," however the issue becomes one of analysis which will not be discussed in this chapter. Another aspect of Winsor's preschool research was the use of the focus groups as a pre-instruction/post-instruction format to get a baseline understanding on each child. Haerle (2006) used think-aloud protocols with elementary students and depicted the results in the form of computer generated concept maps that made the children's thinking, associations, and understanding more visible.

THEORY OF MIND

While personal epistemology research has clearly neglected investigating children many researchers have hypothesized about the onset of personal epistemological development in young children. Other areas of cognitive development have flourished in their investigation of young children (e.g., theory of mind). Theory of mind development is an area of cognitive development research that investigates the nature and development toward understanding of the mental world, which refers to a developmental milestone in which children begin to recognize other's perspectives differ from their own. Individual's inner world consisting of: beliefs, desires, emotions, thoughts, perceptions, intentions, and other states (Flavell, 2004). In contemporary research the term theory of mind surfaced from Piagetian literature and with the work of Premack & Woodruff who investigated chimpanzees and their cognitive ability. Woodruff & Premack (1978) defined theory of mind as a system of inferences that can be used to predict behavior by attributing mental states to

individuals.

Understanding false beliefs demonstrates a child's knowledge or awareness that differences exist between "contents" of the mind and "content" of the world. Wimmer & Perner, (1983) initiated the false-belief-task in which subject (A) puts an object in a certain location (a) but then while subject (A) is away and cannot see what happens, subject (B) moves the location of the object to location (b). Subject (A) returns, and the child is asked; where will subject (A) look for the object; location (a) or (b)? Children who pass the false-belief-task are able to predict that subject (A) will look for the object in location (a) because that is where subject (A) put it and has no knowledge that subject (B) moved it. This infers that the child can adequately distinguish between what they themselves know and what subject (A) knows. Conversely, children who fail the false-belief-task will report that subject (A) will look for the object in location (b); assuming that subject (A) knows that subject (B) has moved the object to location (b). This incorrect prediction on the part of the child indicates an inability to differentiate between what they think/know and what others think/know.

Many researchers have conducted similar false-belief task research, however they have altered the original task in various ways, such that the variety of interpretations are too numerous to elaborate (Astington & Jenkins, 1999; Bartsch & Wellman, 1995; Chandler, Fritz, & Hala, 1989; Call & Tomasello, 1999). The vast findings raise questionable doubt about children's thinking. It may reflect general language or social development, rather than truly reflect their understanding of the mind. In general, most accounts conclude that this developmental criterion is absent in three-year-olds and supposedly emerges closer to age 4, and is in place be age 5. This is not altogether absolutely agreed upon and in some cases noted as inaccurate (Chandler et. al., 1989). Chandler et al. (1989) showed that, at least in some situations on some task variations, 3-year-olds can also demonstrate correct responses on the false-belief-task when they are more actively engaged in deceiving the target person. Lewis & Mitchell (1994) found that 3-year-olds could pass the false-belief-task when the questions are phrased in a certain manner.

Bradmetz & Schneider (2004) used a simplified judgment task with two-year-olds to show that they know that others may have different emotions from their own. Wellman & Woolley (1990) took the same age group and showed children's ability to understand that others may hold different emotions and desires for the identical objects or events. Despite the child's understanding of desires and emotions they consistently fail the false-belief-task. Why? Perhaps it is because the false-belief-task utilizes an incorrect application of a young child's language ability, or misrepresents the role of language in child development. This contrast in a child's ability needs to be investigated from a much closer look at the role of language in the development of theory of mind.

Children use words like happy, sad, want, and like by their second birthday to refer to others internal mental states separate from the individual's external behaviors, physical features, and facial expressions (Bartsch, 2002; Bartsch & Wellman, 1995). Could this be because in early education we tell children this is an appropriate way to think or respond for a given situation. If this is true, could it be that children begin to develop epistemologically at a very early age, however our current education system fails to promote epistemological growth and therefore it is forced into a dormancy? We believe that children do have early epistemological awareness and ability which should be fostered in early childhood settings; increasing teacher's influences and use of technology are two ways that can improve our ability to identify young children's epistemologies. As the child continues to develop and conversational skills advance there is an apparent shift in children's mental states of early understanding of desire and emotion to later understanding of beliefs thoughts and knowledge.

It is not until around three-years-old when children begin to use words like; think and know to refer to thoughts and beliefs. Why the difference between children's connection with emotion and their delayed connection to beliefs? Perhaps emotions are routinely viewed as external based on personal experience (but in reality we cannot feel someone else's pain) whereas beliefs are inherently internal and are not easily monitored.

There is an interesting proposition to deviate from the current theory of mind literature and adopt a "community of mind" (Nelson & Snyder, 2005). The assumption is as follows: in early childhood development an individual is exposed to a large community and attempts to gain membership to this community. This community is synonymous with a person's surrounding and social context, sometimes referred to as social cultural environment. The emphasis is on the minds that interact with and also differ with one another, as well as having certain similarities of structure and content. In the end understanding differences among minds requires understanding the source of the differences among people, their backgrounds, personalities, relationships, and experiences.

Nelson's perspective corresponds to a Vygotskian view which is more compatible in terms of incorporating affect and language as components of an individual's environment. In terms of external associations, a child's receptive language skills such as listening to stories, is largely related to developing representational functions of language. In order to develop these types of skills children are dependent on their environment to provide these experiences and their community is fundamentally pivotal.

This idea of "community of minds" (Nelson & Snyder, 2005) has significant possibilities for assisting research to move forward with attempts to link theory of mind and personal epistemology in young children. Although it emphasizes the role of the external as the innovator of self, the individual remains in an egocentric subjective phase and potentially developing pre-dualistic epistemologies (Burr & Hofer, 2002) which may be more specifically identified in relationship to the child's environment and experiences as a member of their community. Theory of mind researchers have been asking questions such as "How, when, and in what manner does an everyday theory of mind arise" (Wellman, 2001). Researcher, educators, and parents concerned about the impact of personal epistemological development in early childhood need to ask, how, when, and in what manner does personal epistemology arise.

PERSONAL EPISTEMOLOGY AND THEORY OF MIND

Theory of mind (TOM) involves the awareness that others have different perspectives about what is known and this awareness bares significance on the concept of epistemological thought (Hofer and Pintrich, 2002). This is important for understanding personal epistemology, because they focus on the nature of human knowledge and how individuals come to know the world (Burr & Hofer, 2002), and how individuals justify, interpret, and construct knowledge and knowing (Schommer, 1990). Although this section discusses how the two constructs may be linked, there is very little empirical evidence that exists in the current literature.

Mansfield and Clinchy (1985) reported *identifying epistemological beliefs* in 3- to 5-year-olds. It has been suggested by some in the field that personal epistemologies may be developing and even in place prior to TOM. If this is true there may be a pre-dualistic stage of epistemological development that has not been investigated because a child could not hold a belief about knowledge without acknowledging that there are alternative perspectives (Burr & Hofer, 2002).

By successfully completing a false-belief task, understanding that others can/do have different beliefs based on knowledge of their experiences, is equivalent to achieving a dualistic epistemological point of view and acknowledging that there can be competing notions of reality, and understanding that there is no absolute right or wrong interpretation (Kuhn, 2000). Individuals do not simply acquire a full capacity for TOM or personal epistemology all at one time; it is a gradual and continually evolving developmental process. In Piaget's theory of knowledge, he focused on how individuals "progressively reconstruct the relationship between the knower and the known" (Piaget, 1952). The research in this area is in its infancy stage, developmental researchers have raised some questions regarding the order in which these two constructs (TOM and personal epistemologies) occur in development (e.g., Chandler et al., 2002). First, a supposed pre-dualistic phase is characterized by "unwavering egocentric subjectivity," and evokes TOM (Burr & Hofer, 2002). Second and in contrast, Astington, Pelletier, and Homer (2002) suggest from their findings that false-belief understanding is fundamental to children's epistemological development because it underlies their understanding of the epistemic concepts of evidence, inference, and truth.

One problem that consistently surfaces is that of subjective and objective knowledge and knowing (Burr & Hofer, 2002). This is a reoccurring problem in the theory of mind literature as well. Perhaps it is not a development of either/or in terms of one over the other but that both are at a level of incongruence because of changing contexts or environment. This is precisely why, neither, developmental levels; nor dimensions of knowledge may not adequately capture an individual's complete epistemological perspective. In the next section there will be discussion about the integration of developmental levels and dimensions of knowledge.

The prospect of drawing a cognitive link between personal epistemology and theory of mind is an intriguing proposition and could address many of the issues that are emerging in the field of personal epistemology. In order to do develop this theory it will be necessary to shift the ordinary theoretical lens.

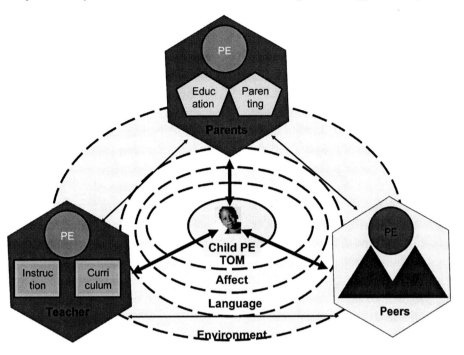

Figure 1. **The Dynamic Systems Framework for Personal Epistemology Development**

A FRAMEWORK FOR RESEARCHING CHILDREN'S PERSONAL EPISTEMOLOGY

This section will briefly introduce and discuss the, *Dynamic Systems Framework for Personal Epistemology Development* (DSFPED) (see Figure 1). This framework depicts the complexity of the many components that affect preschooler's epistemological nature and understanding of knowledge and the process of knowing. The DSFPED integrates critical aspects of several well-known theories: 1) Piaget's (1952) Cognitive Developmental Theory, 2) Vygotsky's (1978) Sociocultural Theory, 3) Bronfenbrenner's (1979, 1988) Ecological Systems Theory, and 4) Minuchin's (1974) Dynamic Family Systems Theory.

In the DSFPED, dynamic refers to the general composition of the system, meaning the components are not isolated. In this dynamic system, the movement within and between the component parts is asynchronous, however, all of the components have interrelationships and

intrarelationships (Vygotsky, 1978). At the center of the DSFPED, the child and his/her personal epistemology; a critical aspect of the framework is that the child is the central focus and all other aspects (i.e., TOM, affect, language, and environment) and subsystems (i.e., parents, teacher, peers) relate back to the child.

Sub-Systems

These external factors; parent, the preschool teacher, and peers represent subsystems within the classroom context who interject their own personal epistemological system. To demonstrate the relationships between the sub-systems and the child, note that there are solid bi-directional arrows going to and from the child and each subsystem. The relationships between the child and their subsystems may be beneficial for identifying patterns in the development of the child's personal epistemological system.

In general, there are two things absent in most developmental theories of human development

189

and specifically in the study of personal epistemology: (1) the understanding of the process; and (2) the mechanism of action at the level of the phenomenon as experienced and interpreted by the individual in the real world (Hofer & Pintrich, 1997).

Minuchin (1974) comes from structural family therapy and may be the least well-known in the field of education. Minuchin (1974) defined the family structure as the invisible set of functional demands that organizes the way in which family members interact. A family is a system that operates through transactional patterns. Repeated transactions establish patterns of how, when, and with whom to relate, then these patterns underpin the system. Once these patterns are underpinned into the family dynamic or structure it is quite difficult to change the role that has been decided for each individual. This role that is designated to each individual is not a conscious or intentionally verbalized event; it occurs based on how the individual can fit into the system and get their needs met. Therefore, an individual can end up with an unsatisfactory role but cannot necessarily escape the role because the system has adapted to and expects certain patterns of behavior or thought from that individual. If the person or pattern within the system changes in the slightest' the whole system changes automatically; Minuchin (1974) called this the "dance."

During early processes of socialization, families model and shape the child's behavior and sense of identity; and perhaps their epistemologies. In this framework the same could apply to the teacher even though the teacher is not a member of the family dynamic; the child can strongly identify or become influenced by the teacher's epistemologies. This sense of belonging occurs when the child makes accommodations that adapt to the family/group; and may consciously or unconsciously commit to perform patterns within the family. The sense of separateness and individuation develops through participation in different family subsystems within different family related contexts

and in groups that are linked to the family but are external to the family system.

According to Bronfenbrenner's (1989) ecological model of human development, nature and nurture interact to describe development as it relates to individual differences that are present between cultures, neighborhoods, and families. Using Bronfenbrenner's systems model, each individual functions within a *Microsystem* which is described by their immediate environment. In the field of personal epistemology research, Schommer-Aikins (2004) introduced an *Embedded Systemic Model* and a coordinated teams approach as an innovative way of conceptualizing epistemological belief and measuring the construct. Her model includes interactions among six systems: (1) cultural relational views, (2) beliefs about "ways of knowing," (3) beliefs about knowledge, (4) beliefs about learning, (5) classroom performance, and (6) self-regulated learning.

The main idea of the Embedded Systemic Model is to link personal epistemology with other cognitive and affective components by superimposing a epistemological belief framework within other cognitive research systems. This idea stems from the assumption that epistemological beliefs do not exist in a vacuum, and she argues that during any point-in-time a learner's beliefs, thoughts, actions, and motivations can be symbolic of multiple systems merging at on time.

Affect

Affect has been considered the least important theoretically in personal epistemology research and may be the most difficult phenomenon to measure. Although, Bendixen & Rule (2004) included affect in their *Integrative Personal Epistemology Model*. The influence of affect on children's personal epistemology, however, has not been considered explicitly. Considering the affective nature in the way children understand knowledge and the process of knowing may provide important information about their epistemic development, this component may be able to offer insights that are deficient due to the limited language ability that exists is early childhood.

Affective traits refer to stable ways or predispositions in emotional responses (Rosenberg, Hammer, & Phelan, 2006), rather than fleeting facial expressions that may be missed or misinterpreted. Affective characteristics in this sense need to focus more on moods or emotions because this is how they are more closely linked to social psychology in terms of cognitive processes. Rosenberg et al. (2006) distinguishes moods and emotions, stating that they are characterized by intensity and duration, this makes evaluating affective dispositions more reliable and valid. Moods are longer lasting than emotions, which are shorter and more intense moments. In addition, Schwarz & Clore (1996) note that moods do not have a specific referent, so the source of the mood is unclear. Therefore, it can be assumed that moods tend to be a reaction or response to a particular event or person. However, most of the research between affect and cognitive processing does not consider what actually stimulates knowledge or investigates the processes involved if activating a mood or emotion. Rather, the research tends to focus on the emotional value associated with a stimulus, in this way affect is viewed as either positive or negative. Viewing it in this manner restricts the connection between affect and cognition to observable behaviors. Perhaps this is the case because we associate a way of knowing the unobservable mental states of an individual and how they know the mental states of others is through external behavior.

According to Tompkins (1991) young children's emotional range and dispositions are strongly influenced by their interactions with others and the reactions that others have to the child's own emotions. Patterns of parental emotional engagement has shown to account for significant variance in preschoolers' emotional and social development Denham (1993) but the impact of others who play significant roles in the preschooler's life have been largely overlooked

(e.g., teachers). Most of the research of young children's emotional development is linked to infant attachment (Fraley & Spieker, 2003) or social competence (Sawyer, Denham, DeMulder, Blair, Auerbach-Major, & Levitas, 2002). There are some studies that involve affective interactions which children have with their teachers (Denham, Blair, DeMulder, Levitas, Sawyer, Auerbach-Major, & Queenan, 2003) and peers (Dunn, Cutting, & Demetriou, 2000), or consideration of the affective influences of siblings (Brody, Stoneman, McCoy, 1994).

It has typically been the theory of mind researchers who have delved into affective traits in terms of social cognition (Flavell, Green, & Flavell, 1998; Gopnik & Wellman, 1994). The research that incorporates affective dispositions with epistemological beliefs is primarily in adulthood (Bendixen & Rule, 2004; Schommer-Aikins, 2000); and sparsely in children (Haerle, 2005; Hofer, 2004 & Schommer-Aikins, 2004). Bendixen & Rule (2004) and Chandler and Lalonde (1996) concluded that individuals experience certain emotions when they experience epistemic doubt. Otherwise, affect within personal epistemological research is as elusive as the idea of researching children.

Moods and emotions of young children are a way for them to communicate *nonverbally* that which they are unable to articulate verbally. It has been used in many different contexts and it applies to working with children as well; 'listen to what they do not say rather than what they do say.' Affective actions go beyond typical compliance behavior (i.e., following rules, being appropriate); much can be gained in learning environments by listening what children tell us with their affective responses and then probing them about their mood or emotion.

Language

The child's language is an additional internal component in the current systems framework (see

Figure 1). Language is a complex concept that has several areas that can be investigated; however, this is an area that no epistemological research has considered. However, language development in children is a source of much debate among theory of mind researchers. The emphasis, for the purpose of the current framework is on the function of language but cannot exclude structure entirely.

First, at a functional level, children use the same system for representing (verbal thought) and communicating (verbal discourse). The later corresponds with pragmatic language, which is the individual's own ability; and the linguistic environment, refers to the social context. Astington & Baird's (2005) approach states it clearly in Vygotskian terms; "Human language is used both as an intra-individual representational system, and as an inter-individual communication system" (p. 339).

Second, at the structural level, children's individual competence and social contexts are reciprocal in nature; each one affecting the other. The theory of mind approach is to control for the child's individual competence while considering the effect of the linguistic environment. This may be beneficial if we want to know what the child can "do," "know," or "understand" at one moment in time. However, looking at multiple systems over the course of instruction needs to view individual competence and social context unitarily. In terms of form and meaning, the distinction needs to be primarily between language in general and mental states. Mental states are frequently referred to as mentalistic language (Dougherty & Sneddon, 2003) that refers to the mind and processes that occur internally. In personal epistemology and theory of mind the key verbs are; "think," "know," and "want." This is a point of debate in theory of mind and early childhood cognitive researchers; some placing emphasis on the meaning or semantics of vocabulary used to tap into mental states abilities (Bartsch & Wellman, 1995; Olson & Astington, 1993; Peterson & Siegal, 2000) while others are more concerned with the way words

are put together or syntax of a phrase (deVilliers & deVilliers, 1999; Tager-Flusberg, 2000).

Language can illustrate a child's relationship to others; it is a form of communication that affords the actions, feelings, and thoughts of the child to be known to others (Fogel, 1993), we do not experience language in isolation. Language connects and defines the relationship between one individual and their cultural environment; it is thought to be fundamental in making sense and understanding both content and process. So then, how do young children use language to become active and motivated participants of their environment that is made up of multiple systems? How does language of others differ and impact young children's ideas about knowledge and knowing? Does language within one system transfer to another; and how does development support the network? These are the types of questions that need to be addressed.

It is also important to note that preschool children have the ability to talk about their feelings and correctly label emotional states; and participate in a considerable amount of pretend play using language that focuses on feelings (Bruner, 1983). Young children are capable of using language to discuss past and future emotions and systematically link their environment to causes and consequences of their emotions (Rogoff, 1982). For example, "That noise was loud, I was scared." "Mommy, you went away. I was sad." It is quite possible that at the preschool age, children can even detect emotional sequences in others (Gopnik, 1984).

THE SUB-SYSTEMS

In considering the child's environment, the external subsystems that comprise the personal epistemology framework include parents, the teacher, and peers (see Figure 1).

Parents

There are several studies that have found, parent beliefs influence child rearing (Sternberg, Wagner, & Okagaki, 1993). Dewey (1991) believed that the parent is the central component of a child's growth and development.

Parenting and the role of parents has changed dramatically in the past half-a-century as we have moved away from authoritarian styles of caring for children (Alwin, 1988). We no longer view physical forms of punishment as routine ways to achieve obedience. For decades there has been an ongoing controversy between the influences of nature versus nurture, this study is grounded in framework that heavily supports the nurture theory, which is strongly supported by most developmental researchers, particularly in areas that are concerned with the influences of parents. For example, Scroufe, Egeland, & Carlson (1999) investigated attachment in infant development and found a strong correlation between the child's emotional bond with their mother and their ease in getting along with peers.

Eisenberg, Cumbrland, & Spinard (1998) studied parents' emotional expressiveness and found that children tend to express their emotions more freely when parents expose their children to emotional vulnerability. These findings can be viewed in two ways: parents teach their children by example or modeling to either appropriately express emotions or keep them bottled up; or children just inherit tendencies to be emotionally expressive or inexpressive.

Parental interactions during early childhood or *proximal processes,* refer to the events and experiences that exist in "life" and are characterized by progressively more complex reciprocal interactions between an individual and the other individuals and objects in which they experience on a regular basis over extended periods of time (Brofenbrenner, 1979). These are central in children's developing epistemologies and theory of mind. The content of these proximal processes a child experiences are products of complex social and physical environments and for this purpose are characterized by affect and language and their interactions with children's personal epistemologies.

Senge (2000) believes that parents are often the most resistive to change in formal classroom instruction and want children to be taught declarative and procedural knowledge for two main reasons; they associate their positive or negative experiences; and/or it is connected to their position/belief within a large family and social dynamic. For example, how their child compares to the neighbors child, what to tell the grandparents, and will their child will be able to get into a competitive college.

Chandler & Chapman (1991) proposes a theory that includes the *domination of children* in which they contextualize the parent-child relationship into four images: (1) domination of child; (2) family disasters [parent objective is to intervene]; (3) living with children; and (4) neglect [parent objective is to understand]. There are also two life paths that the parent and child can travel: separate (corresponds to 1 & 4), or shared (corresponds to 2 & 3). The domination of child position is characterized by the parent objective which is to intervene in the child's life and control all aspects of their development so that it is predictable within the context of the parents' hopes and values. This position has two primary assumptions: parent and child life paths are sufficiently separate or independent, so that parents can intervene without restriction in order to mold the children's development to suit the parents' needs, without concerns for possible negative consequences toward the parents' own development; and the lives of the children have very little intrinsic value or worth. According to the theory, it is possible for parent-child relationships to be separate or shared depending on the family dynamics. The dynamics of a family can be pivotal in many aspects of child development and early childhood education. In early childhood education this theory is significant because the parent-child relationship is the strongest bond the child has or does not have prior to entering any other learning environment. Another point is that parents of young children are typically the most willing and present in their child's lives during this time; as children progress through their academic time, parents become less and less available to educators (this may not apply to all parents, however it is the more common trend). A draw back of needing to know about the parent-child relationship from an educator standpoint, is that time and priorities do not permit teachers to adequately investigate the relationship or even understand what parents know or believe about there child, that is, unless there is a problem. Behavior management seems to be a priority for parents and teachers in early childhood environments, which from an epistemological perspective is unfortunate.

It should be clarified that the relationship between the parent and child is reciprocal in nature, that is, the impact is not solely from the parent to the child in a linear course of action. Children play a central role in their parent's actions and interactions; after parents define the criteria they believe to be acceptable for their child to succeed in life, they set goals and expectations for the child and others involved in the child's life. However, the child's success begins to signify or represent a portion of the parent's self-worth, the degree to which this happens varies according to the parenting style (Burchinal, Peisner-Feinberg, Pianta, & Howes, 2002; Castro, Bryant, Peisner-Feinberg, & Skinner, 2004) and context of the family (Denham, Mitchell-Copeland, Strandberg, Auerbach, & Blair, 1997; Minuchin, 1974). All of these studies have found that the role of parents and gaining knowledge about the family dynamics can impact academic performance, emotional competence, social development, behavior, and motivation. Although Bendixen and Rule (2004) indirectly acknowledge the role of the parents in personal epistemology development, there are no studies conducted within the field of personal epistemology that include parents. Winsor (2005)

attempted to identify evidence that would support Burr & Hofer's (2002) link between theory of mind and personal epistemology using the parent-child relationship. In this study the parents were taught how to administer a false-belief task, rather than the researcher giving the task, the parent administered the task which was videotaped. The purpose was twofold: 1) perhaps the child would feel more at ease with the testing if the parent was in charge, and 2) perhaps the parent would use language that was more familiar to the child. In addition, parents were also given surveys to measure their epistemological beliefs, parent interviews, and family genograms were completed and triangulated with child and teacher data. The parent involvement in the false-belief task yielded more positive results for theory of mind; and interesting parallels and patterns could be seen in many of the child's, parent's, teacher's epistemological data. Knowing about young children's epistemic development in connection with their parents and teacher has a positive influence on student performance and learning.

Teachers

Teachers contribute a great deal to preschool children's education and experience. Yet there very few studies that systematically compare teacher beliefs to parent or child beliefs (Lewitt & Baker, 1995). Teachers' views are particularly important because they impact instruction as well as interactions resulting from individual differences (Vartuli, 1999). Inconsistencies between teacher and parent beliefs can confuse young children and cause various cognitive developmental issues.

Piotrkowski, Botsko, and Matthews (2001) have researched the connection between teacher and parent beliefs about school readiness. They found that inconsistencies create a lack of clarity about what children are expected to know and do at the kindergarten level. Other studies focusing on school readiness (Knudsen-Lindauer & Harris, 1989) found that parents emphasize academic–

oriented skills more than teachers. There are studies that have compared preschool teachers with kindergarten teacher's beliefs about school readiness. Foulks & Morrow (1989) found various differences between beliefs about behavior, whereas another study; Hains, Fowler, Schwartz, Kottwitz, & Rosenkoetter (1998) found that preschool teachers have greater expectations for children in both academic and behavior. Clifford and Green (1996) looked at daycare providers (which included preschool teachers), parents, and kindergarten teachers. The results indicated that all groups differed in their beliefs about school readiness.

The National Education Task Force (1991) revealed that many educators believed that affective characteristics in students and teachers should be considered in part as factors that guide "approaches to learning and instruction." They compared parent and teacher group ratings between interest and engagement; and basic and advanced knowledge. All of the teacher groups viewed interest and engagement to be substantially more important than advanced knowledge. The kindergarten groups were the only participants to view interest and engagement over even basic knowledge. Conversely, parents rated basic knowledge as more important than interest and engagement and the preschool teachers believed that the two domains were equally weighted.

In personal epistemology research the role of the teacher and instruction has had the largest amount of attention of all the sub-systems being investigated in the present study. Schraw & Olafson (2002) studied teacher's epistemological worldviews and educational practices. They compared three worldviews; realist, contextualist, and relativist and consider environmental factors. They point out that far more emphasis is placed on students' beliefs while very little research has focused on the beliefs of the teacher and how they influence instructional practices.

Schraw & Olafson (2002) investigated 24 teachers with one to fifteen years of experience who were enrolled in master level courses. They conducted a battery of questionnaires and conducted interviews. The study involved teacher's beliefs about: knowledge, curriculum, pedagogy, assessment, reality and standards for judging truth, constructivism, role of the teacher, role of the student, and the role of peers. The findings are surprising, they found that most of the teacher's beliefs could be identified as contextual but their classroom practices do not adequately reflect their beliefs. They concluded that this could have three possible causes; (1) pre-service academic programs, (2) the school district, or (3) the culture of teaching.

Preschool teacher's epistemological beliefs need to take a priority seat, particularly because of the growing number of children who are attending preschool today and the literature that supports the importance of early learning and academic outcomes later (e.g., school dropout rates, school attendance, crime). We need to address two of the gaps that Schraw & Olafson (2002) identify as gaps in the research; the teachers' understanding of epistemological views and how she perceives that they are displayed during her instruction, and how she has developed as a teacher as a result of her changing epistemological beliefs.

Alexander, Fives, Buehl, & Mulhern (2002) looked at middle school teachers' instruction. Their study also included an element of interest and utilized the involvement of peers. In an experimental design, Alexander et al. (2002) studied sixth- and seventh-grade science classrooms. They compared a science lesson explained by the principles of persuasion would contribute to how the students understood the content and whether it affected their attitudes about certain scientific premises. Although there is some focus on the student's beliefs Alexander et al. (2002) does address instructional factors. In this study the instructional lesson was void of declarative information that is typically related to the student, it approached the subject of Galileo as a story about a man who struggled to hold onto his beliefs and to promote his scientific discoveries at the risk of being ridiculed and banished. The lesson was conducted in two formats; "teacher-led" and "student-led" (p. 799). They concluded that a one-day persuasive lesson which was student-led had significant impact on student sixth and seventh-grade learning in the domain of science.

In response to the findings of Alexander et al., Sinatra & Kardash (2004) conducted a study of preservice teacher's epistemological beliefs, dispositions, and views of teaching as persuasion. The study investigated 182 preservice teachers enrolled in undergraduate education programs and compared their views about teaching as a persuasion and their views about openness and resistance by measuring their epistemological beliefs and dispositions. Sinatra & Kardash (2004) found that preservice teachers who believed that knowledge evolves, that knowledge can be revised, and that learning is gradual and effortful are more open to persuasive teaching. Such an instructional technique needs to be approached with caution with preservice teachers because the position they take is related to their epistemological beliefs. These findings from Sinatra & Kardash (2004) are indirectly in-line with Schraw & Olafson (2002) in that one of the areas that lead to teacher's epistemological beliefs are related to their preservice preparation.

The role of the teacher and instruction seems to be a rapidly growing area of need and interest in the research of personal epistemologies. Knowing more about the belief's of the teacher in relationship to their instructional approaches can lead to a deeper understanding of how students construct their beliefs. In the earlier chapters of this book you discovered that one of the problems with techonology instruction across cultures is the teacher's belief systems concerning children's capabilities to learn through technology. Another common issue was the confidence and competence of early childhood teachers ability to teach and use technology. Personal epistemologies clearly could be one underlying obstacle to technology use in early childhood programs.

Peers

The influence of peers on personal epistemology development has been proposed in the literature. Flavell et al. (1991) found that children's interactions with peers during play not only constructs a general understanding of their physical and social surrounding but can account for expanding their creative and expressive skills that promote basic dispositions in dealing with life. Although parent's role is vital, when parents limit time the child spends interacting with peers it can hinder a child's sense of autonomy and independence, which is a paradox because this is typically a parent's goal (Chandler & Chapman, 1991).

Children are strongly influenced in many ways by identifying with a group of individuals who are similar to themselves. Social systems of young children have greater limitations that do not exist as people get older; for children, peers are chosen out of convenience (family, neighborhood, parent social circle, or classroom) and usually not with much input from the child. This peer association contributes to the child's co-construction of knowledge through emphasizing the ideas that they groom toward making meaning rather than the acquisition of facts. It is this collaboration with peers that a young child begins to make sense of, understand, interpret, or give significance to their world outside of the family system. Whereas, a family system has a distinctive pattern of its own, when children begin to venture outside of the family network they experience relationships that are distinctively different from what they already know. Within a family there is a hierarchy that is not as malleable as the outside world that exists in peer groups. In many cases this is a child's first experience at impacting a pecking-order and having the opportunity to evaluate information and make decisions (Minuchin, 1974).

Forman (1996) suggests that the most potent link to social development comes from the individual's ability to relate to others at the same level. This social connection is said to manifest effectively because young children respond to each other using: symbols; naïve language and nonverbal communication; practice self-narrating; and think in metaphors. Peer groups support the power of negotiation that is not accessible in families or classrooms because of the authoritarian nature of the hierarchical system. It was Maria Montessori who said: "Our schools show that children of the same age and different ages influence one another (Montessori, 1967, p. 226).

Bendixen & Rule (2004) included peers as part of an individual's epistemological environment in accordance with Piaget's notion that peers are relatively at the same level of power. Alexander et al. (2002) included a comparison of science lessons and found the student-led groups were more effective in achieving a deeper level of understanding because the instruction was divided into small peer groups. The peers were able to present the information in terms that students who may have been unlikely to grasp the concepts in a traditional lecture could understand.

Denham et al. (2003) and Dunn, Cutting, & Demetriou (2000) have researched preschool children's social competence in relationship to cognitive development; both studies indicate that environmental influences resulting from peer interactions advance social competence and cognitive development. In addition, they conclude that peer influences are particularly vulnerable to affect and dispositional traits in preschool children.

TECHNOLOGY IN EARLY CHILDHOOD EPISTEMIC AWARENESS

Research and Technology

Personal epistemology and technical learning environment research is in its infancy and beginning

to draw more attention (Alexander, 2004; Braten, 2008). Braten (2008) summarizes research on the relationship between personal epistemology and internet-based learning activities. To date most of the connections made between personal epistemology and academic learning have been measured from printed text activities, which can be viewed as a limitation in the study of an individual's beliefs about the nature of knowledge and the process of knowing. Braten (2008) argues that personal epistemology may play a more significant role in student learning than previously thought now that researchers are beginning to use internet-based resources.

Consider children growing up in today's society, they are inundated with information from multiple hypermedia sources and often times the information is contradictory. For example, children experience different rules and consequences at home, at school, and at a friend's house; then they see and experience second-hand rules and consequences on television, movies, and games. This can be quite confusing as children attempt to piece this information together so that it is meaningful and makes sense in their life. For young children, figuring out what knowledge is and how it works is as confusing as being newly married. Anyone who has been married, or close to a newly married couple has an understanding of what it is like to learn the rules; and the challenges of trying to make it make sense (i.e., understanding the other person). This is precisely why the role of personal epistemology is so important because children are expected to make decisions, solve problems, and think critically about this information. Children struggle with this implicitly but if personal epistemology were more tangible and explicit in early childhood education, children would be given tools to develop more effective skills and strategies. Children's techniques would be more thoughtful and lead to better understanding of themselves and the world around them, as opposed to thoughtless trial-and-error or strategies that incorporate manipulation.

Children should be taught how the information they are gaining is relevant in their life now and relates to what they experience cognitively, socially, physically, and emotionally. For example, children should know why repetition is so important in learning; children should know why different sources have conflicting information; or why information sometimes changes. Perhaps it is this exact characteristic that is missing in education that prompts toddlers to ask "why" questions that tend to drive parents and teachers crazy. Like Piaget, maybe parents and teachers underestimate the cognitive and epistemological abilities of very young children. Technology use in learning may be the tool that bridges this gap. Research in this area needs attention immediately.

There is limited empirical evidence that links personal epistemology and learning with technology systems. However, it was thought that students holding naïve epistemological ideas, such as, knowledge is simple and certain would have difficulty adapting to the multi-source and multi-dimensionality of many hypermedia materials (Jacobson and Spiro, 1995). Conversely, Hartley and Bendixen (2001) argued the opposite could be true because of the autonomy that students have to control their learning because they might seek additional information and be inclined to use more evaluative strategies while deciding what to believe. Hartley and Bendixen (2003) used a computer tutorial to draw a connection between personal epistemology and the use of self-regulatory comprehension methods. They concluded that when students perceived knowledge as quick or not at all, they relied more heavily on the comprehension devices which were provided, such as, graphic organizers. Hofer (2004) found that students who think out loud while conducting on-line searching generally demonstrate all four dimensions of knowledge; simplicity of knowledge, certainty of knowledge, source of knowledge, and justification for knowledge (Hofer and Pintrich, 1997). Additionally, students who held naïve

epistemological beliefs approached searching on a surface level.

More recently, Braten, Stromso, and Samuelstuen (2005) developed a 36-item questionnaire based on Hofer and Pintrich's (1997) personal epistemological model that focused solely in personal epistemology about internet-based knowledge and knowing to see if epistemological beliefs could predict certain aspects of student's on-line learning. Braten et al. (2005) reported that the dimension of Hofer and Pintrich (1997) were empirically less identifiable. Simple, certain, and source of knowledge bonded together as one way of epistemological thinking, while justification of knowledge presented as its own dimension. Braten et al. (2005) concluded that this may mean, internet-specific epistemological beliefs are not one dimensional or multi-dimension but rather two-dimensional.

Although linking personal epistemology and technology has been jump-started, there needs to be more research that can guide teachers and students across all age levels (Alexander, 2004). More importantly, we need to begin to make this connection in early childhood.

Because many children now enter educational programs with some awareness of technology from their home environments the experiences in childcare centers will either support or conflict their beliefs about its role in learning. The impact of personal epistemology about technology could be an influencing variable on learning and use. As new understanding continues to evolve in this area new approaches to teaching and learning will be needed to address the research.

Teacher Instruction and Technology

It follows that, just as personal epistemology should be more explicit in early childhood education, it should be more explicit in teacher preparation programs. Quality teacher education programs should utilize the information in the field of personal epistemology research as a means of supporting teaching and learning techniques. Teachers should be trained to attend to how they themselves perceive the nature of knowledge and the process of knowing in a manner that makes it evident for them to understand the enormous impact that personal epistemology has for them and their students. This is particularly significant to teacher's beliefs about knowledge and knowing when it comes to the use of technology in the classroom.

How teachers think about knowledge and knowing and the use of technology to promote students beliefs about knowledge and knowing influences their classroom practices and instructional techniques, as well as, influencing student learning and performance. Teachers and preservice teachers should first have a general understanding of personal epistemology (which has been discussed throughout the chapter) and second, understand how this is critical in today's society and can be applied to the use of technology in children's learning.

Often the use of technology in the classroom (including preschool) is avoided by the teacher. It would be easy to say that computers and other technology are just not available but this is not generally the case. For example, during observations in 23 preschool classrooms (for a literacy grant) which were supplied with computers, software, video games, video tapes, and other technology material; my colleagues and I found that, when asked why they did not use the equipment, most of the classroom teachers responded, 'I don't know how to use it' or 'the children don't understand it' or 'they will get plenty of that later, no need to do it now.' Another situation that often arises with technology in the classroom is that, teachers emphasize the mechanics of how to work, for instance, the computer; rather than addressing the information that is available and what that information means as it relates to the student's lives.

Pedagogical use of technologies and hypermedia should be more greatly embraced by teachers so they can foster students toward thinking and reflecting about their own personal epistemological development and how their beliefs relate to learning. Therefore, it goes without saying that teachers should be trained about their own personal epistemological stances influence their students lives. In this way teachers can promote changes in student thinking because it requires teachers to think about teaching in non-traditional ways (Marra, 2005). If teachers become more cognizant and complex about thinking, teaching, and learning, they will be more effective at communicating the implicit and explicit nature of personal epistemology development (Brindley, 2000). The need for epistemological influences and technology in the preschool classroom is essential and has been repeatedly overlooked and devalued in previous research. Brindley (2000) cites research that supports the notion the teacher education programs do not properly, if at all, address learners' existing epistemological beliefs; hence do nothing to challenge relatively simple or naïve epistemological perspectives or promote more complex epistemological development.

Children's Learning and Technology

Braten (2008) states that many adolescent and adult students maintain naïve beliefs (simple and certain) about internet based knowledge and knowing; and in turn tend to be less critical and superficial about their approaches to learning while using internet technologies (i.e., podcasts, educational chat rooms). Also, many students are inclined to shy away from the challenges of computer software programs that incorporate the use of strategies and complex problem-solving abilities. We argue that this avoidant and naïve epistemological approach to knowledge and knowing in technology systems which students adopt may be an outcome that is fostered by teacher's beliefs about knowledge of technologies. We believe that young children are intrigued, curious, and fascinated by technologies (e.g., video games, internet) and have not experienced the stress and frustration that older students may have encountered. Young children's minds are open and malleable to the complexities of the technology age; however, in order to maintain this perspective they should be exposed to educational instruction that utilizes these tools in a way that promotes a deeper understanding of technology to positively shape beliefs about knowledge and the process of knowing. What we mean by this is that, multiple sources of knowledge using a variety of technologies should be used to help student learn how to think critically; make decisions based on warranted assertions; use evidence for making judgments; and develop and use strategies in problem-solving.

Jonassen, Marra, and Palmer (2003) state that students bring predetermined epistemologies or 'scripts' for what they think they can learn or what they expect to learn in college. These positions are a metaphoric lens by which they see and experience learning. This applies to very young children as well; how we choose to influence their academic experiences has a large role in the outcome of their lives. We can standby passively and continue with traditional modes of teacher education and classroom instruction or we can be active participants. Teachers taking the role of active participants, along-side children to promote epistemic awareness and use technology and hypermedia to facilitate and perpetuate higher-order thinking skills in young children could be the conceptual change that education needs to consider. Taking a non-traditional, more contemporary perspective of teaching and learning that integrates the sophistication of personal epistemological development and the advancement of the technology age would equip children with a lens that will allow them to understand the world at it relates to them and their needs as they change and develop in other aspects of human development. A lens that they take with them, to the next level and each level; all the while their focus is on knowledge and knowing as it becomes deeper and broader with every new experience

and interaction.

Having productive and effective teachers for children is like providing positive role models in their lives. Most hypermedia programs and games that are popular with children are linked to an influential pop icon because these are the individuals that children want to emulate in their own life. Fictional or non-fictional children aspire to be like their heroes (i.e., Michael Jordan, Michael Phelps, Spice Girls-all of which have video games or dolls in their honor). Winsor (2008) found that rarely do preschoolers identify the source of their knowledge and if/when they do, they seldom, if ever, identify their teacher as the source of their knowledge. At the end of their first preschool year, preschool children are more likely to label their parents or their peers as the source of their knowledge. We should expect that after a full year of preschool the child-teacher relationship would be potent enough or at least stimulated children thinking to a point that they can attribute some of their knowledge to the teacher.

Winsor (2008) concluded that it was the lack of developmentally appropriate practices that the teacher chose to engage the students during the school year; the emphasis was geared toward play rather than discovery and inquiry. Winsor (2008) stated it could be in part due to the preschool teacher's lack of epistemological insight about his own epistemological beliefs; and his lack of knowledge and experience of how his epistemological stance negatively stimulated the children during their experience in the classroom. Children are sponges, they are eager and excited for learning. When children are not challenged by individuals they lose attention, interest, and motivation to learn. It is our experience that when children's thinking is not challenged they maintain a more naïve view of the world and how others think. Limiting children's capacity to become aware of their surroundings in a structured way allows them to seek the answers to their question in a less structured, less sophisticated way. Both instances breed naïve epistemological development in the early years and may set in motion delayed epistemological development (suppression).

Suppression is another theory of childhood epistemology in which children have the ability and begin to develop epistemic awareness, but when they enter school the epistemological awareness in suppressed and does not surface until late adolescence (Chandler, Hallet, & Sokol, 2002). Therefore, limiting their ability to gain knowledge prevents them from understanding and experiencing the importance of knowledge; and inhibits an early onset of epistemic development. When the epistemological awareness of children is neglected or becomes misguided by the policy of schools and curricula children attend to this need in an unstructured way; these ways operate toward a pleasure principle rather than a cognitive level of development. What we mean by this is that, children do not have the independent cognitive ability, experience, or understanding to know they need to learn to: think critically, make decisions, solve problems, develop and use strategies all on their own. However, children have the cognitive ability with the explicit direction and scaffold of the classroom teacher; and one way that has been advocated for throughout this book is how the use of technology and hypermedia can be a positive tool to promote children's personal epistemological awareness.

How can explicitly making children aware of the presence of knowledge and the process of knowing benefit early learning? There are two ways we see technology can be used as a means to build epistemic awareness in children: 1) making teachers more knowledgeable and cognizant of how hypermedia and technology can build epistemological awareness; and 2) by providing multiple educational (rather than recreational) hypermedia platforms. In other words knowing about and using hypermedia and technological resources during learning activities allows teachers and students multiple opportunities to investigate personal epistemological awareness and understanding.

The implications of better understanding the influences of the nature of knowledge means that, children will *not* view knowledge as absolute (either right or wrong) but will instead gain the ability to evaluate knowledge on the evidence that it is associated with by content (subject domain) and context (the environment); and will not view knowledge as simple, but rather complex and integrated, and that they will be able to understand that some knowledge can be known for certain, while other knowledge is/will always be changing, therefore uncertain. The implications of better understanding the processes of knowing means that children will be able to relate to a broader scope of sources of knowledge, rather than only being able to relate to the sources that they encounter in their daily routine (e.g., they can learn and understand what it is like to live and go to school in China from their peers who are there, by engaging in live chats and podcasts). Also, children can learn how to justify their knowledge based on evidence; they can understand what it means to weigh evidence based on the source and the information provided by that source. By teaching children what it means to have knowledge and know, can enlighten them to many current and future learning opportunities. Hypermedia and technologies have enhanced many of our personal and professional lives, in terms of doing research, looking for a job, finding a date, and completing our taxes. Imagine for a minute the opportunities that young children beginning their education today could have cognitively, epistemologically, and socially if educators used technology as a tool to teach them about the nature of knowledge and the process of knowing. Likewise, what if we could learn more about how young children build epistemological awareness, that is building beliefs about the nature of knowledge and the process of knowing by using hypermedia and technology to grasp the concepts that are needed to understand the influences on their learning potential and performance?

CONCLUSION

Personal epistemology can affect the overall way in which teaching and learning is viewed. The educational significance of personal epistemology can have an important role in improving education for all children. Knowing more about children's epistemological onset and development could have a significant impact on the following: (a) early childhood educational curriculum, (b) classroom instructional techniques, (c) teacher education programs, (d) how parents prepare their children to enter preschool, and (e) use of technology in teaching and learning.

Early Childhood Education Curriculum

The more valid and reliable our research becomes the more likely administrators and government policy makers of early childhood curriculums will be able to consider and implement the value of personal epistemological development. Gaining more knowledge in children's personal epistemologies stands to impact early childhood curriculums but also can guide the current effort to implement preschool standards across the U.S (Martin & Loomis, 2007). The National Association for the Education of Young Children (NAEYC) oversees that national, state, and local education facilities follow strict guidelines in order to obtain funding for their programs. This association developed as a practitioners group based on experience in early childhood programs. The accreditation standards focus on facilities and some pedagogical recommendations more than cognitive acquisition. The problem is further compounded in that each state has different laws regarding early childhood education. For instance, kindergarten is not mandatory in every state; only 41 states require that local school districts offer half-day kindergarten, and nine states require the districts to offer full-day. More alarming than that is that only 14 states in the US require children to have a kindergarten

experience prior to entering first grade; two of those require a full-day of kindergarten (NAEYC, 2007). Further still, in 2006, only 43% of all three-year-olds attended a preschool program, and in the same year only 59% of all four-year-olds attended preschool.

This should alert us that far too many children enter school unprepared to reach their potential. When they begin unprepared, children begin behind and continue to fall further and further behind. This impacts the dropout rate in schools. The government, educators, and parents should be informed about what it takes to enter school ready to succeed. We have long passed the stage of "if" technology belongs in early childhood classrooms and need to find answers to "how" technology impacts learning and development. Knowing about very young children's epistemic development can contribute to other cognitive domain-specific tasks such as improving school performance, raising math and language abilities, sharpening thinking and attention skills, reducing special education placement, and lowering the school drop-out rate. More broadly, the more successfully we educate individuals, the less crime, poverty, mental health issues, dependency addiction, and so on we may see.

It is also possible to add to the list the social and emotional benefits of early childhood education. For example, it improves and strengthens peer interaction, decreases problem behavior, encourages more exploratory behavior, and helps adjustment to the demands of formal schooling. Other long-term benefits include savings in tax dollars, increasing lifelong earning potential, achieving better academic outcomes, and lowering the rates of teen pregnancy and incarceration (Galleghar, 2003).

Classroom Instructional Techniques

Perhaps if there was less of a focus on behavioral factors in early childhood teaching and learning we could more evenly weigh the social, affective, and epistemological factors in preschool learning. It appears that very young children have the propensity to develop epistemologically, but we may not set them up for successfully reaching their potential. How a teacher is trained to teach any grade level is important but especially important in terms of early childhood development. A teacher's teaching philosophy, teaching technique, communication skills, motivation, and even their epistemological beliefs (Schraw & Olafson, 2002) are paramount in the teaching and learning of preschool children. These variables definitely influence the use of technology in instruction.

Preschool teachers should use instructional techniques (i.e., discovery learning, inquiry, block and dramatic play, music and moving activities) that are based on educationally sound research and correspond to the multiple dimensions of learning. Teachers need to experiment and explore how technology fits into these instructional approaches to support learning. Very young children are capable of a plethora of cognitive, emotional, social, and physical activities, and preschool instructional techniques should expose children to all of the modalities of learning so that children can discover what they are good at and where their interests fall. Not all children are going to be good at every task, but they need to experience it. Additionally teachers should be aware of each child's zone of proximal development and how it relates to the zone of advanced development to access current understanding and the potential for extended learning. This will allow the teacher to make quality and informed decisions about pairing students for projects and play and have realistic expectations for each individual child.

Most importantly, the preschool teacher should have a teaching/learning philosophy rather than a play philosophy. Teachers should provide activities that incorporate novel situations that children are familiar with and can relate to. As children work through these activities the teacher should help the child understand the relevance and connections to their world. Teaching and learning

experiences in a preschool classroom should challenge the children to think independently and collectively in solving problems, making decisions, and thinking critically. The teacher is vital to preparing and organizing the environment to allow active engagement and relationships between themselves and each child and promote that relationship building among the peers.

Perhaps the lack of some combination of these techniques speaks to possible contributing factors that limit the children in the Schraw & Olafson study in terms of sources of knowledge. It was expected that the children in this study would have demonstrated their knowledge about external sources similar to those children in the pilot. This did not occur, and this could relate to the philosophies and techniques of the teacher. If teachers are aware of their beliefs about knowledge and knowing and how that relates to learning with preschool children, perhaps children will be to understand their own beliefs more intentionally. For this to occur, teachers would need to explicitly cover themes from an epistemological perspective in the way they ask questions, answer questions, design their lesson plans, and generally approach teaching and learning.

Pre-Service Teacher Education Programs

In order to accommodate more cognitively sophisticated children, we would need to make considerable adjustments to the education of pre-service teachers. Children's personal epistemology is important because it provides valuable insights into what children know and how they learn. The more understanding we have about children's personal epistemology the better we will be able to prepare pre-service teachers to enter the classroom, no matter what level they are teaching. In addition, better prepared teachers will have more solid developmental and cognitive backgrounds and will be more effective and efficient in the classroom. How individuals develop personal epistemologies and the unique relationship they have to learning may assist teacher instruction to follow more closely to theories of learning, hence, bridging the gap between theory and practice. The lack of connection between current research and practice in this field is not unfamiliar to researchers and practitioners. The NRC reports *Eager to Learn* (National Research Council, 2001b) and *From Neurons to Neighborhoods* (National Research Council and Institute of Medicine, 2000) both emphasize the importance of better aligning research and work on translating that research into practice, taking into account the complexities of educational settings. *From Neurons to Neighborhoods* concludes that "as the rapidly evolving science of early child development continues to grow, its complexity will increase and the distance between the working knowledge of service providers and the cutting edge of the science and technology will be staggering.

Teachers need to have an understanding of the importance of child epistemological development, and this may help teachers bring more real-world instruction and assessment into alignment (Schraw & Olafson, 2002). As pointed out earlier, evaluativism is a level of personal epistemology that is not recognizable until later adulthood and is thought to incorporate higher levels of cognition (i.e. metacognition) such as critical thinking, problem-solving, reasoning, and logic (Kuhn, et al, 2002). If we can identify how to cultivate this more sophisticated way of thinking and identify links to epistemological development in early childhood, the results could lead to better understanding of the processes involved in life-long learning. Understanding how very young children can produce evaluativistic thinking as seen in this study is one small step in this process.

The role of preservice teacher preparation is vital to changes in learning and use of technology. Is it well established that these students come to classrooms with pre- and misconceptions about science and technology. This can either be supported or repaired by experience in Colleges of Education (Donovan, M.S. & Bransford, J.D. 2005). The professional challenges that this raises for the early childhood field are formidable" (p. 42).If we accept the idea that young children are capable of inquiry reasoning than it would seem logical that educators would build on this to develop science and technology learning. Individuals have to mount new mental structure as well as accumulate relevant data for the structure. It is as if learners have to get to the middle of the lake without a rowboat. The theoretical task is two-fold: to spell out how new mental structures are acquired and to achieve a theory of environment that that supports such learning (Gelman & Brenneman 2004).

Educate Parents about Preparing Their Children for Preschool and Being Better Learners

Currently many states in the United States do not have educational standards for preschool children, and in some cases families do not even send their children to kindergarten as it is still a choice in many locations. There is a direct relationship between parents' views about education and learning and how they value education (Laosa, 1978). While we train pre-service teachers, parents also need to be educated about the effect of early childhood experiences on later cognitive and emotional abilities. In the chapters about Mexico and Taiwan we learned of the demand from parents in these countries to include technology in early childhood classrooms. Neither country has technology standards for ECE but the parents in Taiwan are eager to enroll their children in private ECE programs that provide technology education. In Ciudad Juárez the CENDI program reported that approximately 35 out of the 40 enrolled children have home computers and that the parents demanded the inclusion of technology education in their curriculum.

This is a difficult area of educational significance to disentangle considering the broad multiculturalism in today's society. Some culturally shaped early learning opportunities have been found to be more conducive than others to preparing children for success in schools, which are typically not designed with diverse configurations of students in mind. One of the challenges that this poses to early childhood educators, in particular, involves striking a balance between demonstrating respect for cultural differences and preparing children to participate successfully in formal school settings (Prince and Lawrence, 1993). A starting point for addressing this dilemma involves understanding how children's cultural backgrounds affect the skills, knowledge, and expectations that they bring to school.

Culture plays a complex role in shaping children's earliest learning opportunities and experiences in the home. Parents' beliefs about when and how children learn school-related skills, their daily interactions with their children, and the social rules that guide these interactions combine in intricate ways to create what Luis Moll has termed "funds of knowledge" that are based in culture (Moll, Amanti, Neff, & Gonzalez, 1992). However, efforts to specify the mechanisms or dimensions of culture that carry its role in learning are in their infancy. There is a need to advance and include cultural beliefs with beliefs about knowledge and knowing. Culture is a complex and multidimensional entity of human development, generally, and epistemological development, specifically. Culture is described by the Board of Children and Families as encompassing economic, ethnic, racial, social, structural, and other dimensions that constitute a constellation of influences on children's early learning opportunities (NAEYC, 2007).

It is critical when examining the research evidence to take careful note of the investigator's definition of culture and its implications for the results from any particular study as it has multiple interpretations. A persistent problem in much of this research is drawing inferences about non-economic dimensions of culture when, in fact,

social class may be the more influential variable (Laosa, 1978). Are differences that are attributed to children's ethnic backgrounds or immigrant status, for example, more accurately ascribed to the educational backgrounds of their parents? Is the socioeconomic status of parents a factor in personal epistemology ?

Parents are most often motivated in their ambitions for the success of their children but do not have the insights to help them along the way. It is common for parents to become less and less engaged in their children's education as they progress. There are many contributing factors to this, but the largest contributing factor that parents will report, with the exception of time, is that they do not understand the material their children are learning followed by an attitude that they do not understand why the material has to be taught because it has no earthly significance to anything useful in the child's life (von Wyl, Perren, Simoni, & Bugin, 2008).

Parents are an important part of the developing epistemologies of young children and an integral part of the *Dynamic Systems Framework for Personal Epistemology Development* (See Figure 1) systems. The current study focused on the child's interactions with his/her peers. The pilot study that was conducted included the parent-child relationship and the parent-teacher relationship. Some of the findings should inform educators that parents have an important role in child development and epistemic development and require some training to inform and empower parents so that they can more adequately prepare their young children for an education and see their role in their child's education for the full term.

Children's personal epistemologies research can foster parent's interpretation of early childhood developmental milestones and transition perceptions away from traditional developmental limitations. Providing parents with a clearer vision of children's cognitive abilities may help parents better prepare their children to enter structured classroom environments. Perhaps if there was less focus on behavior factors in early childhood teaching and learning, we would be more evenly weighting social, affective, and epistemological factors, as opposed to our finding of predominantly social and affective levels.

Use of Technology in Teaching and Learning

Clearly as we explore the implications of epistemic awareness in young children and teachers there will be changes in teacher training and classroom environments. How these structures interact with technology will influence the understanding and use of these tools for learning. The potential for technology based on the epistemic mapping of children's learning could have a major impact on this field. The study in chapter 8 clearly indicates that what teachers say about using technology is contradictory to what is actualized in classrooms. As you read this book you probably noticed three patterns of thinking across most chapters that influence technology use. One common theme is the resistance of teachers to using technology with young children. This connects to the teachers beliefs about learning and their epistemic internal mapping. If we are to change what happens in early childhood classrooms we must look at how the teacher and the child develop learning structures.

Another common theme that has been apparent in this book is the lack of teacher technology training and background. We believe that decisions on how and what we learn are part of the epistemic influence. This lack of training and confidence could come from the internal beliefs that technology is not an appropriate step in the learning process. Because technology development is rapid and constantly evolving it is possible that out thinking has not evolved at a pace to accept this tool as part of our learning structure. It is also possible that as we struggle to acquire technology skills we have not accepted it as something that

enhances learning but an obstacle or a content/skill category without accepting the connections to our personal learning. Until we add technology to our epistemic mapping we cannot help children acquire the necessary thinking to understand and use technology in a constructive manner.

We acknowledge that the other predominant theme of access and equity evident across chapters in this book probably will not be solved through epistemic awareness. We do think that the issues of resistance and acceptance of technology are related to epistemology. As new research continues to explore the idea of epistemic awareness it will our challenge to use the information in an actionable application to teaching.

FUTURE RESEARCH

Researching young children's personal epistemologies is an area that needs a considerable amount of attention. Knowing about the early onset of epistemological thinking will advance research in early childhood development as well as research into adolescence and adulthood (Chandler & Carpendale, 1998; Hofer & Pintrich, 1997). Gopnik, Meltzoff & Kuhn, (1999) found that children younger than two-years-old can use verbal language, watch other individual's reactions to an object and make their own preference judgment, and show empathy and compassion for others. Therefore it is proposed here that future research in young children's personal epistemology continue to investigate children individually and their interactions with others. The *Dynamic Systems Framework for Personal Epistemology Development* (See Figure 1) guides this section of the discussion; suggestions for future research which are closest to children's personal epistemology will be discussed first, followed by some broader issues related to child development in general. Personal epistemology in preschool children is quite exploratory at this point. Future research should include continuing to identify developmental levels and dimensions of knowledge.

Systems Framework

Using a systems approach should be considered in future research as this may be an efficient and effective way to tap into a complex construct with a younger population. Schommer-Aikins (2004) also promotes a systems approach although hers centers on the individual's personal epistemology, and the approach is more domain-specific. In her view, one individual's personal epistemology would be investigated by a professional or scholar from each domain (i.e., math, science, English etc.) then conclusions could be compared for the same individual across multiple domains.

The Dynamic Systems Framework for Personal Epistemological Development (Winsor, 2005) (DSFPED) is a comprehensive perspective on the influences of young children's personal epistemology. The child continues to be the focus of the system; it centers on relationships that impact a child's thinking about knowledge and knowing, such as the relationship between peers as reflected in the current study, but it also includes the relationships that exist between the child and his/her parent(s) and the relationship between the child and their teacher. In addition, the dynamic systems framework integrates the intrinsic and extrinsic facets of the child's development, in terms of cognitive, social, and emotional characteristics. Preschool children are at a cognitive milestone in terms of the theory of mind (TOM) development and with the recent connections between theory of mind and epistemic development in early childhood; TOM is also a cognitive component of the DSFPED.

Future research in children's personal epistemology requires more creative methodologies as a means of investigating their cognitive abilities; traditional survey measures used for adult epistemological inquiry are inadequate due to children's developmental limitations such as reading and writing abilities. Knowing more about young children's source of knowledge, both internal or external, could provide more insights into internal sources such as private speech, pretense, imagination. This would address how it is that, even though much of children's cognitive development is taking place internally and with limited language development at that age, much of what and how they know seems implicit to an outsider but not so implicit to their peers. Source of knowledge is an important dimension of the process of knowing; researching children's sources of knowledge can inform us about developmental patterns and patterns regarding the dimensions of knowledge. This is an area that requires more research in all each levels. In the DSFPED focus on relationships, this is an area that would benefit from more qualitative research, such as phenomenologies or ethnographies (VanMaanen, 1994).

The *Dynamic Systems Framework for Personal Epistemological Development* extrapolates the social dynamic of the individual and accounts for the importance and need for future research to investigate not only the child's relationships but also the relationships of those individuals that directly impact the knowledge and understanding of young children. To clearly and effectively see the child's interactions with others, it is necessary to explore multiple relationships including the relationship between the parent and the teacher; the parent and the child's peers; and the teacher and the child's peers. This becomes quite a complex task, but interactions may be similar among individuals.

Research should be conducted in the children's authentic learning environment. Researching preschooler's personal epistemologies in their classroom environment can be effective and efficient, particularly in these early exploratory studies. Observing or interacting with children in the environment that they know, feel comfortable in, and with all of the objects that they know and love at their fingertips places them in an environment that they will function their best. It also gave the researcher plenty of opportunities to see more natural interactions and perhaps identify unexpected or unanticipated thinking or behaving.

Affect is another construct that is included in the dynamic system approach and is also in its infancy in terms of how it is linked to personal epistemology and future research could address this (Bendixen & Rule, 2004). One's affective nature is particularly poignant in researching young children's epistemologies because it is used in how they choose to communicate. Their emotions, interests, needs, motivations, and attitudes get conveyed through their words and their actions and strongly impact their past, present, and future knowledge and understanding. So, what is the epistemic role of affective dispositions? It is widely agreed upon that being a good moral individual is a result of having sound moral judgment and reasoning ability (Kohlberg, 1984; Kuhn, 1991). Moral judgment requires being emotionally attuned to the world (Gilligan, 1982; Kohlberg, 1984), and moral decision-making is related to epistemic beliefs (Bendixen, Schraw, & Dunkle, 1998; King & Kitchener, 1994).

Future research needs to focus on how the environment impacts what the children know and how they know. This type of social perspective of knowledge is currently accepted in the fields of social psychology and sociology; and termed "social epistemology" (Fuller, 2002, p. 36). The primary difference being that social epistemology involves the social network of the individual, but interestingly, social epistemologists have the same difficulty coming to a consensus about the intricacies of knowledge, just as the personal epistemologists have boundary concerns (i.e., do beliefs about learning predict beliefs about knowledge?). They are two separate domains, but perhaps given the complexities (language, conscious awareness) of tapping into children's personal epistemologies, it may be necessary to get to the root of personal epistemologies through investigations of social networks

The complex construct of language in terms of childhood epistemic development is critical. Future research should focus more on the preschooler's language development more closely and be concerned more with pragmatic and semantic issues. It is in this way that language has been enormously significant in theory of mind (Astington, 1994) and pretend play research (Gopnik & Meltoff, 1989).

Language is a prominent issue in theory of mind development and a controversial one at that (Astington & Baird, 2005; Baron-Cohen, Leslie, & Firth, 1985; Chandler, 1992; Wimmer & Perner, 1983). Astington & Baird (2005) investigate possible explanations for how children acquire their understanding for theory of mind. Likewise, this stands to be an important component for tapping into and understanding children's epistemic development and could also prove to provide significant information in adolescent and adult epistemic thinking as well.

Cognitive constructs may be developing during this critical period of development that have links to personal epistemology and these need to be explored as well. For example, when asking children epistemologically challenging questions, they begin to present metacognitive characteristics in their behaviors that resemble naïve or perhaps metacognitive infancy. Examples include linking past and present knowledge and personal experiences to new information, making associations with reoccurring sources (i.e., parents, peers, books), self-regulated behaviors (i.e., practicing responses in self-talk, repeating others or the story, making-up scenarios when they do not know), self-efficacy, and motivation. Future research should investigate the cognitive constructs that may coincide with epistemic development; and include interactions between the child and components of the DSFPED; and include more systematic and structured cognitive task.

REFLECTIVE QUESTIONS

1. How could personal epistemology influence the use of technology in your classroom?
2. What do you think are the preschooler's beliefs about the nature of knowledge and the process of knowing?
3. What can a child's theory of mind development tell us about their epistemic stance? How would you use this information to develop technology use in your teaching?
4. How do young children demonstrate (e.g., verbally, nonverbally) their personal epistemologies in terms of affect, language, and environment?
5. What evidence have you seen in your classroom that indicate young children may have a personal epistemology about technology?
6. What is the role of parents, teachers, and peers in a preschooler's epistemological understanding of technology?
7. How can informing parents and teachers about epistemological development; and the potential influences on present and future student learning impact parent-child, teacher-student, child-peer, and parent-teacher interactions that will positively affect student learning?
8. How could knowing about early childhood epistemological understanding influence teacher beliefs, teacher practices, teacher instruction, and teacher preparation programs?
9. How can internet technologies or other technological tools contribute to early childhood epistemological understanding?
10. As you learn more about early childhood epistemological understanding by implementing internet technologies or other technological devices in your instruction what steps will you take to inform your colleagues?

REFERENCES

Alexander, P. A. (2004). In the year 2020: Envisioning the possibilities for educational psychology. *Educational Psychologist, 39*, 149–156. doi:10.1207/s15326985ep3903_1

Alexander, P. A., Fives, H., Buehl, M. M., & Mulhern, J. (2002). Teaching as persuasion. *Teaching and Teacher Education, 18*(7), 795–813. doi:10.1016/S0742-051X(02)00044-6

Alwin, D. F. (1988). From obedience to autonomy: Changes in traits desired in children, 1924-1978. *Public Opinion Quarterly, 52*(1), 33–52. doi:10.1086/269081

Astington, J. W., & Baird, J. A. (2005). *Why language matters for theory of mind.* New York, NY: Oxford University Press.

Astington, J. W., & Jenkins, J. M. (1999). A longitudinal study of the relation between language and theory of mind. *Developmental Psychology, 35*, 1311–1320. doi:10.1037/0012-1649.35.5.1311

Astington, J. W., Pelletier, J., & Homer, B. (2002). Theory of mind and epistemological development: the relation between children's second-order false-belief understanding and their ability to reason about evidence. *New Ideas in Psychology, 20*, 131–144. doi:10.1016/S0732-118X(02)00005-3

Baillargeon, R. (1986). Representing the existence and the location of hidden objects: Object permanence in 6-and 8-month-old infants. *Cognition, 23*, 21–41. doi:10.1016/0010-0277(86)90052-1

Bartsch, K. (2002). The role of experience in children's developing folk epistemology: Review and analysis from the theory-theory perspective. *New Ideas in Psychology, 20*, 145–161. doi:10.1016/S0732-118X(02)00006-5

Bartsch, K., & Wellman, H. M. (1995). *Children talk about the mind.* New York: Oxford University Press.

Baxter Magolda, M. B. (1992). Cocurricular influences on college students' intellectual development. *Journal of College Student Development, 33*, 203–213.

Belensky, M., Clinchy, B., Goldberger, N., & Tarule, J. (1986). *Women's ways of knowing: The development of self, voice, and mind.* New York: Basic Books.

Bendixen, L. D., & Rule, D. C. (2004). An integrative approach to personal epistemology: A guiding model. *Educational Psychologist, 39*(1), 69–80. doi:10.1207/s15326985ep3901_7

Bradmetz, J., & Schneider, R. (2004). The role of the counterfactually satisfied Desire in the lag between false-belief and false-emotion attributions in Children aged 4-7. *The British Journal of Developmental Psychology, 22*, 185–196. doi:10.1348/026151004323044564

Braten, I. (2008). Personal epistemology, understanding of multiple texts, and learning within internet technologies. In Khines and Myint Swe (Eds.), *Knowing, knowledge, and beliefs: Epistemological studies across diverse cultures* (pp. 113-133). New York: Springer Science.

Braten, I., Stromso, H. I., & Samuelstuen, M. S. (2005). The relationship between internet-specific epistemological beliefs and learning within internet technologies. *Journal of Educational Computing Research, 33*(2), 141–171. doi:10.2190/E763-X0LN-6NMF-CB86

Brindley, R. (2000). Learning to walk the walk: Teacher educators' use of constructivist epistemology in their own practice. *Professional Educator, 12*(2), 1–14.

Brody, G. H., Stoneman, Z., & McCoy, J. K. (1994). Contributions of protective risk factors to literacy and socioemotional competency in former Head Start children attending kindergarten. *Early Childhood Research Quarterly, 9*(3-4), 407–425. doi:10.1016/0885-2006(94)90017-5

Bronfenbrenner, U. (1979). *The ecology of human development: Experiments by nature and design.* Cambridge, Massachusetts: Harvard University Press.

Bronfenbrenner, U. (1988). Strengthening family systems. In E. F. Zigler & M. Frank (Eds.), *The parental leave crisis: Toward a national policy* (pp. 358-385). New Haven, CT: Yale University Press.

Bruner, J. S. (1983). *The process of education.* Cambridge, MA: Harvard University Press.

Burchinal, M. R., Peisner-Feinberg, E., Pianta, R., & Howes, C. (2002). Development of academic skills from preschool through second grade: Family and classroom predictors of developmental trajectories. *Journal of School Psychology, 40*(5), 415–436. doi:10.1016/S0022-4405(02)00107-3

Burr, J., & Hofer, B. K. (2002). Personal epistemology and theory of mind: Deciphering young children's beliefs about knowledge and knowing. *New Ideas in Psychology, 20*, 199–224. doi:10.1016/S0732-118X(02)00010-7

Call, J., & Tomasello, M. (1999). A nonverbal false belief task: The performance of children and great apes. *Child Development, 70*(2), 381–395. doi:10.1111/1467-8624.00028

Castro, D. C., Bryant, D. M., Peisner-Feinberg, E. S., & Skinner, M. L. (2004). Parent involvement in Head Start programs: The role of parent, teacher, and classroom characteristics. *Early Childhood Research Quarterly, 19*(3), 413–430. doi:10.1016/j.ecresq.2004.07.005

Chandler, M., Fritz, A. S., & Hala, S. (1989). Small scale deceit: Deceptions as a marker of 2-, 3-, and 4-year-olds early theories of mind. *Child Development, 60*, 1263–1277. doi:10.2307/1130919

Chandler, M. J., & Chapman, M. (1991). *Criteria for competence: Controversies in the conceptualization and assessment of children's abilities.* Hillsdale, NJ: Lawrence Erlbaum Associates Inc.

Chandler, M. J., Hallet, D., & Sokol, B. W. (2002). Competing claims about competing knowledge claims. In B. K. Hofer & P. R. Pintrich (Eds.), *Personal epistemology: The psychology of beliefs about knowledge and knowing* (pp. 145-168). Mahwah, NJ: Lawrence Erlbaum Associates.

Chandler, M. J., & Lalonde, C. E. (1996). Shifting to an interpretive theory of mind: 5-to-7-year-olds changing conceptions of mental life. In A. Sameroff & M Haith (Ed.), *The five to seven year shift: The age of reason and responsibility* (pp. 111-139) Chicago, Il: University of Chicago Press.

Clark, A. S., McQuail, R., & Moss, P. (2003). *Exploring the field of listening to and consulting with young children.* London: Thomas Coram Research, London Institute of Education.

Clifford, E. F., & Green, V. P. (1996). The mentor-protégé relationship as a factor in preservice teacher education: A review of the literature. *Early Child Development and Care, 125,* 73–83. doi:10.1080/0300443961250107

Denham, S. A. (1993). Preschoolers' likability as cause or consequence of their social behavior. *Developmental Psychology, 29*(2), 271–275. doi:10.1037/0012-1649.29.2.271

Denham, S. A., Blair, K. A., DeMulder, E., Levitas, J., Sawyer, K., Auerbach-Major, S., & Queenan, P. (2003). Preschool emotional competence: Pathway to social competence. *Child Development, 74*(1), 238–256. doi:10.1111/1467-8624.00533

Denham, S. A., Mitchell-Copeland, J., Strandberg, K., Auerbach, S., & Blair, K. (1997). Parental contributions to preschoolers' emotional competence: Direct and indirect effects. *Motivation and Emotion, 21*(1), 65–86. doi:10.1023/A:1024426431247

deVilliers, J. G., & deVilliers, P. A. (1999). Language development. In M. H. Bornstein & M. E. Lamb (Eds.), *Developmental psychology: An advanced textbook (4th ed.)* (pp. 466-480). Mahwah, NJ: Lawrence Erlbaum Associates.

Dewey, J. (1991). *How we think.* Amerst, NY: Great Books In Philosophy, Prometheus Books.

Doherty-Sneddon, G. (2003). *Children's unspoken language.* New York: Kingsley Publishing Ltd.

Donovan, M. S., & Bransford, J. D. (2005) How Students Learn. National Research Council. National Academies Press.

Dunn, J., Cutting, A. L., & Demetriou, H. (2000). Moral sensibility, understanding others, and children's friendship interactions in the preschool period. *The British Journal of Developmental Psychology, 18*(2), 159–177. doi:10.1348/026151000165625

Eisenberg, N., Cumberland, L. A., & Spinard, P. C. (1998). Relations of young children's agreeableness and resiliency to effortful control and impulsivity. *Social Development, 13*(2), 193–212.

Elder, A. D. (2002). Characterizing fifth grade students' epistemological beliefs in science. In B. K. Hofer & P. R. Pintrich (Eds.), *Personal epistemology: The psychology of beliefs about knowledge and knowing* (pp. 347-363). Mahwah, NJ: Lawrence Erlbaum Associates Publishers.

Ellis, S., & Rogoff, B. (1982). The strategies and efficacy of child versus adult teachers. *Child Development, 53*(3), 730–735. doi:10.2307/1129386

Flavell, J. H. (2004). Theory of mind development. *Merrill-Palmer Quarterly, 50*(3), 274–290. doi:10.1353/mpq.2004.0018

Flavell, J. H., Green, F. L., & Flavell, E. R. (1995). Young children's knowledge about Thinking. *Monographs of the Society for Research in Child Development, 16*(1, Serial No. 243).

Flavell, J. H., Green, F. L., & Flavell, E. R. (1998). The mind has a mind of its own: Developing knowledge about mental uncontrollability. *Cognitive Development, 13*(1), 127–138. doi:10.1016/S0885-2014(98)90024-7

Fogel, A. (1993*). Developing through relationships: Origins of communication, self, and culture.* Chicago, IL: University of Chicago Press.

Fraley, R. C., & Spieker, S. J. (2003). Are infant attachment patterns continuously or categorically distributed? A taxometric analysis of strange situation behavior. *Developmental Psychology, 39*(3), 387–404. doi:10.1037/0012-1649.39.3.387

Gelman, R. (1979). Preschool thought. *The American Psychologist, 34*(10), 900–905. doi:10.1037/0003-066X.34.10.900

Gelman, S. A. (2000). The role of essentialism in children's concepts. In H. Reese (Ed.), *Advances in child development and behavior* (pp. 269-283). San Diego, CA: US Academic Press.

Gelman, R. & Brenneman. (2004). Mathematic and science cognitive development. In Mathematical and Scientific Development in Early Childhood: A Workshop Summary (2005). National Academies Press.

Gopnik, A. (1984). The acquisition of gone and the development of the object concept. *Journal of Child Language, 11*(2), 273–292. doi:10.1017/S0305000900005778

Gopnik, A., & Meltzoff, A. (1986). Relations between semantic and cognitive in the one word stage: The specificity hypothesis. *Child Development, 57*(4), 1040–1053. doi:10.2307/1130378

Gopnik, A., & Wellman, H. M. (1994). The theory-theory. In L Hirschfeld & S. Gelman (Eds.), *Mapping the mind: Domain specificity in cognition and culture* (pp. 257-293). New York: Cambridge University Press.

Greig, A., & Taylor, J. (1999). *Doing research with children.* Thousand Oaks: Sage.

Haerle, F. C. (2005). *Personal epistemologies of 4th graders: Their beliefs about knowledge and knowing.* Unpublished doctoral dissertation, Carl von Ossietzky University, Oldenburg, Germany.

Haerle, F. C. (2006). Personal epistemologies of fourth graders: Their belief about knowledge and knowing. Oldenburg: Didaktisches Zentrum.

Hammer, D., & Elby, A. (2002). On the form of a personal epistemology. In B. K. Hofer & P. R. Pintrich (Eds.), *Personal epistemology: The psychology of beliefs about knowledge and knowing* (pp. 169-190). Mahwah, NJ: Lawrence Erlbaum Associates.

Hartley, K., & Bendixen, L. D. (2001). Educational research in the Internet age: Examining the role of individual characteristics. *Educational Researcher, 30*(9), 22–26. doi:10.3102/0013189X030009022

Hartley, K., & Bendixen, L. D. (2003). The use of comprehension aids in a hypermedia environment: Investigating the impact of metacognitive awareness and epistemological beliefs. *Journal of Educational Multimedia and Hypermedia, 12,* 275–289.

Hofer, B. K. (2000). Dimensionality and disciplinary differences in personal epistemology. *Contemporary Educational Psychology, 25*, 378–405.doi:10.1006/ceps.1999.1026

Hofer, B. K. (2001). Personal epistemology research: Implications for learning and teaching. *Journal of Educational Psychology Review, 13*(4), 353–383. doi:10.1023/A:1011965830686

Hofer, B. K. (2004a). Epistemological understanding as a metacognitive process: Thinking aloud during online searching. *Educational Psychologist, 39*(1), 1–3. doi:10.1207/s15326985ep3901_1

Hofer, B. K. (2004b). Exploring the dimensions of personal epistemology in differing classroom contexts: Student interpretations during the first year of college. *Contemporary Educational Psychology, 29*, 129–163. doi:10.1016/j.cedpsych.2004.01.002

Hofer, B. K., & Pintrich, P. R. (1997). The development of epistemological theories: Beliefs about knowledge and knowing and their relation to learning. *Review of Educational Research, 67*, 88–140.

Hofer, B. K., & Pintrich, P. R. (Eds.). (2002). *Personal epistemology: The psychology of beliefs about knowledge and knowing.* Mahwah, NJ: Erlbaum.

Jacobson, M. J., & Spiro, R. J. (1995). Hypertext learning environments, cognitive flexibility, and transfer of complex knowledge: An empirical investigation. *Journal of Educational Computing Research, 12*(4), 301–333.

Jonassen, D. H., Marra, R. M., & Palmer, B. (2003). Epistemological development: An implicit entailment of constructivist learning environments. In N. M. Seel & S. Dijkstra (Eds.), *Curriculum, plan, and processes of instructional design: International perspectives* (p. 75-88). Mahwah, NJ: Lawrence Erlbaum.

King, P. M., & Kitchener, K. S. (1994). *Developing reflective judgment.* San Fransico: Jossey-Bass, John Wiley & Sons, Inc.

Knudsen-Lindauer, S. L., & Harris, K. (1989). Priorities for kindergarten curricula: views of parents and teachers. *Journal of Research in Childhood Education, 4*(1), 51–61.

Kuhn, D. (1991). *The skills of argument.* New York: Cambridge University Press.

Kuhn, D. (2000). Theory of mind, metacognition and reasoning: A life-span perspective. In P. Mitchell, & K. J. Riggs (Eds.), *Children's reasoning and the mind* (pp. 301-326). Hove, England: Psychology Press.

Kuhn, D., Cheney, R., & Weinstock, M. (2000). The development of epistemological understanding. *Cognitive Development, 15*, 309–328. doi:10.1016/S0885-2014(00)00030-7

Kuhn, D., & Pearsall, R. (1998). Relations between metastrategic knowledge and strategic performance. *Cognitive Development, 13*(2), 227–247. doi:10.1016/S0885-2014(98)90040-5

Kuhn, D., & Pearsall, S. (2000). Developmental origins of scientific thinking. *Journal of Cognition and Development, 1*, 113–129. doi:10.1207/S15327647JCD0101N_11

Kuhn, D., & Weinstock, M. (2002). What is epistemological thinking and why does it matter? In B. K. Hofer & P. R. Pintrich (Eds.), *Personal epistemology: The psychology of beliefs about knowledge and knowing* (pp. 121-144). Mahwah NJ: Lawrence Erlbaum.

LeCompte, M., & Preissle, J. (1992). Toward an ethnology of student life in schools and Classrooms: Synthesizing the qualitative research tradition. In M. D. LeCompte, W. L. Millroy, & J. Preissle (Eds.), *The handbook of qualitative research in education.* San Diego, CA: Academic Press.

Lewis, C., & Mitchell, P. (1994). *Children's early understanding of mind: Origins and development.* Hillsdale, NJ: Lawrence Erlbaum Associates

Mansfield, A., & Clinchy, B. (1985). *Early growth in multiplism in the child.* Paper submitted at the 15th annual symposium of the Jean Piaget Society, Phildelphia.

Mansfield, A. F., & Clinchy, B. (2002). Toward the integration of objectivity and subjectivity: epistemological development from 10 to 16. *New Ideas in Psychology, 20*(2-3), 225–262. doi:10.1016/S0732-118X(02)00008-9

Marra, R. (2005). Teacher beliefs: The impact of the design of constructivist learning environments on instructional epistemologies. *Learning Environments Research, 8*, 135–155. doi:10.1007/s10984-005-7249-4

Minuchin, S. (1974). *Families and family therapy.* Cambridge, MA: Harvard University Press.

Montessori, M. (1967). *The absorbent mind.* NY: Dell.

Moschner, B., Anschuetz, A., Wernke, S., & Wagener, U. (2008). Measurement of epistemological beliefs and learning strategies of elementary school children. In Khines and Myint Swe (Eds.), *Knowing, knowledge, and beliefs: Epistemological studies across diverse cultures* (pp. 113-133). New York: Springer Science.

Muis, K. R., Bendixen, L. D., & Harle, F. C. (2006). Domain-generality and domain-specificity in personal epistemology research: Philosophical and empirical reflections in the development of a theoretical framework. *Educational Psychology Review, 18*, 3–54. doi:10.1007/s10648-006-9003-6

National Research Council. (2001). *Adding it up: Helping children learn mathematics.* Mathematics Learning Study Committee. J. Kilpatrick, J. Swafford, & B. Findell (Eds.), *Center for Education, Division of Behavioral and Social Sciences and Education.* Washington, D.C: National Academy Press.

National Research Council. (2001a). *Eager to learn: Educating out preschooler.* Committee on Early Childhood Pedagogy. B.T. Bowman, M.S. Donovan, & M.S. Burns (Eds.), *Commission on Behavioral and Social Science Education.* Washington, DC: National Academy Press.

Nelson, C. A., & Snyder, K. (2005). The segregation of face and object processing in development: A model system of categorization? In L. Gershoff-Stowe & D. H. Rakison (Eds.), *Building object categories in developmental time* (pp. 1-32). Mahwah, NJ: Lawrence Erlbaum Associates.

Nelson, C. M. (2003). Through a glass Darkly: Reflections on our field and its future. *Education & Treatment of Children, 26*(4), 330–336.

O'Neill, D. K., Astington, J. W., & Flavell, J. H. (1992). Young children's understanding of the role that sensory experiences play in knowledge acquisition. *Child Development, 63*(2), 474–490. doi:10.2307/1131493

Olson, D. R., & Astington, J. W. (1993). Thinking about thinking: Learning how to take statements and hold beliefs. *Educational Psychologist, 28*(1), 7–23. doi:10.1207/s15326985ep2801_2

Perner, J. (1991). *Understanding the representational mind.* Cambridge, MA: MIT Press.

Perry, W. G., Jr. (1970). *Forms of intellectual and ethical development in the college years: A scheme.* New York: Holt, Rinehart and Winston.

Peterson, C. C., & Siegal, M. (2000). Insights into theory of mind from deafness and autism. *Mind & Language, 15*(1), 123–145. doi:10.1111/1468-0017.00126

Piaget, J. (1952). *The origins of intelligence in children* (Cook, M., Translation). New York: International University Press. (Original work published in 1936).

Piaget, J. (1964). Development and learning. *Journal of Research in Science Teaching, 2*, 176–186. doi:10.1002/tea.3660020306

Piaget, J., & Inhelder, J. (1966/1969). La psychologie de l'enfant. Paris: Presses Universitaries de France/*The psychology of the child*. London: Routledge & Kegan Paul.

Piotrkowski, C. S., Botsko, M., & Matthews, E. (2000). Parents' and teachers' beliefs about children's school readiness in a high need community. *Early Childhood Research Quarterly, 15*(4), 537–558. doi:10.1016/S0885-2006(01)00072-2

Poole, D. A., & Lamb, M. E. (1998*). Investigative interviews of children: A guide for helping professionals.* Washington, DC: American Psychological Association.

Rosenberg, S., Hammer, D., & Phelan, J. (2006). Multiple epistemological coherences in an Eighth-grade discussion of the rock cycle. *Journal of the Learning Sciences, 15*(2), 261–292. doi:10.1207/s15327809jls1502_4

Sawyer, K. S., Denham, S., DeMulder, E., Blair, K., Auerbach-Major, S., & Levitas, J. (2002). The contribution of older siblings' reaction to emotions to preschoolers' emotional and social competence. *Marriage & Family Review, 34*(3-4), 183–212.

Schommer, M. (1990). Effects of beliefs about the nature of knowledge on comprehension. *Journal of Educational Psychology, 82*(3), 498–504. doi:10.1037/0022-0663.82.3.498

Schommer-Aikins, M. (2000). Understanding middle students' beliefs about knowledge and learning using a multidimensional paradigm. *The Journal of Educational Research, 94*(2), 774–784.

Schommer-Aikins, M. (2004). Explaining the epistemological belief system: Introducing the embedded systemic model and coordinated research approach. *Educational Psychologist, 39*(1), 19–29. doi:10.1207/s15326985ep3901_3

Schraw, G., & Lehman, S. (2001). Situational interest: A review of the literature and directions for future research. *Educational Psychology Review, 13*(1), 23–52. doi:10.1023/A:1009004801455

Schraw, G., & Olafson, L. (2003). Teacher's epistemological worldviews and educational practices. *Issues in Education, 8*(2), 99–148.

Senge, P. (2000). Systems citizenship: The leadership mandate for this millennium. In H. Frances & M. Goldsmith (Eds.), *The leader of the future 2: Visions, strategies, and practices for the new era.* (pp. 31-46). San Francisco, CA: Jossey-Bass.

Siegler, R. S. (1998). Developmental differences in rule learning: A microgenetic analysis. *Cognitive Psychology, 36*(3), 273–310.doi:10.1006/cogp.1998.0686

Sinatra, G. M., & Kardash, C. A. M. (2004). Teacher candidates' epistemological beliefs, dispositions, and views on teaching as persuasion. *Contemporary Educational Psychology, 29*(4), 483–498. doi:10.1016/j.cedpsych.2004.03.001

Sternberg, R. J., Wagner, R. K., & Okagaki, L. (1993). Practical intelligence: The nature and role of tacit knowledge in work and at school. In J. M. Puckett & H. W. Reese (Eds.), *Mechanisms of everyday cognition* (pp. 257-398). Hillsdale, NJ: Lawrence Erlbaum Associates.

Tager-Flusberg, H. (2000). The challenge of studying language development in children with autism. In L. Menn & R. N. Bernstein (Eds.), *Methods for studying language production* (pp. 194-197). Mahwah, NJ: Lawrence Erlbaum Associates.

Tangen, R. (2008). Listening to children's voices in educational research: Some theoretical and methodological problems. *European Journal of Special Needs Education, 23*(2), 157–166. doi:10.1080/08856250801945956

Vartuli, S. (1999). How early childhood teacher beliefs vary across grade levels. *Early Childhood Research Quarterly, 14*(4), 489–514. doi:10.1016/S0885-2006(99)00026-5

Vygotsky, L. S. (1978). *Mind in society: The development of higher psychological processes.* Cambridge, MA: Harvard University Press.

Wellman, H. M., Cross, D., & Watson, J. (2001). Meta-analysis of theory-of-mind development: The truth about false belief. *Child Development, 72*(3), 655–684. doi:10.1111/1467-8624.00304

Wellman, H. M., & Woolley, J. D. (1990). From simple desires to ordinary beliefs: The early development of everyday psychology. *Cognition, 35,* 245–275. doi:10.1016/0010-0277(90)90024-E

Wimmer, H., & Perner, J. (1983). Beliefs about beliefs: Representation and constraining function of wrong beliefs in young children's understanding of deception. *Cognition, 13,* 103–128. doi:10.1016/0010-0277(83)90004-5

Winsor, D. L. (2006). Inter-relatedness of theory of mind and epistemology in young children. Paper presented in F.C. Haerle (Chair), *Measuring Children's Personal Epistemology and Its Relevance for Education.* Symposium conducted at the American Educational Research Association Annual Meeting, San Francisco, CA, USA.

Woodruff, G., & Premack, D. (1979). Intentional communication in the chimpanzee: The development of deception. *Cognition, 7,* 333–362. doi:10.1016/0010-0277(79)90021-0

Chapter 11
Technology Resources and Software Recommended for Young Children and Teachers

Lee Allen
University of Memphis, USA

Sally Blake
University of Memphis, USA

Candice Burkett
University of Memphis, USA

Rene Crow
University of Central Arkansas,
USA

Andrew Neil Gibbons
New Zealand Tertiary College,
New Zealand

Michael M. Grant
University of Memphis, USA

Satomi Izumi-Taylor
University of Memphis, USA

Yu-Yuan Lee
University of Memphis, USA,
& Nan Kai University of
Technology, Taiwan

Jorge Lopez
University of Texas at El Paso,
USA

María Eugenia López
Centro de Desarrollo Infantil,
México

Zelda McMurtry
Arkansas State University, USA

Clif Mims
University of Memphis, USA

Vivian Gunn Morris
University of Memphis and
Harding Academy, USA

Cheri Lewis Smith
University of Memphis and
Harding Academy, USA

Denise Winsor
University of Memphis and
Harding Academy, USA

ABSTRACT

Technology is being designed for children of all ages, even as young as nine months (Morrison, 2007).
The software market is growing rapidly for children from infant to preschool age, with programs for
children under five representing the fastest-growing educational softwarea area (Morrison 2007). The
Internet provides access to a great collection of resources available for young children and teachers.

DOI: 10.4018/978-1-60566-784-3.ch011

The following pages may be of interest to educators of young children. There are web sites included for software and articles of interest related to issues concerning technology and young children selected by all authors of our book.

LINKS TO ONLINE RESOURCES ON TECHNOLOGY AS A LEARNING TOOL

- (NAEYC and Authors) http://www.journal.naeyc.org/btj/200311/links.asp
- **ACTTive Technology**, a quarterly publication of Macomb Projects, features articles about technology application for young children and curriculum activities. www.wiu.edu/users/mimacp/wiu/articles.html
- **"Adobe Photoshop"** can be used to create slideshows and class books using digital photos taken in the classroom. Slideshows are a great way to document a school year, or special event, in pictures. Slideshows can be saved to disk and are keepsakes that parents are sure to enjoy. By making class books using Adobe Photoshop, teachers can help students retell their own classroom experiences through writing. Children love to take the books home to share with friends and family!
- **"Alphabet Express,"** a software program by School Zone Publishing Company, is recommended for children from ages three to six. After logging on to this program, children can choose to listen to an alphabet song, play early literacy games, or select a letter of the alphabet to learn about via games and coloring pages. Printable handwriting pages are available for each letter of the alphabet. The bright colors and lively music capture the interest of the very youngest learners. (Available at www.schoolzone.com)
- **The America Connects Consortium** (ACC) supports the work of community technology centers (CTCs) across the country. Through training, evaluation, resource development, and information referral, ACC supports the use of information technology to improve adult literacy and achievement in education. In this article, "With Computers, Children Learn the 3 Rs Plus the S: Self-Esteem," by Carolyn Moore, parents and teachers in a Head Start program in Connecticut are surprised at the changes taking place in the students. www.americaconnects.net/field/F7abcd.asp
- **Apple Learning Interchange's** extensive use of digital video ignites conversation, imagination, and improvement in education by showcasing the exemplary content that educators deliver in classrooms every day. http://ali.apple.com/ali_sites/ali/new_elem.html
- **Bailey's Book House** by Edmark is recommended for children from the ages of two to five. When interacting with the software, children select from seven early literacy activities that focus on letter recognition, rhyming, and vocabulary development. Children also can create printable cards for various occasions and "write" stories. The program also encourages the development of basic computer skills. The software can be purchased from Edmark (1-800-362-2890 or www.edmark.com).
- "Business Leaders Warn of Early Learning Gap; Urge States, Federal Government to Build High-Quality Early Childhood Education Programs" is a **Business Roundtable** Press Release dated May 7, 2003. www.brt.org/press.cfm/902
- **Candy's Project Website**—Walking

through the spring 2000 project on chickens a visitor can see an excellent example of a teacher-created Website showcasing a preschool class's project. www.cds-sf.org/cproject/index.htm

- **CAST (Center for Applied Special Technology)** uses technology to expand opportunities for all people, including those with disabilities. www.cast.org/index.cfm
- **Center for Media Education** is dedicated to creating a quality electronic media culture for children and youth, their families and communities. CME's research focuses on the potential—and peril—for children and youth of the rapidly evolving digital media culture. www.cme.org
- **Center for Media Literacy** provides clear explanations and relevant connections about media and technology and their impact on our culture, our schools, and ourselves—especially children and young people. www.medialit.org
- **Child Care plus+**: The Center on Inclusion in Early Childhood offers a number of free and inexpensive resources, including an Adapting Toys Tool Kit that contains materials and instructions for adapting toys, adding sensory input, and promoting independent play. www.ccplus.org
- **Children and Computers** site contains developmental software and Website evaluation tools, award winning software suggestions, and articles and research pertaining to young children and technology. www.childrenandcomputers.com
- "Children and Computer Technology" is the theme of this special issue of **The Future of Children** (Fall/Winter 2000, vol. 10, no. 2). www.futureofchildren.org/pubs-info2825/pubs-info.htm?doc_id=69787
- **Children Now's** Children and the Media program works to improve the quality of news and entertainment media both for children and about children's issues, with

particular attention to media images of race, class, and gender. www.childrennow.org

- "Connected to the Future: A Report on Children's Internet Use from the **Corporation for Public Broadcasting**." American children, regardless of their age, ethnicity, or income, greatly increased their Internet use from home, school, or library between 2000 and 2002. Even so, children from underserved populations still significantly lag behind more advantaged children, both in home and school access. This report discusses the trends and implications for the future. www.cpb.org/pdfs/ed/resources/connected/03_connect_report.pdf
- "Connecting Kids to Technology: Challenges and Opportunities," by Tony Wilhelm, Delia Carmen, and Megan Reynolds; Annie E. Casey Foundation and Benton Foundation. July 8, 2002. This report, presented on the **Digital Divide Network**, examines the demographics of the digital divide, discusses some implications of current trends, and highlights a few efforts to bridge the divide and provide a level playing field for all children. www.digitaldividenetwork.org/content/stories/index.cfm?key=244
- **Content bank** guides teachers to a wealth of education resources, including links to Websites with lesson plans, grammar lessons, puzzles, and games— for example, sites where users can build a Webpage without knowing any html. www.content-bank.org/firsttime/index.asp
- **CyberStart** Pennsylvania, a unique multiyear state initiative, has for its goal making technology and educational programs available to expand the learning opportunities for young children. www.cyberstart.org
- **Division of Early Childhood** of the

Council for Exceptional Children (DEC/CEC) is an international organization for those who work with young children with special needs from infancy through age eight. www.dec-sped.org "Early Childhood Research and Practice" is an Internet journal on the development, care, and education of young children. http://ecrp.uiuc.edu

- The **Early Childhood Technology Literacy Project** won the Computerworld Smithsonian Award in Education and Academia in 2000 for focusing on using technology to enhance early literacy. Lesson plans, vignettes, suggested software, Websites, professional development resources, and articles can be found here. www.ectlp.org

- **Early Connections: Technology in Early Childhood Education** (a project of the Northwest Educational Technology Consortium and Northwest Regional Educational Laboratory's Child & Family Program) connects technology with the way young children learn. Find resources and information for educators and care providers here. www.netc.org/earlyconnections/index.html

- **Encarta Encyclopedia** can be used formally and informally to research topics in which children are interested. More than 4,500 articles are available, from aardvark to Zambia. www.encarta.msn.com/encnet/refpages/artcenter.aspx

- The **International Society for Technology in Education** project developed standards to guide educational leaders in recognizing and addressing the essential conditions for effective use of technology to support pre-K–12 education. The Website includes performance indicators, lesson examples, and scenarios to help guide the use of technology as a tool for learning. http://cnets.iste.org/students

- "Internet Access in U.S. Public Schools and Classrooms: 1994–2001," from the **National Center for Education Statistics** (NCES) of the U.S. Department of Education. Since 1994, NCES has surveyed public schools to estimate access to information technology in schools and classrooms. Each fall a new nationally representative sample of approximately 1,000 public schools has been surveyed about Internet access and Internet-related topics. Read here about the results. www.nces.ed.gov/pubs2002/internet

- The **Kaiser Family Foundation** report, "Zero to Six: Electronic Media in the Lives of Infants, Toddlers, and Preschoolers," by Victoria J. Rideout, Elizabeth A. Vandewater, and Ellen A. Wartella, presents the finding of one of the only large-scale national studies on the role of media in the live of young children. www.kff.org/content/2003/3378/0to6Report.pdf

- "**Kid Pix Studio Deluxe**" by Broderbund allows children to create artwork using the computer. The creativity toolbox provides resources so that children can draw, paint, and animate artwork. Their artwork can also be accompanied by music and sound. Artwork can be saved, combined to form a slideshow, or sent to friends and family via e-mail. Skills addressed in the program include colors, shapes, numbers, and letters. Early vocabulary usage is also encouraged.

- "**Kidspiration**" by Inspiration Software, Inc. allows children to create graphic organizers using pictures, texts, and spoken language. The program can help children to develop study skills by helping them to create visual representations of important concepts. Kidspiration can aid student in the development of the following skills: categorization, communication, and estimation. The program is intended for children in kindergarten through fifth grade and is available from Inspiration Software, Inc (1-800-877-4292 or http://www.kidspiration.com).

- **Kids' Space**, a children's educational foundation, provides high quality yet commercial-free Websites for learning and collaboration among students and teachers. It seeks to make a difference in understanding people and ourselves. www.kids-space.org

- **Kidsmart** Guide to Early Learning and Technology for Home and School has sections for parents and teachers, offered in eight languages, with areas titled Learning and Playing Together, Integrating Technology, and Access for All. www.kidsmartearlylearning.org

- **The Lion and Lamb Project's** mission is to stop the marketing of violent toys, games, and entertainment to children, working with parents and concerned adults to reduce the demand for violent entertainment products and with industry and government to reduce the supply. www.lion-lamb.org

- At **Mrs. Feldman's Kindergarten Homepage** you will find Websites that can be used with young children as well as articles and technology integration ideas. http://homepage.mac.com/dara_feldman

- **NAEYC Position Statement: Technology and Young Children—Ages 3 through 8.**www.naeyc.org/resources/position_statements/pstech98.htm

- The **NAEYC Technology and Young Children Interest Forum** is available to NAEYC members through the Get Involved section of NAEYC's Website. The Interest Forum's mission is to lead discussions, share research and information, and demonstrate best practices regarding technology so it can be used to benefit children

from birth through age eight. www.naeyc.org/Getinvolved/getinvolved.asp

- **National Center for Technology Innovation**, funded by the U.S. Office of Special Education Programs, is a catalyst for cutting-edge technology developed by educators for students with disabilities, their teachers, and their parents. Look for the launch of their Website. www.nationaltechcenter.org

- **National Early Childhood Technical Assistance Center** provides information on various types of assistive technology, funding resources, and current legislation. http://nectas.unc.edu/topics/atech/atech/asp

- **National Institute on Media and the Family** offers tools and resources to help families and educators maximize the benefits and minimize the harm of mass media on children through research, education, and advocacy. www.mediaandthefamily.org

- **North Central Regional Education Laboratory** offers a one-stop guide to online publications and Websites on educational technology. www.ncrel.org

- **PBS Kids** Website has interactive games, stories, music, and coloring for children, plus sections with activities for families and classroom activities for teachers. www.pbskids.org

- **"Reader Rabbit Learns to Read with Phonics"** by the Learning Company is a software program suitable for children ages three to six. The software uses a dual approach, using both phonics and sight word identification, to encourage reading readiness skills. Activities included in the program support the development of letter-sound recognition, blending skills, and patterning ability. The program also aids in the development of vocabulary skills. The *Road to Reading* mission, a component of the software program, features Mat the Mouse. Mat the Mouse is a young mouse who wishes there were no more words in the world during a moment of frustration at her inability to read. He children help Mat the Mouse to restore the alphabet to the world, one letter at a time. (Available at www.learningcompany.com)

- **"Reading Success"** by Smithson-Berry Publications is a software program that takes children on a journey through the "Itty Bitty City" while offering them multiple interactive visual and auditory learning experiences. The research-based program focuses on early literacy skills including phonemic awareness, language development, phonics, fluency, comprehension, and vocabulary. Prereading skills addressed in the program include sequencing, categorizing, rhyming, recognition of letters, development of language and vocabulary, and identification of colors and shapes. Reading readiness activities include categorizing, vocabulary and language development activities, patterning, letter sequencing, capital and lower case letter identification, blending letter sounds, and sight word identification. Early readers can practice previously learned skills while increasing their sight vocabulary, creating simple sentences, exploring homophones and diphthongs, practicing verb tense, and actually reading early readers. (Available from Smithson-Berry Publications at 1-877-732-3935 or www.smithson-berry. org)

- **Sammy's Science House** by Edmark encourages children to think scientifically while learning about the weather, seasons of the year, animal habitats, and other basic concepts. Sequencing, sorting, and classifying skills are addressed. The children love that the program allows them to manipulate various characteristics of the

environment to create different animated scenes. For example, children can select different precipitation and wind levels and observe their effects. Creativity is encouraged throughout the program. (Available from Edmark at 1-800-362-2890 or www. edmark.com).

- "Technology: A Key to the Future," *Head Start Bulletin* special issue, February 2000. Issue no. 66 describes some of the ways Head Start programs are making innovative use of technology to achieve program goals. Focus is on the Internet, with articles such as Head Start programs and the World Wide Web, designing a useful Website, and ensuring young children's access to the Web. www.headstartinfo.org/publications/ hsbulletin66/cont_66.htm

- **THE (Technology Helping Educators) Consortium** project seeks to improve the quality of early childhood teacher education programs by enhancing Head Start teachers' academic opportunities through increased exposure to and use of technology in authentic and culturally relevant contexts. www.thecol.org

- **Tots 'n' Tech Research Institute** offers ideas for equipment and materials that can help children with special needs be more independent in caring for themselves, making friends, communicating, and doing the things that other young children do in child care and community activity settings. http://tnt.asu.edu

- "Universal Design for Learning: From the Start," by Bonnie Blagojevic, Deb Twomey, & Linda Labas; University of Maine's **Center for Community Inclusion**. The phrase universal design for learning (UDL) was adopted by educators at CAST (Center for Applied Special Technology) to reflect the important difference between universal design for access, which makes information and materials available to children, and universal design for learning, which takes into account an actual gain in knowledge or skills. The authors discuss the concept, history, and use of UDL for children with disabilities. www.ume.maine.edu/~cci/facts/facts6/udl.htm

- "Use of Computer Technology to Help Students with Special Needs," by Ted S. Hasselbring and Candyce H. Williams Glaser. In the special Fall/Winter 2000 issue (on children and technology) of ***The Future of Children***, this article provides an overview of the various ways computer technology can help the nearly five million students with disabilities in the U.S. become active learners in the classroom alongside their nondisabled peers. www.futureofchildren.org/pubs-info2825/pubsinfo.htm?doc_id=69787

- **www.4teachers** helps teachers who are integrating technology into the curriculum and classroom. The Website offers free Web-based programs (many also in Spanish) to help them create a Web page, make a poster, write rubrics, and so on. http://4teachers.org

- www.aolatschool.com contains resources for students, educators, and parents. Students can access information including games, lessons, and tutorials to enhance learning in math, science, language arts, social studies, the arts, and other elective subjects. Reference tools such as atlases, almanacs, dictionaries, and encyclopedias are available as well as news sources, educational games, and weather forecasts. For educators, lesson plan builders, flashcards, worksheet and puzzle makers, clip art resources, and rubric generators are available. Tips for integrating technology into the classroom, creating Web sites, online collaborative projects, and Internet safety can also be found at this Web site.

- www.bbc.co.uk/cbeebies/ is a website that

is based on the underlying belief that children learn through play. Interactive stories and games are available at this site. Several games and stories have been modified to better accommodate special needs children.

- www.bookhive.com offers information on various children's books for children ages birth through 12. Book reviews, along with parental notes, can be found for a wide variety of books. Searches may be conducted based on author, illustrator, title, interest area, reading level, or number of pages. This site is a valuable resource for both parents and educators.

- www.educationworld.com provides educators with a plethora if information that is organized according to the following topics: lesson planning, professional development, technology integration, school issues, and Education World at home. Tips for the classroom, management tools, and printable ideas and activities can be found at this site. Links to other professional resources are also available.

- www.internet4classrooms.com is a site where educators can access a wide variety of educational resources including:
  - Assessment assistance to aid in test preparation
  - Practice modules/tutorials to support the development of technological skills needed to use multiple software programs including PowerPoint, Word, Excel, Inspiration, Internet Explorer, Dreamweaver, HyperStudio, Macintosh, Windows/PC, WebQuest, Works, Netscape, and Claris
  - Links to frequently updated sites containing notable quotes, trivia questions, and other interesting facts
  - Guidelines for effective searching of the Internet
  - Links to numerous sites that can be

used to enhance learning in the classroom (the links are grouped according to subject area, grade level, and topic)

- www.lego.com is a site where children can play games, solve puzzles, and view the latest lego products. Games include memory match and hide and seek. Children can also create their own lego scenes and draw or paint pictures.

- www.literacycenter.net/, started with a small business innovation search (SBIR) contract from the U.S. Department of Education, offers free resources for parents and educators to aid in the development of early literacy skills. Resources are available in English, Spanish, Dutch, and French. Interactive activities available at this site provide young children with the opportunity to learn about colors, letters, numbers, shapes, phonemes, rhyming, and writing. At this site, additional information on the importance of each skill addressed is available.

- www.netc.org/earlyconnections/, developed by the Northwest Educational Technology Consortium, is a site that provides resources and information for educators on the use of technology in early childhood education. Information on how technology relates to children's development during different stages can be found at this site. Also, information on how to incorporate technology into the classroom and links to additional information can be found.

- www.pbskids.org is a site that contains games and activities related to children's favorite PBS characters. The activities include coloring pages, matching activities, and sing-alongs. Letter and number identification and rhyming are some of the skills addressed at this site. Portions of the site provide resources for parents and teachers.

- www.playhousedisney.com has a portion of the site dedicated to educators where they can search for classroom activities, recipes, puzzles, games, and songs. When at this site, the educator is able to search for information by selecting specific skills to be addressed, themes to be reflected, and age levels (from two to five) to be included in the activities. Each search generates age-appropriate activities that can be used in the classroom.

- www.scholastic.com has a section of the site designed for teachers where they can find subject-related online activities, lesson plans, and teaching tools. Teachers can generate flashcards, make rubrics, create class home pages, and find age-appropriate lesson plans. With Scholastic's Global Classport, educators can connect to classrooms and collaborate with teachers in 182 countries!

- www.school.discovery.com is a site where educators can find lesson plans, create puzzles, download free clip art, and create custom quizzes and worksheets. By signing up for an online account, teachers are able to store their online creations for future use. An entire section of this site focuses on Science Fairs, offering project ideas and multiple links where further information can be found. "Brain Booster" word puzzles that require higher order thinking skills are also available for educators to use in their classrooms.

- www.starfall.com is a website where parents and educators can find activities, handouts, and interactive games that support children's learning at the pre-reading, beginning reading, intermediate reading, and advanced reading levels. Very young children can discover the letters and the sounds that the letters make while exploring the site. Animated pictures that reinforce the sounds made by the particular letters are available for each letter, and short jingles help to teach the sounds. Beginning reading acquisition is encouraged by the interactive books available at this site. The children can manipulate the pages of the available books while working on the computer, and the computer will "read" the books to the children, highlighting each individual word as it is read. Printable books and skill-building worksheets are available to reinforce the skills learned via the computer. For more advanced readers, various genres of interactive books are available including plays, comics, myths, folk tales, and fables. Fictional and nonfictional works are also available.

- www.storyplace.org, a website available in both English and Spanish, provides children with an opportunity to explore interactive books. The digital library contains selections for preschool and elementary-aged children. Both online and printable activities are available at this site.

- www.teachyoungchildren.org is the official site of the NAEYC Technology and Young Children Interest Forum. The site offers information on the best practices for using technology with children, a technology information exchange, research references on the use of technology with young children, resources for funding technology, and tips for using the Internet.

HELPFUL WEBSITES FOR FAMILIES

1. PBS Parents: http://www.pbs.org/parents/childrenandmedia. Helps parents learn how media such as TV, movies, computers and video games can shape their child's development. Also includes definitions for the slang used in instant messages as well as other media terms.

2. Zero to Three: http://www.zerotothree. org/site/PageServer. Provides information especially for parents of children from birth to age 3. Many topics are explored, including how to choose quality child care and developmental milestones.

3. Parents Guide to the Internet: U.S. Department of Education: http://www. ed.gov/pubs/parents/internet/index.html. This guide is ideal for parents with very little knowledge of the Internet and how it works. Includes sections about setting limits and keeping children safe from the Internet's potential dangers.

4. Disney Online Safety: http://home.disney. go.com/guestservices/safety. Excellent site with advice for parents on how to keep their children safe on the Internet. Includes specific questions that parents can ask their children about their Internet use.

5. Fathering Magazine: http://www.fathermag. com. Website focusing on the important role of fathers in the lives of children. Contains excellent articles on "cyberbullying" focusing on what parents can do to protect their children.

6. KidsHealth for Parents: http://kidshealth. org/parent. Information and advice for parents on a variety of topics. Internet topics include how parents can take an active role in protecting their children from Internet predators and sexually explicit materials. Information for kids and teens also.

7. Education Resources for Spanish Speakers: U.S. Department of Education: http://www. ed.gov/espanol/bienvenidos/es/index.html. Wonderful resource for Spanish speaking families. Information on a variety of educational topics.

8. Internet 4 Classrooms: http://www.internet-4classrooms.com/parents.htm. An extensive list of websites to help parents help their children succeed. Categories include reading, math, discipline, internet safety, and planning for the future. Many Spanish sites available also.

9. SuperKids: Education for the Future: http://www.superkids.com/. In addition to presenting unbiased software reviews, SuperKids also features stories and interviews on subjects related to education, technology, and parenting.

10. KidSites: http://www.kidsites.com/sites-grownups/parents.htm. One of the leading guides to the best websites for children and parents. Every website listed is checked and approved by the staff of KidSites to ensure that the site is family friendly.

11. ChildFun: http://childfun.com/. Fun activities and printable resources for families to enjoy.

HELPFUL WEBSITES FOR TEACHERS

1. NAEYC Technology and Young Children Interest Forum: http://www.techandyoungchildren.org/index.html. NAEYC website designed to lead discussions, share research, and demonstrate best practices regarding technology so it can be used to enhance the learning of children aged 0-8.

2. Early Connections: Technology in Early Childhood Education: http://www.netc.org/earlyconnections/. Resources and information on the appropriate and effective use of technology with young children.

3. PBS Teachers: http://www.pbs.org/teachers/earlychildhood/. Valuable resource designed especially for early childhood teachers. Addresses media literacy and copyright laws and includes information on connecting school and home.

4. Scholastic Teachers: http://www2.scholastic.com/browse/article.jsp?id=3749732. Presents 5 keys to successful parent-teacher communication. Other excellent resources for teachers are available on this website also.

5. PowerPoint in the Classroom: http://www.actden.com/PP/. An easy to use tutorial on PowerPoint for beginners. Would be an excellent tutorial even for children because of the animated site guides.

6. Internet 4 Classrooms: http://www.internet-4classrooms.com/teacher.htm. This website features an extensive list of websites that help teachers use the internet effectively.

7. Kathy Schrocks Guide for Educators: http://school.discoveryeducation.com/schrockguide/gadgets.html. Excellent list of useful websites for teachers specifically addressing the use of "digital gadgets" in education, such as using digital cameras and camcorders in the classroom, podcasting, and using iPods with young children.

8. Discovery Education Classroom Resources: http://discoveryeducation.com/survival/parent_communication.cfm. Lists specific ideas for effective parent communication from email to parent conferences.

9. Web for Teachers: http://www.4teachers.org/. Online tools and resources for helping teachers integrate technology into the curriculum. Also includes valuable resources for supporting English language learners.

10. National Educational Technology Standards (NETS): http://www.iste.org/AM/Template.cfm?Section=NETS. NETS for students includes national technology standards and describes what students should know and be able to do with technology.

11. Early Childhood Technology Literacy Project: http://www.montgomeryschoolsmd.org/curriculum/littlekids/. Website designed as a parent/teacher resource for the Early Childhood Technology Literacy Project, an award-winning project designed to integrate technology into K-2 instruction. Many helpful links for kids, parents, and teachers.

RESEARCH AVAILABLE ONLINE

Special Issues on Technology and Young Children

- Early Education and Development, Vol. 17(3), 2006. Technology in Early Childhood Education, Edited by X. Christine Wang and Jim Hoot.
- Young Children, November 2003. Using Technology as a Teaching and Learning Tool.
- Contemporary Issues in Early Childhood, Vol. 3(2), 2002. Technology Special Issue. Edited by Nicola Yelland & John Siraj-Blatchford.
- The Future of Children, Vol. 10(2), 2000. Children and Computer Technology. Edited by Richard E. Behrman

Early Childhood Research or Technology Related Journals

- Early Childhood Development and Care
- Early Childhood Research Quarterly
- Early Education and Development
- He Kupu eLearning
- Information Technology in Childhood Education Annual
- Journal of Computer Assisted Learning
- Journal of Educational Computing Research
- Journal of Educational Technology Systems
- Journal of Research in Childhood Education
- Young Children

Evaluation Criteria for Websites

Evaluation of web sites is an important part of technology use. The following sites and references are designed to help you determine the appropriate site for use with your children.

Critically Analyzing Information Sources from the Cornell University Library:

- Author
- Date of Publication
- Edition or Revision
- Publisher
- Title of Journal
- Intended Audience
- Objective Reasoning
- Coverage
- Writing Style
- Evaluative Reviews

Evaluating Web Pages: Questions to Ask & Strategies for Getting the Answers: An eight-point evaluation checklist from the UC Berkeley Library.

- What can the URL tell you?
- Who wrote the page? Is he, she, or the authoring institution a qualified authority?
- Is it dated? Current, timely?
- Is information cited authentic?
- Does the page have overall integrity and reliability as a source?
- What's the bias?
- Could the page or site be ironic, like a satire or a spoof?
- If you have questions or reservations, how can you satisfy them?

Evaluating Information Found on the Internet from Johns Hopkins University (Elizabeth E. Kirk):

- Authorship
- Publishing body
- Point of view or bias
- Referral to other sources
- Verifiability
- Currency

- How to distinguish propaganda, misinformation and disinformation
- The mechanics of determining authorship, publishing body, and currency on the Internet

Five Criteria for Evaluating Web Pages (Jim Kapoun):

- Accuracy
- Authority
- Currency
- Objectivity
- Coverage

To evaluate Web sites go to this table of criteria and questions to ask when judging the reliability of information on the Web.

Generic Criteria for Evaluation (Hope Tillman):

- Stated criteria for inclusion of information
- Authority of author or creator
- Comparability with related sources
- Stability of information
- Appropriateness of format
- Software / hardware / multimedia requirements

Other resources:

- Criteria for the Evaluation of Internet Information Resources (Alastair Smith)
- ICYouSee: T is for Thinking (John Henderson)
- BUBL Information Service
- The WWW Virtual Library
- Yahoo's Home Page and Yahoo's Magazines section
- Selection by librarians:
  - Librarians' Index to the Internet [UC Berkeley]
  - Internet Reference Resources [Cornell University]

RECOMMENDED READING

Ching, C. C., Wang, X. C., & Kedem, Y. (2006). Digital photo journals in a K-1 classroom: A novel approach to addressing early childhood technology standards and recommendations. In S. Tettegah & R. Hunter (Eds.), *Technology: Issues in administration, policy, and applications in K-12 classrooms* (pp. 253-269). Oxford, UK: Elsevier.

Clements, D., & Sarama, J. (2003). *Strip Mining for Gold: Research and Policy in Educational Technology: A Response to "Fool's Gold (in PDF)"* or Strip Mining for Gold: Research and Policy in Educational Technology: A Response to "Fool's Gold (in HTML). *AACE Journal, 11*(1), 7–69.

Clements, D. H. (1991). Current technology and the early childhood curriculum. In B. Spodek & O. N. Saracho (Eds.), *Yearbook in early childhood education, Volume 2: Issues in early childhood curriculum* (pp. 106-131). New York: Teachers College Press.

Clements, D. H. (1993). Computer technology and early childhood education. In J. L. Roopnarine & J. E. Johnson (Eds.), *Approaches to early childhood education* (2nd ed.) (2nd ed., pp. 295-316). New York: Merrill.

Clements, D. H. (1993). Early education principles and computer practices. In C. G. Hass & F. W. Parkay (Eds.), *Curriculum planning: A new approach* (6th ed.). Boston: Allyn and Bacon.

Clements, D. H., & Nastasi, B. K. (1992). Computers and early childhood education. In M. Gettinger, S. N. Elliott, & T. R. Kratochwill (Eds.), Advances in school psychology: *Preschool and early childhood treatment directions* (pp. 187-246). Hillsdale, NJ: Lawrence Erlbaum Associates.

Debate on Appropriateness of Technology for Young Children Alliance for Childhood. (2004). *Tech Tonic: Towards a New Literacy of Technology, Alliance for Childhood.* College Park, MD: Publisher Cordes, C., & Miller, E. (2000). *Fool's gold: A critical look at computers in childhood.* College Park, MD: Alliance for Childhood.

Haugland, S. W. (1999). What roles should technology play in young children's learning? *Young Children, 54*(6), 26–32.

Hutinger, P., Bell, C., Beard, M., Bond, J., Johanson, J., & Terry, C. (1998). Final Report: The early childhood emergent literacy technology research study. Macomb, IL: Western Illinois University, Macomb Projects.

Hutinger, P., Bell, C., Daytner, G., & Johanson, J. (2005). *Disseminating and replicating an effective emergent literacy technology curriculum: A final report.* Macomb, IL: Western Illinois University, Center for Best Practices in Early Childhood. Available in html: http://www.wiu.edu/thecenter/reports.php or PDF: http://www.wiu.edu/thecenter/finalreports/ELiTeCFinalRpt2.pdf

Sarama, J., & Clements, D. H. (2002). Learning and teaching with computers in early childhood education. In O. N. Saracho & B. Spodek (Eds.), *Contemporary Perspectives in Early Childhood Education* (pp. 171-219). Greenwich, CT: Information Age Publishing, Inc.

Wartella, E. A., & Jennings, N. (2000). Children and Computers: New Technology-Old Concerns (in PDF) or Children and Computers: New Technology-Old Concerns (in HTML). *The Future of Children: Children and Computer Technology, 10*(2). *Review Articles on Technology & ECE*

Yelland, N. (1995). Mindstorms or a storm in a teacup? A review of research with Logo. *International Journal of Mathematical Education in Science and Technology, 26*(6), 853–869.

IMPACT OF TECHNOLOGY ON CHILDREN'S COGNITIVE DEVELOPMENT

Calvert, S. L., Strong, B. L., & Gallagher, L. (2005). Control as an engagement feature for young children's attention to the learning of computer content. *The American Behavioral Scientist, 48*(5), 578–589.

Nastasi, B., & Clements, D. H. (1994). Effectance motivation, perceived scholastic competence, and high-order thinking in two cooperative computer environments. *Journal of Educational Computing Research, 10,* 249–275.

Wright, & D. D. Shade (Eds.), *Young children: Active learners in a technological age.* Washington, D.C.: National Association for the Education of Young Children.

IMPACT OF TECHNOLOGY ON CHILDREN'S SOCIAL DEVELOPMENT

Buckleitner, W. (2000). Sharing at the computer: Software that promotes socialization and cooperation. *Scholastic Early Childhood Today, 6-7.*

Calvert, S. L. (2002). Identity construction on the Internet. In S. L. Calvert, A. B. Jordan & R. R. Cocking (Eds.), *Children in the digital age: Influences of electronic media on development* (pp.57-70). Westport, CT: Praeger.

Freeman, N. K., & Somerindyke, J. (2001). Social play at the computer: Preschoolers scaffold and support peers' computer competence. *Information Technology in Childhood Education Annual,* 203–213.

Heft, T., & Swaminathan, S. (2002). The effects of computers on the social behavior of preschoolers. *Journal of Research in Childhood Education, 16*(2), 162–174.

Lomangino, A. G., Nicholson, J., & Sulzby, E. (1999). The influence of power relations and social goals on children's collaborative interactions while composing on computers. *Early Childhood Research Quarterly, 14*(2), 197–228.

Wang, X. C., & Ching, C. C. (2003). Social construction of computer experience in a first-grade classroom: Social processes and mediating artifacts. *Early Education and Development, 14*(3), 335–361.

TECHNOLOGY AND CONTENT AREAS

Clements, D. H. (1999). Young children and technology. In G. D. Nelson (Ed.), *Dialogue on early childhood science, mathematics, and technology education* (pp. 92-105). Washington, DC: American Association for the Advancement of Science.

Clements, D. H., & Sarama, J. (2004). Building Blocks for early childhood mathematics. *Early Childhood Research Quarterly, 19*, 181–189.

Clements, D. H., & Sarama, J. (2005). Young children and technology: What's appropriate? In W. Masalski & P. C. Elliott (Eds.), *Technology-supported mathematics learning environments: 67th Yearbook* (pp. 51-73). Reston, VA: National Council of Teachers of Mathematics.

Dyson, A. (1999). The ninja's, the ladies, and the X-men: Text as a ticket to play. From *Writing Superheroes: Contemporary childhood, popular culture, and classroom literacy* (pp. 47-65). New York: Teachers College Press.

Labbo, L. D., & Ash, G. E. (1998). What is the role of computer-related technology in early literacy? In S. B. Neuman & K. A. Roskos (Eds.), *Children Achieving: Best Practices in Early Literacy.* Newark, DE: International Reading Association.

Pelletier, J., Reeve, R., & Halewood, C. (2006). Young Children's Knowledge Building and Literacy Development Through Knowledge Forum®. *Early Education and Development, 17*(3).

Sarama, J., & Clements, D. H. (2002). Building Blocks for young children's mathematical Steve Clements, D. H. (2002). Computers in early childhood mathematics. *Contemporary Issues in Early Childhood, 3*(2), 160–181.

TECHNOLOGY USE IN SCHOOL

Changing How and What Children Learn in School with Computer-Based Technologies (in PDF) or Changing How and What Children Learn in School with Computer-Based Technologies (in HTML). by Jeremy M. Roschelle, Roy D. Pea, Christopher M. Hoadley, Douglas N. Gordin, and Barbara M. Means.

Cuban, L. (2001). *Oversold and underused: Computers in the Classroom.* Boston, MA: Harvard U. Press.

Gillespie, C. W. (2004). Seymour Papert's vision for early childhood education? A descriptive study of preschoolers and kindergarteners in discovery-based, Logo-rich classrooms. *Early Childhood Research and Practice, 6*(1). Available online at http://ecrp.uiuc.edu/

Gillespie, C.W., & Beisser, S. R. (2001). Developmentally appropriate LOGO computer programming with young children. *Information Technology in Childhood Education*, 232-247

Good, L. (2005/06). Snap it up!: Using digital photography in early childhood. *Childhood Education, 82*(2), 79–85.

Haugland, S. (2005). Selecting or Upgrading Software and Web Sites in the Classroom. *Early Childhood Education Journal, 32*(5), 329–340.

Haugland, S. W. (2004). Early childhood classrooms in the 21st century: Using computers to maximize learning. In J. Hirschbuhl (Ed.). *Computers in Education Annual Edition*. New York: McGraw Hill.

Haugland, S. W., Ruiz, E. L., & Gong, Y. (2004) Animals on-line: Using information technologies to locate pets, learn about their care, and communicate with others. In Jalongo, M.R. *The World's Children and Their Companioon Animals: Developmental and Educational Implications of the Child/Pet Bond*. Association for Childhood Education International, 127-137.

Hutinger, P., & Johanson, J. (2000). Implementing and maintaining an effective early childhood comprehensive technology system. *Topics in Early Childhood Special Education, 20*(3), 159–173.

Hutinger, P., Johanson, J., & Rippey, R. (2000). Final report: Benefits of comprehensive technology system in an early childhood setting: Results of a three-year study. Macomb, IL: Western Illinois University, Center for Best Practices in Early Childhood.

Plowman, L., & Stephen, C. (2005). Children, play, and computers in pre-school education. *British Journal of Educational Technology, 36*(2), 145–157.

Wang, X. C., Kedem, Y., & Hertzog, N. (2004). Scaffolding young children's reflections with student-created PowerPoint presentations. *Journal of Research in Childhood Education, 19*(2).

YOUNG CHILDREN'S TECHNOLOGY EXPERIENCE OUTSIDE OF SCHOOL

Calvert, S. L., & Rideout, V. J., et al. (2005). Age, ethnicity and socioeconomic patterns in early computer use: A national survey. *The American Behavioral Scientist, 48*(5), 590–607.

Kerawalla, L., & Crook, C. (2002). Children's computer use at home and at school: Context and continuity. *British Educational Research Journal, 28*(6), 751–771.

Resnick, M., Rusk, N., & Cooke, S. (1998). The Computer Clubhouse: Technological Fluency in the Inner City (in PDF) or The Computer Clubhouse: Technological Fluency in the Inner City (in HTML).

The Impact of Home Computer Use on Children's Activities and Development (in PDF) or The Impact of Home Computer Use on Children's Activities and Development (in HTML). Kaveri Subrahmanyam, Robert E. Kraut, Patricia M. Greenfield, and Elisheva F. Gross

RESEARCH ON TEACHER & TECHNOLOGY

Beisser, S. R., & Gillespie, C. W. (2003). Kindergartners can do it so can you: A case study of a constructionist technology-rich first year seminar for undergraduate college students. *Information Technology in Childhood Education Annual*, 243–260.

Bers, M., Ponte, I., Juelich, K., Viera, A., & Schenker, J. (2002). Teachers as Designers: Integrating Robotics in Early Childhood Education. *Information Technology in Childhood Education Annual*, AACE 123-145.

Hutinger, P., Robinson, L., Schneider, C., Daytner, G., & Bond, J. (2006). Effectiveness of online workshops for increasing participants' technology knowledge, attitude, and skills: A final report of the Early Childhood Technology Integrated Instructional System. Macomb, IL: Western Illinois University, Center for Best Practices in Early Childhood.

Izumi-Taylor, S., Sluss, D., & Turner, S. (2007). Three views of learning experiences using technology-enhanced teaching: How online video conferencing sessions can promote students' construction of knowledge. *He Kupu eLearing,* 1(2), 6-17.

Taylor, S. I., & Hsuey, Y. (2005). Implementing a constructivist approach in higher Education through technology. *Journal of Early Childhood Teacher Education, 26,* 127–132.

DIGITAL DIVIDE, GENDER, & EQUITY ISSUES

Assistive Technology: Supporting the Participation of Children with Disabilities by Sarah A. Muligan

Becker, H. J. (2000). Who's Wired and Who's Not: Children's Access to and Use of Computer Technology (in PDF) or Who's Wired and Who's Not: Children's Access to and Use of Computer Technology in HTML). The Future of Children: Children and Computer Technology, 10(2).

Judge, S., Puckett, K., & Cabuk, B. (2004). Digital equity: New findings from the early childhood longitudinal study. *Journal of Research on Technology in Education, 36*(4), 383–396.

Tech-Savvy: Educating Girls in the New Computer Age (in PDF) or Tech-Savvy: Educating Girls in the New Computer Age (in HTML)

Use of Computer Technology to Help Students with Special Needs (in PDF) or Use of Computer Technology to Help Students with Special Needs (in HTML) by Ted S. Hasselbring and Candyce H. Williams Glaser

REFERENCES

Alexander, J. E., & Tate, M. A. (2001, July 25). *Evaluating Web Resources.* Widener University, PA.

Barker, J., & Obromsook, S. (2004, July 27). *Evaluating Web Pages: Questions to Ask & Strategies for Getting the Answers.* University of California, Berkeley.

Henderson, J. R. (2003, November 11). *The ICYouSee Critical Thinking Guide.* Ithaca College, NY.

Kapoun, J. (1998, July/August). Teaching Undergrads WEB Evaluation: A Guide for Library Instruction. C&RL News (pp. 522-523).

Kirk, E. E. (1996). *Evaluating Information Found on the Internet.* The Sheridan Libraries, Johns Hopkins University.

Smith, A. G. *Testing the Surf: Criteria for Evaluating Internet Information Resources.* The *Public-Access Computer Systems Review, 8*(3). Victoria University of Wellington, New Zealand.

Tillman, H. (2003, March 28). *Evaluating Quality on the Net.* Babson College, MA.

Appendix A

THINKING ABOUT TECHNOLOGY: A REFLECTIVE GUIDE FOR TEACHERS

1. What types of technology have you used?
   o Computers for word processing
   o Internet for information search
   o Internet for blogging
   o Internet for Chat Rooms
   o Internet for My Space or have a web page
   o E-mail
   o Digital Camera
   o Digital Video Camera
   o Educational software
   o Spreadsheet
   o Educational Reporting System
   o Smart Boards or other forms of educational technology
   o Cell Phones
   o Text Messaging
   o Other. _____
2. How long have I been using technology at home?   At School?
3. How do I learn about how to use technology?
   o My children or family
   o Read instructional manual
   o Professional In-service
   o Classes
   o A friend
   o Other. _____

4. Are you secure when you use technology? __yes __ no
5. List five things you like about using technology.

6. List five concerns you have about using technology.

7. How do I use technology in my classroom?

8. What would best help you learn to use technology in your classroom?

9. How could I improve the use of technology in my classroom?

10. Make a plan to integrate technology into your class.

Subject	Type of Technology	Activity
Social Development		
Cognitive Development		
Physical Development		
Literacy		
Mathematics		
Science		
Social Studies		

11. How can I share ideas about technology with my peers?

12. How can I use technology to assess student work and my own program?

Appendix B

FAMILY TECHNOLOGY INFORMATION SHEET

Please take a few minute to fill out the information on this sheet. We are trying to get information about family technology use so we might plan how best to serve your child's learning needs in our class.

Caregiver Name._____ Child's Name._____

What types of technology do you use in your home?

1. What types of technology does your family use? (Please fill in or check the circles by each statement.)

O Computers for word processing	O Internet for information search
O Internet for blogging	O Internet for Chat Rooms
O Internet for My Space or have a web page	O E-mail
O Digital Camera	O Digital Video Camera
O Educational software	O Spreadsheet
O Educational Reporting System	O Cell Phones
O Text Messaging	O Other. _____
O None of the above.	

2. Are there any special concerns about your child using technology at school? If yes, please explain.

3.   Would you be interested in participating in technology training sessions with your child?

4.   Please list times that would be convenient for you to come to technology workshops.

5.   Would you be interested in using school computers after school hours? If yes, what times would be convenient for you?

6.   Do you have any questions about our work with technology?

Thank you.

Appendix C

EPISTEMIC BELIEF SURVEY

ID Number: _____

Put an X on the circle that best describes what you think about each set of statements.

EXAMPLE

| I work best in the morning. | ● | ● | ○ | ● | ● | I work best in the evening. |

Most like what I think.	Somewhat like what I think.	Neither are like what I think.	Somewhat like what I think.	Most like what I think.
●	●	○	●	●

1	I think that I understand an idea if I know the circumstances around it.	●	○	○	○	●	I think I understand an idea if I can recall specific details about it.
2	What I learn that is true today will still be true in the future.	●	○	○	○	●	The things I learn as true today will likely change in the future.
3	I think knowledge comes from both outside and inside of me.	●	○	○	○	●	I think knowledge comes from what other people have discovered.
4	I think all people's ideas are equally correct.	●	○	○	○	●	I think some people's ideas are more correct than others.
5	I think that today's fact may be tomorrow's fiction.	●	○	○	○	●	I think people's view of reality changes over time.

6	I think knowledge in a subject is a collection of facts.	● ○ ○ ○ ●	I try my best to connect knowledge from different subjects.
7	What I think about a subject is how I determine the truth about it.	● ○ ○ ○ ●	I think that experts in a subject are best able to determine the truth.
8	What I think about something is different from what other people think about it.	● ○ ○ ○ ●	I think something is real if I can see, hear, feel, smell, or taste it.
9	I think what is true is a matter of opinion.	● ○ ○ ○ ●	I think expert's ideas are the most true.
10	I think all true ideas can be linked together.	● ○ ○ ○ ●	I think there are as many ways to organize ideas as there are people in the world.
11	What I think is true in one subject will be unique from what all others think about that subject.	● ○ ○ ○ ●	When I don't know something, I ask someone who I think will know about that subject.
12	I think some facts remain the same while most change.	● ○ ○ ○ ●	I think facts remain the same.
13	When I don't know something, I don't bother asking other people about it.	● ○ ○ ○ ●	I think knowledge comes from both knowledgeable people and my own thoughts.
14	I think that to know the truth I need to examine different perspectives.	● ○ ○ ○ ●	I think that what is true is always based on facts.
15	I think two people can believe different truths and both be correct.	● ○ ○ ○ ●	I think people's understanding of truth changes over time.
16	I think most words have one clear meaning.	● ○ ○ ○ ●	I think most words have different meanings based on their contexts.
17	I think knowledge comes from outside of myself.	● ○ ○ ○ ●	When I don't know something, I use information from both myself and others.
18	When I study, I try to understand the big ideas in the material.	● ○ ○ ○ ●	When I study, I look for the specific facts.
19	I think an expert's idea is no more correct than my idea.	● ○ ○ ○ ●	I think the most correct idea can be found out by examining the proof for the ideas.
20	I think facts in a subject can change.	● ○ ○ ○ ●	I think facts in a subject remains the same over time.

Compilation of References

Ainsa, P. A., Murphy, D., Thouvenelle, S., & Wright, J. L. (1994). Listen to the Children: Observing Young Children's Discoveries with the Microcomputer. In J. L. Wright, & D. D. Shade (Eds.), Young Children: Active Learners in a Technological Age (pp. 3-17). Washington D.C.: National Association for the Education of Young Children.

Albert, L. (1996). *Cooperative discipline*. Shoreview, MN: AGS Publishing.

Alexander, J. E., & Tate, M. A. (2001, July 25). *Evaluating Web Resources*. Widener University, PA.

Alexander, P. A. (2004). In the year 2020: Envisioning the possibilities for educational psychology. *Educational Psychologist*, *39*, 149–156. doi:10.1207/s15326985ep3903_1

Alexander, P. A., Fives, H., Buehl, M. M., & Mulhern, J. (2002). Teaching as persuasion. *Teaching and Teacher Education*, *18*(7), 795–813. doi:10.1016/S0742-051X(02)00044-6

Alliance for Technology Access. (2004). *Computer resources for people with disabilities: A guide to assistive technologies, tools and resources for people of all ages.* (4th ed.) Alameda, CA: Hunter House, Inc.

Alwin, D. F. (1988). From obedience to autonomy: Changes in traits desired in children, 1924-1978. *Public Opinion Quarterly*, *52*(1), 33–52. doi:10.1086/269081

Americans with Disabilities Act of 1990, 42 U.S.C.A. 12101.

ANUIES. (2001). Anuario Estadístico 2000. Población escolar de posgrado, México.

ANUIES. (2003). *Mercado laboral de profesionistas en México. Diagnóstico* (1990-2000), México, ANUIES(Biblioteca de la educación superior. Serie Investigaciones. Arnaut, A. (1998). Historia de una profesión. *Los maestros de educación primaria en México*, 1887-1994, México, SEP (Biblioteca del normalista).

Arnaut, A. (2003). Sistema de Formación de Maestros en México. Continuidad, reforma y cambio en. Educación 2001. Revista mexicana de educación, año IX, núm. 102, nueva época, noviembre, México.

Ashton & Webb. (1986) *Making a Difference: Teacher Efficacy and Student Achievement*. Monogram. White Plains, NY: Longman.

Ashton, P. (1984). Teacher efficacy: A motivational paradigm for effective teacher education. *Journal of Teacher Education*, *35*(5), 28–32. doi:10.1177/002248718403500507

Astington, J. W., & Baird, J. A. (2005). *Why language matters for theory of mind*. New York, NY: Oxford University Press.

Astington, J. W., & Jenkins, J. M. (1999). A longitudinal study of the relation between language and theory of mind. *Developmental Psychology*, *35*, 1311–1320. doi:10.1037/0012-1649.35.5.1311

Astington, J. W., Pelletier, J., & Homer, B. (2002). Theory of mind and epistemological development: the relation between children's second-order false-belief understanding and their ability to reason about evidence. *New Ideas in Psychology*, *20*, 131–144. doi:10.1016/S0732-118X(02)00005-3

Attewell, P., Suazo-Garcia, & Battle, J. (2003). Computers and young children: Social benefit or social problems? *Social Forces, 82*(1), 277–296. doi:10.1353/sof.2003.0075

Babb, J. (1999). Chips with everything. *Taiwan Review*. Retrieved January 20, 2008, from http://taiwanreview.nat.gov.tw/site/Tr/ct.asp?xItem=1440&ctNode=119

Bacon, W., & Ichikawa, V. (1988). Maternal expectations, classroom experiences, and achievement among kindergartners in the United States and Japan. *Human Development, 31*, 378–383.

Bagrit, L. (1965). The age of automation. *The Reith Lectures, 1964*. Harmondsworth: Penguin Books.

Bailey, B. A. (2001). *Conscious discipline: Seven basic skills for brain smart classroom management*. (Rev. Ed.) Oviedo, FL: Loving Guidance.

Baillargeon, R. (1986). Representing the existence and the location of hidden objects: Object permanence in 6-and 8-month-old infants. *Cognition, 23*, 21–41. doi:10.1016/0010-0277(86)90052-1

Ballard, M. E., & West, J. R. (1996). The effects of violent videogames play on male' hostility and cardiovascular responding. *Journal of Applied Social Psychology, 26*, 717–730. doi:10.1111/j.1559-1816.1996.tb02740.x

Bandura, A. (1977). Self-efficacy: Toward a unifying theory of behavioral change. *Psychological Review, 84*, 191–215.doi:10.1037/0033-295X.84.2.191

Bandura, A. (1986). *Social foundations of thought and action: A social cognitive theory*. Upper Saddle River, New Jersey: Prentice-Hall.

Bandura, A. (1988). Perceived self-efficacy: Exercise of control through self-belief. In J. P. Dauwalder, M. Perrez, & V. Hobi (Eds.), *Annual series of Euporean research in behavior therapy, 2*, 27-59. Lisse, The Netherlands: Swets & Zeitlander.

Bandura, A. (1991). Self-regulation of motivation through anticipatory and self- regulatory mechanisms. In R. A. Dienstbier (Ed.), *Perspectives on motivation: Nebraska symposium on motivation, 38*, 69-164. Lincoln: University of Nebraska Press.

Bandura, A. (1993). Perceived self-efficacy in cognitive development and functioning. *Educational Psychologist, 28*(2), 117–148. doi:10.1207/s15326985ep2802_3

Bandura, A. (1997). *Self-efficacy: The exercise of control*. New York: Freeman.

Bandura, A., & Schunk, D. H. (1981). Cultivating competence, self-efficacy, and intrinsic interest through proximal self-motivation. *Journal of Personality and Social Psychology, 41*, 586–598. doi:10.1037/0022-3514.41.3.586

Barker, J., & Obromsook, S. (2004, July 27). *Evaluating Web Pages: Questions to Ask & Strategies for Getting the Answers*. University of California, Berkeley.

Barrett, H. (2000). *Electronic teaching portfolios: Multimedia skills + portfolio development = powerful professional development*. Paper presented at the Society for Technology and Teacher Education (SITE) conference, San Diego, CA. Available online: http://transition.alaska.edu/www/portfolios/site2000.html.

Barron, A. E., Kemker, K., Harmes, C., & Kalaydjian, K. (2003). Large-scale research study on technology in K-12 schools: Technology integration as it relates to the National Technology Standards. *Journal of Research on Technology in Education, 35*(4), 489–507.

Bartlett, A. (2002). Preparing preservice teachers to implement performance assessment and technology through electronic portfolios. *Action in Teacher Education, 24*(1), 90–97.

Bartlett, A., & Sherry, A. C. (2006). Two views of electronic portfolios in teacher education: Non-technology undergraduate and technology graduate students. *International Journal of Instructional Media, 33*(3), 245–252.

Bartsch, K. (2002). The role of experience in children's developing folk epistemology: Review and analysis from the theory-theory perspective. *New Ideas in Psychology, 20*, 145–161. doi:10.1016/S0732-118X(02)00006-5

Bartsch, K., & Wellman, H. M. (1995). *Children talk about the mind*. New York: Oxford University Press.

Bauserman, K. L., Cassady, J. C., Smith, L. L., & Stroud, J. C. (2005). Kindergarten literacy achievement: The effects of the PLATO integrated learning system. *Reading Research and Instruction, 44*(4), 49–60.

Baxter Magolda, M. B. (1992). Cocurricular influences on college students' intellectual development. *Journal of College Student Development, 33*, 203–213.

Bayardo-Moreno, M. G. (2003). *El posgrado para profesores de educación básica*, México, SEP(Cuadernos de discusión, 5).

Becker, H. (2000). Who's wired and who's not: Children's access to and use of computer Computer. *The Future of Children, 10*(2), 44–75.doi:10.2307/1602689

Becker, H. J. (2001, April). *How are teachers using computers in instruction?* Paper presented at the annual meeting of the American Educational Research Association, Seattle, WA.

Becker, J. D. (2006). Digital equity in education: A multilevel examination of differences in and relationships between computer access, computer use and state-level technology policies. *Education Policy Analysis Archives, 15*(3). Retrieved November 24, 2008 from http://epaa.asu.edu/epaa/v15n3/

Behrmann, M. (1988). Assistive technology for young children in special education. In C. Dede (Ed.), *Learning with Technology. 1998 ASCD Yearbook* (pp. 73-93). Alexandria, Virginia: Association for Supervision and Curriculum Development.

Belensky, M., Clinchy, B., Goldberger, N., & Tarule, J. (1986). *Women's ways of knowing: The development of self, voice, and mind*. New York: Basic Books.

Bendixen, L. D., & Rule, D. C. (2004). An integrative approach to personal epistemology: A guiding model. *Educational Psychologist, 39*(1), 69–80. doi:10.1207/s15326985ep3901_7

Bers, M. U., New, R. S., & Boudreau, L. (2004). Teaching and learning when no one is expert: Children and parents explore technology. *Early Childhood Research and Practice, 6*(2). Retrieved 22 January, 2005, http://ecrp.uiuc.edu/v6n2/bers.html

Bers, M., New, B., & Boudreau, L. (2004). Teaching and learning when no one is expert: Children and parents explore technology. *Early Childhood Research and Practice, 6*(2). Retrieved April 16, 2008. http://ecrp.uniuc.edu/v62n2/bers.html

Bessell, A., Sinagub, J., Lee, O., & Schumm, J. (2003). Engaging families with technology. *T.H.E. Journal, 31*(5), 7–13.

Better than people. (2005, December 24th). *The Economist* (pp. 58-59).

Bickford, A., Tharp, S., McFarling, P., & Beglau, M. (2002). Finding the right fuel for new engines of learning. *Multimedia Schools, 9*(5), 18–26.

Bird, K. (2006, February 1). How do you spell parental involvement? S-I-S: student information systems are engaging parents, benefiting kids, and finally winning over teachers, too. *Technological Horizons in Education Journal.* Retrieved October 5, 2008 from http://www.highbeam.com

Bolstad, R. (2004). *The role and potential for ICT in early childhood education: A review of New Zealand and international literature*. Wellington: New Zealand Council for Educational Research.

Bouffard, S. (2008, July). Tapping into technology: The Role of the Internet in family-school communication. *Family Involvement Research Digests: Harvard Family Research Projects.* Retrieved July 30, 2008 from http://www.hfrp.org/family-involvement/fine-family-involvement-network-of-educators/fine-newsletter-archive/july-fine-newsletter-the-role-of-technology-in-family-involvement.

Bowers, C. (1988). *The cultural dimensions of educational computing: Understanding the non-neutrality of technology*. New York: Teachers College Press.

Bowers, C. (2000). *Let them eat data: How computers affect education, cultural diversity and the prospects of ecological sustainability*. Athens, GA: The University of Georgia Press.

Bradmetz, J., & Schneider, R. (2004). The role of the counterfactually satisfied Desire in the lag between false-belief and false-emotion attributions in Children aged 4-7. *The British Journal of Developmental Psychology, 22*, 185–196. doi:10.1348/026151004323044564

Braten, I. (2008). Personal epistemology, understanding of multiple texts, and learning within internet technologies. In Khines and Myint Swe (Eds.), *Knowing, knowledge, and beliefs: Epistemological studies across diverse cultures* (pp. 113-133). New York: Springer Science.

Braten, I., Stromso, H. I., & Samuelstuen, M. S. (2005). The relationship between internet-specific epistemological beliefs and learning within internet technologies. *Journal of Educational Computing Research, 33*(2), 141–171. doi:10.2190/E763-X0LN-6NMF-CB86

Bredekamp, S., & Rosengrant, T. (1994). Learning and teaching with technology. In J. L. Wright, & D. D. Shade (Eds.), *Young children: Active learners in a technological age* (pp. 53-61). Washington D.C.: National Association for the Education of Young Children.

Brendekamp, S., & Rosegrant, T. (Eds.). (1995). Reaching potentials: Transforming early childhood curriculum and assessment. (Vol. 2). Washington, DC: National Association for the Education of Young Children.

Brindley, R. (2000). Learning to walk the walk: Teacher educators' use of constructivist epistemology in their own practice. *Professional Educator, 12*(2), 1–14.

Brody, G. H., Stoneman, Z., & McCoy, J. K. (1994). Contributions of protective risk factors to literacy and socioemotional competency in former Head Start children attending kindergarten. *Early Childhood Research Quarterly, 9*(3-4), 407–425. doi:10.1016/0885-2006(94)90017-5

Brogden, L. M., & Couros, A. (2007). Toward a philosophy of technology and education. *The Delta Kappa Gamma Bulletin, 2*(73). Retrieved May 1, 2008, from http://vnweb.hwwilsonweb.com.proxy.lib.odu.edu/ hww/results/getResults.jhtml?_DARG S=/hww/results/results_common.jhtml.7#record_6

Bronfenbrenner, U. (1979). *The ecology of human development: Experiments by nature and design*. Cambridge, Massachusetts: Harvard University Press.

Bronfenbrenner, U. (1988). Strengthening family systems. In E. F. Zigler & M. Frank (Eds.), *The parental leave crisis: Toward a national policy* (pp. 358-385). New Haven, CT: Yale University Press.

Brooks-Young, S. (2007). Are document cameras the next big thing? *T.H.E. Journal, 34*(6), 20–23.

Brown, K. (2002). *The right to learn: Alternatives for a learning society*. London: Routledge Falmer. Buckingham, M. (2007). *Go put your strengths to work: 6 powerful steps to achieve outstanding performance*. New York, NY: Free Press.

Bruner, J. S. (1983). *The process of education*. Cambridge, MA: Harvard University Press.

Buckleitner, W. (1999). The state of children's software evaluation: Yesterday, today, and in the 21st Century. *Information Technology in Childhood Education Annual*. Retrieved March 21, 2002, from http://web2.infotrac.galegroup.com

Burchinal, M. R., Peisner-Feinberg, E., Pianta, R., & Howes, C. (2002). Development of academic skills from preschool through second grade: Family and classroom predictors of developmental trajectories. *Journal of School Psychology, 40*(5), 415–436. doi:10.1016/S0022-4405(02)00107-3

Burr, J., & Hofer, B. K. (2002). Personal epistemology and theory of mind: Deciphering young children's beliefs about knowledge and knowing. *New Ideas in Psychology, 20*, 199–224. doi:10.1016/S0732-118X(02)00010-7

Butler, S. (1970). *Erewhon*. Harmondsworth: Penguin Books.

Calderoni, J. (June 1998). Telesecundaria: Using TV to Bring Education to Rural Mexico. *World Bank Human Development Network: Education Group-Education and Technology Team*.

Call, J., & Tomasello, M. (1999). A nonverbal false belief task: The performance of children and great apes. *Child Development, 70*(2), 381–395. doi:10.1111/1467-8624.00028

Calvo-Pontón, B., et al. (2002), Tendencias en supervisión escolar. *La supervisión escolar de la educación primaria en México: prácticas, desafíos y reformas,* México, UNESCO/Instituto Internacional de Planeamiento de la Educación.

Cardelle-Elawar, M., & Wetzel, K. (1995). Students and computers as partners in developing students' problem solving skills. *Journal of Research on Computing in Education, 29*(4), 378–401.

Carmona, J. (1996). Presentation devices extend reach of information to entire groups. *T.H.E. Journal, 23*(6), 12–15.

Castañeda-Salgado, A., et al. (2003). *La UPN y la formación de maestros de educación básica,* México, SEP (Cuadernos de discusión, 15).

Castellani, J., & Tsantis, L. (2002). Cross-cultural reactions to using computers in the early childhood classroom. *Contemporary Issues in Early Childhood, 3*(2). Retrieved October 14, 2003, from http://www.triangle.co.uk/ciec/

Castro, D. C., Bryant, D. M., Peisner-Feinberg, E. S., & Skinner, M. L. (2004). Parent involvement in Head Start programs: The role of parent, teacher, and classroom characteristics. *Early Childhood Research Quarterly, 19*(3), 413–430. doi:10.1016/j.ecresq.2004.07.005

CBBC NEWSROUND. (2004, July 30). *Poor Eyesight Links to Genetics.* Retrieved May 28, 2008, form http://news.bbc.co.uk/cbbcnews/hi/sci_tech/news-id_3938000/3938193.stm

Cervantes-Galván, E. (2003). *Los desafíos de la educación en México.* ¿Calidad en la escuela, México, FUNDAP.

Chaboudy, R., & Jameson, P. (2001, September 1). Connecting families and schools through technology. *The Book Report.* Retrieved October 5, 2008 from http://www.highbeam.com/doc/1G1-96306627.html

Chandler, M. J., & Chapman, M. (1991). *Criteria for competence: Controversies in the conceptualization and assessment of children's abilities.* Hillsdale, NJ: Lawrence Erlbaum Associates Inc.

Chandler, M. J., & Lalonde, C. E. (1996). Shifting to an interpretive theory of mind: 5-to-7-year-olds changing conceptions of mental life. In A. Sameroff & M Haith (Ed.), *The five to seven year shift: The age of reason and responsibility* (pp. 111-139) Chicago, Il: University of Chicago Press.

Chandler, M. J., Hallet, D., & Sokol, B. W. (2002). Competing claims about competing knowledge claims. In B. K. Hofer & P. R. Pintrich (Eds.), *Personal epistemology: The psychology of beliefs about knowledge and knowing* (pp. 145-168). Mahwah, NJ: Lawrence Erlbaum Associates.

Chandler, M., Fritz, A. S., & Hala, S. (1989). Small scale deceit: Deceptions as a marker of 2-, 3-, and 4-year-olds early theories of mind. *Child Development, 60,* 1263–1277. doi:10.2307/1130919

Chang, N. (2001). Is it Developmentally Inappropriate to Have Children Work Alone at the Computer? [Norfolk, VA: AACE.]. *Information Technology in Childhood Education Annual, 2001*(1), 247–265.

Charney, R. (2002). *Teaching children to care: Classroom management for ethical and academic growth.* (Rev. ed.). Greenfield, MA: Northeast Foundation for Children.

Chen, M. (2000, Fall/Winter). Five commentaries: Looking to the future. *The future of children, Children and Computer Technology, 10*(2), 168-171. Retrieved August 6, 2008 from http://www.futureofchildren.org.

Children and Computer Technology. (2001). Analysis and Recommendations. *The Future of Children, 10*(2), 4–30. doi:10.2307/1602687

Ching, C. C., Wang, X. C., Shih, M., & Kedem, Y. (2006). Digital photography and journals in a K-1 classroom: Toward meaningful technology integration in early childhood education. *Early Education and Development, 17,* 347–371. doi:10.1207/s15566935eed1703_3

Chittenden, E., & Jones, J. (1998). *Science assessment in early childhood programs. Dialogue on early childhood science, mathematics, and technology education.* Washington, DC: Project 2061, American Association for the Advancement of Science.

Chiu, S. (2005, Feburary). Wan chu zhi hui- ru he shen xuan you zhi de you jiao ruan ti [Playing Games for IQ development - how to select a good education software for young children]. *You jiao jian xun, 28,* 9-13.

Chiu, S. (2006). Zhe pian ruan ti shi wo yao de ma? Cong xiao fei zhe de guan dian kan you jiao ruan ti shi chang [Is this software the one I wanted? Examining the education software market from consumers' perspectives]. *Jiao xiao ke ji yu mei ti, 76,* 4-19.

Chiu, S., & Chuang, M. (2004). Computer integration in kindergarten teaching: Teachers' practices and beliefs. *Journal of Taiwan Normal University: Mathematics &Science Education, 49*(2), 35–60.

Clark, A. S., McQuail, R., & Moss, P. (2003). *Exploring the field of listening to and consulting with young children.* London: Thomas Coram Research, London Institute of Education.

Clements, D. (1998). *Young children and technology. Dialogue on early childhood science, mathematics, and technology education.* Washington, DC: Project 2061, American Association for the Advancement of Science.

Clements, D. H. (1994). The uniqueness of the computer as a learning tool: Insights from research and practice. In J. L. Wright & D.D. Shade (Eds.), *Young Children: Active Learners in a Technological Age.* Washington, DC: NAEYC.ED 380 242.

Clements, D. H. (1999). *The future of educational computing research: The case of computer programming.* The Association for the Advancement of Computing in Education. Retrieved October 20, 2001, from http://web7.infotrac.galegroup.com

Clements, D. H. (2004). Young children and technology. In K.M. Paciorek & J.H. Munro (Eds.) *Annual Editions:*

Early Childhood Education (24th ed.). Guilford, CT: McGraw-Hill.

Clements, D. H., & Sarama, J. (2002). The role of technology in early childhood learning. *Teaching Children Mathematics, 8*(6), 340–346.

Clifford, A. C., & Grant, M. M. (2008, November). *Teachers: Shaping professionally and becoming technology integrators.* Paper presented at the annual meeting of the Association for Educational Communications and Technology, Orlando, FL.

Clifford, E. F., & Green, V. P. (1996). The mentor-protégé relationship as a factor in preservice teacher education: A review of the literature. *Early Child Development and Care, 125,* 73–83. doi:10.1080/0300443961250107

Conapo (2002). *Proyecciones de la población de México 2000-2050,* México, Conapo (Prospectiva demográfica).

Conapo (2003). *Informe de Ejecución del Programa de Acción de la Conferencia Internacional sobre la Población y el Desarrollo 1994-2003.* México, México.

Congreso de la Unión. (2002). *Título Sexto del trabajo y de la Previsión Social,* Artículo 123, Fracción XX", en Constitución Política de los Estados Unidos Mexicanos, México, Porrúa.

Cook, D., & Finlayson, H. (1999). *Interactive children, communicative teaching: ICT and classroom teaching.* Buckingham, UK: Open University Press. Limits of Software. Reading, MA: Addison-Wesley.

Cooper, M. (2005). *Bound and determined to help children with learning disabilities succeed.* Weston, MA: Learning Disabilities Worldwide.

Coordinación General de Actualización y Capacitación para Maestros en Servicio. (2003), Centros de Maestros. Un acercamiento a su situación actual, México, SEP (Cuadernos de discusión, 14). DGI-SEP (s/f), Direcciones generales de la SEP. Dirección General de Educación Indígena. *Información básica,* México, en: http://sep.gob.mx/wb2/sep/sep_4413_informacion_basica_g.

Copple, C., & Bredekamp, S. (2006). *Basics of developmentally appropriate practice: An introduction for teachers of children 3 to 6.* Washington, DC: The National Association for the Education of Young Children.

Cordeau, C., & Miller, E. (Eds.). (1999). *Fool's Gold: A Critical Look at Computers in Childhood. Alliance For Childhood.* Retrieved July 11, 2008 from http://www.allianceforchildhood.net/projects/ computers/computers_reports_fools_gold_download.htm

Corporation for Public Broadcasting. (2002). *Connected to the future: A report on children's Internet use from the Corporation for Public Broadcasting.* Washington, DC: Author.

Couse, L., & Chen, D. (2008). Exploring the potential uses of the Tablet computer as a tool for young children to represent ideas. In K. McFerrin et al. (Eds.), *Proceedings of Society for Information Technology and Teacher Education International Conference 2008* (pp. 3450-3455). Chesapeake, VA: AACE.

Crow, R. (2007). *You ought to be in pictures: Using behavior picture stories with preschoolers with challenging behaviors.* Paper presented at Annual Conference of the Southern Early Childhood Association, Jacksonville, Florida

Cuban, L. (1986). *Teachers and machines: The classroom use of technology since 1920.* New York: Teachers College Press.

Cuban, L. (2001). *Oversold and underused: Computers in the classroom.* Cambridge, MA: Harvard University Press.

Dahl, A., & Lopez-Claros, A. (2005). The impact of information and communication technologies on the economic competitiveness and social development of Taiwan. *Global Technology Information Report 2005-2006.* Retrieved May 23, 2008, from http://www.weforum.org/en/initiatives/gcp/Global%20Information%20Technology%2 0Report/index.htm

Damon, W. (1988). *The moral child.* New York: Free Press.

Davidson, J. I., & Wright, J. L. (1994). The potential of the microcomputer in the early childhood classroom. In J. L. Wright & D. D. Shade (Eds.), *Young children: Active learners in a technological age* (pp. 77-91). Washington D.C.: National Association for the Education of Young Children.

del Rufugo, M., & Gonzalez, L. E. (2004). *Country Background Report. Attracting, developing and retaining effective teachers.* Franciso Deceano, National Coordinator. OECD.

Denham, S. A. (1993). Preschoolers' likability as cause or consequence of their social behavior. *Developmental Psychology, 29*(2), 271–275. doi:10.1037/0012-1649.29.2.271

Denham, S. A., Blair, K. A., DeMulder, E., Levitas, J., Sawyer, K., Auerbach-Major, S., & Queenan, P. (2003). Preschool emotional competence: Pathway to social competence. *Child Development, 74*(1), 238–256. doi:10.1111/1467-8624.00533

Denham, S. A., Mitchell-Copeland, J., Strandberg, K., Auerbach, S., & Blair, K. (1997). Parental contributions to preschoolers' emotional competence: Direct and indirect effects. *Motivation and Emotion, 21*(1), 65–86. doi:10.1023/A:1024426431247

deVilliers, J. G., & deVilliers, P. A. (1999). Language development. In M. H. Bornstein & M. E. Lamb (Eds.), *Developmental psychology: An advanced textbook (4th ed.)* (pp. 466-480). Mahwah, NJ: Lawrence Erlbaum Associates.

DeVries, R., Zan, B., Hildebrant, R., Edmiaston, R., & Sales, C. (2002). *Developing constructivist early childhood curriculum.* New York: Teachers College Press.

Dewey, J. (1991). *How we think.* Amerst, NY: Great Books In Philosophy, Prometheus Books.

DGPPP-SEP. (2003), Estadística Básica del Sistema Educativo Nacional. *Inicio de cursos 1970 a 2002*, México.

Dick, P. K. (1964). *Martian Time Slip.* London, UK: Millenium.

Dodge-Hall, A., & Chau, M. (2007). *Basic facts about low-income families: Birth to age six.* National Center for Children in Poverty. Washington, DC: Columbia University. Mailman School of Public Health.

Doherty-Sneddon, G. (2003). *Children's unspoken language.* New York: Kingsley Publishing Ltd.

Donovan, M. S., & Bransford, J. D. (2005) How Students Learn. National Research Council. National Academies Press.

Duhaney, D. C. (2001). Teacher education: Preparing teachers to integrate technology. *International Journal of Instructional Media, 28*(1), 23–33.

Dunn, J., Cutting, A. L., & Demetriou, H. (2000). Moral sensibility, understanding others, and children's friendship interactions in the preschool period. *The British Journal of Developmental Psychology, 18*(2), 159–177. doi:10.1348/026151000165625

Dunn, S., & Morgan, V. (1987). *The impact of the computer on education: A course for teachers.* Hemel Hempstead: Prentice Hall.

Dylak, S., & Kaczmarska, D. (2001). Foreign language, technology, and science. *TechTrends, 45*(6), 35–39. doi:10.1007/BF02772020

Educación Primaria, Plan 1997. (2002). *Lineamientos Académicos para Organizar el Proceso de Titulación.* Licenciatura en Educación Secundaria, Plan 1999, México.

Educación Primaria, Plan 1997. (2002). *Lineamientos para la Organización del Trabajo Académico durante Séptimo y Octavo Semestres.* Licenciatura en Educación Primaria, Plan 1997, México.

Educación Primaria, Plan 1997. (2002). *Plan de Estudios 2002.* Licenciatura en Educación Física, México.

Educación Primaria, Plan 1997. (2002). *Plan de Estudios 1997.* Licenciatura en Educación Primaria, México.

Educación Primaria, Plan 1997. (2002). *Programa Nacional de Fortalecimiento de la Educación Especial y de la Integración Educativa,* México.

Educación Primaria, Plan 1997. (2003). *Documento base, México, SEP* (Cuadernos de discusión, 1).

Educación Primaria, Plan 1997. (2003. *Informe de Labores 2002-2003,* México.

Educación Primaria, Plan 1997. (2003c). *Lineamientos Académicos para Organizar el Proceso de Titulación.* Licenciatura en Educación Primaria, Plan 1997, México.

Educación Primaria, Plan 1997. (2003). *Principales cifras y avances del sector educativo reportadas en el tercer informe de gobierno,* México.

Educación Primaria, Plan 1997. (2004). *El seguimiento y la evaluación de las prácticas docentes: una estrategia para la reflexión y la mejora en las escuelas normales,* México, SEP (Serie Evaluación interna, 1).

Educación Primaria, Plan 1997. (2004). *Documento Rector,* México, SEP (Política nacional para la formación y el desarrollo profesional de los maestros de educación básica) (en prensa). SG (1993), "Acuerdo Secretarial 179. Instructivo general para su aplicación", en *Diario Oficial de la Federación.*

Education Trust. (2004). Measured Progress. Achievement rises and gaps narrow, but too slowly. Washington, DC: Author.

Edyburn, D. L. (2003). *What every teacher should know about assistive technology.* Allyn and Bacon Smart Series. Boston, MA: Allyn and Bacon.

Eisenberg, N., Cumberland, L. A., & Spinard, P. C. (1998). Relations of young children's agreeableness and resiliency to effortful control and impulsivity. *Social Development, 13*(2), 193–212.

Elder, A. D. (2002). Characterizing fifth grade students' epistemological beliefs in science. In B. K. Hofer & P. R. Pintrich (Eds.), *Personal epistemology: The psychology of beliefs about knowledge and knowing* (pp. 347-363). Mahwah, NJ: Lawrence Erlbaum Associates Publishers.

Eldridge, D. (2001). Parent Involvement: It's worth the effort. *Young Children, 56*(4), 65–69.

Ellis, K., & Blashki, K. (2004). Toddler techies: A study of young children's interaction with computers. [Norfolk, VA: AACE.]. *Information Technology in Childhood Education Annual, 2004*(1), 77–96.

Ellis, S., & Rogoff, B. (1982). The strategies and efficacy of child versus adult teachers. *Child Development, 53*(3), 730–735. doi:10.2307/1129386

Ensalaco, M., & Majka, L. C. (2000). Acuerdo Secretarial 252. In *Diario Oficial de la Federación*, México.

Ensalaco, M., & Majka, L. C. (2002). Decreto por el que se adiciona el Artículo 3°, en su párrafo primero y el Artículo 31 de la Constitución Política de los Estado Unidos Mexicanos. In *Diario Oficial de la Federación*, México.

Ensalaco, M., & Majka, L. C. (2002). Decreto por el que se reforma el artículo 25 de la Ley General de Educación. In *Diario Oficial de la Federación*, México.

Ensalaco, M., & Majka, L. C. (2005). *Children's Human Rights*. Lanham, Maryland: Rowman & Littlefield Publishers, Inc.

Epper, R. M., & Bates, A. W. (2001). *Teaching faculty how to use technology: Best practices from leading institutions*. Westport, CT: Oryx Press.

Epstein, J. (2000). *School and family partnerships: Preparing educators and improving schools*. Boulder, CO: Westview.

Epstein, J. (2007). Families, schools, and community partnerships. In D. Koralek (Ed.), *Spotlight on young children and families* (p. 37). Washington: National Association for the Education of Young Children.

Fang, H. (2003, September). You er xiao dian nao hao bu hao [Using computer: Is it good or bad for young children]? *You jiao zi xun, 154*, 2-10.

Fang, H. (2004). A case study on implementation of computer and information education for public kindergarten. *Journal of National Taipei Teachers College, 17*(1), 51–78.

Farmer, L. (2002, January 1). Teaming parents with technology. *The Book Report*. Retrieved October 5, 2008 from http://www.highbeam.com/doc/1G183077440.html

Feenberg, A. (1999). *Questioning technology*. London: Routledge.

Felix, G. (2007, February 28). Mexican education. In *El Diario de Juarez*.

Ferdig, R. E. (2006). Assessing technologies for teaching and learning: understanding the importance of technological pedagogical content knowledge. *British Journal of Educational Technology, 37*(5), 749–760. doi:10.1111/j.1467-8535.2006.00559.x

File, N. (2001). Family-professional partnerships: Practice that matches philosophy. *Young Children, 56*(4), 70–74.

Finley, L., & Hartman, D. (2004). Institutional change and resistance: Teachers preparatory faculty and technology integration. *Journal of Technology and Teacher Education, 12*(3), 319–330.

Fish, A. M., Li, X., McCarrick, K., Butler, S. T., Stanton, B., & Brumitt, G. A. (2008). Early Childhood Computer Experience and Cognitive Development among Urban Low-Income Preschoolers. *Journal of Educational Computing Research, 38*(1), 97–113. doi:10.2190/EC.38.1.e

Fisher, M. (2000). Technology, pedagogy and education. *Journal of Information Technology for Teacher Education, 9*(1), 109–123.

Fitzsimons, P. (2002). Enframing education. In M. A. Peters (Ed.), *Heidegger, education, and modernity* (pp. 171-190). Lanham, MD: Rowman & Littlefield Publishers.

Flavell, J. H. (2004). Theory of mind development. *Merrill-Palmer Quarterly, 50*(3), 274–290. doi:10.1353/mpq.2004.0018

Flavell, J. H., Green, F. L., & Flavell, E. R. (1995). Young children's knowledge about Thinking. *Monographs of the Society for Research in Child Development, 16*(1, Serial No. 243).

Flavell, J. H., Green, F. L., & Flavell, E. R. (1998). The mind has a mind of its own: Developing knowledge about mental uncontrollability. *Cognitive Development, 13*(1), 127–138. doi:10.1016/S0885-2014(98)90024-7

Fogel, A. (1993*). Developing through relationships: Origins of communication, self, and culture.* Chicago, IL: University of Chicago Press.

Foreman, J. (2003). Next-generation educational technology versus the lecture. *EDUCAUSE Review, 38*(4), 12-22. Retrieved June 10, 2006, from http://www.educause.edu/LibraryDetailPage/666?ID=ERM0340

Fraley, R. C., & Spieker, S. J. (2003). Are infant attachment patterns continuously or categorically distributed? A taxometric analysis of strange situation behavior. *Developmental Psychology, 39*(3), 387–404. doi:10.1037/0012-1649.39.3.387

Freeman, N., & Somerindyke, J. (2001). *Social play at the computer: preschoolers scaffold and support peers computer competence Information Technology in Childhood Education Annual.* [Online]. Available USCA Library System Directory Discus. http://web3.infotrac.galegroup.com.

Furlan, A., et al. (2003). Investigaciones sobre disciplina e indisciplina. In J. M. Piña et al. (coords.), Acciones, actores y prácticas educativas. Libro 2, México, Grupo Ideograma (La investigación educativa en México 1992-2004).

Gadel, J. (1997). Education. Available at: http://www.tulane.edu/~rouxbee/children/mexico1.html (Reviewed 27 December 2008).

Gates, N. C. (2007). Technology integration for the savvy teacher. *Journal of the Tennessee Association for the Education of Young Children*, 21-22.

Gee, J. P. (2003). *What video games have to teach us about learning and literacy.* New York: Palgrave Macmillan.

Gelernter, D. (1994, September 19-26). Unplugged: The myth of computers in the classroom. *The New Republic* (pp. 14-15).

Gelman, R. & Brenneman. (2004). Mathematic and science cognitive development. In Mathematical and Scientific Development in Early Childhood: A Workshop Summary (2005). National Academies Press.

Gelman, R. (1979). Preschool thought. *The American Psychologist, 34*(10), 900–905. doi:10.1037/0003-066X.34.10.900

Gelman, R., & Brenneman (2004). Mathematic and science cognitive development. In *Mathematical and Scientific Development in Early Childhood: A Workshop Summary.* National Academies Press.

Gelman, S. A. (2000). The role of essentialism in children's concepts. In H. Reese (Ed.), *Advances in child development and behavior* (pp. 269-283). San Diego, CA: US Academic Press.

Gestwicki, C. (2007). *Home, school, and community relations* (6th ed.). Clifton Park, NY: Thomson Delmar Learning.

Ghiraldelli, P. Jr. (2000). The fundamentals of Gepeto's philosophy of education: Neopragmatism and infancy in the postmodern world. *Educational Philosophy and Theory, 32*(2), 201–207. doi:10.1111/j.1469-5812.2000.tb00444.x

Gibbons, A. N. (2006). The politics of technology in early childhood in Aotearoa/New Zealand: Fitting early childhood educators in the ICT grid. *Australian Journal of Early Childhood, 31*(4), 7–14.

Gibson, S., & Dembo, M. (1984). Teacher efficacy: A construct validation. *Journal of Educational Psychology, 76*, 569–582. doi:10.1037/0022-0663.76.4.569

Goddard, R. D., Hoy, W. K., & Woolfolk Hoy, A. (2000). Collective teacher efficacy: Its meaning, measure, and impact on student achievement. *American Educational Research Journal, 37*, 479–507.

Goode, S. (2006). Assistive technology and diversity issues. *Topics in Early Childhood Special Education, 26*(1), 51–54. doi:10.1177/02711214060260010501

Gopnik, A. (1984). The acquisition of gone and the development of the object concept. *Journal of Child Language, 11*(2), 273–292. doi:10.1017/S0305000900005778

Gopnik, A., & Meltzoff, A. (1986). Relations between semantic and cognitive in the one word stage: The specificity hypothesis. *Child Development, 57*(4), 1040–1053. doi:10.2307/1130378

Gopnik, A., & Wellman, H. M. (1994). The theory-theory. In L Hirschfeld & S. Gelman (Eds.), *Mapping the mind: Domain specificity in cognition and culture* (pp. 257-293). New York: Cambridge University Press.

Gray, C. (2000). *The new social story book*. Arlington, TX: Future Horizons.

Greig, A., & Taylor, J. (1999). *Doing research with children.* Thousand Oaks: Sage.

Gwynn, R. (1986). Towards a pedagogy of information. In R. Ennals., R. Gwyn, & L. Zdravchev (Eds.), *Information technology and education: The changing school* (pp. 29-44). Chichester: Ellis Horwood Ltd.

Haerle, F. C. (2005). *Personal epistemologies of 4th graders: Their beliefs about knowledge and knowing.* Unpublished doctoral dissertation, Carl von Ossietzky University, Oldenburg, Germany.

Hamm, E. M., Mistrett, S. G., & Ruffino, A. G. (2006). Play outcomes and satisfaction with toys and technology of young children with special needs. *Journal of Special Education Technology, 21*(1), 29–34.

Hammer, D., & Elby, A. (2002). On the form of a personal epistemology. In B. K. Hofer & P. R. Pintrich (Eds.), *Personal epistemology: The psychology of beliefs about knowledge and knowing* (pp. 169-190). Mahwah, NJ: Lawrence Erlbaum Associates.

Hammond, L. D., et al. (2005). Educational goals and purposes: developing a curricular vision for teaching. In Linda Darling-Hammond and John Bransford (Eds.), *Preparing teachers for a changing world, what teachers should learn and be able to do* (pp.169-200). San Francisco, CA: Jossey-Bass.

Hao, Y. (2000). *Relationship between teachers' use of reflection and other selected variable and preschool teachers' engagement in developmentally appropriate practice.* Retrieved 25 February, 2008, from http://www.eric.ed.gov/ERICDocs/data/ericdocs2sql/content_storage_01/0000019b/80/16/e2/3b.pdf

Harbeck, J. D., & Sherman, T. M. (1999). Seven principles for designing developmentally appropriate web sites for young children. *Educational Technology, 39*(4), 39–44.

Hardman, M. J., Drew, C. J., & Egan, M. W. (2008). *Human exceptionality: School, community and family.* (5th ed.) Boston, MA: Houghton Mifflin.

Hartley, K., & Bendixen, L. D. (2001). Educational research in the Internet age: Examining the role of individual characteristics. *Educational Researcher, 30*(9), 22–26. doi:10.3102/0013189X030009022

Hartley, K., & Bendixen, L. D. (2003). The use of comprehension aids in a hypermedia environment: Investigating the impact of metacognitive awareness and epistemological beliefs. *Journal of Educational Multimedia and Hypermedia, 12,* 275–289.

Hastie, M., Chen, N.-S., & Kuo, Y.-H. (2007). Instructional Design for Best Practice in the Synchronous Cyber Classroom. *Educational Technology & Society, 10*(4), 281–294.

Hauge, M. R., & Gentile, D. A. (2003, April). *Video game addiction among adolescents: Associations with academic performance and aggression.* Paper presented at Society for Research in Child Development Conference, Tampa, FL. Retrieved May 07, 2007 from http://www.psychology.iastate.edu/FACULTY/dgentile/SRCD%20Video%20Game%20Addiction.pdf

Haugland, S. (1992). The effect of computer software on preschool children's developmental gains. *Journal of Computing in Childhood Education, 3*(1), 15–30.

Haugland, S. W. (1997). How teachers use computers in early childhood classrooms. *Journal of Computing in Childhood Education, 8*(1), 3–14.

Haugland, S. W. (2000). Early childhood classrooms in the 21st century: Using computers to maximize learning. *Young Children, 55*(1), 12–18.

Haugland, S. W. (2005). Selecting or upgrading software and web sites in the classroom. *Early Childhood Education Journal, 32*(5), 329–340. doi:10.1007/s10643-005-4401-9

Haugland, S., & Wright, J. (1997). *Young children and technology: A world of discovery.* New York: Allyn & Bacon.

Haynes, J. (2002). *Children as philosophers: Learning through enquiry and dialogue in the primary classroom.* London: RoutledgeFalmer.

Heidegger, M. (1977). The question concerning technology. (W. Lovitt, Trans.). In M. Heidegger (Ed.), *The question concerning technology and other essays* (pp. 1-49). New York: Harper & Row.

Henderson, A. T., & Mapp, K. L. (2002). *A new wave of evidence: The impact of School, family, and community connections on student achievement.* Austin, TX: Southwest Education Educational Development Laboratory. Retrieved August 21, 2008 from: http://www.sedl.org/connections/resources/evidence.pdf.

Henderson, J. R. (2003, November 11). *The ICYouSee Critical Thinking Guide.* Ithaca College, NY.

Henson, R. K. (2001). *Teacher Self-Efficacy: Substantive Implications and Measurement Dilemmas.* 1337Invited keynote address given at the annual meeting of the Educational Research Exchange. Texas A&M University, College Station, Texas.

Hernandez, S., & Leung, B. (2004). Using the Internet to boost parent-teacher relationships. *Kappa Delta Pi Record, 40*(3), 136–138.

Hess, J., Gutierrez, A. M., Peters, J., & Cerreta, A. (2005). *Family information guide to assistive technology.* Washington, D.C.: United States Department of Education Office of Special Education Programs (OSEP).

Hey, big-spender. (2005, December 5th). *The Economist* (pp. 60-61).

Hofer, B. K. (2000). Dimensionality and disciplinary differences in personal epistemology. *Contemporary Educational Psychology, 25,* 378–405.doi:10.1006/ceps.1999.1026

Hofer, B. K. (2001). Personal epistemology research: Implications for learning and teaching. *Journal of Educational Psychology Review, 13*(4), 353–383. doi:10.1023/A:1011965830686

Hofer, B. K. (2004). Epistemological understanding as a metacognitive process: Thinking aloud during online searching. *Educational Psychologist, 39*(1), 1–3. doi:10.1207/s15326985ep3901_1

Hofer, B. K. (2004). Exploring the dimensions of personal epistemology in differing classroom contexts: Student interpretations during the first year of college. *Contemporary Educational Psychology, 29,* 129–163. doi:10.1016/j.cedpsych.2004.01.002

Hofer, B. K., & Pintrich, P. R. (1997). The development of epistemological theories: Beliefs about knowledge and knowing and their relation to learning. *Review of Educational Research, 67,* 88–140.

Hofer, B. K., & Pintrich, P. R. (Eds.). (2002). *Personal epistemology: The psychology of beliefs about knowledge and knowing.* Mahwah, NJ: Erlbaum.

Hourcade, J. J., Parette, H. P., & Huer, M. B. (1997). Family and cultural alert! Considerations in assistive technology assessment. *Exceptional Children, 30*(1), 40–44.

Howard, J., Greyrose, E., Kehr, K., Espinosa, M., & Beckwith, L. (1996). Teacher-facilitated microcomputer activities: Enhancing social play and affect in young children with disabilities. *Journal of Special Education Technology, 13*(1), 37–47.

Hsieh, C. (2004, January). You zhi yuan ke cheng zhi fan si yu zhan wang [*The introspection and envision of preschool education curriculum*]. *You jiao jian xun, 15.* Retrieved May 13, 2008, from http://www.ece.moe.edu.tw/preschool.html

Hsieh, M. F. (2004). Teaching practices in Taiwan's education for young children: complexity and ambiguity of developmentally appropriate practices and/or developmentally inappropriate practices. *Contemporary*

Issues in Early Childhood, *5*(3), 309–329. doi:10.2304/ciec.2004.5.3.5

Hughes, D. R. (1998). *Kids online: Protecting your children in cyberspace*. Minnesota: Fleming H. Revell.

Hung, A. M. (2004). *A study of the effects of phonics instruction on English word pronunciation & memorization of vocational senior high school students in Taiwan.* Unpublished master's thesis. National Taiwan Normal University, Taipei: Taiwan.

Husén, T., & Postlethwaite, N. (Eds.). (1994). *The International Encyclopedia of Education* (2nd ed.). Oxford: Pergamon Press.

Huseth, M. (2001). The school-home connection. *Learning and Leading with Technology*, *29*(2), 6–17.

Hutinger, P. L., & Johnson, J. (2000). Implementing and maintaining an effective early childhood comprehensive technology system. *Topics in Early Childhood Special Education*, *20*(3), 159–173. doi:10.1177/027112140002000305

Hutinger, P., & Johanson, J. (1998). Software for young children. In S.L. Judge & H.P. Parette (Eds.), *Assistive technology for young children with disabilities* (pp. 76-126). Cambridge, MA: Brookline Books.

Hutinger, P., Robinson, L., & Schneider, C. (2004). *Early Childhood Technology Integrated Instructional System (EC-TIIS) Phase 1: A final report*. Macomb, IL: Center for Best Practices in Early Childhood, Western Illinois University. (ERIC Document Reproduction Service No. ED 489166).

IDEA. (1997). H.R. 5 Public Law 105-17. U.S.C. Sections 1400-1485 (also known as P.L.94-142). Washington, DC. Johnson, J. (1998*). Perspectives: The dialogue on Early Childhood science, mathematics, an technology education*. Washington, DC: Project 2061, American Association for the Advancement of Science.

Iikura, H. (2007). *Nihonjinno shikitari* [Japanese customs]. Tokyo, Japan: Seishun Shupansha.

Illich, I. (1976). *Deschooling Society*. Harmondsworth: Penguin Books.

Individuals with Disabilities Education Improvement Act of 2004, Pub. L. No. 108-446, 118, STAT. 2647 (2006).

INEE. (2004). *Informe Anual 2003*, México, en http://capacitacion.ilce.edu.mx/inee/estadisticas.htm. (Accessed November 2008).

International Society for Technology and Education (ISTE) Accreditation Committee. (1992). *Curriculum guidelines for accreditation of educational computing and technology programs*. Eugene: ISTE.

International Society for Technology in Education. (2007). *The ISTE national educational technology standards (NETS•S) and performance indicators for students*. Eugene, OR: author.

International Society for Technology in Education. (2008). *The ISTE national educational technology standards (NETS•T) and performance indicators for teachers*. Eugene, OR: author.

Izumi-Taylor, S. (2006). Play of Japanese preschoolers in constructivist environments. *PlayRights*, *27*(1), 24–29.

Izumi-Taylor, S. (2008). Play and technology in group-oriented Japanese early childhood educational settings. *He Kupu*, *1*(4), 9–15.

Izumi-Taylor, S. (2008). Sunao (cooperative) children: How Japanese teachers Nurture autonomy. *Young Children*, *63*(3), 76–79.

Izumi-Taylor, S. (2009). *Pre-service teachers' perceptions of teaching technology To young children in Japan and the United States*. Unpublished manuscript.

Izumi-Taylor, S., & Taylor, J. W. (2009). I am the boss of me! *An intuitive approach to constructivism in Japanese childhood education*. Unpublished manuscript.

Izumi-Taylor, S., Rogers, C., & Samuelsson, I. (2007). *Teachers' perspectives on play in Japan, the US, and Sweden*. Paper presented at the annual meeting of the International Play Association/the Association of Study of Play Conference. Rochester, NY.

Izumi-Taylor, S., Sluss, D., & Lovelace, A. (2006). Nurturing children's love of learning through play and technology. *He Kupu*, *1*(1), 35–46.

Izumi-Taylor, S., Sluss, D., & Turner, S. (2007). Three views of learning experiences using technology-enhanced teaching: How online video conferencing sessions can promote students' construction of knowledge. *He Kupu*, *1*(2), 6–48.

Jacobson, M. J., & Spiro, R. J. (1995). Hypertext learning environments, cognitive flexibility, and transfer of complex knowledge: An empirical investigation. *Journal of Educational Computing Research*, *12*(4), 301–333.

Jonassen, D. H., Marra, R. M., & Palmer, B. (2003). Epistemological development: An implicit entailment of constructivist learning environments. In N. M. Seel & S. Dijkstra (Eds.), *Curriculum, plan, and processes of instructional design: International perspectives* (p. 75-88). Mahwah, NJ: Lawrence Erlbaum.

Jordan, A. (2008). Children's media policy. *The Future of Children*, *18*(1), 235–249. doi:10.1353/foc.0.0003

Judge, S. (2006). Constructing an assistive technology toolkit for young children: Views from the field. *Journal of Special Education Technology*, *21*(4), 17–24.

Judge, S. L. (1998). Providing access to assistive technology for young children and families. In S.L. Judge & H.P. Parette (Eds.), *Assistive technology for young children with disabilities* (pp. 1-15). Cambridge, MA: Brookline Books.

Judge, S. L., & Lahm, E. A. (1998). Assistive technology applications for play, mobility, communication, and learning for young children with disabilities. In S.L. Judge & H.P. Parette (Eds.), *Assistive technology for young children with disabilities* (pp. 16-44). Cambridge, MA: Brookline Books.

Judge, S. L., & Parette, H. P. (1998). Assistive technology decision-making strategies. In S.L. mJudge & H.P. Parette (Eds.), *Assistive technology for young children with disabilities* (pp.127-147). Cambridge, MA: Brookline Books.

Judge, S. L., & Parette, H. P. (1998). Family-centered assistive technology decision making in infant-toddler intervention. *The Transdisciplinary Journal*, *8*(2), 185–206.

Kaczmarek, L. (2007). A team approach: Supporting families of children with disabilities in inclusive programs. *Spotlight on Young Children and Families* (pp. 28-36).

Kagan, S. L., Moore, E., & Bredekamp, S. (1995). Reconsidering children's early development and learning: Toward common views and vocabulary. National Education Goals Panel, Goal 1. Technical Planning Group Report, 95-03. Washington, DC: National Education Goals Panel. (ERIC Document Reproduction Service No. ED 391 576).

Kajder, S. (2004). Plugging in: What technology brings to the English/language arts classroom. *Voices from the Middle*, *11*(3), 6–9.

Kapoun, J. (1998, July/August). Teaching Undergrads WEB Evaluation: A Guide for Library Instruction. C&RL News (pp. 522-523).

Kariuki, M., & Duran, M. (2004). Using anchored instruction to teach preservice teachers to integrate technology in the curriculum. *Journal of Technology and Teacher Education*, *12*(3), 431–450.

Kaufman, H. (2001). Skills for working with all families. *Young Children*, *56*(4), 81–83.

Kearsley, G. (2000). *Online education: learning and teaching in cyberspace*. Belmont, CA: Wadsworth Publishing

Kennedy, K. (Producer). (2001). *AI*. US: Warner Brothers.

Kerr, S. T. (1996). Toward a sociology of educational technology. In D.H. Jonassen (Ed.), *Handbook of research for educational communications and technology* (pp. 143-169). New York: Simon & Schuster.

Keyser, J. (2006). *From parents to parents: Building a family-centered early childhood program*. St. Paul: MN. Redleaf Press.

Kieff, J., & Wellhousen, K. (2000). Planning family involvement in early childhood programs. *Young Children*, *55*(3), 18–25.

King, P. M., & Kitchener, K. S. (1994). *Developing reflective judgment*. San Fransico: Jossey-Bass, John Wiley & Sons, Inc.

Kirk, E. E. (1996). *Evaluating Information Found on the Internet*. The Sheridan Libraries, Johns Hopkins University.

Klien, A. (2000). *Culturally Consonant Education: An analysis of techniques that are academically empowering for children of immigrant and guest workers*. A paper presented at the International Congress on Challenges to Education. Mexico City - Aug. 30-Sept. 1, 2000.

Knezek, G., & Christensen, R. (2007). Effect of technology-baed programs on first- and second-grade reading achievement. *Computers in the Schools, 24*(3/4), 23–41.

Knudsen-Lindauer, S. L., & Harris, K. (1989). Priorities for kindergarten curricula: views of parents and teachers. *Journal of Research in Childhood Education, 4*(1), 51–61.

Kubrick, S. (Writer/Director). (1968). *2001: A space odyssey*. US: MGM.

Kuhn, D. (1991). *The skills of argument*. New York: Cambridge University Press.

Kuhn, D. (2000). Theory of mind, metacognition and reasoning: A life-span perspective. In P. Mitchell, & K. J. Riggs (Eds.), *Children's reasoning and the mind* (pp. 301-326). Hove, England: Psychology Press.

Kuhn, D., & Pearsall, R. (1998). Relations between metastrategic knowledge and strategic performance. *Cognitive Development, 13*(2), 227–247. doi:10.1016/S0885-2014(98)90040-5

Kuhn, D., & Pearsall, S. (2000). Developmental origins of scientific thinking. *Journal of Cognition and Development, 1*, 113–129. doi:10.1207/S15327647JCD0101N_11

Kuhn, D., & Weinstock, M. (2002). What is epistemological thinking and why does it matter? In B. K. Hofer & P. R. Pintrich (Eds.), *Personal epistemology: The psychology of beliefs about knowledge and knowing* (pp. 121-144). Mahwah NJ: Lawrence Erlbaum.

Kuhn, D., Cheney, R., & Weinstock, M. (2000). The development of epistemological understanding. *Cognitive Development, 15*, 309–328. doi:10.1016/S0885-2014(00)00030-7

Kurahashi, S. (1935). *Gangu kyoikuhen* [Education with toys]. Tokyo, Japan: Yuzankaku.

Lai, Y., & Chiu, S. (2006). Examining factors related to Taichung kindergarten mangers' decision-making on selecting computer application approaches. *Proceedings of The Second Conference on Computer and Network Technology in Education (CNTE 2006)*, May 23-24, 2006, Chung Hua University, Hsinchu, Taiwan.

Lankshear, C., Snyder, I., & Green, B. (2000). *Teachers and technoliteracy:- Managing literacy, technology and learning in schools*. St Leonards, NSW: Allen & Unwin.

LeCompte, M., & Preissle, J. (1992). Toward an ethnology of student life in schools and Classrooms: Synthesizing the qualitative research tradition. In M. D. LeCompte, W. L. Millroy, & J. Preissle (Eds.), *The handbook of qualitative research in education*. San Diego, CA: Academic Press.

Lee, Y., & Key, S. (2008). Playing videogames: Do students choose specific foreign language learning strategies in playing these games? *TNTESOL Journal*, 30-37.

Lee, Y., Cheon, J., & Key, S. (2008). Learners' perceptions of video games for second/foreign language learning. In C. Crawford et al. (Eds.), *Proceedings of Society for Information Technology and Teacher Education International Conference 2008* (pp. 1733-1738). Chesapeake, VA: AACE.

Lesar, S. (1998). Use of assistive technology with young children with disabilities: Current status and training needs. *Journal of Early Intervention, 21*, 146–159. doi:10.1177/105381519802100207

Levin, D., Stephens, M., Kirshstein, R., & Birman, B. (1998). *Toward assessing the effectiveness of using technology in K-12 education*. U.S. Department of Education. Washington, DC: Office of Educational Research and Improvement.

Levin, T., & Wadmany, R. (2008). Teachers' views on factors affecting effective integration of information technology in the classroom: Developmental scenery. *Journal of Technology and Teacher Education, 16*(2), 233–263.

Lewis, A. (2003). Using communications technology and parental involvement to improve homework completion and quality. *Action Research Exchange, 2*(1).

Lewis, C. (1986). Children's social development in Japan. In H. Stevenson, H. Azuma, & K. Hakuta (Eds.), *Child development and education in Japan* (pp. 186-200). New York: W. H. Freeman and Company.

Lewis, C. (1995). *Educating hearts and minds.* New York: Cambridge University Press.

Lewis, C., & Mitchell, P. (1994). *Children's early understanding of mind: Origins and development.* Hillsdale, NJ: Lawrence Erlbaum Associates

Li, X., & Atkins, M. S. (2004). Early Childhood Computer Experience and Cognitive and Motor Development. *Pediatrics, 113*(6), 1715–1722. doi:10.1542/peds.113.6.1715

Liang, J., & Tsai, C. (2008). Internet self-efficacy and preference toward constructivist internet-based learning environments: A study of pre-school teachers in Taiwan. *Educational Technology & Society, 11*(1), 226–237.

Liang, P. H., Wang, J. Y., & Tsuei, E. M. (2005). *Young children and technology: a study of integrating information technology into thematic teaching in kindergarten.* Paper presented at the Academic Conference in Department of Early Childhood and Education, Chaoyang University of Technology, Taichung, Taiwan. Retrieved May 10 2008, from http://atecce.org/d/d1-3.htm

Lichtman, M. (2006). *Qualitative research in education: A user's guide.* Thousands Oaks, CA: Sage Publications.

Lichtman, M., & Taylor, S. I. (1993). *Conducting and reporting case studies.* ([]. East Lansing, ML: National Center for Research on Teacher Learning.]. *Report No. TM, 019,* 956.

Lin, Y. W., & Tsai, M. L. (1996). Culture and the kindergarten curriculum in Taiwan. *Early Child Development and Care, 123,* 157–165. doi:10.1080/0300443961230111

Lindstrand, P. (2001). Parents of children with disabilities evaluate the importance of the computer in child development. *JSET E. Journal, 16*(2).

Lipper, L. A., & Lazarus, W. (2000). Five commentaries: Looking to the future. *The Future of Children, Children and Computer Technology, 10*(2), 175-178. Retrieved August 6, 2008 from http://www.futureofchildren.org.

Lowther, D. L., & Ross, S. M. (1999). *Survey of Computer Use: Reliability analysis.* Memphis, TN: Center for Research in Educational Policy, The University of Memphis.

Lü, S., Zhang, L., Lin, S., & Xu, F. (2007). You zhi yuan da ban jin hang guo ji wang lu jiao bi you huo dong zhi ge an yan jiu [A case study on the implementation of the "*International Netpal Project*" in kindergarten]. *Proceedings of Taiwan Academic Network Conferenc 2007.* Retrieved May 23, 2008, from http://itech.ntcu.edu.tw/Tanet%202007/index1.html

Lucas, G. (Executive Producer and Director). (2005). *Star wars episode III: Revenge of the Sith.* US: Twentieth Century Fox.

Lutterman-Aguilar, A. (2000). *Challenges Faced by Academic Programs Abroad: Breaking Stereotypes & Promoting Intercultural Awareness.* A paper presented at the International Congress on Challenges to Education. Mexico City - Aug. 30-Sept. 1, 2000.

Maddox, C., & Cummings, R. (2004). Fad, fashion and the weak role of theory and research in information technology in education. *Journal of Technology and Teacher Education, 12*(4), 511–528.

Male, M. (2003). *Technology for inclusion: Meeting the special needs of all students.* Boston, MA: Allyn & Bacon.

Mansfield, A. F., & Clinchy, B. (2002). Toward the integration of objectivity and subjectivity: epistemological development from 10 to 16. *New Ideas in Psychology, 20*(2-3), 225–262. doi:10.1016/S0732-118X(02)00008-9

Mansfield, A., & Clinchy, B. (1985). *Early growth in multiplism in the child.* Paper submitted at the 15ᵗʰ annual symposium of the Jean Piaget Society, Phildelphia.

Marra, R. (2005). Teacher beliefs: The impact of the design of constructivist learning environments on instructional epistemologies. *Learning Environments Research, 8,* 135–155. doi:10.1007/s10984-005-7249-4

Marshall, J. D. (1999). Technology in the New Zealand curriculum. *New Zealand Journal of Educational Studies, 34*(1), 165–175.

Mayer, R. E., & Moreno, R. (2003). Nine ways to reduce cognitive load in multimedia learning. In E.M. Wills, R.H. Bruning, C.A. Horn, & L.M. PytlikZillig (Eds.), *Web-based learning: What do we know? Where do we go?* Greenwich, CT: Information Age Publishing.

McCarrick, K., Li, X., Fish, A., Holtrop, T., Bhavnagri, N.P., Stanton, B., Brumitt, G.A., Butler, S., & Partridge, T. (2007). *Parental involvement in young children's computer use and cognitive development, 10*(2), 67-82. NHSA Dialog: A Research-to-Practice Journal for the Early Intervention Field.

McNeely, B. (2005). Using technology as a learning tool, not just the cool new thing. In D.G. Oblinger & J.L. Oblinger (Eds.), *Educating the Net Generation* (pp. 4.1-4.10). Washington, DC: Educause.

Merrill, T. L., & Miró, R. (Eds.). (June 1996). Mexico: a country study. In *Education: Section 7 of Chapter 2. Federal Research Division: Library of Congress.* Available at: http://lcweb2.loc.gov/frd/cs/cshome.html. (Reviewed 25 November 2008).

Meyer, A., & Rose, D. H. (2000). Universal design for individual differences (2000). *Educational Leadership, 58*(3), 39–43.

Milbrath, Y. L., & Kinzie, M. B. (2000). Computer technology training for prospective teachers: Computer attitudes and perceived self-efficacy. *Journal of Technology and Teacher Education, 8*(4), 373–384.

Mims, C., Polly, D., Shepherd, C. E., & Inan, F. A. (2006). From campus to the field: Examining PT3 proj-ects designed to improve preservice teachers' methods courses and field experiences. *TechTrends, 50*(3), 16–24. doi:10.1007/s11528-006-7599-5

Ministry of Education, Department of Elementary Education. (2003). *General Guidelines of Grades 1-9 Curriculum for Elementary and Junior high school Education.* Retrieved May 01, 2008, from http://www.edu.tw/eje/content.aspx?site_content_sn=4420

Ministry of Education. Culture, Sports, Science, and Technology. (2000).

Ministry of Education. Republic of China. (2005, January 23). *Education for Primary and Junior High School Students.* Retrieved April 02, 2008, from http://english.moe.gov.tw/ct.asp?xItem=245&ctNode=502&mp=1

Ministry of Education. Republic of China. (2005, January 23). *Information and Internet education.* Retrieved May 23, 2008, from http://english.moe.gov.tw/ct.asp?xItem=7190&ctNode=514&mp=1

Ministry of Education. Republic of China. (2005, January 23). *Education for preschool children.* Retrieved May 23, 2008, from http://english.moe.gov.tw/ct.asp?xItem=7089&ctNode=502

Ministry of Education. Republic of China. (2006, July 4). *Policy White Paper on Media Literacy Education.* Retrieved February 01, 2008, from http://english.moe.gov.tw/ct.asp?xItem=1282&ctNode=784&mp=3

Ministry of Education. Te Tahuhu o te Matauranga (1996). Te whāriki: He whāriki matauranga mō ngā mokopuna o Aotearoa, early childhood curriculum. Wellington: Learning Media.

Minuchin, S. (1974). *Families and family therapy.* Cambridge, MA: Harvard University Press.

Montessori, M. (1967). *The absorbent mind.* NY: Dell.

Morris, V. G., & Taylor, S. I. (1998). Alleviating barriers to family involvement in education: The role of teacher education. *Teaching and Teacher Education, 14*(2), 219–231. doi:10.1016/S0742-051X(97)00037-1

Morrison, G. (2007). *Early childhood education today* (10th ed). Upper Saddle River, NJ: Pearson Merrill Prentice Hall.

Morrison, G. (2009). *Early Childhood Education Today.* Upper Saddle River, NJ: Pearson.

Morrison, G. R., & Lowther, D. L. (2002). *Integrating computer technology in the classroom* (2nd ed.). Upper Saddle River, NJ: Merrill Prentice Hall.

Morrison, G. S. (2006). *Fundamentals of early childhood education* (4th ed.). Columbus, OH: Pearson Merrill Prentice Hall.

Morrison, G. S. (2007). *Early childhood education today* (10th ed.). Columbus, OH: Pearson Merrill Prentice Hall.

Moschner, B., Anschuetz, A., Wernke, S., & Wagener, U. (2008). Measurement of epistemological beliefs and learning strategies of elementary school children. In Khines and Myint Swe (Eds.), *Knowing, knowledge, and beliefs: Epistemological studies across diverse cultures* (pp. 113-133). New York: Springer Science.

Moss, P. (2006). Structures, understandings and discourses: Possibilities for re-visioning the early childhood worker. *Contemporary Issues in Early Childhood, 7*(1), 30–41. doi:10.2304/ciec.2006.7.1.30

Muis, K. R., Bendixen, L. D., & Harle, F. C. (2006). Domain-generality and domain-specificity in personal epistemology research: Philosophical and empirical reflections in the development of a theoretical framework. *Educational Psychology Review, 18,* 3–54. doi:10.1007/s10648-006-9003-6

Mulligan, S. A. (2003). Assistive technology: Supporting the participation of children with disabilities. *YC Young Children, 58*(6), 50–51.

Munoz, J. P. (1986). The significance of fostering play development in handicapped children. In *Play: A skill for life* (pp. 1-12). Rockville, MD: American Occupational Therapy Association.

Murphy, D. (Producer). (2007). *Transformers.* US: Paramount.

Muto, T. (Ed.). (2004). *Early childhood education handbook.* Tokyo, Japan: Yoshimi Kohsan.

Myers, R. Yoshikawa, H., McCartney, K., Bub, K.L., Lugo-Gil, J., Ramos, M., Knaul, F., & UNICEF Innocenti Research Centre (2007). *Early childhood education in Mexico: expansion, quality improvement, and curricular reform,* Innocenti Working Papers:inwopa07/40, UNICEF Innocenti Research Centre.

Nagasaki, I., Kaneda, T., Taylor, S. I., Watanabe, Y., & Goshiki, T. (2002). How the quality of early childhood education affects the social development of American and Japanese children. *Research Bulletin of Tokoha Junior College, 33,* 123–134.

Nagel, D. (2007, February 2007). Groups respond to proposed EETT Cuts. *T.H.E. Journal.* Retrieved June 6, 2008 from: http://thejournal.com/articles/20166.\

Narvaez, A., Feldman, J., & Theriot, C. (2006). Virtual pre-k: Connecting home, school, and community. *Young Children, 61*(1), 52–53.

National Association for the Education of Young Children. (1996). *Technology and young children – Ages 3 through 8: A position statement of the National Association for the Education of Young Children.* Washington, D.C.: NAEYC.

National Association for the Education of Young Children. (1997). *Developmentally appropriate practice in early childhood programs serving children from birth through age 8.* Washington, DC: National Association for the Education of Young Children. Retrieved April 14, 2008, http://naeyc.org/about/positions/pdf/PSDAP98.PDF

National Association for the Education of Young Children. Position Statement Office of Technology Assessment (1988, September). *Power on! New tools for teaching and learning* (p. 7). Washington DC: U.S. Government Printing Office, OTA-SET-379.

National Center for Education Statistics (NCES). (2000). *Teachers' tools for the 21st century: a report on teachers' use of technology.* Washington, DC: U.S. Department of Education.

National Council for Accreditation of Teacher Education (NCATE). (2000) *NCATE Standards: Unit standards.* Washington: NCATE. Also available at: http://www.ncate.org/2000/pressrelease.htm

National Council for Accreditation of Teacher Education (NCATE). (2000). *Program standards for elementary teacher preparation.* Washington: NCATE. Also available at: http://www.ncate.org/standard/elemstds/pdf.

National Curriculum Standards for Kindergarten. Retrieved from http://www.mext.go.jp/a_menu/shotou/youji/english/youryou/ mokuji.htm

National Research Council. (2000). *From neurons to neighborhoods: The science of early childhood development.* Committee on Integrating Science of Early Childhood Development. In J.P. Shonkoff & D.A. Phillips (Eds.), *Board on Children, Youth, and Families, Commission on Behavioral and Social Science and Education.* Washington, DC: National Academy Press.

National Research Council. (2001). *Adding it up: Helping children learn mathematics.* Mathematics Learning Study Committee. J. Kilpatrick, J. Swafford, & B. Findell (Eds.), *Center for Education, Division of Behavioral and Social Sciences and Education.* Washington, D.C: National Academy Press.

National Research Council. (2001). *Eager to learn: Educating out preschooler.* Committee on Early Childhood Pedagogy. B.T. Bowman, M.S. Donovan, & M.S. Burns (Eds.), *Commission on Behavioral and Social Science Education.* Washington, DC: National Academy Press.

National Research Council. (2005). *Mathematical and scientific development in early childhood.* Washington, DC: The National Academies Press. Text Citation: (NRC, 2005).

Nelms, E. (2002). The effects of a teacher-created web page on parent communication: An action research study. *Action Research Exchange, 1*(2).

Nelsen, J. (1996). *Positive discipline.* New York: Ballantine Books.

Nelson, C. A., & Snyder, K. (2005). The segregation of face and object processing in development: A model system of categorization? In L. Gershoff-Stowe & D. H. Rakison (Eds.), *Building object categories in developmental time* (pp. 1-32). Mahwah, NJ: Lawrence Erlbaum Associates.

Nelson, C. M. (2003). Through a glass darkly: Reflections on our field and its future. *Education & Treatment of Children, 26*(4), 330–336.

Nelson, C., Duvergé, H. A., Gary, B. M., & Price, G. J. (2003). *Using computers in family literacy programs.* Louisville, KY: National Center for Family Literacy.

Nisan-Nelson, P. D. (2001). Technology integration: A case of professional development. *Journal of Technology and Teacher Education, 9*(1), 83–103.

No, C. L. B. (2002). (NCLB) Act of 2001, Pub. L. No. 107-110, § 115 . *Stat,* 1425.

Norris, C., Sullivan, T., Poirot, J., & Soloway, E. (2003). No access, no use, no impact: Snapshot surveys of educational technology in k-12. *Journal of Research on Technology in Education, 36*(1), 15–27.

O'Neill, D. K., Astington, J. W., & Flavell, J. H. (1992). Young children's understanding of the role that sensory experiences play in knowledge acquisition. *Child Development, 63*(2), 474–490.doi:10.2307/1131493

Olson, D. R., & Astington, J. W. (1993). Thinking about thinking: Learning how to take statements and hold beliefs. *Educational Psychologist, 28*(1), 7–23. doi:10.1207/s15326985ep2801_2

Olson, J. L., Platt, J. C., & Dieker, L. A. (2008). *Teaching children and adolescents with special needs.* (5th ed.) Upper Saddle River, NJ: Pearson.

Ortiz Jiménez, M. (2003). *Carrera Magisterial. Un proyecto de desarrollo profesional,* México, SEP (Cuadernos de discusión, 12).

Pajares, F. (1996). Self-efficacy beliefs and mathematical problem solving of gifted students. *Contemporary Educational Psychology, 21*(4), 325–344. doi:10.1006/ceps.1996.0025

Pajares, F. (1996). Self-efficacy beliefs and mathematical problem solving of gifted students. *Contemporary Educational Psychology, 21*(4), 325–344.doi:10.1006/ceps.1996.0025

Pajares, F. (1996). Self-efficacy beliefs in achievement settings. *Review of Educational Research,* (66): 543–578.

Pajares, F., & Graham, L. (1999). Self-efficacy, motivation constructs, and mathematics performance of entering middle school students. *Contemporary Educational Psychology, 24*(2), 124–139.doi:10.1006/ceps.1998.0991

Papert, S. (1993). Situating constructionism. In I. Harel & S. Papert. (Eds.). *Constructionism.* (pp. 1- 12). Norwood, NJ: Ablex Publishing Corporation.

Papert, S. (1993). *The children's machine: Rethinking school in the age of the computer.* New York: Basic-Books.

Papert, S. (1998). Technology in schools: To support the system or render it obsolete? *The Milken Family Foundation.* Retrieved March 01, 2008, from http://www.mff.org/edtech/article.taf?_function=detail&Content_uid1=106

Parette, H. P. (1997). Family-centered practice and computers for children with disabilities. *Early Childhood Education Journal, 25*(1), 53–55. doi:10.1023/A:1025690032730

Parette, H. P., & Petch-Hogan, B. (2000). Approaching families: Facilitating culturally/linguistically diverse family involvement. *Exceptional Children, 33*(2), 4–10.

Parette, P., & McMahan, G. A. (2002). What should we expect of assistive technology? Being sensitive to family goals. *Teaching Exceptional Children, 35*(1), 56–61.

Paterson, W. A., Henry, J., O'Quin, K., Ceprano, M. A., & Blue, E. V. (2003). Investigating the effectiveness of an integrated learning system on early emergent readers. *Reading Research Quarterly, 38*(2), 172–207. doi:10.1598/RRQ.38.2.2

Perner, J. (1991). *Understanding the representational mind.* Cambridge, MA: MIT Press.

Perry, W. G., Jr. (1970). *Forms of intellectual and ethical development in the college years: A scheme.* New York: Holt, Rinehart and Winston.

Peters, M. A. (1998). Education and the shift from knowledge to information: Virtual classrooms or automated diploma mills? *Access, 17*(1), 65–78.

Peterson, C. C., & Siegal, M. (2000). Insights into theory of mind from deafness and autism. *Mind & Language, 15*(1), 123–145. doi:10.1111/1468-0017.00126

Piaget, J. (1952). *The origins of intelligence in children* (Cook, M., Translation). New York: International University Press. (Original work published in 1936).

Piaget, J. (1962). *Play, dreams, and imitation in childhood.* New York: Norton.

Piaget, J. (1964). Development and learning. *Journal of Research in Science Teaching, 2,* 176–186. doi:10.1002/tea.3660020306

Piaget, J., & Inhelder, J. (1966/1969). La psychologie de l'enfant. Paris: Presses Universitaries de France/*The psychology of the child.* London: Routledge & Kegan Paul.

Piotrkowski, C. S., Botsko, M., & Matthews, E. (2000). Parents' and teachers' beliefs about children's school readiness in a high need community. *Early Childhood Research Quarterly, 15*(4), 537–558. doi:10.1016/S0885-2006(01)00072-2

Polloway, E. A., Patton, J. R., & Serna, L. (2008). *Strategies for teaching learners with special needs.* (9th ed.). Upper Saddle River: New Jersey.

Poole, D. A., & Lamb, M. E. (1998). *Investigative interviews of children: A guide for helping professionals.* Washington, DC: American Psychological Association.

Popham, W. J. (2008). *Classroom assessment: What teachers need to know* (5th Ed.). Boston: Allyn and Bacon.

Position Statement, NAEYC: Technology and Young Children-Ages Three Through Eight. (1996). *Young Children, 51*(6), 11-16.

Prairie, A. (2005). *Inquiry into math, science, and technology for young children*. Clifton Park, NY: Thomson Delmar Learning.

Prensky, M. (2001). *Digital game-based learning*. New York: McGraw-Hill.

Prensky, M. (2001). Digital natives, digital immigrants part I. *Horizon, 9*(5), 1–6. doi:10.1108/10748120110424816

Prensky, M. (2001). Digital natives, digital immigrants part 2: Do they really think differently? *Horizon, 9*(6), 1–6. doi:10.1108/10748120110424843

Purushotma, R. (2005, January). Commentary: you're not studying, you're just... [Electronic version]. *Language Learning & Technology, 9*(1), 80–96.

Ramirez, F. (2001, September/October). Technology and parental involvement. *The Clearing House*. Retrieved October 5, 2008 from http://www.highbeam.com

Rao, S. M., & Gagie, B. (2006). Learning through seeing and doing: Visual supports for children with autism. *Teaching Exceptional Children, 38*(6), 26–33.

Ray, J. (2006). Welcome to the blogosphere: The educational use of blogs (aka edublogs). *Kappa Delta Pi Record, 42*(4), 175–177.

Ray, J., & Shelton, D. (2004). Connecting with families through technology. *Young Children*, 30–31.

Renzulli, J.S. (2007). The Renzulli learning system: Assessing and developing children's interest. *Duke Gifted Letter for Parents of Gifted Children, 7*(3) Spring

Robinson, L. (2003). Technology as a scaffold for emergent literacy: Interactive storybooks for toddlers. *Young Children, 58*(6), 42–48.

Robinson, L. (2007, March). *FCTD Newsletter*. The Family Center on Technology and Disability. Retrieved June 24, 2008 from http://www.fctd.info/resources/newsletters/displayNewsletter.php?newsletterID=10045

Rosas, R., Nussbaum, M., Cumsille, P., Marianov, V., Correa, M., & Flores, P. (2003). Beyond Nintendo: Design and assessment of educational video games for first and second grade students. *Computers & Education, 40*(1), 71–94. doi:10.1016/S0360-1315(02)00099-4

Rose, D., & Meyer, A. (2000). Universal design for learning. *Journal of Special Education Technology, 15*(1), 67–70.

Rosenberg, S., Hammer, D., & Phelan, J. (2006). Multiple epistemological coherences in an Eighth-grade discussion of the rock cycle. *Journal of the Learning Sciences, 15*(2), 261–292. doi:10.1207/s15327809jls1502_4

Ross, S. M., Smith, L. J., & Alberg, M. (1999). *The School Observation Measure*. Memphis, TN: Center for Research in Educational Policy, The University of Memphis.

Sakamoto, A. (1995). *Moricimidiajidainokodomotachi* [Children in the era of multi-media]. Tokyo, Japan: Sanchou Shupan.

Sakamoto, H. (1976). *Kurhashi Shozo sonohitoto shisou* [Kuahashi Shozo, the person and his thoughts]. Tokyo, Japan: furuberusha.

Salas Garza, E. (May 1998). *Mexico-Basic Education Development Project*. Washington, D.C.: The World Bank.

Sandoval Flores, E. (2002). *La trama de la escuela secundaria: institución, relaciones y saberes*, México, UPN.

Santibáñez, L. (2002). Están mal pagados los maestros en México? Estimado de los salaries relativos del magisterio. In *Revista Latino americana de Estudios Educativos, 33*(2), México, Centro de Estudios Educativos.

Savín Castro, M. A. (2003). *Escuelas normales: propuestas para la reforma integral*, México, SEP (Cuadernos de discusión, 13).

Sawyer, K. S., Denham, S., DeMulder, E., Blair, K., Auerbach-Major, S., & Levitas, J. (2002). The contribution of older siblings' reaction to emotions to preschoolers' emotional and social competence. *Marriage & Family Review, 34*(3-4), 183–212.

Schneider, B., & Lee, Y. (1990). A model for academic success: The school and home environment of East Asian students. *Anthropology & Education Quarterly, 21*(4), 358–377. doi:10.1525/aeq.1990.21.4.04x0596x

Schommer, M. (1990). Effects of beliefs about the nature of knowledge on comprehension. *Journal of Educational Psychology, 82*(3), 498–504. doi:10.1037/0022-0663.82.3.498

Schommer-Aikins, M. (2000). Understanding middle students' beliefs about knowledge and learning using a multidimensional paradigm. *The Journal of Educational Research, 94*(2), 774–784.

Schommer-Aikins, M. (2004). Explaining the epistemological belief system: Introducing the embedded systemic model and coordinated research approach. *Educational Psychologist, 39*(1), 19–29. doi:10.1207/s15326985ep3901_3

Schraw, G., & Lehman, S. (2001). Situational interest: A review of the literature and directions for future research. *Educational Psychology Review, 13*(1), 23–52. doi:10.1023/A:1009004801455

Schraw, G., & Olafson, L. (2003). Teacher's epistemological worldviews and educational practices. *Issues in Education, 8*(2), 99–148.

Schunk, D. H. (1984). Self-efficacy perspective on achievement behavior. *Educational Psychologist, 19*(1), 48–59.

Schunk, D. H. (1987). Peer models and children's behavior change. *Review of Educational Research, 57*(2), 149–174.

Schunk, D. H. (1995). Self-efficacy and education and instruction. In J.E. Maddux (Ed.) *Self-Efficacy, Adaptation, and Adjustment: Theory, Research, and Application* (pp.281-303). New York: Plenum Press.

Schunk, D. H., Hanson, A. R., & Cox, P. D. (1987). Peer-model attributes and children's achievement behaviors. *Journal of Educational Psychology, 79*(1): 54–61. doi:10.1037/0022-0663.79.1.54

Schunk, D.H., & Hanson, A. R. (1985). Peer models: Influence on children's self-efficacy and achievement. *Journal of Educational Psychology, 77*(3): 313–322. doi:10.1037/0022-0663.77.3.313

Schwalje, C. (2001). Empowering our youngest learners. *Principal, 80*(5), 40–41.

Secretaría de Educación Pública (SEP) (1999). *Profile of Education in Mexico* (2nd ed). Mexico City: SEP.

Section for Early Childhood and Inclusive Education Division of Basic Education, Education Sector. (2003, December 19-21). *Early Childhood Care and Education in E-9 Countries: Status and Outlook.* A report for the Fifth E-9 Ministerial Meeting. Cairo: Egypt.

Seki, H. (Producer). (2000). *Digimon: The movie.* US: Twentieth Century Fox.

Senge, P. (2000). Systems citizenship: The leadership mandate for this millennium. In H. Frances & M. Goldsmith (Eds.), *The leader of the future 2: Visions, strategies, and practices for the new era.* (pp. 31-46). San Francisco, CA: Jossey-Bass.

SEP (2004). Balance del proceso de la Reforma Integral de la Educación Secundaria.

SEP/Heurística Educativa. (2003). Evaluación cualitativa del Programa Escuelas de Calidad. *Reunión para el estudio del reporte descriptivo de la línea de base de la evaluación cualitativa del PEC*, México.

Shaffer, D. W., & Gee, J. P. (2005, September). *Before every child is left behind: How epistemic games can solve the coming crisis in education* (WCER Working Paper): University of Wisconsin-Madison, Wisconsin Center for Education Research Retrieved March 10, 2006, from http://www.wcer.wisc.edu/publications/workingPapers/Working_Paper_No_2005_7.hp

Shaffer, D. W., Squire, K. R., Halverson, R. H., & Gee, J. P. (2005). Video games and the future of learning. *Phi Delta Kappan, 87*(2), 104–111.

Shepard, L., Kagan, S. L., & Wurtz, E. (1997). *Principles and recommendations for early childhood assessments.* Unpublished Draft. Washington, DC: National Educational Goals Panel.

Shigaki, I. (1983). Child care practices in Japan and the United States: How do they reflect cultural values in young children? *Young Children, 38*(4), 13–24.

Shinji, R. (1996). Nuyojino seiriteki hatsutatsu [Young children's physical development]. In M. Takauchi (Ed.), *Shoji hoken jushu* [Health practices for young children] (pp. 27-49). Osaka, Japan: Hoiku Shpansha.

Siegler, R. S. (1998). Developmental differences in rule learning: A microgenetic analysis. *Cognitive Psychology, 36*(3), 273–310. doi:10.1006/cogp.1998.0686

Simons, C. (1987, March). They get by with a lot of help from their kyoiku mamas. *Smithsonian*, 44–53.

Sinatra, G. M., & Kardash, C. A. M. (2004). Teacher candidates'epistemological beliefs, dispositions, and views on teaching as persuasion. *Contemporary Educational Psychology, 29*(4), 483–498. doi:10.1016/j.cedpsych.2004.03.001

Skau, L., & Cascella, P. W. (2006). Using assistive technology to foster speech and language skills at home and in preschool. *Teaching Exceptional Children, 38*(6), 12–17.

Skinner, B. F. (1965). Reflections on a decade of teaching machines. In R. Glaser (Ed.), *Teaching machines and programmed learning: Data and directions* (pp. 5-20). Washington: Association for Educational Communications and Technology.

SMART Technologies. (2008). http://www2.smarttech.com/st/en-US/Products/SMART+Boards/.

Smeets, E. (2005). Does ICT contribute to powerful learning environments in primary education? *Computers & Education, 44*, 343–355. doi:10.1016/j.compedu.2004.04.003

Smith, A. G. *Testing the Surf: Criteria for Evaluating Internet Information Resources*. The *Public-Access Computer Systems Review, 8*(3). Victoria University of Wellington, New Zealand.

Socha, D. E. (1997). *Perspectives on the Mexican Education System: Prejudices, Problems, Possibilities.* Fulbright-Hays Summer Seminar Abroad.

Spiegel-McGill, P., Zippiroli, S., & Mistrett, S. (1989). Microcomputers as social facilitators in integrated pre-

schools. *Journal of Early Intervention, 13*(3), 249–260. doi:10.1177/105381518901300306

Squire, K. D. (2004). *Replaying history: Learning world history through playing Civilization III.* Unpublished doctoral dissertation, Indian University.

Sterbinsky, A., Ross, S. M., & Burke, D. (2004). *Tennessee EdTech Accountability Model (TEAM) reliability study.* Alexandria, VA: The CNA Corporation.

Sternberg, R. J., Wagner, R. K., & Okagaki, L. (1993). Practical intelligence: The nature and role of tacit knowledge in work and at school. In J. M. Puckett & H. W. Reese (Eds.), *Mechanisms of everyday cognition* (pp. 257-398). Hillsdale, NJ: Lawrence Erlbaum Associates.

Swaminathan, S., & Wright, J. (2003). Educational Tech in the early to primary years. In J. Isenberg & M. Jalongo (Eds.), *Major trends & issues in ECE.* (pp. 136-146). NY: Teachers College Press.

Tager-Flusberg, H. (2000). The challenge of studying language development in children with autism. In L. Menn & R. N. Bernstein (Eds.), *Methods for studying language production* (pp. 194-197). Mahwah, NJ: Lawrence Erlbaum Associates.

Taiwan Review. (2004, March, 01). Changing role, a high-tech adventure. [Electronic version] *Taiwan Review, 54*(3). Retrieved May 20, 2008 from http://taiwanreview.nat.gov.tw/site/Tr/ct.asp?xItem=939&CtNode=128

Tangen, R. (2008). Listening to children's voices in educational research: Some theoretical and methodological problems. *European Journal of Special Needs Education, 23*(2), 157–166. doi:10.1080/08856250801945956

Tapscott, D. (1998). *Growing up digital: The rise of the Net generation.* New York: McGraw-Hill.

Taylor, S. I. (2004). Let it be: Japanese preschoolers rule the classroom. *Young Children, 59*(5), 20–25.

Taylor, S. I., Ogawa, T., & Wilson, J. (2002). Moral development of Japanese children. *International Journal of Early Childhood, 43*(3), 12–18.

Taylor, S. I., Rogers, C., Dodd, A., Kaneda, T., Nagasaki, I., Watanabe, Y., & Goshiki, T. (2004). The meaning of play: A cross-cultural study of American and Japanese teachers' perspective on play. *Journal of Early Childhood Teacher Education, 24*, 311–321. doi:10.1080/1090102040240411

Teacher intern handbook. (2006). State University, AR: Arkansas State University.

Technology-Related Assistance for Individuals with Disabilities Act of 1988 (Tech Act) (P.L. 100-407, 102 Stat. 1044, 29 U.S.C. §§ 2201 *et seq.*). *Id.* § 705(3) and (4).

Tillman, H. (2003, March 28). *Evaluating Quality on the Net.* Babson College, MA.

Tobin, J., Wu, D., & Davidson, D. (1989). *Preschool in three cultures.* New Haven: Yale University Press.

Tobolka, D. (2006). Connecting teachers and parents through the Internet. *Tech Directions, 66*(5), 24–26.

Trinkle, D. A. (2005). The 361° Model for transforming teaching and learning with technology. *EDUCAUSE Quarterly, 28*(4), 18–25.

Tschannen-Moran, M., & Woolfolk Hoy, A. (2003). *Teacher efficacy: Capturing an elusive construct.* Teaching and Teacher Education. http://www.unesco.org/

Tschannen-Moran, M., Woolfolk Hoy, A., & Hoy, W. K. (1998). Teacher efficacy: Its meaning and measure. *Review of Educational Research, 68*, 202–248.

Tseng, Y., & Liang, C. (2002). The impact of online game and internet café on the school policy. *Audio-Visual Education Bimonthly, 44*(2), 2–12.

Turiel, E. (1998). The development of morality. In W. Damon, & N. Eisenberg. (Eds.), *Handbook of child psychology, 3*, (5th ed.) (pp. 863-932). New York, NY: John Wiley.

Turing, A. (1992). *Mechanical Intelligence: Collected Works of A M Turing.* Amsterdam: North Holland.

U.S. Department of Justice. (2005). *A guide to disability rights laws.* Washington, DC: Civil Rights Division. U.S. Department of Justice.

Ulman, J. G. (2005). *Making technology work for learners with special needs: Practical skills for teachers.* Boston, MA: Allyn and Bacon.

United Nations Educational, Scientific and Cultural Organization (UNESCO) (2006). *Address by Mr Koïchiro Matsuura, Director-General of UNESCO, on the theme of education, the university and cultural diversity Universidad Nacional Autónoma de México.*

United States Department of Commerce. (1999). *Falling through the net: Defining the digital divide.* Washington, DC: U.S. Dept. of Commerce, National Telecommunications and Information Administration.

United States Department of Education. (2000, December). *E-Learning: Putting a world-class education at the fingertips of all children.* The National Educational Technology Plan. Darby, PA: Diane Publishing.

UNUM Provident Insurance Company. (1999). *Assistive Technology Decision Tree.* Retrieved June 21, 2008 from http://www.microsoft.com/enable/download/default.aspx#righttech

US Department of Education. (2003). *Early Childhood Education in Developing Countries.* Education Around the World: Mexico. http://www.ed.gov/offices/OUS/PES/int_mexico.html

Van Eck, R. (2006). Digital game-based learning: It's not just the digital natives who are restless. *EDUCAUSE Review, 41*(2), 16-30. Retrieved June 8, 2006, from http://www.educause.edu/apps/er/erm06/erm0620.asp

Van Hoorn, J., Nourot, P., Scales, B., & Alward, K. (2007). *Play at the center of curriculum* (4th ed.). Upper saddle River, NJ: Pearson Merrill Prentice Hall.

Van Scoter, J., Ellis, D., & Railsback, J. (2001). *Technology in early childhood education: Finding the balance.* Portland, OR: Northwest Regional Educational Laboratory.

Vartuli, S. (1999). How early childhood teacher beliefs vary across grade levels. *Early Childhood Research Quarterly, 14*(4), 489–514. doi:10.1016/S0885-2006(99)00026-5

Voogt, J., & McKenney, S. (2007). Using ICT to foster (pre) reading and writing skills in young children. *Computers in the Schools, 24*(3/4), 83–94.

Vossler, K., Waitere-Ang, H., & Adams, P. (2005). Becoming an educator. In P. Adams, K. Vossler, & C. Scrivens (Eds.), *Teachers work in Aotearoa New Zealand* (pp. 17-27). Victoria, Australia: Thomson/Dunmore Press.

Vygotsky, L. S. (1978). *Mind in society: The development of higher psychological processes.* Cambridge, MA: Harvard University Press.

Walker, T., & White, C. (2002). Technorealism: The rhetoric and reality of technology in teacher education. *Journal of Technology and Teacher Education, 10*(1), 63–71.

Wang, X. C., & Hoot, J. L. (2006). Introduction: Information and communication technology in early childhood education. *Early Education and Development, 17*(3), 317–322. doi:10.1207/s15566935eed1703_1

Wartella, E. A., & Jennings, N. (2000). *Children and computers: New technology-old concerns.* Children and Computer Technology. Fall.

Wayne, A., Zucker, A., & Powell, T. (2002). *So what about the "digital divide" in K-12 schools? Educational technology and equity in U.S. K-12 schools.* Menlo Park, CA: SRI International.

Weikle, B., & Hadadian, A. (2003). Can assistive technology help us to not leave any child behind? *Preventing School Failure, 47*(4), 181–194.

Wellman, H. M., & Woolley, J. D. (1990). From simple desires to ordinary beliefs: The early development of everyday psychology. *Cognition, 35*, 245–275. doi:10.1016/0010-0277(90)90024-E

Wellman, H. M., Cross, D., & Watson, J. (2001). Meta-analysis of theory-of-mind development: The truth about false belief. *Child Development, 72*(3), 655–684. doi:10.1111/1467-8624.00304

Wershing, A., & Symington, L. (1998). Learning and growing with assistive technology. Judge & H.P. Parette (Eds.), *Assistive technology for young children with disabilities* (pp. 45-75). Cambridge, MA: Brookline Books.

Wimmer, H., & Perner, J. (1983). Beliefs about beliefs: Representation and constraining function of wrong beliefs in young children's understanding of deception. *Cognition, 13*, 103–128. doi:10.1016/0010-0277(83)90004-5

Winn, J. (2003, July). Avoiding death by powerpoint. *Journal of Professional Issues in Engineering Education and Practice*, 116–118.

Winsor, D. L. (2006). Inter-relatedness of theory of mind and epistemology in young children. Paper presented in F.C. Haerle (Chair), *Measuring Children's Personal Epistemology and Its Relevance for Education.* Symposium conducted at the American Educational Research Association Annual Meeting, San Francisco, CA, USA.

Wood, E., Willoughby, T., Schmidt, A., Porter, L., Specht, J., & Gilbert, J. (2004). Assessing the Use of Input Devices for Teachers and Children In Early Childhood Education Programs. *Information Technology in Childhood Education Annual, (1)*, 261-280. AACE.

Woodruff, G., & Premack, D. (1979). Intentional communication in the chimpanzee: The development of deception. *Cognition, 7*, 333–362. doi:10.1016/0010-0277(79)90021-0

Wortham, S. C. (2008). *Assessment in Early Childhood Education.* Columbus, OH: Pearson Merrill Prentice Hall.

Yamamura, Y. (1986). The child in Japanese society. In H. Stevens, H. Azuma, & K. Hakuta (Eds.), *Child development and education in Japan* (pp. 28-34). New York, NY: W. H. Freeman and Company.

Yang, X. (1998, December). Man tan dian nao zai you er jia ting jiao yu de gong neng [The educational role of home computers in young children's family Education]. *You Jiao Zi Xun, 97*, 50–53.

Yang, X. H. (2005, March). Gong li you zh yuan mian lin de jing zheng ya li [Competitive pressure on public kindergartens]. *Early Childhood Education, 277*, 18–19.

Yelland, N. (2002). Playing with ideas and games in early mathematics. *Contemporary Issues in Early Childhood, 3*(2). Retrieved October 23, 2002, from http://www.triangle.co.uk/ciec/

Young, D., & Behounek, L. (2006). Kindergarteners use PowerPoint to lead their own parent-teacher conferences . *Young Children, 61*(2), 24–26.

Zhang, S. Y., & Carrasquillo, A. (1995). Chinese parents' influence on academic performance . *New York State Association for Bilingual Education Journal, 10*, 46–53.

Zhao, Y., Byers, J., Mishra, P., Topper, A., Chen, H., & Enfield, M. (2001). What do they know? A comprehensive portrait of exemplary technology-using teachers. *Journal of Computing in Teacher Education, 17*(2), 25–37.

Zheng, M. (2004, January). Yin ying jiao gai tan you jiao ke cheng zhi fa zhan cu shi [In responding to education reform: the curriculum development trend in early childhood education]. *You Jiao Jian Xun, 15*, 6–7.

Zorrilla Fierro, M., & Lorenza Villa, L. (2003). *Políticas educativas. La investigación educative en México. 1992-2002.* Libro 8, México, Grupo Ideograma (La investigación educativa en México, 1992-2004).

About the Contributors

Sally Blake is an Associate Professor in Early Childhood at the University of Memphis. Sally has been the PI on more than $600,000 dollars of Eisenhower funds and $700,000 of NASA funds for teacher training and professional development. Sally Blake was the Director and Co-PI of the NSF sponsored Partnership for Excellence in Teacher Education (PETE) and the Noyce Scholarship program at the University of Texas at El Paso. She was also a research fellow with the NSF Center for Research on Educational Reform,(MSP project) a teaching fellow with the NSF Center for Effective Teaching and Learning(MIE project), co-developer of the Research Pedagogical Labs and the MAT degree in the College of Science (MSP project), and Co-PI on the NSF GK-12 grant. She is the Faculty Research Director of the Barbara K. Lipman Early Childhood School and Research Institute.

Satomi Izumi-Taylor is a professor of early childhood education in the Department of Instruction and Curriculum Leadership at the University of Memphis. She received her doctorate in family and child development from Virginia Polytechnic Institute and State University and her mater's degree in early childhood education from San Francisco State University. She was awarded the College of Education Outstanding Award for Research in 2003, the Dean's Excellence Award in Teaching in 2004, the Dean's Excellence Award in Mentoring in 2005, the College of Education's Ellery Earl Crader Professor of Education Award in 2006, and the Dean's Excellence Award in Service in 2008. She has published numerous articles and book chapters on cognitive, social, and moral development in children, pre-service teacher education, play, Japanese early childhood education, and reflection. Her current research interests include cross-cultural studies of childcare in China, Japan, the United States, and Sweden; pre-service teachers' notion of technology in Japan; New Zealand, the US, and Taiwan; and American and Japanese pre-service teachers' teaching science.

* * *

Lee Allen is an Assistant Professor of Instructional Design and Technology and Information Science at the University of Memphis. Dr. Allen has previously served as an assistant superintendent for technology services in the Dallas, TX public school district, and as a teacher, school librarian, technology trainer, and director of instructional technology in Santa Fe, NM. Dr. Allen's primary research interests are technology as a vehicle for organizational/institutional change, online teaching and learning, electronic portfolio development, and situated learning in communities of practice. He is currently developing the first 100% online Master's of Science degree program for the College of Education, and serves as technology consultant for the NCLB Memphis Striving Readers Project.

Candice Burkett is the Research Assistant for the SPIRIT research team and a mathematics education student at the University of Memphis. She has worked with the Texas Pre-freshman Engineering Project in Texas, co-authored articles in professional journals and plans be a researcher in Early Childhood Education.

Rene Crow is an assistant professor at the University of Central Arkansas in Conway, Arkansas, where she teaches in the undergraduate and graduate teacher education program. Her expertise is in early childhood special education and she has a research interest in assisting young children with behavioral challenges to develop social and emotional competencies.

Andrew Gibbons is the Academic Dean at New Zealand Tertiary College, a provider of specialist early childhood teacher education in New Zealand. He graduated from the Auckland College of Education with his diploma of teaching early childhood education in 1992, and has since worked in a wide range of educational settings in both London and Auckland. His research interests connect the philosophy of education with contemporary early childhood education theory and practice, including the recently published book, *The Matrix Ate My Baby*, exploring the role of new technologies in early education, and arguing for a philosophy of technology. Andrew is Executive Committee Member and Membership Secretary of the Philosophy of Education Society of Australasia, and co-program chair of the 2009 Reconceptualizing Early Childhood Education Conference.

Michael M. Grant is an associate professor in the Instructional Design and Technology program at the University of Memphis. He has been working with elementary and secondary educators for over ten years. His research considers how to best help faculties implement technology integration and how students represent their learning with computer technologies in different ways. Dr. Grant earned his Ph.D. from The University of Georgia in Instructional Technology.

Yu-Yuan Lee is faculty at the Nan Kai University of Technology, Taiwan and a doctoral candidate and a graduate assistant in the Instruction and Curriculum Leadership Department of the College of Education at the University of Memphis. She is from Taiwan and holds the position as an instructor at the Kan Kai University of Technology, where she taught EFL. Her research interests include the application of commercial video games in EFL curricula, technology integration in EFL curricula, and language learning strategies. She has made presentations in technology and ESL related conferences, such as *Society for Information Technology and Teacher Education International Conference (SITE), Tennessee TESOL Conference, and Student Research Forum at the University of Memphis. Her papers are included in the SITE proceedings and published in TN Journal.*

Jorge Lopez is the chair of Physics at the University of Texas at El Paso and a native Mexican. He became involved with early childhood education through his work with the National Science Foundation. He has developed and piloted early childhood and primary physical science projects in El Paso and the Juarez, Mexico schools. Has written one book, one chapter in a book, edited two books, and written two articles included in books on Nuclear physics. He has 63 articles published in 48 journal publications and in 15 conference proceedings, as well as 10 web and unpublished articles, and 83 abstracts. Has given 97 presentations in 40 national and international meetings, 11 Regional Meetings and 46 Seminars.

María Eugenia López grew up in Mexico. She is currently the director of the Centro de Desarrollo Infantil No. 4 in Cd. Juarez, Chihuahua, Mexico. She has worked with early childhood programs in Mexico for more than 15 years. She is dedicated to the belief that all children have the right to the best possible education and is an activist for children's rights. She has been a major influence in the reform of preschool education in Chihuahua.

Zelda McMurtry is an assistant professor of Early Childhood in the Department of Teacher Education at Arkansas State University. Dr. McMurtry serves as a university supervisor for student teachers in addition to teaching early childhood undergraduate and graduate students. She serves as the Coordinator of Early Childhood Education programs for all campuses in the ASU system. Dr. McMurtry's research interests include studying student teaching and cooperating teachers, and children's literature and the impact of reading aloud.

Clif Mims is a former elementary and middle school teacher. He is currently an assistant professor of Instructional Design and Technology at The University of Memphis. His research interests include teacher education and technology integration. He and his wife have three children.

Vivian Gunn Morris holds the Ph.D. degree in Inner City Education, Early Childhood Education Emphasis, from Peabody College of Vanderbilt University. She is Professor of Education, Assistant Dean for Faculty and Staff Development in the College of Education and Director of the New Teacher Center at the University of Memphis. She was awarded the College of Education's Ellery Earl Crader Professor of Education Award in 2008, the Faudree Professor, a prestigious professorship at the University of Memphis, and held the Lillian and Morrie Moss Chair of Excellence in Urban Education from 2004-06. She was a recipient of the Association of Teacher Educators' 1997 Distinguished Research Award in Teacher Education for her research in family involvement in education. The New Teacher Center was the recipient of the Tennessee Board of Regents' Award in Academic Excellence in March 2006. She received the College of Education's Dean's Award for Excellence in Research and Scholarship in 2005 and the Outstanding Teacher Education Award for Service in 1995. Dr. Morris' areas of expertise and research include family involvement in education, early childhood and elementary teacher education, school improvement planning, urban education, mentoring, and the education of African American children. Her most recent research and publications are related to early childhood education, mentoring new teachers and segregation/desegregation of schools in the south and appear as books, book chapters, and journal articles.

Testuya Ogawa is the director of Kawasaki Futaba Kindergarten in Kawasaki City in Japan and is also an instructor of a trade school where he trains future early childhood teachers. Since the early 1980's he has studied technology in early childhood education and is one of the first researchers in Japan to implement technology in the classroom. He has published numerous articles and book chapters in Japan and the United States. As a director of a kindergarten in an urban city, he focuses on the education of young children through the use of technology.

Cheri Smith is an early childhood doctoral candidate in the department of Instruction and Curriculum Leadership at the University of Memphis. She is also an assistant professor of early childhood education at Harding University in Searcy, Arkansas. Her research interests include using children's literature to create nurturing environments and designing classroom environments for young children that promote growth and learning.

Denise Winsor had joined academe community after working as a clinical psychologist. She piloted the Family Builders and Family Preservation grants in the 1980's. She has developed the *Dynamic Systems Framework for Personal Epistemology Development* (Winsor, 2005), a systems model which aids the understanding early childhood cognitive development. Her research interests include an emphasis on preschool-age children's knowledge and understanding; and how to more effectively educate preschool children using developmentally appropriate practices in early childhood classrooms. Currently, Dr. Winsor is working in collaboration with multiple research teams to develop a science curriculum for preschool using science inquiry methods; and utilizing a systems approach (i.e., child, teacher, parent, and peer interactions) to better understand the epistemological development of very young children as they become school-ready. She is interested in teacher preparation methods specifically metacognitive strategies that integrate theoretical, conceptual, and applied tasks that aid students in high-order thinking related to real world settings.

Index

A

American with Disabilities Act (ADA) 134
assistive technology 114–130, 134, 135, 136
Assistive Technology Act 114, 115, 116, 117
assistive technology device
        115, 116, 120, 126
assistive technology service 116
augmentative communication 121, 122, 126
available cognitive capacity 133

B

backwardness 78
blogs 22, 66, 152, 154, 161

C

Center for Applied Special Technology (CAST)
        219, 222
Centros de Desarrollo Infantil (CENTI)
        83, 84, 85, 204
child initiated play 57
cognitive development 21, 22, 27, 28, 30,
        32, 59, 80, 90, 110, 118, 126, 127,
        133, 134, 136, 145, 146, 178, 181,
        182, 185, 186, 197, 207, 212
community of mind 187
Confucianism 21, 26
Consejo Nacional de Fomento Educativo
        (CONAFE) 84
Consejo Nacional de Población (Conapo)
        73, 74, 91
constructivist 163, 164, 172, 173, 174,
        210, 213, 214
cooperative learning 136
cram schools 26

D

critical reflection 2, 3, 4, 5, 9, 12, 13, 15
culturalness 7
curriculum development 95, 98
CyberStart 219

D

deschooling 15, 16
developmentally appropriate 3, 4, 18, 131,
        136, 138, 145, 160, 162, 200
didactic situations 86
digital divide 141, 142, 147, 148, 156,
        219, 232
Digital Generation Gap 155–156
digital immigrants 20, 34
digital native 22, 23
diploma mills 15, 16, 18

E

early childhood education (ECE) 177, 204
electronic communication 152, 156
electronic portfolio 102, 103
Embedded Systemic Model 190
extrinsic 173, 207

F

functional performance 134

G

gait trainers 120
group-oriented environment
        49, 50, 57, 58, 60, 61, 62, 66

H

Head Start 132, 133, 150, 210